T0235125

Lecture Notes in Computer Science 10471

Commenced Publication in 1973
Founding and Former Series Editors:
Gerhard Goos, Juris Hartmanis, and Jan van Leeuwen

Editorial Board

More information about this series at http://www.springer.com/series/7408

Laure Petrucci · Cristina Seceleanu
Ana Cavalcanti (Eds.)

Critical Systems: Formal Methods and Automated Verification

Joint 22nd International Workshop
on Formal Methods for Industrial Critical Systems
and 17th International Workshop
on Automated Verification of Critical Systems, FMICS-AVoCS 2017
Turin, Italy, September 18–20, 2017
Proceedings

 Springer

Editors
Laure Petrucci
Paris 13 University
Villetaneuse
France

Ana Cavalcanti
University of York
York
UK

Cristina Seceleanu
Mälardalen University
Västerås
Sweden

ISSN 0302-9743   ISSN 1611-3349   (electronic)
Lecture Notes in Computer Science
ISBN 978-3-319-67112-3   ISBN 978-3-319-67113-0   (eBook)
DOI 10.1007/978-3-319-67113-0

Library of Congress Control Number: 2017952389

LNCS Sublibrary: SL2 – Programming and Software Engineering

Printed on acid-free paper

This Springer imprint is published by Springer Nature
The registered company is Springer International Publishing AG
The registered company address is: Gewerbestrasse 11, 6330 Cham, Switzerland

Preface

This volume contains the papers presented at the International Workshop on Formal Methods for Industrial Critical Systems and Automated Verification of Critical Systems (FMICS-AVoCS), held in Turin, Italy, September 18–20, 2017. FMICS-AVoCS 2017 combines the 22nd International Workshop on Formal Methods for Industrial Critical Systems and the 17th International Workshop on Automated Verification of Critical Systems.

The aim of the FMICS workshop series is to provide a forum for researchers who are interested in the development and application of formal methods in industry. In particular, FMICS brings together scientists and practitioners who are active in the area of formal methods and interested in exchanging their experiences in the industrial usage of these methods. The FMICS workshop series also strives to promote research and development that targets the improvement of formal methods and tools for industrial applications.

The aim of the AVoCS workshop series is to contribute to the interaction and exchange of ideas among members of the international research community on tools and techniques for the verification of critical systems. The subject is to be interpreted broadly and inclusively. It covers all aspects of automated verification, including model checking, theorem proving, SAT/SMT constraint solving, abstract interpretation, and refinement pertaining to various types of critical systems (safety-critical, business-critical, performance-critical, etc.) that need to meet stringent dependability requirements.

This year we received 30 submissions, out of which 8 were submitted to the new special track on "Formal methods for mobile and autonomous robots", focusing on the design, verification, and implementation of mobile and autonomous robots based on formal methods.

Each of these submissions went through a rigorous review process in which each paper was reviewed by at least three researchers from a strong Program Committee of international reputation. We selected 14 papers, 4 of them for the special track, for presentation during the workshop and inclusion in the workshop's proceedings, which resulted in an acceptance rate of 47%.

The regular track papers span various topics on system modeling and verification, such as deductive verification of code, automata learning techniques, event-based timing constraints verification, and model checking software components, as well as topics related to testing and scheduling, such as automatic conformance testing of industrial systems, model-based testing of asynchronous systems, and formal-methods-backed schedulability analysis.

The papers accepted for the special track cover recent results and open problems related to verifying mobile and autonomous robots.

The workshop also featured keynotes by Prof. Parosh Abdullah (Uppsala University, Sweden) and Prof. Kerstin Eder (University of Bristol, UK), and a tutorial offered by Prof. Tiziana Margaria (University of Limerick and Lero - The Irish Software Research Centre, Ireland) and Prof. Bernhard Steffen (TU Dortmund, Germany). We hereby thank the invited speakers for having accepted our invitation, and the tutors for organizing the tutorial.

We are grateful to the editorial staff of Springer for publishing the workshop's proceedings, EasyChair for assisting us in managing the complete process from submission to proceedings, as well as ERCIM and EASST for their support. Finally, we would like to thank the Program Committee members and the external reviewers, for their accurate and timely reviews, all authors for their submissions, and all attendees of the workshop for their participation.

July 2017

Laure Petrucci
Cristina Seceleanu
Ana Cavalcanti

Organization

Program Committee

María Alpuente	Universitat Politècnica de València, Spain
Jiří Barnat	Masaryk University, Czech Republic
Ana Cavalcanti	University of York, UK
Michael Dierkes	Rockwell Collins, France
Kerstin Eder	University of Bristol, UK
Alessandro Fantechi	Università degli Studi di Firenze, Italy
Michael Fisher	University of Liverpool, UK
Francesco Flammini	Ansaldo STS, Naples, Italy
María Del Mar Gallardo	University of Málaga, Spain
Michael Goldsmith	University of Oxford, UK
Gudmund Grov	Heriot-Watt University, UK
Matthias Güdemann	Diffblue Ltd., Oxford, UK
Marieke Huisman	University of Twente, The Netherlands
Gerwin Klein	NICTA and University of New South Wales, Australia
Lars Kristensen	Bergen University College, Norway
Anna-Lena Lamprecht	University of Limerick, Ireland
Peter Gorm Larsen	Aarhus University, Denmark
Thierry Lecomte	ClearSy, Aix-en-Provence, France
Radu Mateescu	Inria Grenoble - Rhône-Alpes, France
David Mentré	Mitsubishi Electric R&D Centre Europe, Rennes, France
Stephan Merz	Inria Nancy, France
Manuel Núñez	Universidad Complutense de Madrid, Spain
Charles Pecheur	Université catholique de Louvain, Belgium
Marielle Petit-Doche	Systerel, Aix-en-Provence, France
Laure Petrucci	Université Paris 13 and CNRS, France
Markus Roggenbach	Swansea University, UK
Matteo Rossi	Politecnico di Milano, Italy
Marco Roveri	FBK-irst, Italy
Thomas Santen	Microsoft Research Advanced Technology Labs Europe, Germany
Cristina Seceleanu	Mälardalen University, Sweden
Bernhard Steffen	University of Dortmund, Germany
Jun Sun	Singapore University of Technology and Design, Singapore
Maurice Ter Beek	ISTI-CNR, Pisa, Italy
Helen Treharne	University of Surrey, UK
Xavier Urbain	Université Claude Bernard Lyon 1, France

Jaco van de Pol   University of Twente, The Netherlands
Peter Ölveczky   University of Oslo, Norway

Additional Reviewers

Armand, Michaël	Kamali, Maryam
Basile, Davide	Lang, Frédéric
Bendík, Jaroslav	Linker, Sven
Boudjadar, Jalil	Longuet, Delphine
Boyer, Benoît	Macedo, Hugo Daniel
Bozzano, Marco	Marsso, Lina
Brecknell, Matthew	Merino, Pedro
Carnevali, Laura	Micheli, Andrea
Cousineau, Denis	Murray, Toby
Cruanes, Simon	Panizo, Laura
Dennis, Louise	Pardo, Daniel
Dixon, Clare	Poskitt, Christopher M.
Griggio, Alberto	Potop-Butucaru, Maria
Guérin Lassous, Isabelle	Salmerón, Alberto
Happa, Jassim	Tixeuil, Sébastien
Insa, David	Wang, Jingyi

Replacing Store Buffers by Load Buffers in Total Store Ordering (Invited Lecture)

Parosh Aziz Abdulla[1], Mohamed Faouzi Atig[1], Ahmed Bouajjani[2], and Tuan Phong Ngo[1]

[1] Uppsala University, Uppsala, Sweden
{parosh,mohamed_faouzi.atig,tuan-phong.ngo}@it.uu.se
[2] IRIF, Université Paris Diderot, Paris, France
abou@irif.fr

To gain more efficiency and save energy, almost all modern multi-processor architectures execute instructions in an out-of-order fashion. This means that processors execute instructions in an order governed by the availability of input data rather than by their original order in the program. The out-of-order execution does not affect the behavior of *sequential* programs. However, in the concurrent setting, many new (and unexpected) behaviors may be observed in program executions. We can no longer assume the classical Sequential Consistency (SC) semantics that has for decades been the standard semantics for concurrent programs. Sequential consistency means that "the result of any execution of the program is the same as if the operations of all the processors were executed in some sequential order, and the operations of each individual processor appear in this sequence in the order specified by its program" [8]. In fact, even well-known concurrent algorithms such as mutual exclusion and producer-consumer protocols that are correct under the SC semantics, may not satisfy their specifications any more when run on modern architectures. This means that it is relevant to carry out program verification in order to to ensure correctness under these new premises.

To carry out formal verification, we need to have a well-defined semantics for the program under consideration. The inadequacy of the SC semantics has led to the invention of new program semantics, so called *Weak, (or relaxed) Memory Models*, by allowing permutations between certain types of memory operations [4–6]. One of the most popular memory models is Total Store Ordering (TSO) that corresponds, among others, to the relaxation adopted by Sun's SPARC multiprocessors [11] and formalizations of the Intel x86-tso memory model [9, 10]. The TSO model inserts an unbounded non-lossy (perfect) FIFO buffer (queue), called a *store buffer*, between each processor and the main memory. When a processor performs a write operation, the memory will not be immediately updated as is the case in the SC semantics. Instead, the write operation will be appended to the tail of the store buffer of the processor. In such a case, we say that the write operation is *pending*. A pending write operation is only visible to the processor that has issued it, but not to the rest of the processors. At any point during the execution of the program, the memory may be *updated*, i.e., the write operation at the head of the store buffer of one of the processors may non-deterministically be fetched and used to update the memory. The update operation overwrites the memory position corresponding to the variable on which the write operation is performed.

After the update operation, the write operation will be visible to all the processors. If a processor performs a read operation, then it searches first its own store buffer for the latest pending write operation on the same variable. If no pending write operation exists on that variable in the buffer, the processor fetches the value from the memory.

In this lecture, we describe an alternative semantics called the *dual TSO* semantics [3]. The new semantics is equivalent to the classical TSO semantics but more amenable for efficient algorithmic verification. The main idea is to replace the store buffers of the processors by *load buffers*. The load buffer of a processor contains pending read operations instead of write operations. Intuitively, the read operation at the end of a buffer can be consumed and used to perform a local read operation by the processor. The flow of information will now be in the reverse direction, i.e., write operations by processors will immediately update the memory, while the values of the variables are propagated non-deterministically from the memory to the load buffers of the processors. When a processor performs a read operation, it fetches its value from the tail of its buffer.

One interesting aspect of the dual semantics is that it presents a new (yet equivalent) view of the classical memory model of TSO. Furthermore, the model allows to incorporate *lossiness* into the semantics. More precisely, if we extend the semantics by allowing the load buffers of the processors to lose messages non-deterministically, then the set of reachable processor states will remain the same. The equivalent lossy semantics allows the application the framework of well-structured systems [1, 2, 7] in a straightforward manner leading to a simple proof of decidability of safety properties for finite-state programs operating on Dual-TSO.

References

1. Abdulla, P., Cerans, K., Jonsson, B., Tsay, Y.: General decidability theorems for infinite-state systems. In: LICS 1996, pp. 313–321. IEEE Computer Society (1996)
2. Abdulla. P.A.: Well (and better) quasi-ordered transition systems. Bull. Symb. Log. **16**(4), 457–515, (2010)
3. Abdulla, P.A., Atig, M.F., Bouajjani, A., Ngo, T.P.: The benefits of duality in verifying concurrent programs under TSO. In: Desharnais, J., Jagadeesan, R. (eds.) 27th International Conference on Concurrency Theory, CONCUR 2016, 23–26 August 2016, Québec City, Canada, vol. 59. LIPIcs, pp. 5:1–5:15. Schloss Dagstuhl - Leibniz-Zentrum fuer Informatik (2016)
4. Adve, S., Gharachorloo, K.: Shared memory consistency models: a tutorial. Computer **29** (12) 1996
5. Adve, S., Hill, M.D.: Weak ordering - a new definition. In: ISCA (1990)
6. Dubois, M., Scheurich, C., Briggs, F.A.: Memory access buffering in multiprocessors. In: ISCA (1986)
7. Finkel, A., Schnoebelen, P.: Well-structured transition systems everywhere! Theor. Comput. Sci. **256**(1–2), 63–92 (2001)

8. Lamport, L.: How to make a multiprocessor computer that correctly executes multiprocess programs. IEEE Trans. Comp. **C-28**(9) (1979)
9. Owens, S., Sarkar, S., Sewell, P: A better x86 memory model: x86-tso. In: TPHOL (2009)
10. Sewell, P., Sarkar, S., Owens, S., Nardelli, F.Z., Myreen, M.O.: x86-tso: a rigorous and usable programmer's model for x86 multiprocessors. CACM **53** (2010)
11. Weaver, D., Germond, T. (eds.): The SPARC Architecture Manual Version 9. PTR Prentice Hall (1994)

Contents

Modeling and Analysis Techniques

Automated Verification Techniques

Deductive Functional Verification of Safety-Critical Embedded C-Code: An Experience Report

Dilian Gurov[1], Christian Lidström[2(✉)], Mattias Nyberg[1,2], and Jonas Westman[1,2]

[1] KTH Royal Institute of Technology, Stockholm, Sweden
[2] Systems Development Division, Scania AB, Södertälje, Sweden
christian.lidstrom@scania.com

Abstract. This paper summarizes our experiences from an exercise in deductive verification of functional properties of automotive embedded C-code in an industrial setting. We propose a formal requirements model that supports the way C-code requirements are currently written at SCANIA. We describe our work, for a safety-critical module of an embedded system, on formalizing its functional requirements and verifying its C-code implementation by means of VCC, an established tool for deductive verification. We describe the obstacles we encountered, and discuss the automation of the specification and annotation effort as a prerequisite for integrating this technology into the embedded software design process.

1 Introduction

While Formal Methods are in general only slowly making their way into industrial practice for quality assurance, their adoption in the domain of embedded, safety-critical systems has seen much progress over the last years. One reason for this development, from an industry perspective, is the increased analyses effort advocated by standards to achieve functional safety of such systems. For example, automotive functional safety standard ISO 26262 recommends formal verification for higher levels of criticality. The smaller size of embedded code as compared to arbitrary applications, and the constraints on how code is structured in order to safeguard against potential unwanted behaviours, are also enabling factors for the application of the typically more expensive formal analysis techniques.

SCANIA is a leading manufacturer of commercial vehicles, and specifically heavy trucks and buses. A large part of the embedded C-code developed at SCANIA is safety-critical, and a considerable effort is spent during code development and deployment on quality assurance. On top of the traditional testing methods, SCANIA is exploring the possibility for integrating deductive verification and model checking into the code design and quality assurance process.

Work partially funded by VINNOVA within the KLOSS AKUT initiative, which sent academics out to Industry one day a week for half a year during 2015/2016.

L. Petrucci et al. (Eds.): FMICS-AVoCS 2017, LNCS 10471, pp. 3–18, 2017.
DOI: 10.1007/978-3-319-67113-0_1

The main motivation for this are the increased safety requirements resulting from innovative trucking solutions such as platooning and autonomous driving.

Motivating Factors. The starting point for the work described here were the following general findings and concrete observations made from studying a particular C-module and its associated requirements document [1].

1. Many of the requirements of the module are *functional*, in the sense that they express output values as a function of input values (i.e., as a mathematical function). A common case is that two or more outputs of the same module depend on intersecting sets of inputs. This leads to a natural *functional decomposition* that allows the functionality of modules to be understood conceptually through the metaphor of a *combinational logic circuit*.
2. The well-known and established logic and deductive system called *Hoare logic* has been developed precisely for formally specifying and proving this type of properties [12]. Program verification in this style is based on *logical assertions*, which are essentially state properties expressed as first-order formulas over program and (additional) logical variables, typically in the form of pre- and postconditions to C-functions, or loop invariants. The assertions are tied to specific control points of the program, usually by means of program annotations provided by the programmer. The annotated program is then translated by purely symbolic means (based on computation of so-called weakest preconditions, or on symbolic execution) to a first-order logic formula, called verification condition, which is true exactly when the assertions hold for the annotated program. The generated verification condition is then passed on to an automated (back-end) theorem prover to be checked for validity.
3. The typical control flow of embedded code, and the used datatypes, follow certain constraints, described through guidelines following MISRA C and ISO 26262, which render the given correctness problem *decidable*. For instance, most of the code we examined does not involve any looping constructs, which typically require loop invariants to be provided by the programmer, and most of the data is of enumerable (i.e., non-inductive) types, and thus no datatype invariants need to be provided.
4. There exist mature tools such as VCC [4,5] and Frama-C [8] that support the automated deductive verification of C-code supplied with annotations.

All these observations and findings were a strong indication that the formal specification of requirements and their deductive functional verification can be automated to a degree that makes them a viable option for increased quality assurance of the safety-critical embedded C-code. This lead to the present pre-study, which builds on the findings of two Master theses [10,13].

Goals of the Study. The main question that the present pre-study addresses is: is it feasible, and what would be needed, to push formal requirement specification and deductive functional verification into an embedded software design process, such as the one at SCANIA?

Our concrete questions concern:

1. Formalization of functional requirements: how user-friendly can it be made, and how much effort does it take?
2. Verification tool: what is the code coverage regarding the given code base, how easy is it to use the tool and to make sense and use of the feedback it provides on failed verifications, and how efficient is it in practice?
3. Annotation of the code: how much effort does it take, what annotation overhead does this incur, and how automatable is the annotation process?

Structure of the Paper. The remainder of the paper is organized as follows. In Sect. 2 we describe the type of requirements we found in the requirements document, and propose a formal requirements model, based on mathematical functions, for capturing such requirements. In Sect. 3 we describe the verification tool VCC, the verification method it supports, and the specifics of its use. In Sect. 4 we discuss (without, however, revealing proprietary code or information) the module which we considered in our pre-study, its requirements, the annotation process, and the obstacles which we encountered. Our findings are summarized in Sect. 5, together with a proposal for a semi-automated specification and verification process based on these findings. Related work we describe in Sect. 6, and conclude with Sect. 7.

2   Formalizing Functional Requirements

In this section we describe the character of the requirements as we encountered in the requirements document of the module we considered [1], and propose a formal requirements model.

Requirements. The requirements in the provided requirements document are written in terms of a set of *requirements variables*, which are (model) variables distinct from the program variables. This follows a clean discipline of separating specifications from implementations.

A significant number of the requirements are presented in a format illustrated by the following concrete example:

```
While SecondaryCircuitHandlesSteering == True
    If ParkingBrakeSwitch == ParkingBrakeNotSet
        ElectricMotor = On
```

which could be described as a *conditional assignment form*. On its own, such a requirement does not specify completely the value of the variable being set (here, `ElectricMotor`). Since the same variable may be assigned a value by more than one requirement, this immediately raises the questions of whether the set of requirements is *complete* (i.e., it specifies, for all values of the input variables, a value for every output variable) and whether it is *consistent* (i.e., specifies at most one such value), together guaranteeing the well-definedness of the specified data transformation. While specifications may be incomplete by intention, inconsistency is always a problem that needs to be resolved.

Further noteworthy to observe is that, while some of the requirements variables used in the specifications do correspond to global *module interface* ones (i.e., variables through which the module interacts with its environment), most do not; instead they are *intermediate* requirements variables. This corresponds conceptually to a *function decomposition* of the functions computed by the module. Such a break-down of requirements constitutes a natural representation of a multi-output function when its outputs depend on intersecting sets of inputs, and makes the reading of requirements easier. It also allows the functionality of modules to be understood conceptually, and visualized, through the metaphor of a (multiple-valued) *combinational logic circuit*.

Many of the intermediate requirements variables have corresponding counterparts in the code in the form of local variables or struct fields (sometimes even more than one, as certain values are transferred by reference via calls to helper functions). These observations raise the question whether one should aim to verify every requirement individually, or only the induced functional dependence of the output variables on the input ones. The first option can only be realized by referring in the code annotations to the local code artifacts, and thus ties the verification to the implementation. This goes against the principle of separating specifications from implementation details, which allows the implementation to evolve without necessarily changing the requirements. On the other hand, the second option may result in considerably worse verification times, as it is usually the case when verifying a specification in a "black-box" manner, not utilizing the implementation information.

Formal Requirements Model. To formalize the requirements, one has first to define a *formal requirements model.* In the present case of purely functional data transformation, it is suitable to base the formal model on the standard discrete-mathematical notion of *(partial) function.*

As an example, consider variables $x_1, x_2 \in \{7, -3\}$ and $x_3, y \in \{-2, 6\}$, and let the value of variable y depend functionally on the values of the variables x_1, x_2 and x_3, as defined by the table on the left of Fig. 1. We shall use this (rather trivial) example to discuss possible presentations of such functions.

Function Views. One can distinguish between two views on mathematical functions. First, there is the *black-box* view, which describes the functions computed by a module via *interface variables* only, i.e., as module *contracts*. This view is important for *modular verification* (say, in an assume/guarantee style), as it is the view of the module that is exported to the rest of the system. In principle, this is the view to be verified, since it specifies just the data transformation to be computed by a module and nothing more. And then, there is the *white-box* view, which decomposes the functions by introducing *intermediate variables*. This view is important for readability and simplicity of module specifications. However, as explained above, the verification of the individual requirements resulting from the breakdown is problematic. Ideally, intermediate variables should only be

(a) Function.

x_1	x_2	x_3	y
7	7	-2	6
-3	7	-2	6
7	-3	-2	6
-3	-3	-2	-2
7	7	6	-2
-3	7	6	-2
7	-3	6	-2
-3	-3	6	6

(b) Function decomposition.

x_1	x_2	f
7	7	7
-3	7	7
7	-3	7
-3	-3	-3

z	x_3	g
7	-2	6
-3	-2	-2
7	6	-2
-3	6	6

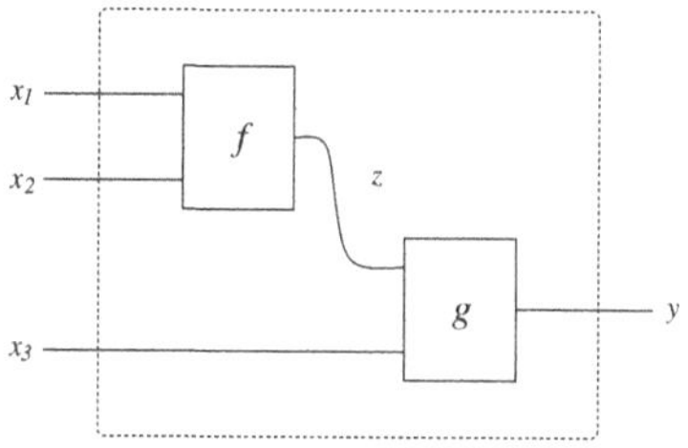

(c) Function architecture.

Fig. 1. A function and its decomposition.

used as a vehicle to relate output values to input values. The two views have a simple mathematical connection by means of *function decomposition* in the one direction, and *function substitution* in the other.

For instance, the example function defined above can be decomposed according to the equations:

$$z = f(x_1, x_2)$$
$$y = g(z, x_3)$$

introducing the intermediate requirements variable $z \in \{7, -3\}$ and the functions f and g defined by the tables in the middle of Fig. 1. The "architecture" of this decomposition, or white-box view of the function, is depicted on the right of Fig. 1, in the style of a combinational logic circuit.

3 The Verification Tool VCC

VCC, standing for Verified Concurrent C, is a tool for the formal verification of programs written in the C language [5]. As the name suggests, it supports verification of concurrent code. It has been developed at Microsoft Research, and is available for Windows under the MIT license via GitHub[1].

The assertions to be verified, such as *function contracts* and *data invariants*, are to be specified by the programmer directly in the C source code in the form of *annotations*. VCC has its own syntax for this: annotations are always enclosed in parentheses and preceded by an underscore '_(...)', but otherwise follow a syntax similar to the one of the C language itself.

The contract of a function is a set of annotations located between the function header and its body. The set typically includes a *precondition* expressing an assumption on the values of the actual parameters and global variables at the time of invoking the function, and a *postcondition* relating the return value and the values of the global variables at the time of returning from the function

---

[1] See `github.com/Microsoft/vcc`.

```
#include <vcc.h>

void swap(int *p, int *q)
  _(writes p,q)
  _(ensures *p == \old(*q) && *q == \old(*p))
{
  int tmp;
  tmp = *p;
  *p = *q;
  *q = tmp;
}
```

Fig. 2. A simple C-function annotated with a contract.

call to the former values. The remaining annotations essentially specify other side-effects of executing the function body.

An example of a contract for a simple C function is given in Fig. 2. The header file vcc.h is included in order to make the compiler ignore the VCC annotations. In the contract, the **ensures** clause specifies a postcondition, where an expression appearing within an \old clause refers to its value at function invocation time (for preconditions this is the default mode). The postcondition states that the value pointed to by p upon return from the method call will equal the value pointed to by q before execution, and *vice versa*. Preconditions are specified with the keyword **requires**. There is no precondition provided in this specification, meaning that the contract should hold for any values of the actual parameters and global variables at the time of invoking the function. The **writes** clause specifies the side-effect that both argument pointers are writable, and no other memory locations. It also serves to give notice to any calling function that (only) the contents of the specified memory locations may change during the call. In contrast, the lack of a **writes** clause tells the caller that this function will not have any visible side-effects w.r.t. the specified variables.

Contracts can be specified not only for functions, but for any block of code. Assertions can be inserted at any control point of executable code, and are useful both to provide hints to VCC and for troubleshooting. Finally, one can specify invariants for both loops and data structures.

Verification Method. VCC is a deductive verifier. The annotations are translated into an intermediate language and provided to another tool, BOOGIE, from which proof obligations are generated; these are then discharged by an automated theorem prover, the default being Z3.

The verification of function contracts is *modular*: when checking the body of a function, and a call to another function is encountered, the tool asserts that the caller fulfills the preconditions of the callee, and assumes that the callee's postconditions hold right after the call statement. This function modularity ensures scalability of the verification method w.r.t. the number of C functions.

The verification performed by VCC is claimed to be *sound*, in the sense that verified assertions do indeed hold, but is not guaranteed to be complete, meaning that assertions that could not be verified may still hold. Sometimes the programmer can "help" the tool by rewriting assertions to equivalent formulas that can be handled by the back-end reasoning engine.

Ghost Code. During verification, VCC keeps track of an internal state referred to as the *ghost* state [5]. Apart from logical representations of all actual program variables, this state also includes many other abstract data structures and functions that are needed to provide a model in which to reason about the program. In addition to function contracts, VCC provides numerous other ways of manipulating the ghost state, allowing the programmer to assist the reasoning engine in performing a successful verification.

Ghost functions can be defined with the keyword `def`. Such functions must have no side effects, and may only be used in specifications. Also regular (but side-effect free) C functions can be marked with the keyword `pure` to allow them to be used in specifications. Ghost variables are declared with the keyword `ghost` preceding an ordinary C declaration. For ghost variables, any native or user created C type can be used, as well as a number of types built into VCC. For example, there are mathematical integers (`\integer`), natural numbers (`\natural`), and true Booleans (`\bool`), to name a few.

Memory Model. C is often referred to as a low-level programming language, because of the similarity between its primitive objects and those of hardware. In addition, C has explicit memory (de)allocation, pointer arithmetic and aliasing, and a weak type system that can be easily circumvented, all of which makes reasoning about memory harder. VCC, however, has a stricter memory model and stronger typing for its ghost state [7]. System memory is represented as a set of typed objects, and is maintained in the ghost memory as pointers to all valid objects. One guarantee of this model is that valid objects are always separated. VCC can thus efficiently take advantage of well-written C code and elevate it to its own stronger model. In cases where it is not able to do this, verification will fail, and additional annotations regarding the usage of memory are needed.

Because of its focus on concurrent code, ownership and closedness information is also stored for each object in ghost memory [6]. For example, threads are only allowed to make sequential writes to memory of which they are the owner, and sequential reads to memory that they own or can be proved not to change. Ownership is represented as a tree structure. The system heap is organized as a set of trees, where each root node represents a thread and each edge represents ownership by the source node. A thread is the direct owner of its local variables, whereas a struct owns its fields and is itself owned by some higher-level object.

4   The Case Study

Our case study is based on a C-code module that is part of the embedded system controlling the SCANIA trucks, and is considered safety-critical. More specifically, the module deals with the secondary power steering function that must take over in the case of a malfunction in the primary power steering function. Since the C-code itself is proprietary, we shall only describe its relevant aspects here, and will not be able to show any parts of it.

The code base of the analyzed module has 1,400 lines of code, consisting of 10 C-functions, one main and 9 helper functions. The analyzed code is strictly *sequential* (although the larger system is not), and the control flow consists solely of if- and switch-statements, and function calls (i.e., it does not involve any loops). The module interacts with two other modules: one primarily concerned with diagnostics, and one performing the I/O to the larger system. We had no access to the source code for the first of these, and could therefore not perform any reasoning about variables that depended on it. In the case of the latter, 9 small functions concerning reading, writing and status checking of signals were annotated as part of the verification. Additionally, the analyzed code makes much use of type definitions and macros imported from several external files, none of which were taken into account in our quantitative assessment.

SCANIA has its own internal programming rules for embedded systems, most of which are identical to the MISRA C development guidelines. Because of this, the analyzed code base avoids many of the C constructs which may cause problem in the stricter model which VCC operates in.

Requirements. Our starting point for annotating the code base was an internal document, containing 27 requirements. Of these, 14 were not considered for verification: 6 were not specific to the module itself (they had to do with initialization, and should be specified on another module), 3 were of a temporal nature (and thus could not be captured through VCC assertions), and the remaining 5 depended on output from other modules (and would need more modules to be included in the verification effort). Thus, 13 requirements were considered, of which 10 were verified due to time constraints. No functional errors were found in the code base during this verification.

The requirements are given in two formats: some are expressed in natural language only, and some in a semi-formal form, making use of logical statements and operators, such as if, else, and, and = (although the precise semantics of these operators is left unspecified). The document provides no details as to how variables referred to in requirements are related to system memory. After careful analysis we found that they could refer to globally available signals, local program variables, or not exist as explicit variables in the code at all.

An example of a semi-formal requirement was given above, in the beginning of Sect. 2. An example for a requirement in natural language could be: "*If the vehicle is moving without primary power steering, then the secondary circuit should handle power steering.*" The requirement can be seen formalized and

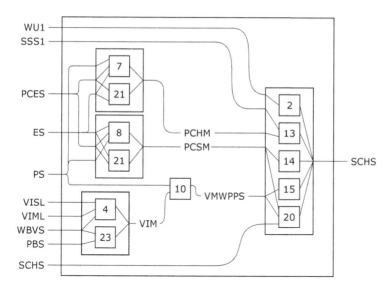

Fig. 3. Combinational logic circuit of case study requirements.

annotated in Fig. 5, and represented as a numbered box in Fig. 3, as requirement number 15.

A representation of some of the requirements in the form of a *combinational logic circuit* is shown in Fig. 3. The circuit models all requirements that define the value of the variable SCHS (the complete model is over 35 requirements variables, of which 6 output, 17 input and 12 intermediate variables). Outside the larger box are the interface variables, with input variables to the left and the output ones to the right. Requirements are represented by small boxes with numbers corresponding to the number of the requirement according to the document. These boxes are (sometimes cloned and) grouped together in "gates", so that each gate has a single output "wire" modelling a requirements variable.

The requirements did not form a complete specification of the module. We also found that under a naive interpretation two of the requirements were contradictory. Upon further investigation we found that this was a case of imprecise specification, and that they were intended to be evaluated in a certain order. Formal verification generally helps with detecting and resolving such issues, as two contradictory requirements can not both be verified on the same code base.

Code Preprocessing. Before verifying the requirements, the code had first to be prepared in order to pass VCC as it is, without any annotations concerning the application-specific requirements. First of all, some preprocessor directives concerning conditional inclusion of platform-specific headers and compiler-specific language extensions had to be either rewritten or removed. Furthermore, VCC always tries to prove validity and ownership of all accessed memory, which means that annotations for that purpose had to be inserted. We also chose to insert annotations for verification of termination of all functions before verifying the requirements, which was easily achieved because of the simplicity of the module's control flow.

Code Annotation: Main Function. Since the analyzed module contains a single entry-point function, all requirements chosen for verification had to be specified in the contract of this particular function. The requirements were specified according to the white-box view described in Sect. 2, and were verified individually. To achieve this, ghost variables were used in the annotations to reason about the variables that do not exist as memory in the scope of the top-level function, such as local variables within a function, and about the requirements variables that are not implemented in the module. Variables of the former kind were referred to directly by their memory location. An example of a contract specified according to the white-box view is shown in Fig. 5. Some requirements were also specified according to the black-box view, in order to compare the readability of the resulting contracts. This was performed by substitution of model variables for the expressions which defined them.

Code Annotation: Ghost Variable Assignment. In order to successfully verify the white-box view contracts, the ghost variables have to be assigned the correct values during execution of the function. During the case study, we came up with two distinct methods to achieve this.

The first of these is to simply assign to the ghost variable the value of the local program variable or expression that it represents, within the functions where it changes. For manual annotation this is relatively straight-forward. The verification is also fast since the ghost representations are continuously synchronized with the actual code, and as such there is less work for the verification tool to prove the correlation. However, because of the tight connection to the code this method does not lend itself well to automation, since the relation between intermediary requirement variables and expressions in the code can not be inferred without human instruction.

In the second method, we define a separate ghost program that computes the complete combinational logic circuit discussed in Sect. 2, from program input variables. The ghost program can then be inserted in the body of the top-level function through inlining. Because VCC will need to infer the relation between the ghost circuit and the actual code, the performance of the verification is worse (how much worse depends largely on the number of intermediate variables, i.e., how much VCC needs to infer that would otherwise be explicit). On the other hand, the construction of such a ghost program from a formal requirements specification is far easier to automate. Another drawback of this method is that incomplete specifications cause problems, since VCC is not able to infer any relation between the ghost circuit and the software for input values that are not specified, whereas in the first method this relation can be made explicit even if not specified, provided ghost variables are always assigned values in the code.

```
int state[NUM_SIGNALS]; // Global state

int _(pure) read(int idx)
  _(requires \thread_local_array(state, NUM_SIGNALS))
  _(requires 0 <= idx && idx < NUM_SIGNALS)
  _(ensures  \result == state[idx])
{
  if (idx >= 0 && idx < NUM_SIGNALS)
    return state[idx];
}
```

Fig. 4. A fully specified function.

Code Annotation: Helper Functions. Since the requirements only specify the behaviour of the module as a whole and not how individual functions should behave, and because VCC performs its verification function-modularly, it was necessary to decompose and propagate the top-level requirements through the call hierarchy of the module. We utilized two complementary approaches to this, which we term *bottom-up* and *top-down.*

In the bottom-up approach, we give a complete specification of the computations performed by the functions, starting at the bottom of the call hierarchy, working upwards. This approach is suitable for small functions, which many other functions depend on, such as setters and getters, since giving a complete specification for these is relatively easy, and we get much value out of having one. An example of a fully specified, simple read function is given in Fig. 4.

In the top-down approach, on the other hand, we instead work with one requirement at a time, follow the trail of execution affecting that requirement through the functional hierarchy, and add the appropriate annotations, or partial specifications. This approach is suited for large and high-level (w.r.t. the call hierarchy) functions, where giving a complete specification is complex and not much value is gained from having one. An example of a partial contract of a high-level function, where annotations for only certain requirements have been supplied, is given in Fig. 5. These annotated requirements are represented as boxes within gates in Fig. 3, with their respective numbers.

Obstacles. Apart from the previously mentioned challenges with the requirements themselves, we also identified several obstacles to verification that could occur from how the code is written. Most importantly, the code should be written in a *type-safe* manner. To perform its reasoning, VCC must be able to lift the code to its own stronger model. If the code is not written in a well-typed manner, such as making use of implicit type conversions or aliasing of distinct memory objects, VCC will be unable to do this lifting and verification will not be possible without assistance in the form of additional annotations.

Another obstacle that may occur is code that depends on previous executions, for example in the form of local *static variables.* Such variables are outside the scope of the contract and can therefore not be used to directly specify

```
_(ghost \bool model_vehicleIsMoving) // Intermediate ghost variable
_(ghost \bool model_VehicleMovingWithoutPrimaryPowerSteering)

void steering()
  _(writes \array_range(state, NUM_SIGNALS))
  _(writes &model_vehicleIsMoving)
  _(writes &model_VehicleMovingWithoutPrimaryPowerSteering)
  // Req. 4
  _(ensures \old(state[WHEEL_BASED_SPEED]) > VEH_MOVING_LIMIT
        ==> model_vehicleIsMoving == \true)
  _(ensures \old(state[WHEEL_BASED_SPEED]) < VEH_STATIONARY_LIMIT
        ==> model_vehicleIsMoving == \false)
  // Req. 10
  _(ensures \old(state[POS_SENSOR]) == NO_FLOW
        && model_vehicleIsMoving == \true
        ==> model_VehicleMovingWithoutPrimaryPowerSteering == \true)
  // Req. 15
  _(ensures model_VehicleMovingWithoutPrimaryPowerSteering == \true
        ==> state[SECONDARY_CIRCUIT_HANDLES_STEERING] == \true)
```

Fig. 5. A partially specified function.

properties of the function; but at the same time changes to their values may affect future invocations of the function. It is possible to work around this, for example by connecting static variables to ghost variables that exist in the scope of the contract, but a much simpler solution is just to try to avoid them.

Variables of the enumerable and Boolean types can also make verification difficult in some cases, since in the C language they are in reality backed by the integer type, and may assume all the same values. While these types of variables are common and may not be easily avoided, they introduce some additional annotation effort; for a successful verification of requirements referring to such variables, annotations for proving that the variables never assume values outside of their expected domain are usually needed.

5   Discussion

Summary of Findings. We now return to the questions raised in the Introduction.

1. We found the *formalization* of functional requirements intuitive to achieve, and without much effort. We also found that the formalization helped clarify the requirements, as we were forced to resolve ambiguities and contradictions in order to achieve a valid verification.
2. The *code coverage* of the verification tool VCC for the given code base was almost complete. It is relatively easy to use the tool, especially as it can be configured as a plug-in to Visual Studio, but requires a certain training and knowledge of the underlying verification technology to make full use of it.

VCC turns out to be relatively *efficient*: it took 165 sec to verify the whole annotated module, of which 65 sec went to the "worst" function. On the negative side, the *feedback* provided from the tool when verification fails only highlights the specific assertions that failed to verify, without any hints as to why. Depending on the type and complexity of the assertion, this feedback may not always be useful, and careful analysis of the code and the annotations is usually required to understand what went wrong.

3. The *annotation overhead* of the code was about 50%, or roughly 700 lines of annotations. The annotation was performed manually, but we observe a clear potential for automation of (most of) the annotation process (see below). Manual annotation of the code, even after having formalized the requirements and understood the tool and code base, required much effort; we estimate it roughly to have taken between 1 and 1.5 person-months. In particular, finding and inserting appropriate annotations for all memory accesses, as well as figuring out how each function affects the individual requirements or, alternatively, giving a full specification for the function, are time consuming tasks.

Towards Semi-automated Specification and Verification. Based on findings from the case study, we propose the following work process that automates most of the specification and verification effort, as a prerequisite of integrating our technology into the development process for safety-critical embedded C-code.

Our proposal is to start from a (potentially graphical) combinational logic circuit-like description of the computed functions, according to a chosen function decomposition (i.e., a white-box view as illustrated on Fig. 3), together with descriptions of the individual "gates" of this circuit, created with the help of a tool. The tool has to support specifying interface requirements variables in terms of references to the actual global program variables, or otherwise allow this mapping to be provided by the user separately. This description can be seen as the *requirements model*, and is then to be translated to a VCC "ghost program" computing the functions, by introducing a ghost variable for each requirements variable. In this way we can utilize the existing syntax and operational semantics of VCC ghost code, and are thus relieved from the need to have to define such a semantics for a new formal requirements language. This ghost program can thus be seen as an *executable specification*.

From the requirements model, including the mapping of interface requirements variables to actual global program variables, a *contract* for the main function of the given module is to be generated. The tool should support generating both the white-box and black-box view contracts. In the white-box view, global program variables should be used in the specification of interface requirements, in order to enable modular verification. The generated executable specification is to be inlined in the top-level function of the module, so that the value of the intermediate requirements variables can be computed. As a fallback strategy, intermediate requirements variables may instead be manually synchronized with their program counterparts, in cases where verification proves unfeasible.

What then remains to be annotated are the helper functions. One way of handling these is to *inline* them successively into the main function. While this eliminates the need for annotation of helper functions altogether, its drawbacks are the potential explosion of code (which may result in an inability of VCC to verify it), and the need to maintain a verified code base separately from the actual code base, creating a potential gap and making more difficult the interpretation of the feedback from the tool.

The preprocessing phase described in Sect. 4 is to be assisted by dedicated static analyses, which are to generate annotations for the different types of implicit requirements. Certain postprocessing may also be needed in order to help the programmer in making sense of and reacting to the messages that VCC issues on unsuccessful verifications.

6   Related Work

VCC has been used in a number of software verification initiatives. It was in fact built with verification of the Microsoft Hyper-V hypervisor in mind [5,7]. In a case study [2], VCC was also used to verify another hypervisor, although a less complex one. The study presents techniques for verification using automated methods. It describes modeling of interaction between hardware and software, and shows that functional verification of simulation of guest machines is feasible. In another case study [3], VCC is used to verify system calls in a micro-kernel based operating system targeted at safety-critical embedded systems. The study was part of an avionics project, and describes the verification process as well as how the underlying hardware architecture was modelled. In addition, it is shown that assembly code can be semantically specified and integrated in the verification through VCC.

Within the same avionics project, a case study utilizing the verification tool Frama-C was also performed [9]. The study evaluates several aspects of modern formal verification, such as how formalization of requirements can be achieved and when it is feasible, and the complexity of the formal languages of verification tools in comparison to programming languages. Solutions to many obstacles that commonly occur in formal verification are proposed. Of the encountered case studies, this is the only one with a starting point similar to ours, i.e. informal requirements specifying functional relations between input and output states. Our approach is different in that we formalize the requirements as a circuit, which can then be executed in ghost code, as well as handle requirements variables without explicit counter-parts in the software.

A methodology for reasoning about timed and hybrid systems in VCC is presented in [4]. The approach uses what is referred to as *Timers* and *Deadlines*, and can provide a solution to the verification of temporal requirements in a functional setting. Another work examines the incorporation of strongest post-conditions in the verification process, and how symbolic execution can be used to calculate them [11]. Such a framework could provide a basis for automation of much of the C code annotation process, particularly the (complete) specification of function contracts.

7   Conclusion

In this paper we summarize our findings and experiences with specifying and verifying deductively the functional requirements of an embedded safety-critical C-code module, by using the VCC tool. The main specifics of the verified code is that it computes a multi-output function over variables from finite domains that has a non-trivial, multi-level decomposition. The main challenge then is how to deal with intermediate requirements variables.

The pre-study indicates that deductive functional verification can be a viable option for increased quality assurance of safety-critical embedded C-code. For its integration into an *embedded C-code development process*, however, a number of issues need to be resolved. First, a formal requirements language needs to be adopted and guidelines for writing requirements need to be formulated and supported by a tool. Second, the coding rules that are prerequisite for successful verification need to be enforced. Third, the annotation process needs to be automated almost completely, with clear hints to the programmer where he or she has to provide annotations, and of what type. And fourth, support for interpreting and handling the feedback from the verification tool needs to be provided in a way that allows unsuccessful verifications to be resolved adequately and without requiring deep knowledge of the inner workings of the tool. Our work currently focuses on addressing these issues.

References

1. Allocation Element Requirement AE417 Dual-Circuit Steering. Scania Technical Product Data (2015)
2. Alkassar, E., Hillebrand, M.A., Paul, W., Petrova, E.: Automated verification of a small hypervisor. In: Leavens, G.T., O'Hearn, P., Rajamani, S.K. (eds.) VSTTE 2010. LNCS, vol. 6217, pp. 40–54. Springer, Heidelberg (2010). doi:10.1007/978-3-642-15057-9_3
3. Baumann, C., Beckert, B., Blasum, H., Bormer, T.: Formal verification of a microkernel used in dependable software systems. In: Buth, B., Rabe, G., Seyfarth, T. (eds.) SAFECOMP 2009. LNCS, vol. 5775, pp. 187–200. Springer, Heidelberg (2009). doi:10.1007/978-3-642-04468-7_16
4. Cohen, E.: Modular verification of hybrid system code with VCC. CoRR abs/1403.3611 (2014)
5. Cohen, E., Dahlweid, M., Hillebrand, M., Leinenbach, D., Moskal, M., Santen, T., Schulte, W., Tobies, S.: VCC: a practical system for verifying concurrent C. In: Berghofer, S., Nipkow, T., Urban, C., Wenzel, M. (eds.) TPHOLs 2009. LNCS, vol. 5674, pp. 23–42. Springer, Heidelberg (2009). doi:10.1007/978-3-642-03359-9_2
6. Cohen, E., Moskal, M., Schulte, W., Tobies, S.: A practical verification methodology for concurrent programs. Technical report MSR-TR-2009-15, Microsoft Research, February 2009
7. Cohen, E., Moskal, M., Schulte, W., Tobies, S.: A precise yet efficient memory model for C. In: Workshop on Systems Software Verification (SSV 2009). Electronic Notes in Theoretical Computer Science, vol. 254, pp. 85–103. Elsevier (2009)

8. Cuoq, P., Kirchner, F., Kosmatov, N., Prevosto, V., Signoles, J., Yakobowski, B.: Frama-C. In: Eleftherakis, G., Hinchey, M., Holcombe, M. (eds.) SEFM 2012. LNCS, vol. 7504, pp. 233–247. Springer, Heidelberg (2012). doi:10.1007/978-3-642-33826-7_16

9. Dordowsky, F.: An experimental study using ACSL and Frama-C to formulate and verify low-level requirements from a DO-178C compliant avionics project. In: Formal Integrated Development Environment (F-IDE 2015), pp. 28–41 (2015)

10. Eriksson, J.: Formal Requirement Models for Automotive Embedded Systems. Master's thesis, KTH Royal Institute of Technology, School of Computer Science and Communication (2016)

11. Gordon, M., Collavizza, H.: Forward with Hoare. In: Roscoe, A., Jones, C., Wood, K. (eds) Reflections on the Work of C.A.R. Hoare, pp. 101–121. Springer, London (2010). doi:10.1007/978-1-84882-912-1_5

12. Hoare, C.A.R.: An axiomatic basis for computer programming. Commun. ACM **12**(10), 576–580 (1969)

13. Lidström, C.: Verification of Functional Requirements of Embedded Automotive C Code. Master's thesis, KTH Royal Institute of Technology, School of Computer Science and Communication (2016)

Verifying Event-Based Timing Constraints by Translation into Presburger Formulae

Björn Lisper[✉]

School of Innovation, Design, and Engineering,
Mälardalen University, 721 23 Västerås, Sweden
bjorn.lisper@mdh.se

Abstract. Abstract modeling of timing properties is often based on events. An event can be seen as a sequence of times. Timing constraints can then be expressed as constraints on events: an example is the TADL2 language that has been developed in the automotive domain.

Event-based constraints can express timing properties of implementations as well as timing requirements. An important step in timing verification is then to show that any events that comply with the properties of the implementation, i.e., that describe the timings of its possible behaviours, also satisfy the requirements.

Real-time software is often organised as a set of periodically repeating tasks, especially in domains with time-critical systems like automotive and avionics. This implementation naturally yields periodic events, where each event occurrence belongs to a periodically repeating time window. An interesting question is then: if some events are periodic in this fashion, will they then fulfil a timing constraint that describes a timing requirement? We show, for a number of TADL2 timing constraints, how to translate this implication into an equivalent Presburger formula. Since Presburger logic is decidable, this yields an automated method to decide whether the periodic implementation satisfies the timing requirements or not. Initial experiments with a Presburger solver indicate that the method is practical.

1 Introduction

Timing behavior descriptions exist in many different forms. Classical real-time scheduling theory defines the basic *periodic* [18] and *sporadic* [19] patterns to describe task activations, along with the simple notion of *relative deadlines* for capturing the desired behavior of a system's response. Digital circuits are often accompanied by *timing diagrams* [4], where selected scenarios from an infinitely repeating behavior are depicted graphically, specifically indicating the minimum and maximum distances between key events. In the automotive domain, the model-based development frameworks of AUTOSAR [6] and EAST-ADL [12] offer a rich palette of *built-in timing patterns* and constraints, commonly specified in terms of typical-case timing diagrams. On the theoretical side, *temporal* and *real-time logics* concentrate on a few basic building blocks, from which more complex timing formulae can be constructed using logical connectives.

© Springer International Publishing AG 2017
L. Petrucci et al. (Eds.): FMICS-AVoCS 2017, LNCS 10471, pp. 19–33, 2017.
DOI: 10.1007/978-3-319-67113-0_2

An important class of timing behavior descriptions is based on *events*: examples are TADL2 [10], a revised version of the *Timing Augmented Description Language* (TADL) [15] that forms the basis for timing specifications in AUTOSAR and EAST-ADL, and the CCSL language of the UML real-time profile MARTE [5]. Events are sequences (or sets) of times. A rich variety of timing properties, for single as well as multiple events, can be expressed in this fashion. An advantage with this way of describing timing properties is that it abstracts away from the underlying system by describing its possible timing behaviours through constraints on events. Once this is done, it can be checked in the event domain whether the system fulfils its timing requirements or not. If the possible timing behaviours of the system are described by a predicate *impl* on the events $e^1, \ldots, e^n$, and if the requirements are expressed by the predicate *req* on the same events, then the property that the system fulfils its timing requirements is expressed by the formula

$$\forall e^1, \ldots, e^n.[impl(e^1, \ldots, e^n) \Rightarrow req(e^1, \ldots, e^n)] \tag{1}$$

We have studied a case where formulae of this kind can be decided. Systems are often implemented in a fashion that gives rise to *periodic* events, where each event occurrence belongs to a regularly repeating time window of fixed size. The class of periodic events has certain mathematical properties that, when the *impl* predicate in (1) is expressed as a conjunction of periodic event constraints, allows many instances of (1) to be translated into an equivalent Presburger formula. We exemplify this by translating a number of instances of (1), where $req(e^1, \ldots, e^n)$ is given by different TADL2 constraints, into equivalent Presburger formulae. Since Presburger logic is decidable, this yields a route to automatic verification of these instances.

An important case where periodic events appear is for *periodic preemptive fixed priority based scheduling*, where real-time tasks are triggered periodically and higher priority tasks can preempt lower-priority tasks. The time windows for events marking the completions of such tasks can be established by a best- and a worst-case response-time analysis, well-known from classical real-time scheduling theory. The task model is very common in areas like automotive and avionics, and many real-time operating systems implement this scheduling policy.

In the widely used AUTOSAR standard [6] for development of automotive software, the smallest software entities that can be associated with events are *runnables*. These are grouped into tasks, which can be executed by the AUTOSAR Basic Software Layer according to this scheduling policy. Events arising from runnables will then be periodic. Timing requirements can be expressed over these events using constraints from the *AUTOSAR Timing Extensions* [7], which are directly based on the TADL timing constraints. This opens the possibility to verify timing constraints for AUTOSAR software automatically using our approach.

A concern, however, is the potentially very high complexity for deciding Presburger formulae. This could render the verification method impractical. We have performed some simple experiments with the the `iscc` calculator[1], which can handle general Presburger formulae. In all cases, the translated formulae were solved instantaneously. This indicates that the method may indeed be practical.

The rest of this paper is organised as follows. In Sect. 2 we define events, and introduce a syntax for timing constraints as a simple logic "TiCS" for sequences of times. Section 3 introduces TADL2, and we define the TADL2 constraints in TiCS. In Sect. 4 we show how to translate statements of form (1) into Presburger formulae, and we prove the equivalence of the translated formula for some typical cases where the events are periodic and the requirements are expressed as TADL2 constraints. In Sect. 5 we give an account for some initial experiments with a Presburger solver. We discuss related work in Sect. 6, and the paper is concluded with some reflections on future work in Sect. 7.

2   Events

Definition 1. *An* event *e is a strictly increasing, possibly infinite sequence of times* $\langle e_0, e_1, \ldots \rangle$*. Each time* e_i *is an* occurrence *of the event.*

We consider times to be integers. This is not a serious restriction: all results shown here are also valid for events with real-valued occurrences. For a *periodic* event, each occurrence belongs to a regularly appearing, fixed size time window:

Definition 2. *An event* $\langle e_0, e_1, \ldots \rangle$ *is* periodic *with* start time t_s*, jitter* $j \geq 0$*, and* periodicity $p > j$*, iff for all* $i \geq 0$ *holds that* $t_s + i \cdot p \leq e_i \leq t_s + i \cdot p + j$*. We write* $Per(e, t_s, p, j)$ *to denote that e is a periodic event with start time* t_s*, periodicity p, and jitter j.*

Fig. 1. Time windows for a periodic event.

Periodic events with jitter correspond to the periodic task model with output jitter [8]. Figure 1 provides an illustration of the time windows to which the occurrences of a periodic event must belong.

We define a simple, formal syntax for constraints on events in the form of a first-order logic, see Fig. 2, where we also give a standard denotational semantics with semantic functions mapping expressions and environments "ρ" to values. We label the logic "TiCS" ("Timing Constraints for Sequences"). It is a variation of the event logic "TiCL" [17], which has been used to give a formal semantics to

---

[1] https://dtai.cs.kuleuven.be/cgi-bin/barvinok.cgi.

the TADL2 timing constraints: the main difference between TiCS and TiCL is that in TiCL events are sets of times, whereas TiCS defines events as sequences of times.

TiCS allows timing constraints to be expressed as conditions on arithmetic expressions involving event occurrences. There are three kinds of variables: event variables e, arithmetic variables t, and index variables i. Event occurrences are of the form e_{i+n}, where n is a natural number. Quantification can be done over all three kinds of variables.

$$
\begin{array}{ll}
n \in \mathbb{N} \text{ (natural numbers)} & o \in \textbf{Eocc} \text{ (event occurrences)} \\
z \in \mathbb{Z} \text{ (integers)} & t \in \textbf{Avar} \text{ (arithmetic variables)} \\
e \in \textbf{Evar} \text{ (event variables)} & a \in \textbf{AExpr} \text{ (arithmetic expressions)} \\
i \in \textbf{Ivar} \text{ (index variables)} & c \in \textbf{CExpr} \text{ (constraint expressions)}
\end{array}
$$

$$
\begin{aligned}
o &\rightarrow e_{i+n} \\
a &\rightarrow z \mid t \mid i \mid o \mid a_1 + a_2 \mid a_1 - a_2 \mid a_1 \cdot a_2 \mid a_1/a_2 \\
c &\rightarrow T \mid F \mid a_1 \geq a_2 \mid c_1 \wedge c_2 \mid c_1 \vee c_2 \mid \neg c \mid \forall e.c \mid \forall i.c \mid \forall t.c \mid \exists e.c \mid \exists i.c \mid \exists t.c
\end{aligned}
$$

$$
\begin{aligned}
\epsilon &\in \textbf{Event} = \mathbb{N} \rightarrow \mathbb{Z} \text{ (events)} \\
\rho &\in \textbf{Env} = (\textbf{Avar} \rightarrow \mathbb{Z}) \cup (\textbf{Ivar} \rightarrow \mathbb{N}) \cup (\textbf{Evar} \rightarrow \textbf{Event}) \text{ (environments)} \\
\mathcal{A} &\in \textbf{AExpr} \rightarrow \textbf{Env} \rightarrow \mathbb{Z} \\
\mathcal{C} &\in \textbf{CExpr} \rightarrow \textbf{Env} \rightarrow \mathbb{B}
\end{aligned}
$$

$$
\begin{aligned}
\mathcal{A}[z]\rho &= z \\
\mathcal{A}[t]\rho &= \rho(t) \\
\mathcal{A}[i]\rho &= \rho(i) \\
\mathcal{A}[e_{i+n}]\rho &= \rho(e)(\rho(i) + n) \\
\mathcal{A}[a_1 \oplus a_2]\rho &= \mathcal{A}[a_1]\rho \oplus \mathcal{A}[a_2]\rho, \\
&\qquad \oplus \in \{+, -, \cdot, /\} \\
\mathcal{C}[T]\rho &= T \\
\mathcal{C}[F]\rho &= F
\end{aligned}
$$

$$
\begin{aligned}
\mathcal{C}[a_1 \geq a_2]\rho &= \mathcal{A}[a_1]\rho \geq \mathcal{A}[a_2]\rho \\
\mathcal{C}[c_1 \wedge c_2]\rho &= \mathcal{C}[c_1]\rho \wedge \mathcal{C}[c_2]\rho \\
\mathcal{C}[c_1 \vee c_2]\rho &= \mathcal{C}[c_1]\rho \vee \mathcal{C}[c_2]\rho \\
\mathcal{C}[\neg c]\rho &= \neg(\mathcal{C}[c]\rho) \\
\mathcal{C}[\forall e.c]\rho &= \forall \epsilon.\mathcal{C}[c]\rho[e \mapsto \epsilon] \\
\mathcal{C}[\exists e.c]\rho &= \exists \epsilon.\mathcal{C}[c]\rho[e \mapsto \epsilon] \\
\mathcal{C}[\forall i.c]\rho &= \forall n.\mathcal{C}[c]\rho[i \mapsto n] \\
\mathcal{C}[\exists i.c]\rho &= \exists n.\mathcal{C}[c]\rho[i \mapsto n] \\
\mathcal{C}[\forall t.c]\rho &= \forall z.\mathcal{C}[c]\rho[t \mapsto z] \\
\mathcal{C}[\exists t.c]\rho &= \exists z.\mathcal{C}[c]\rho[t \mapsto z]
\end{aligned}
$$

Fig. 2. Syntactic categories, abstract syntax, and semantics

We will make free use of derived operators like $\Rightarrow$, $>$, $=$, $\neq$, which are definable in the language. We will write e_i for e_{i+0}. We will write $a \leq a' \leq a''$ for $a \leq a' \wedge a' \leq a''$. We will sometimes use set inclusion $x \in S$ when this formula can be expressed as a predicate in TiCS: for instance, given an interval $[l, u]$ we may write $x \in [l, u]$ for $l \leq x \leq u$. We will use the the shorthands $\forall p(x).c$ and $\exists p(x).c$ for $\forall x.(p(x) \Rightarrow c)$ and $\exists x.(p(x) \wedge c)$, respectively. We will allow ourselves the use of the infinity symbol "∞" in lieu of integers, when the semantics is clear: for instance, $\infty \geq z$ will always be true whenever $z \in \mathbb{Z}$. Using this notation we can express the property of being a periodic event as the following constraint:

$$
Per(e, t_s, p, j) = \forall i \geq 0.[t_s + i \cdot p \leq e_i \leq t_s + i \cdot p + j]
$$

When defining TADL2 constraints below we will allow nonrecursive "macros" defined in this way to appear in the formulae: their semantics can be defined by simple substitution. Finally we will use metanotation like "$e^1, \ldots, e^n$", or "$c_1 \wedge \cdots \wedge c_n$", to describe a varying number of arguments, or expressions.

TiCS, being a first-order logic containing basic arithmetics, is undecidable. Presburger arithmetic is a decidable fragment.

3   TADL2

The *Timing Augmented Description Language* (TADL2) [10] is a constraint language for describing timing requirements and properties within the automotive domain. It was originally defined in the TIMMO project, and was subsequently revised and formalised within the TIMMO-2-USE project[2]. The syntax of TADL is compliant to the AUTOSAR meta-model, but the TADL2 constraints can also be understood through a textual syntax.

TADL2 defines constraints on events, which are simply (finite or infinite) sequences of strictly increasing times. The definition does not specify whether times are integers or reals: the constraints have meaningful interpretations in both cases.

The TADL2 constraints can be divided into three groups: *repetition rate constraints*, which concern single events, *delay constraints*, which concern the timing relation between *stimuli* and *responses*, and *synchronisation constraints*, which require that corresponding occurrences of a group of events appear in sufficiently tight clusters.

All repetition rate constraints can be seen as instances of a *generic repetition rate constraint*. This constraint is specified by four parameters *lower*, *upper*, *jitter*, and *span* where $span > 0$. An event $\langle t_0, t_1, \ldots \rangle$ satisfies a generic repetition rate constraint iff there exists a sequence of times $\langle x_0, x_1, \ldots \rangle$ such that for all $i \geq 0$,

$$x_i \leq t_i \leq x_i + \textit{jitter}, \quad \text{and} \quad \textit{lower} \leq x_{i+span} - x_i \leq \textit{upper}$$

A *periodic* repetition constraint is a generic repetition rate constraint where $span = 1$, and $lower = upper$. This uniquely decides x_i to be $x_0 + i \cdot \textit{lower}$, and we can write the constraint as $\exists x_0. Per(\langle t_0, t_1, \ldots \rangle, x_0, \textit{lower}, \textit{jitter})$ with *Per* given by Definition 2. A *sporadic* repetition constraint has $span = 1$, and $upper = \infty$. TADL2 also defines more complex *pattern* repetition constraints, and *arbitrary* repetition constraints, see [10].

(The reason why we define a slightly different periodic constraint "*Per*" in Sect. 2 is that the TADL2 *Periodic* constraint is too weak to allow the results that we prove in Sect. 4. These results rely on knowledge about the relative offsets of periodic events, and this information is not present for the *Periodic* constraint.)

---

[2] https://itea3.org/project/timmo-2-use.html.

Delay constraints relate two events, called stimulus and response, by demanding that each occurrence of the stimulus is matched by at least one occurrence of the response within some time window. The basic delay constraint takes the parameters *lower*, and *upper*, and relates the stimulus event $\langle s_0, s_1, \ldots \rangle$ and the response event $\langle r_0, r_1, \ldots \rangle$ through the following constraint: for all i there exists a j such that

$$s_i + lower \leq r_j \leq s_i + upper$$

Synchronisation constraints concern a group of events S, characterised by a single parameter *tolerance*. The basic synchronisation constraint is fulfilled if there are time windows of size *tolerance* such that (1) each time window contains at least one occurrence of each event in S, and (2) there are no "spurious" event occurrences outside these windows. In other words, this constraint is satisfied iff there is a sequence of times $\langle x_0, x_1, \ldots \rangle$ such that (1) for all events $\langle s_0, s_1, \ldots \rangle \in S$ and for all i there exists a j such that

$$x_i \leq s_j \leq x_i + tolerance$$

and (2) for all i there exists a j such that

$$s_i - tolerance \leq x_j \leq s_i$$

Following [10, 17] the twelve most important TADL2 constraints are expressed below in TiCS. First, the repetition rate constraints:

$$Repeat(e, l, u, s) = \forall i \geq 0.[l \leq e_{i+s} - e_i \leq u] \quad (s > 0)$$
$$Repetition(e, l, u, s, j) = \exists e'.[Repeat(e', l, u, s) \wedge StrongDelay(e', e, 0, j)]$$
$$Sporadic(e, l, u, j, m) = Repetition(e, l, u, 1, j) \wedge Repeat(e, m, \infty, 1)$$
$$Periodic(e, p, j, m) = Sporadic(e, p, p, j, m) \quad (p > 0)$$
$$Pattern(e, p, o_1, \ldots, o_n, j, m) = \exists e'.[Periodic(e', p, 0, 0) \wedge Repeat(e, m, \infty, 1) \wedge$$
$$Delay(e', e, o_1, o_1 - j) \wedge$$
$$\cdots$$
$$Delay(e', e, o_n, o_n - j)]$$
$$Arbitrary(e, l_1, \ldots, l_n,$$
$$u_1, \ldots, u_n) = Repeat(e, l_1, u_1, 1) \wedge \cdots \wedge Repeat(e, l_n, u_n, n)$$
$$Burst(e, l, o, m) = Repeat(e, l, \infty, o) \wedge Repeat(e, m, \infty, 1)$$

Then, the delay constraints:

$$Delay(e, e', l, u) = \forall i \geq 0.\exists k \geq 0.[l \leq e'_k - e_i \leq u]$$
$$StrongDelay(e, e', l, u) = \forall i \geq 0.[l \leq e'_i - e_i \leq u]$$
$$Order(e, e') = \forall i \geq 0.[e_i < e'_i]$$

Finally, the synchronisation constraints:

$$Synch(e^1, \ldots, e^n, w) = \exists e'.[Delay(e', e^1, 0, w) \wedge Delay(e^1, e', -w, 0) \wedge$$
$$\cdots$$
$$Delay(e', e^n, 0, w) \wedge Delay(e^n, e', -w, 0)]$$
$$StrongSynch(e^1, \ldots, e^n, w) = \exists e'.[StrongDelay(e', e^1, 0, w) \wedge$$
$$\cdots$$
$$StrongDelay(e', e^n, 0, w)]$$

In addition, TADL2 contains five constraints that cannot always be expressed in TiCS: an *execution time constraint*, and four constraints that are variations of basic constraints but where these constraints are restricted to hold only between certain event occurrences as specified by an auxiliary *causality relation* on these. As TADL2 does not define the nature of this relation further, we cannot guarantee that these constraints are always expressible in TiCS. However note that if the causality relation can be expressed in the TiCS syntax, then the full constraint can be as well and the verification machinery developed here can be applied. We will not consider these constraints further here: see [10] for details.

In addition to the constraints TADL2 also allows timing expressions to be symbolic. Symbolic variables can be defined, or constrained, and used in timing constraints. Typical usages are to parameterise timing requirements for easy update, to constrain the ranges of parameters, and to aid time budgeting by specifying bounds on sums of delays. TiCS supports symbolic timing expressions right away, and constraints on symbolic variables can simply be conjoined with the timing constraints.

4   Transforming TADL2 Constraints into Presburger Formulae

We will now show how to transform statements of the form (1), where the antecedent specifies events to be periodic according to Definition 2, and the consequent is chosen from a selection of TADL2 constraints, into equivalent Presburger formulae. The correctness of the transformation depends on a certain property of the repeating time windows for the periodic events. We now define this property, and show that it holds for these time windows.

Definition 3. *Let $R = \langle R_0, R_1, \ldots \rangle$ be a sequence of sets of times. Let E be a set of events.*

1. *R is a sequence of regions for E iff for all $i \geq 0$, and all $e \in E$, holds that $e_i \in R_i$.*
2. *R is tight for E iff it is a sequence of regions for E, and for any event e, where $e_i \in R_i$ for all $i \geq 0$, holds that $e \in E$.*

Lemma 1. *If R is tight for E, then $e \in E \iff \forall i.e_i \in R_i$.*

Proof. $\Rightarrow$: since if R is tight for E, then R is a sequence of regions for E. $\Leftarrow$: by the definition of tightness.

Let us write $win(t_s, p, j, i)$ for the ith time window $[t_s + i \cdot p, t_s + i \cdot p + j]$ containing the ith occurrence of a periodic event according to Definition 2.

Lemma 2. *$\{\, win(t_s, p, j, i) \mid i \geq 0 \,\}$ is tight for $\{\, e \mid Per(e, t_s, p, j) \,\}$.*

Proof. Immediate from Definition 2.

A tight sequence of regions fully characterises its set of events: each event occurrence belongs to the corresponding region, and any event in the set can be generated by picking a time from each region as the corresponding occurrence.

The transformation into a Presburger formula follows a common pattern. The first step is to transform the consequent in (1), i.e., the formula specifying the requirements, by replacing event occurrences with arithmetic variables to obtain a formula free of such occurrences:

- If the consequent contains the term $\forall i.C(e_{i+n})$, where $Per(e, t_s, p, j)$, then this term is replaced by $\forall i.\forall t \in win(t_s, p, j, i + n).C(t)$. That is: e_{i+n} is replaced by the arithmetic variable t throughout, where t ranges over the interval of e_{i+n}.
- If there are several distinct event occurrences indexed by the same quantified index variable, then each occurrence is replaced by a distinct arithmetic variable ranging over its interval. For instance, $\forall i.C(e_{i+n}, e'_{i+m})$ is translated into $\forall i.\forall t \in win(t_s, p, j, i + n).\forall t' \in win(t'_s, p', j', i + m).C(t, t')$ (given that $Per(e, t_s, p, j)$, and $Per(e', t'_s, p', j')$).
- Terms with existentially quantified index variables are transformed in the same way.

We now give a formal definition. The translation is defined relative to a function R mapping event variables to sequences of regions, and we denote it "P_R". We define it for a fragment of TiCS without quantification over events, and where formulas w.l.o.g. are in prenex normal form (all quantifiers are at the outermost level). The first restriction is important, whereas the second is merely for convenience as it allows a more succinct definition of the translation. In Fig. 3 we define the syntax of this fragment.

$$
\begin{aligned}
a &\rightarrow z \mid t \mid i \mid e_{i+n} \mid a_1 + a_2 \mid a_1 - a_2 \mid a_1 \cdot a_2 \mid a_1/a_2 \quad \textbf{AExpr} \\
c^- &\rightarrow T \mid F \mid a_1 \geq a_2 \mid c_1^- \wedge c_2^- \mid c_1^- \vee c_2^- \mid \neg c^- \quad \textbf{CExpr}^- \\
c &\rightarrow c^- \mid \forall t.c \mid \exists t.c \mid \forall i.c \mid \exists i.c \quad \textbf{CPExpr}
\end{aligned}
$$

Fig. 3. Abstract syntax for restricted constraint expressions

First we introduce some notation. $FVI(c)$ denotes the set of index variables that are free in c:

Definition 4. *For any expression c and index variable i, $Eo(c, i)$ is the set of event occurrences in c of the form e_{i+n}, for some event variable e and natural number n. Furthermore $Eo(c) = \bigcup_{i \in FVI(c)} Eo(c, i)$.*

For instance, if $r, s \in \textbf{Evar}$, then $Eo(s_i + l \leq r_j \leq s_i + u, i) = \{s_i\}$, $Eo(s_i + l \leq r_j \leq s_i + u, j) = \{r_j\}$, $Eo(s_i + l \leq r_j \leq s_i + u) = \{s_i, r_j\}$, and $Eo(e_i \leq e_{i+1}, i) = \{e_i, e_{i+1}\}$.

Next, we assume a function $t: \textbf{Eocc} \rightarrow \textbf{Avar}$ that maps each event occurrence e_{i+n} to a syntactic arithmetic variable $t(e_{i+n}) \in \textbf{Avar}$. Our transformation replaces each e_{i+n} with $t(e_{i+n})$. We assume that all variables $t(e_{i+n})$ are fresh.

Definition 5. *(Substitution of event occurrences) Let $c^- \in \mathbf{CExpr}^-$, and let EO be a set of event occurrences: then $c^-[e_{i+n} \leftarrow t(e_{i+n}) \mid e_{i+n} \in EO]$ is the expression resulting when every occurrence of e_{i+n} in c, where $e_{i+n} \in EO$, is concurrently replaced by the variable $t(e_{i+n})$.*

(We could make a fully formal, recursive definition over the structure of c^-.) Basically this is a first order substitution, the only difference being that we replace syntactic event instances e_{i+n} rather than single variables. Since there never can be any overlaps between the expressions e_{i+n} to be replaced, and since the substitution does not introduce such expressions, this kind of substitution is well-defined. We need some more meta-notation to define the translation:

Definition 6. *For any finite set of event occurrences $EO = \{o_1, \ldots, o_n\}$, arithmetic variables $t(o_1), \ldots, t(o_n)$, sets of integers $T(o_1), \ldots, T(o_n)$, and constraint expression c, we define:*

$$\forall(\, t(o) \in T(o) \mid o \in EO \,).c =$$
$$\forall t(o_1) \cdots \forall t(o_n).(t(o_1) \in T(o_1) \wedge \cdots \wedge t(o_n) \in T(o_n) \Rightarrow c)$$

Thus, the meta-notation denotes a formula where the variables $t(o_1), \ldots, t(o_n)$ are universally quantified over c while ranging over the sets $T(o_1), \ldots, T(o_n)$.

We now define our transformation P_R for expressions in **CPExpr**. We assume that for each $e \in \mathbf{Evar}$ there is a set of events $E(e)$ such that $R(e)$ is a sequence of regions for $E(e)$:

Definition 7.

$$P_R(c^-) = c^-[e_{i+n} \leftarrow t(e_{i+n}) \mid e_{i+n} \in Eo(c^-)], \quad c^- \in \mathbf{CExpr}^-$$
$$P_R(\forall t.c) = \forall t.P_R(c)$$
$$P_R(\exists t.c) = \exists t.P_R(c)$$
$$P_R(\forall i.c) = \forall i.\forall(\, t(e_{i+n}) \in R(e)_{i+n} \mid e_{i+n} \in Eo(c, i) \,).P_R(c)$$
$$P_R(\exists i.c) = \exists i.\forall(\, t(e_{i+n}) \in R(e)_{i+n} \mid e_{i+n} \in Eo(c, i) \,).P_R(c)$$

It is clear that $P_R(c)$ will contain no event occurrences. If all numerical subexpressions in c are linear in the index variables, arithmetic variables and event occurrences, and if the set memberships $t(e_{i+n}) \in R(e)_{i+n}$ can be expressed as Presburger formulae, then $P_R(c)$ will be a Presburger formula. For instance, if $i, k \in \mathbf{Ivar}$ and $r, s \in \mathbf{Evar}$ then

$$P_R(\forall i.\exists k.(s_i + l \leq r_k \leq s_i + u)) = \forall i.\forall t \in R(s)_i.\exists k.\forall t' \in R(r)_k.(t + l \leq t' \leq t + u)$$

Here, we have written t for $t(s_i)$ and t' for $t(r_k)$. If the conditions $t \in R(s)_i$ and $t' \in R(r)_k$ can be expressed by Presburger formulae then the transformed formula is also a Presburger formula.

The translation does not handle terms with quantified events. Such events appear in the definitions of the *Repetition, Pattern, Synch,* and *StrongSynch* constraints. To translate such constraints, the quantified events have to be eliminated. For the *Repetition* constraint, if $l = u = p$ and $s = 1$ then the constraint $Repeat(e', p, p, 1)$ will uniquely determine $e'_i = e'_0 + i \cdot p$. Then, the quantification over e' can be replaced by a quantification over an arithmetic variable e'_0, and e'_i can be replaced by $e'_0 + i \cdot p$ throughout. This situation appears for the *Periodic* constraint, which calls *Repetition* through *Sporadic*.

For the synchronisation constraints, *Synch*, and *StrongSynch*, the instances e'_i of the existentially quantified event e' specify starting times of time windows of size w, where some occurrences of all events $e^1, \ldots, e^n$ belong to each window, and no occurrence of any event is outside such a time window. For these constraints, the existence of such a window can instead be expressed by the condition that for all pairs of synchronised events, all distances between the involved event occurrences are less than or equal to the size w of the window. We omit the details.

By eliminating quantified events in the manner described above, all constraints listed in Sect. 3 except the general *Sporadic* and *Repetition* constraints can be written in a form where (1) can be translated into a formula free from event occurrences according to above. What remains is to prove the *correctness* of the translation. We exemplify by proving the correctness for the *Delay* constraint.

Theorem 1.

$$\forall e, e'.[Per(e, t_s, p, j) \wedge Per(e', t'_s, p', j') \Rightarrow Delay(e, e', l, u)]$$
$$\Longleftrightarrow$$
$$\forall i \geq 0. \forall t \in win(t_s, p, j, i). \exists k \geq 0. \forall t' \in win(t'_s, p', j', k).[l \leq t' - t \leq u]$$

Proof. $\Leftarrow$: assume that the statement to the right of the equivalence holds. Consider any events e, e' such that $Per(e, t_s, p, j)$, and $Per(e', t'_s, p', j')$. Then it holds for any $i, k \geq 0$ that $e_i \in win(t_s, p, j, i)$, and $e'_k \in win(t'_s, p', j', k)$. Then, by instantiating $t = e_i$ and $t' = e'_k$ in the right-hand side we obtain $\forall i \geq 0. \exists k \geq 0.[l \leq e'_k - e_i \leq u]$, that is: $Delay(e, e', l, u)$.

$\Rightarrow$: assume that the statement does not hold. We show existence of e, e' where $Per(e, t_s, p, j)$, $Per(e', t'_s, p', j')$, and $\neg Delay(e, e', l, u)$. Since the statement does not hold, there exists an $i \geq 0$ and $t \in win(t_s, p, j, i)$ such that for all $k \geq 0$ there is a $t' \in win(t'_s, p', j', k)$ where $\neg(l \leq t' - t \leq u)$. Another way to express this is that there is a sequence of times $\{t'_k \mid k \geq 0\}$ where for all elements t'_k holds that $t'_k \in win(t'_s, p', j', k)$ and $\neg(l \leq t'_k - t \leq u)$. By tightness and Lemma 1 there is an event e such that $e_i = t$ and $Per(e, t_s, p, j)$. Similarly, by tightness and Lemma 1 we can construct an event e' where $Per(e', t'_s, p', j')$, by letting $e'_k = t_k$ for each $k \geq 0$. Thus, $\exists i \geq 0. \forall k \geq 0. \neg(l \leq e'_k - e_i \leq u)$, that is: $\neg Delay(e, e', l, u)$.

Theorem 1 is illustrated in Fig. 4. It shows two time windows, for the events e and e', respectively, and indicates how the distance between any t, t' drawn from the respective time window must be kept between l and u. The theorem

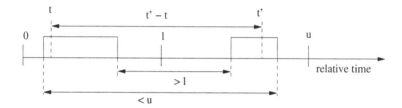

Fig. 4. An illustration of Theorem 1.

does not guarantee that the translated formula is a Presburger formula. For this to hold, the periodicities p, p' of the events e, e' must be constants.

For all the TADL2 constraints listed in Sect. 3, except *Sporadic* and *Repetition*, the equivalence of the translation can be proved in a similar manner as for Theorem 1. This suggests that it should be possible to prove, in a similar way, a correctness result for the translation P_R of *any* constraint in **CPExpr**. However, counterexamples can be found where the equivalence between statement and translated statement does not hold. To prove such a result we need to find a nontrivial fragment of TiCS, which is smaller than the one defined in Fig. 3, for which such a result holds. This is a topic for further research.

5   An Experiment: The Box Service Generic-External

We have tried our method by verifying parts of the timing requirements for the "Box Service Generic-External" (BSG-E) [10], which manages the fog lights in cars. It also handles the electrical protection of downstream wires, diagnostics, and the dialogue with the main car ECU over a CAN network. The total specification of the timing requirements includes ten events, five delay constraints, two periodic constraints, and one synchronisation constraint involving two events. We selected a subset of these with two events, and one delay constraint: the selection was made to provide an example with periodic events. The events are: EMA_PERM3, (filtered) voltage reading from the power supply, and CAR_CDE_BSE, the arrival of the first frame on the CAN bus from the main ECU. EMA_PERM3 is periodic, with periodicity 15 ms and zero jitter, and the nature of CAR_CDE_BSE is not specified. The delay constraint specifies a requirement that whenever a rising edge is detected on the power supply, the first frame from the CAN bus must be read within 40 ms. For this example we assume that CAR_CDE_BSE is periodic. We obtain the following timing constraints:

$$AcqPerm = 5$$
$$T\_init = 40$$
$$Per(EMA\_PERM3, t_2, 3 \cdot AcqPerm, 0)$$
$$Per(CAR\_CDE\_BSE, t_3, 3 \cdot AcqPerm, jitter)$$
$$Delay(EMA\_PERM3, CAR\_CDE\_BSE, 0, T\_init)$$

As the start time t_2 for EMA_PERM3 is not specified, we leave it open. Similarly, since CAR_CDE_BSE is not specified at all, we leave its start time t_3 and jitter open. (We cannot leave its periodicity as a parameter, as this would create a nonlinear expression in the transformed constraint.) For this example we set it to the periodicity of EMA_PERM3, but any value could be chosen.

We have verified the *Delay* constraint, transformed according to Sect. 4, with the iscc[3] calculator [22]. iscc can simplify sets defined by Presburger formulae using Fourier-Motzkin variable elimination. Sets defined by formulae without free variables reduce either to the empty or the universal set (that is, false or true): if the defining formula has free variables then the result will be a set defined by a simplified, quantifier-free formula in the same variables. Thus, iscc can be used as a Presburger solver with the ability to return parametric results.

The experiment was carried out on a Dell Optiplex 7010, with a dual-core 64 bit Intel i5-3570 processor running at 3.40 GHz, 8 GB memory, three levels of cache (256 kB, 1 MB, 6 MB) running Xubuntu linux v. 14.04.5.

```
AcqPerm = 5 and T_init = 40 and
t2 >= 0 and t3 >= 0 and jitter >= 0 and
(not exists i : not (not (i >= 0) ||
(not exists t : not (not (t2 + i*3*5 <= t <= t2 + i*3*5 + 0) ||
(exists k : k >= 0 and
(not exists t' : not (not (t3 + k*3*5 <= t' <= t3 + k*3*5 + jitter) ||
0 <= t' - t and t' - t <= T_init)))))))
```

Fig. 5. iscc encoding of the Presburger formula for the *Delay* constraint.

The encoding of the Presburger formula for the *Delay* constraint, in the textual language of iscc, is shown in Fig. 5. The formula includes constraints on the auxiliary variables as well as non-negativity constraints on the starting times and the jitter. When run with this input, iscc will instantaneously return the following, simplified set expression:

```
{ [AcqPerm = 5, T_init = 40, t2, t3, jitter] :
    t2 >= 0 and t3 >= 0 and 0 <= jitter <= 40 + t2 - t3 and
    15*floor((14t2 + t3)/15) >= -40 + 14t2 + t3 + jitter }
```

We thus obtain constraints on the unknown parameters of the periodic events. We can also make runs with different periodicities of CAR_CDE_BSE to explore how this parameter affects the ability to find a solution that satisfies the constraint. In all, the ability to produce symbolic solutions facilitates a design space exploration where the system is designed as to meet its timing constraints.

---

[3] Our version was built using version 0.40 of the **barvinok** library.

6   Related Work

Logics for expressing and reasoning about real-time properties are mostly expressed as modal logics [1,3,11]. Decidable such logics allow for verification of real-time properties of systems by model-checking. In particular Timed Automata [2] have become much used for this purpose. UPPAAL [16] is a well-known tool for modeling and verification using timed automata. Jagadish [21] used UPPAAL to verify some TADL timing constraints, transformed into timed automata, for periodic events. Examples include the delay constraint. UPPAAL has also been used for verifying timing constraints expressed in the AUTOSAR Timing Extensions [7,9], which build on the TADL timing constraints.

Our approach, using translations into Presburger formulae, is quite different from model checking. It allows the use of decision procedures that eliminate quantifiers through projections, which allows parametric solutions in the form of quantifier-free formulas. For timing verification this can be valuable in early design phases where system parameters are not yet fixed. Possibly parametric model checking of timed automata can be used for the same purpose [14], but this remains to be investigated. Furthermore our approach can be directly extended to continuous time. For this kind of time the use of projection-based decision procedures will yield a lower complexity, whereas the opposite holds for model checking.

We know few other attempts to verify timing properties by deciding Presburger formulae. Amon et al. [4] capture the logic of timing diagrams in a form that resembles our constraint language but without event variables. This sublanguage corresponds to Presburger formulas.

CCSL [5] is a timing constraint language in the UML profile MARTE [20] for modeling and analysis of real-time systems. CCSL can specify *clocks*, and relations between them. Yin et al. [23] describe how to translate a specification in a subset of CCSL into a Promela model for verification in the model checker SPIN. Ning and Pantel [13] proposed a framework for verifying timing properties of MARTE models through model checking over Timed Petri Nets.

7   Conclusions and Further Research

We have shown how to verify a number of TADL2 timing constraints under the condition that the constrained events are periodic with jitter. The TADL2 constraints then express timing requirements, whereas the periodicity and jitter of the events may stem from an implementation where tasks are triggered with some fixed periodicity. Such implementations are common in safety-critical systems, in domains like automotive and avionics. TADL2 has been developed within the automotive domain, with its typical timing requirements mind, and it forms the basis for the AUTOSAR Timing Extensions. It can therefore be of great practical interest to have methods to verify whether or not such periodically scheduled systems will meet their timing requirements expressed as TADL2 constraints. Our work provides a step towards this goal.

The translations to Presburger formulas, and their proofs of correctness, follow a common pattern. An obvious topic for future research is to find a larger fragment of TiCS for which the translation is correct.

We believe that the ability to obtain symbolic results, constraining design parameters, can be very useful. This is convenient in early design phases where all parts of the system are not yet fixed, and it facilitates a design space exploration where the system is optimised under the given timing constraints.

A possible concern is the extremely high worst-case complexity for solving Presburger formulas. However, our experience is that timing constraints in domains like automotive often are gathered into a conjunction of rather simple constraints, like delay or synchronisation constraints. The translated Presburger formula will then be a conjunction of simple constraints, each involving only a few variables. The solver can then solve these individually and intersect the results, which is likely to be much faster than the worst case. A topic for future research is to make larger case studies to see whether this is indeed the case.

Acknowledgments. This work was partially supported by VINNOVA through the ITEA2 TIMMO-2-USE and ITEA3 ASSUME projects. We would also like to thank Johan Nordlander for interesting discussions.

References

1. Abadi, M., Lamport, L.: An old-fashioned recipe for real time. ACM Trans. Program. Lang. Syst. **16**(5), 1543–1571 (1994)
2. Alur, R., Courcoubetis, C., Dill, D.: Model-checking for real-time systems. In: Proceeding of Logic in Computer Science, pp. 414–425. IEEE (1990)
3. Alur, R., Henzinger, T.A.: A really temporal logic. J. ACM **41**(1), 181–203 (1994)
4. Amon, T., Borriello, G., Hu, T., Liu, J.: Symbolic timing verification of timing diagrams using Presburger formulas. In: Proceeding of 34th Annual Design Automation Conference, pp. 226–231. ACM, New York (1997)
5. André, C., Mallet, F.: Clock constraints in UML/MARTE CCSL. Research report, INRIA, May 2008
6. AUTOSAR: Homepage of the AUTOSAR project (2009). www.autosar.org/
7. AUTOSAR: Specification of timing extensions (2011). www.autosar.org/
8. Baruah, S., Buttazzo, G., Gorinsky, S., Lipari, G.: Scheduling periodic task systems to minimize output jitter. In: Proceeding of Sixth International Conference on Real-Time Computing Systems and Applications (RTCSA 1999), pp. 62–69 (1999)
9. Beringer, S., Wehrheim, H.: Verification of AUTOSAR software architectures with timed automata. In: Beek, M.H., Gnesi, S., Knapp, A. (eds.) FMICS/AVoCS 2016. LNCS, vol. 9933, pp. 189–204. Springer, Cham (2016). doi:10.1007/978-3-319-45943-1_13
10. Blom, H., Feng, L., Lönn, H., Nordlander, J., Kuntz, S., Lisper, B., Quinton, S., Hanke, M., Peraldi-Frati, M.A., Goknil, A., Deantoni, J., Defo, G.B., Klobedanz, K., Özhan, M., Honcharova, O.: D11 language syntax, semantics, metamodel v2. Technical report, August 2012. https://itea3.org/project/timmo-2-use.html
11. Chaochen, Z., Hoare, C.A.R., Ravn, A.P.: A calculus of durations. Inf. Process. Lett. **40**(5), 269–276 (1991)

12. Cuenot, P., et al.: 11 The EAST-ADL architecture description language for automotive embedded software. In: Giese, H., Karsai, G., Lee, E., Rumpe, B., Schätz, B. (eds.) MBEERTS 2007. LNCS, vol. 6100, pp. 297–307. Springer, Heidelberg (2010). doi:10.1007/978-3-642-16277-0_11

13. Ge, N., Pantel, M.: Time properties verification framework for UML-MARTE safety critical real-time systems. In: Vallecillo, A., Tolvanen, J.-P., Kindler, E., Störrle, H., Kolovos, D. (eds.) ECMFA 2012. LNCS, vol. 7349, pp. 352–367. Springer, Heidelberg (2012). doi:10.1007/978-3-642-31491-9_27

14. Hune, T., Romijn, J., Stoelinga, M., Vaandrager, F.W.: Linear parametric model checking of timed automata. J. Log. Algebr. Program. **52–53**, 183–220 (2002). http://dx.doi.org/10.1016/S1567-8326(02)00037-1

15. Johansson, R., Frey, P., Jonsson, J., Nordlander, J., Pathan, R.M., Feiertag, N., Schlager, M., Espinoza, H., Richter, K., Kuntz, S., Lönn, H., Kolagari, R.T., Blom, H.: TADL: timing augmented description language, version 2. Technical report, October 2009

16. Larsen, K.G., Pettersson, P., Yi, W.: UPPAAL in a nutshell. Int. J. Softw. Tools Technol. Transfer **1**, 134–152 (1997)

17. Lisper, B., Nordlander, J.: A simple and flexible timing constraint logic. In: Margaria, T., Steffen, B. (eds.) ISoLA 2012. LNCS, vol. 7610, pp. 80–95. Springer, Heidelberg (2012). doi:10.1007/978-3-642-34032-1_12

18. Liu, C., Layland, J.: Scheduling algorithms for multiprogramming in a hard-real-time environment. J. ACM **20**(1), 46–61 (1973)

19. Mok, A.K.: Fundamental design problems of distributed systems for the hard-real-time environment. Ph.D. thesis, Massachusetts Institute of Technology, May 1983

20. UML profile for MARTE: modeling and analysis of real-time embedded systems. Technical report, OMG, November 2009

21. Suryadevara, J.: Validating EAST-ADL timing constraints using UPPAAL. In: Proceeding 39th Euromicro Conference on Software Engineering and Advanced Applications (SEAA), September 2013. http://www.es.mdh.se/publications/2988-22

22. Verdoolaege, S.: barvinok: user guide. Technical report, January 2016. barvinok.gforge.inria.fr/barvinok.pdf

23. Yin, L., Mallet, F., Liu, J.: Verification of MARTE/CCSL time requirements in Promela/SPIN. In: Proceeding of 16th IEEE International Conference on Engineering of Complex Computer Systems (ICECCS 2011), pp. 65–74, April 2011

Query Checking for Linear Temporal Logic

Samuel Huang and Rance Cleaveland[(✉)]

University of Maryland, College Park, USA
srhuang@cs.umd.edu, rance@cs.umd.edu

Abstract. The query-checking problem for temporal logic may be formulated as follows. Given a Kripke structure M and a temporal-logic *query* of form $\phi\,[\mathtt{var}]$, which may be thought of as a temporal formula with a missing propositional subformula $\mathtt{var}$, find the most precise propositional formula f that, when substituted for $\mathtt{var}$ in $\phi\,[\mathtt{var}]$, ensures M satisfies the resulting temporal property. Query checking has been used for system comprehension, specification reconstruction, and other related applications in the formal analysis of systems.

In this paper we present an automaton-based methodology for query checking over linear temporal logic (LTL). While this problem is known to be hard in the general case, we show that by exploiting several key observations about the interplay between the input model M and the query $\phi\,[\mathtt{var}]$, we can produce results for many problems of interest. In support of this claim, we report on preliminary experimental data for an implementation of our technique.

1   Introduction

Temporal logics [9] are widely used to specify desired properties of system behavior. Such logics permit the description of how systems should execute over time; tools such as model checkers [4,8] can then be used automatically to determine whether or not certain types of system possess given temporal properties.

The practical utility of model checking and other temporal-logic-based verification technologies relies on the ability of users to define correctly the properties they are interested in. To assist users in this regard, researchers have looked into various forms of automated *temporal-property reconstruction* [1,11,17,18] as a means of helping users to devise temporal specifications from given system specifications. Users may then use these as specifications for the system (useful when systems subsequently have new functionality added, as the new system can be checked against the old specification to ensure backward compatibility); they may also review them as a means of gaining insight into the behavior of a system that may not have been formally specified or verified. One of the most influential lines of work in this area is so-called *temporal logic query checking* [6], which aims to solve the following general problem: given a system, and a temporal formula with a missing (propositional) subformula, "solve" for the missing subformula. As originally formulated by Chan [6], the temporal logic in question was a subset of the branching-time temporal logic CTL [10], for which he gave

© Springer International Publishing AG 2017
L. Petrucci et al. (Eds.): FMICS-AVoCS 2017, LNCS 10471, pp. 34–48, 2017.
DOI: 10.1007/978-3-319-67113-0_3

efficient algorithms for computing most-precise missing formulas. Others have considered different variants of this problem, by considering multiple missing subformulas, for instance, or different logics [5,7,15].

In this paper we consider the problem of *query checking for linear temporal logic* (LTL) [10]. LTL differs from branching-time logics in that one specifies properties of executions, rather than states in a system, and it is often viewed as an easier formalism to master for this reason. It is also the basis for specification languages, such as FORSPEC [2], used in digital hardware design. In the current work we show how automaton-based model-checking techniques may be adapted to yield a solution to the query-checking problem that, while computationally complex in the worst case, exploits structure in the space of possible query solutions to yield better performance. To this end, after reporting on related work and developing needed mathematical preliminaries, we present our technique and report on a preliminary implementation that we are developing.

2   Related Work

Temporal-logic query checking was initially defined and explored by William Chan [6], who considered the problem in the context of the branching-time temporal logic CTL [10]. Chan initially considered a subset of CTL and showed that queries in this subset, which allows the universal path quantifier and places restrictions on the modal operators, can be solved in linear time. This work was subsequently extended to more expressive branching-time logics via alternating-tree automaton constructions [5] and three-valued model checking [15]; this last paper also describes several applications of the technique in areas such as invariant inference and test generation. Other work has studied the problem for classes of infinite-state systems [21].

In contrast to branching time, linear-time query checking has remained relatively unstudied. Chokler et al. [7] consider several variants of LTL query checking and prove complexity results for these problems; however, no implementation or experimental results were reported.

Other researchers have considered the problem of so-called specification mining, in which temporal properties are inferred not from system models, but from execution behavior, using techniques from data mining and machine learning. Such properties hold of the data from which they are generated, but not necessarily of all system behaviors. Emblematic of this work is the dynamic-invariant generation work of Ernst et al. [11], which uses program instrumentation to obtain state information as a program executes and then data mining to identify possible invariants. Other work in this vein couples data mining of execution data with retesting to attempt to remove invalid invariants in the case of Simulink models [1]. Other work has considered the mining of general LTL formulas from run-time data [16].

3   LTL, Kripke Structures and Büchi Automata

This section defines the syntax of LTL and reviews the notions of Kripke structure, Büchi automata, and model checking in LTL. In what follows, we fix a finite non-empty set $\mathcal{A}$ of atomic propositions.

3.1   LTL and Kripke Structures

The syntax of LTL formulas is given by the following grammar.

$$\phi := a \in \mathcal{A} \mid \neg\phi \mid \phi \vee \phi \mid \mathbf{X}\,\phi \mid \phi\,\mathbf{U}\,\phi$$

In addition to the propositional constructs a, $\neg$ and $\vee$, LTL formulas also include the modal operators $\mathbf{X}$, or "next state", and $\mathbf{U}$, or "until". The derived propositional operations $\wedge$, $\rightarrow$, etc. are defined in the usual manner; we also write tt as an abbreviation for $a \vee \neg a$ for a designated $a \in \mathcal{A}$ and ff for $\neg$tt. We additionally use the following derived temporal operators in the sequel.

$$\mathbf{F}\,\phi \triangleq \mathtt{tt}\,\mathbf{U}\,\phi$$
$$\mathbf{G}\,\phi \triangleq \neg(\mathbf{F}\,\neg\phi)$$
$$\phi_1\,\mathbf{R}\,\phi_2 \triangleq \neg((\neg\phi_1)\,\mathbf{U}\,(\neg\phi_2))$$

$\mathbf{F}$ and $\mathbf{G}$ are the "eventually" and "always" operators, while $\mathbf{R}$ is sometimes called the "release" operator. We write Φ for the set of LTL formulas.

The semantics of LTL is given as a relation $\models\,\subseteq (2^{\mathcal{A}})^\omega \times \Phi$. Intuitively, $\pi \models \phi$ holds if $\pi \in (2^{\mathcal{A}})^\omega$, which is an infinite sequence of subsets of $\mathcal{A}$, makes ϕ true. In what follows, if $\pi = A_0 A_1 \ldots$ then we write $\pi[i] \in 2^{\mathcal{A}}$ for $A_i \subseteq \mathcal{A}$ and $\pi[i..] \in (2^{\mathcal{A}})^\omega$ for the suffix $A_i A_{i+1} \ldots$. The relation $\models$ may now be defined as follows.

- $\pi \models a$ $(a \in \mathcal{A})$ iff $a \in \pi[0]$.
- $\pi \models \neg\phi$ iff $\pi \not\models \phi$.
- $\pi \models \phi_1 \vee \phi_2$ iff $\pi \models \phi_1$ or $\pi \models \phi_2$.
- $\pi \models \mathbf{X}\,\phi$ iff $\pi[1..] \models \phi$.
- $\pi \models \phi_1\,\mathbf{U}\,\phi_2$ iff there is a $j \geq 0$ such that $\pi[j..] \models \phi_1$ and for all $0 \leq i < j$, $\pi[i..] \models \phi_2$.

We often write $\llbracket \phi \rrbracket \triangleq \{\pi \in (2^{\mathcal{A}})^\omega \mid \pi \models \phi\}$ for the set of sequences satisfying ϕ.

LTL formulas are often used to specify properties of systems modeled as *Kripke Structures*.

Definition 1. *A* Kripke Structure *is a quadruple* (S, R, L, i) *where:*

- *S is a non-empty set of states;*
- *$R \subseteq S \times S$ is the transition relation;*
- *$L \in S \rightarrow 2^{\mathcal{A}}$ is the labeling function; and*
- *$i \in S$ is the initial state.*

A Kripke structure encodes the behavior of a system, with S representing system states and the transition relation recording the possible execution steps that are possible when a system is in a given state: when the system is in state s it can evolve in one step to state s' iff $(s, s') \in R$. The labeling function indicates which atomic propositions are true in any given state; if $a \in L(s)$ then a is deemed true s, while if $a \notin L(s)$ it is false. State i is the initial state. In what follows we require Kripke structures to be *left-total*: for every $s \in S$ it must be the case that there is an $s' \in S$ such that $(s, s') \in R$. We also call a Kripke structure *finite-state* if its state set is finite. Semantically, left-total Kripke structure $K = (S, R, L, i)$ gives rise to a subset $[\![K]\!]$ of $(2^A)^\omega$ as follows.

- Infinite sequence $s_0 s_1 \ldots \in S^\omega$ is an *execution* of K if $s_0 = i$ and $(s_i, s_{i+1}) \in R$ for all $i \geq 0$.
- K *generates* $\pi = A_0 A_1 \ldots$ iff there is an execution $s_0 s_1 \ldots$ of K such that $A_i = L(s_i)$.
- $[\![K]\!] = \big\{ \pi \in (2^A)^\omega \mid K \text{ generates } \pi \big\}$.

We then write $K \models \phi$, where K is a Kripke structure and ϕ is an LTL formula, iff $[\![K]\!] \subseteq [\![\phi]\!]$.

3.2   Büchi Automata and LTL Model Checking

The LTL model-checking problem may be formulated as follows.

Given: Kripke structure K, LTL formula ϕ
Determine: Does $K \models \phi$?

When K is finite-state the model-checking problem is decidable in time proportional to $|K|$, where $|K|$ is the size of Kripke structure K. A common approach for LTL model checking relies on the use of *Büchi automata*. This section defines these automata and explains their use in LTL model checking.

Büchi automata. Büchi automata are used to recognize so-called ω-regular languages, which are sets of infinite-length sequences of alphabet symbols.

Definition 2. *A Büchi automaton is a quintuple $(Q, \Sigma, \delta, q_I, F)$, where:*

- *Q is a finite, non-empty set of states;*
- *Σ is a finite, non-empty set of alphabet symbols;*
- *$\delta \subseteq Q \times \Sigma \times Q$ is the transition relation;*
- *q_I is the initial state; and*
- *$F \subseteq Q$ is the set of accepting states.*

Let B be a Büchi automaton $(Q, \Sigma, \delta, q_i, F)$. We define the language, $L(B) \subseteq \Sigma^\omega$, of B as follows.

- Given ω-word $w = \alpha_0 \alpha_1 \ldots \in \Sigma^\omega$, define a *run* of B on w to be a sequence $q_0 q_1 \ldots \in Q^\omega$ such that $q_0 = q_I$ and $(q_i, \alpha_i, q_{i+1}) \in \delta$ for all $i \geq 0$.

– A run $q_0 q_1 \ldots \in Q^\omega$ of B on w is *accepting* iff for all $i \geq 0$ there exists $j \geq i$ such that $q_j \in F$.
– $L(B) = \{w \in \Sigma^\omega \mid B \text{ has an accepting run on } w\}$.

The subsets $W \subseteq \Sigma^\omega$ such that $W = L(B)$ for some Büchi automaton B coincide with the so-called ω-regular languages. This class of languages is closed with respect to complementation and intersection; both of these operations can be realized as constructions on Büchi automata. In addition, checking for emptiness of the language of B is decidable in time proportional to the size of B. Algorithmically, this can be done by computing the strongly connected components of B and determining if there is one such component reachable from the start state, containing an accepting state, and having at least one edge from a state in the component to another state in the component. This ensures the existence of at least one accepting run in B, and hence the non-emptiness of $L(B)$.

LTL model checking using Büchi automata. Büchi automata may be used as a basis for *model checking* of finite-state Kripke structures against LTL formulas [19]. Recall the model-checking problem in this case: given finite-state Kripke structure K and LTL formula ϕ, determine whether or not $K \models \phi$. This problem may be solved algorithmically using Büchi automata as follows.

– From K, construct Büchi automaton B_K such that $L(B_K) = [\![K]\!]$.
– From ϕ, construct Büchi automaton $B_{\neg\phi}$ such that $L(B_{\neg\phi}) = [\![\neg\phi]\!]$.
– Construct the Büchi automaton $B_{K,\neg\phi}$ such that $L(B_{K,\neg\phi}) = L(B_K) \cap L(B_{\neg\phi})$ and check if $L(B_{K,\neg\phi}) = \emptyset$. This is true iff $K \models \phi$.

Note that both B_K and $B_{\neg\phi}$ must have alphabet sets $\Sigma = 2^{\mathcal{A}}$. Specifically, transitions in both of these Büchi automata are labeled by subsets of $\mathcal{A}$.

For $K = (S, R, L, i)$, the construction B_K is straightforward: define $B_K = (S, 2^{\mathcal{A}}, \delta_K, i, S)$, where

$$\delta_K = \{(s, A, s') \mid (s, s') \in R \text{ and } A = L(s)\}.$$

The construction of B_ϕ for LTL formula ϕ is more complex, and a number of approaches may be found in the literature [3,12–14]. The best techniques yield automata that are $O(3^{|\phi|})$, where $|\phi|$ is the size of formula ϕ.

We close this section by giving an alternative formulation of Büchi automata whose alphabets are $2^{\mathcal{A}}$. The edges in these automata are labeled by propositional formulas constructed from $\mathcal{A}$, rather than subsets of $\mathcal{A}$; the interpretation of such an edge $q \xrightarrow{\gamma} q'$ is that $q \xrightarrow{A} q'$ for every A satisfying γ. These notions are formalized as follows.

– Define the set of propositional formulas Γ over $\mathcal{A}$ by the following grammar.

$$\gamma ::= a \in \mathcal{A} \mid \neg\gamma \mid \gamma \vee \gamma$$

Note that $\Gamma \subsetneq \Phi$. We use the usual encodings of $\mathtt{tt}$, $\wedge$, etc.
– If $A \subseteq \mathcal{A}$ and $\gamma \in \Gamma$ then define $A \models \gamma$ as follows.

- $A \models a$ iff $a \in A$
- $A \models \neg\gamma$ iff $A \not\models \gamma$
- $A \models \gamma_1 \vee \gamma_2$ iff $A \models \gamma_1$ or $A \models \gamma_2$.

We write $[\![\gamma]\!]$ for $\{A \subseteq \mathcal{A} \mid A \models \gamma\}$. Note that $A \models \gamma$ iff $\pi \models \gamma$ for all π such that $\pi[0] = A$.

We sometimes use $A \subseteq \mathcal{A}$ as short-hand for the formula $(\bigwedge_{a \in A} a) \wedge (\bigwedge_{a \notin A} \neg a)$. Note that $[\![A]\!] = \{A\}$ in this case.

Definition 3. *Given $\mathcal{A}$, a Büchi propositional automaton is a tuple (Q, δ, q_I, F), where:*

- *Q is a finite non-empty set of states, with $q_I \in Q$ and $F \subseteq Q$.*
- *$\delta \subseteq (Q \times \Gamma \times Q)$ is the transition relation.*

Based on our interpretation of sets $A \subseteq \mathcal{A}$ as propositions it is easy to see that every Büchi automaton is also a Büchi propositional automaton. An arbitrary Büchi propositional automaton $B = (Q, \delta, q_I, F)$ may also be translated into a traditional Büchi automaton $B' = (Q, 2^{\mathcal{A}}, \delta', q_I, F)$ by defining

$$\delta' = \{(q, A, q') \mid \exists \gamma. (q, \gamma, q') \in \delta \wedge A \in [\![\gamma]\!]\}.$$

We define $L(B) = L(B')$. The traditional tableau-based constructions for converting LTL formulas into Büchi automata may easily be adapted to generate Büchi propositional automata with the property that for every pair of automaton states q, q' there is exactly one γ such that $(q, \gamma, q') \in \delta$.

Finally, we give a construction for Büchi propositional automaton B_{12} with $L(B_{12}) = L(B_1) \cap L(B_2)$ for the special case of Büchi propositional automata B_1 and B_2, with every state in B_1 accepting.

Theorem 1. *Let $B_1 = (Q_1, \delta_1, q_1, Q_1)$ and $B_2 = (Q_2, \delta_2, q_2, F_2)$ be Büchi propositional automata. Then $L(B_{12}) = L(B_1) \cap L(B_2)$, where*

$$B_{12} = (Q_1 \times Q_2, \delta_{12}, (q_1, q_2), Q_1 \times F_2)$$

and $((q_1, q_2), \gamma_1 \wedge \gamma_2, (q_1', q_2')) \in \delta_{12}$ iff $(q_1, \gamma_1, q_1') \in \delta_1$ and $(q_2, \gamma_2, q_2') \in \delta_2$.

4   The LTL Query Checking Problem

In LTL query checking we are interested in Kripke structures and LTL formula *queries*, which are formulas containing a missing propositional subformula. The goal in LTL query checking is to construct solutions for the missing subformula. This section defines the problem precisely and proves results that will be used later in our algorithmic solution.

LTL queries correspond to LTL formulas with a missing propositional subformula, which we denote var. It should be noted that var stands for an unknown proposition over $\mathcal{A}$; it is *not* a propositional variable. The syntax of queries is as follows.

$$\phi := \mathtt{var} \mid a \in \mathcal{A} \mid \neg\phi \mid \phi \vee \phi \mid \mathbf{X}\,\phi \mid \phi\,\mathbf{U}\,\phi$$

In this paper we only consider the case of a single propositional unknown, although the definitions can naturally be extended to multiple such unknowns. We often write $\phi[\mathtt{var}]$ for LTL query with unknown $\mathtt{var}$, and $\phi[\phi']$ for the LTL formula obtained by replacing all occurrences of $\mathtt{var}$ by LTL formula ϕ'. We also say that an occurrence of $\mathtt{var}$ within $\phi[\mathtt{var}]$ is *positive* if it appears within an even number of instances of $\neg$, and *negative* otherwise. If all occurrences of $\mathtt{var}$ in $\phi[\mathtt{var}]$ are positive we say $\mathtt{var}$ is *positive* in $\phi[\mathtt{var}]$; if all are negative we say $\mathtt{var}$ is *negative* in $\phi[\mathtt{var}]$; if there are both positive and negative occurrences of $\mathtt{var}$ in $\phi[\mathtt{var}]$ then $\mathtt{var}$ is *mixed* in $\phi[\mathtt{var}]$.

The query-checking problem may now be formulated as follows.

Given: Finite-state Kripke structure K, LTL query $\phi[\mathtt{var}]$
Compute: All $\gamma \in \Gamma$ (i.e. all propositional formulas over $\mathcal{A}$) with $K \models \phi[\gamma]$.

If γ is such that $K \models \phi[\gamma]$, then we call γ a *solution* for K and $\phi[\mathtt{var}]$, and in this case we say that $\phi[\mathtt{var}]$ is solvable for K. Computing all solutions for query checking problem K and $\phi[\mathtt{var}]$ cannot be done explicitly, since the number of propositional formulas is infinite. However, if we define $\gamma_1 \equiv \gamma_2$ to hold if $[\![\gamma_1]\!] = [\![\gamma_2]\!]$, then it is clear that there are only finitely many distinct equivalence classes for Γ. We also say that γ_1 is at least as strong (weak) as γ_2 if $[\![\gamma_1]\!] \subseteq [\![\gamma_2]\!]$ ($[\![\gamma_2]\!] \subseteq [\![\gamma_1]\!]$). We now have the following.

Theorem 2. *Let K be a finite-state Kripke structure and $\phi[var]$ an LTL query.*

1. *If var is positive in $\phi[var]$ then there is a finite set (modulo $\equiv$) of strongest solutions for $\phi[\gamma]$.*
2. *If var is negative in $\phi[var]$ then there is a finite set (modulo $\equiv$) of weakest solutions to $\phi[\gamma]$.*

In some cases these sets of maximal solutions contain a single solution.

Definition 4. *Let $\phi[var]$ be an LTL query. Then $\phi[var]$ is:*

– conjunctively covariant *iff for all γ_1, γ_2, $\phi[\gamma_1 \wedge \gamma_2] \equiv \phi[\gamma_1] \wedge \phi[\gamma_2]$; and*
– conjunctively contravariant *iff for all γ_1, γ_2, $\phi[\gamma_1 \vee \gamma_2] \equiv \phi[\gamma_1] \wedge \phi[\gamma_2]$.*

Theorem 3. *Let K be a finite-state Kripke structure, and let $\phi[var]$ be solvable for K. Then the following hold.*

1. *If var is positive in $\phi[var]$ and $\phi[var]$ is conjunctively covariant, then there is a unique strongest solution (modulo $\equiv$) for $\phi[var]$.*
2. *If var is negative in $\phi[var]$ and $\phi[var]$ is conjunctively contravariant, then there is a unique weakest solution (modulo $\equiv$) for $\phi[var]$.*

As examples, note that $\mathbf{G}\,\mathtt{var}$ is conjunctively covariant and solvable for every K, and that $\mathtt{var}$ is positive; it is guaranteed to have a unique strongest solution for any K. So does $\mathbf{G}\,\mathbf{F}\,\mathtt{var}$. On the other hand, $\mathbf{G}(\mathtt{var} \implies \mathbf{F}\,\phi')$ is conjunctively contravariant and solvable for every K, and $\mathtt{var}$ appears negatively. Thus, every K has a unique weakest solution for this query.

5 Automaton-Based LTL Query Checking

In this section we show how LTL query checking can be formulated as a problem on Büchi propositional automata whose propositional labels may contain instances of var. In this paper we only consider LTL queries in which var is either negative or positive; the mixed case will not be dealt with. The approach is based on LTL model checking in that we generate Büchi propositional automata from both a Kripke structure and the negation of an LTL query and compose them; we then search for solutions to var that make the language of the composition automaton empty. To formalize these notions, we introduce the following definitions.

5.1 Propositional Queries

Definition 5. *Let* var *be an unknown proposition. Then propositional queries are generated by the following grammar.*

$$\gamma ::= var \mid a \in \mathcal{A} \mid \neg\gamma \mid \gamma \vee \gamma$$

We write $\gamma[var]$ *for a generic instance of a propositional template, and* $\Gamma[var]$ *for the set of all propositional templates involving* var.

It is easy to see that propositional queries form a subset of LTL queries, and that notions of $\gamma[\gamma']$, positive and negative occurrences of var, etc., carry over immediately. A *shattering formula* for query $\gamma[var]$ is a propositional formula γ' with the property that $[\![\gamma[\gamma']]\!] = \emptyset$; that is, γ' "makes" $\gamma[var]$ unsatisfiable. We call $\gamma[var]$ *shatterable* if it has a shattering formula. The following is a consequence of the fact that the set of propositional formulas form a Boolean algebra.

Theorem 4. *Let* $\gamma[var]$ *be shatterable.*

1. *If* var *is positive in* $\gamma[var]$ *then there is a unique (modulo $\equiv$) weakest shattering formula for* $\gamma[var]$.
2. *If* var *is negative in* $\gamma[var]$ *then there is a unique strongest (modulo $\equiv$) shattering formula for* $\gamma[var]$.

Intuitively, if $\gamma[var]$ is shatterable and var is positive, then $\gamma[var]$ can be rewritten as $var \wedge \gamma'$ for some propositional formula γ' (i.e. γ' contains no occurrences of var). In this case the weakest shattering formula for $\gamma[var]$ is $\neg\gamma'$. A dual argument holds in the case that var is negative in $\gamma[var]$.

5.2 Büchi Query Automata

Büchi query automata are propositional automata with propositional queries labeling transitions.

Definition 6. *Let var be a propositional unknown. A* Büchi query automaton
has form (Q, δ, q_I, F), *with finite state set* Q, *initial state* $q_I \in Q$, *accepting*
states $F \subseteq Q$, *and transition relation* $\delta \subseteq Q \times \Gamma[\textbf{var}] \times Q$.

Intuitively, a Büchi query automaton is like an LTL query in that it contains a
propositional unknown, var, that can be used to change the language accepted
by the automaton. Specifically, if var is set to a condition γ' that shatters the
edge label $\gamma[\textbf{var}]$, then any query-automaton edge of form $(q, \gamma[\textbf{var}], q')$ is no
longer available for use in constructing runs of the automaton. Figure 1 illustrates
this phenomenon. Thus, by varying var we can thus affect the language accepted
by the query automaton.

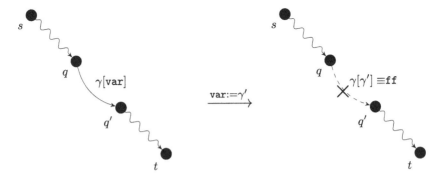

Fig. 1. Shattering edges in a Büchi query automaton. Proposition γ' shatters $\gamma[\textbf{var}]$,
and consequently the edge $(q, \gamma[\textbf{var}], q')$ is removed.

Formally, if $B[\textbf{var}]$ is a Büchi query automaton then define $B[\gamma]$ to be the
Büchi propositional automaton obtained by replacing all occurrences of var by
γ in any edge label within $B[\textbf{var}]$. We say that γ *shatters* $B[\textbf{var}]$ if $L(B[\gamma]) = \emptyset$,
i.e. if γ renders the language of $B[\textbf{var}]$ empty. Notions of positive and negative
occurrences of var in $B[\textbf{var}]$, etc., carry over in the obvious manner.

We now note the following correspondence between LTL queries and Büchi
query automata.

Theorem 5. *Let* $\phi[\textbf{var}]$ *be an LTL query. Then there exists a Büchi query*
automaton $B_\phi[\textbf{var}]$ *such that the following hold.*

1. *For all* $\gamma \in \Gamma$, $[\![\phi[\gamma]]\!] = L(B_\phi[\gamma])$.
2. *If var is positive in* $\phi[\textbf{var}]$ *then var is positive in* $B_\phi[\textbf{var}]$.
3. *If var is negative in* $\phi[\textbf{var}]$ *then var is negative in* $B_\phi[\textbf{var}]$.

The construction of $B_\phi[\textbf{var}]$ is a straightforward adaptation of the construction
of Büchi propositional automata from LTL formulas ϕ.

5.3 LTL Query Checking via Büchi Query Automata

We now explain our approach to LTL query checking. Given finite-state Kripke structure K and LTL query $\phi[\text{var}]$, we perform the following.

1. Construct Büchi (propositional) automaton B_K.
2. Construct Büchi query automaton $B_{\neg\phi}[\text{var}]$.
3. Construct the product query automaton, $B_{K,\neg\phi}[\text{var}]$.
4. Solve for shattering conditions for $B_{K,\neg\phi}[\text{var}]$.

Because of Theorem 5 we know the following. If $\phi[\text{var}]$ is conjunctively covariant and var is positive in $\phi[\text{var}]$, then var is negative in $B_{K,\neg\phi}[\text{var}]$, and the strongest solution for var in $\phi[\text{var}]$ with respect to K coincides with the weakest shattering condition for $B_{K,\neg\phi}[\text{var}]$. The dual result holds in case var is negative in $\phi[\text{var}]$. Thus, solving for shattering conditions in $B_{K,\neg\phi}[\text{var}]$ yields appropriate query solutions for K and $\phi[\text{var}]$.

6 Implementing an LTL Query Checker

Based on the developments given earlier in the paper, to develop a query checker for finite-state Kripke structures and LTL queries $\phi[\text{var}]$ it suffices to construct the product query automaton $B_{K,\neg\phi}[\text{var}]$ and then search for γ that shatter $B_{K,\neg\phi}[\text{var}]$. In this section we highlight some of the algorithmic aspects of this strategy and report on preliminary results of a prototype implementation.

At the outset, we can note that there is one immediate algorithmic solution: enumerate γ and test to see if $L(B[\gamma]) = \emptyset$ by computing the strongly connected components of $B[\gamma]$ and seeing if the start state can reach a successful component (i.e. one with an accepting state and at least one edge from the component back to itself). As there are $2^{2^{|\mathcal{A}|}}$ semantically distinct such γ, this procedure terminates; indeed, this is the basis of the approach outlined in [7]. The complexity of this approach is prohibitive, however, as a sample implementation of ours has shown: even Kripke structures with 10s of states and 10 atomic propositions failed to complete successfully. This is to be expected, given that there are $2^{2^{10}} \geq 1.75 \times 10^{308}$ semantically distinct propositions in this case.

Instead, the approach outlined below pursues two different strategies to reduce the computational effort associated with shattering. One involves exploiting the lattice structure of $2^{2^{\mathcal{A}}}$ to reduce the number of propositions that must be considered; the second combines this idea with a weakening of the problem to require the computation of a single shattering proposition, rather than all such propositions. The next sections provide further details regarding our approach.

6.1 Construct Büchi Automaton B_K

Given a Kripke structure K, constructing the corresponding Büchi automaton B_K is done using the traditional method as described above. There is no query component to the model input, it should be noted.

6.2   Construct Büchi Query Automaton $B_{\neg\phi}[\text{var}]$

The LTL3BA package performs translations from standard LTL formulas to Büchi propositional automata. For a given query $\phi[\text{var}]$ we convert the formula into a Büchi query automaton by treating var as a normal atomic proposition. By default, LTL3BA attempts to remove non-determinism from the output Büchi query automaton, which can increase the number of edges in the automaton containing var on their labels. We configure LTL3BA so that removal of non-determinism is not required in order to avoid this extra overhead.

6.3   Construct Product Query Automaton $B_{K,\neg\phi}[\text{var}]$

As mentioned before, there is a well-known product construction for composing two Büchi automata into a single one accepting the intersection of the languages of the component automata. We adapt this composition operation to automaton B_K and query automaton $B_{\neg\phi}[\text{var}]$, yielding composite query automaton $B_{K,\neg\phi}[\text{var}]$, as follows. States in $B_{\neg\phi}[\text{var}]$ are pairs of states from B_K and $B_{\neg\phi}[\text{var}]$. Tuple $((q_1, q_2), A \wedge \gamma[\text{var}], (q_1', q_2'))$ is a transition in $B_{K,\neg\phi}[\text{var}]$ iff (q_1, A, q_1') is a transition in B_K and $(q_2, \gamma[\text{var}], q_2')$ is a transition in $B_{\neg\phi}[\text{var}]$. It should be noted that the transition label in this case, $A \wedge \gamma[\text{var}]$, has a special property: for any var, either $[\![A \wedge \gamma[\text{var}]]\!] = \{A\}$, or $[\![A \wedge \gamma[\text{var}]]\!] = \emptyset$. This is a consequence of the fact that our treatment of A as a proposition means that $[\![A]\!] = \{A\}$. The initial state of $B_{K,\neg\phi}[\text{var}]$ is the pair consisting of the start states of B_K and $B_{\neg\phi}[\text{var}]$, respectively; states are accepting in $B_{K,\neg\phi}[\text{var}]$ if and only if the state component coming from $B_{\neg\phi}[\text{var}]$ is accepting.

6.4   Solve for Shattering Conditions of $B_{K,\neg\phi}[\text{var}]$

Given $B_{K,\neg\phi}[\gamma]$, we now must find a proposition γ such that $L(B_{K,\neg\phi}[\gamma]) = \emptyset$. One approach [7] is to enumerate all possible γ and compute whether or not $L(B_{K,\neg\phi}[\gamma]) = \emptyset$ for each such γ. Because of the number of possible γ, this approach is infeasible for all but trivial $\mathcal{A}$.

Our approach instead focuses on determining when sets of edges in $B_{K,\neg\phi}[\text{var}]$ can be shattered via a common proposition γ in such a way that $L(B_{K,\neg\phi)}[\gamma])$ is empty. Our procedure may be summarized as follows.

1. Pre-process $B_{K,\neg\phi}[\text{var}]$ to eliminate all strongly connected components that have no outgoing edges from the component and that do not contain any accepting states. Call the reduced query automaton $B'[\text{var}]$.
2. Identify all unique edge labels $S = \{\gamma_1[\text{var}], \dots, \gamma_n[\text{var}]\}$ in $B'[\text{var}]$.
3. Process Γ appropriately to determine how $B'[\text{var}]$ can be shattered.

We now expand on the last step of the above procedure. In this work our interest is only for LTL queries $\phi[\text{var}]$ in which var appears only positively or only negatively; we do not consider queries in which var is mixed. Based on the construction of $B_{K,\neg\text{var}}[\text{var}]$ it follows that var is either positive in all of the

$\gamma_i[\text{var}]$ or negative in all of the $\gamma_i[\text{var}]$. In what follows we assume that var is positive; the negative case is dual.

The first step in processing the $\gamma_i[\text{var}]$ (var is positive) is to determine if $\gamma_i[\text{var}]$ is shatterable, and if so, to compute its weakest shattering condition γ_i'. Propositional queries $\gamma_i[\text{var}]$ that are not shatterable are removed from future consideration, as they cannot contribute to shattering $B'[\text{var}]$. In what follows we assume that each $\gamma_i[\text{var}]$ is shatterable, with weakest shattering condition γ_i'.

The next step S is to search for subsets of S that, when all shattered, shatter $B'[\text{var}]$. More specifically, suppose $S' \subseteq S$ and γ'' is such that γ'' shatters each $\gamma'[\text{var}] \in S'$. In $B'[\gamma'']$ none of the edges labeled by elements of S' would be present; if enough edges are eliminated, $L(B[\gamma'']) = \emptyset$, and γ'' would shatter $B'[\text{var}]$. In this case we say that S' *shatters* $B'[\text{var}]$. This search procedure is facilitated by the following observations.

1. If S' shatters $B'[\text{var}]$ and $S' \subseteq S''$, S'' also shatters $B'[\text{var}]$.
2. If S' does not shatter $B'[\text{var}]$ and $S'' \subseteq S'$, S'' does not shatter $B'[\text{var}]$.

These observations can be exploited to develop a modified breadth-first search (BFS) strategy for finding all minimal subsets of S that shatter $B'[\text{var}]$. The BFS algorithm maintains a work set, $W \subseteq 2^S$, of subsets of S that need processing. Initially, $W = \{\emptyset\}$. The algorithm then repeatedly does the following. It selects a minimum-sized $S' \in W$ and checks if S' shatters $B[\text{var}]$. If it does, then it removes all supersets of S' from W and adds S' to the set of minimal shattering subsets of S. If it does not, then every superset of S' that contains one more element than S' is added to W. The procedure terminates when W is empty. Note that the approach does not add to W when S' is found to be a shattering set; the correctness of this approach is based on the first observation above.

The BFS algorithm in the worst-case can still require examination of all subsets of S, so we also consider a different algorithm whose goal is to compute a single minimal shattering subset of S. This approach, which we call GREEDY_SET_SEARCH (GSS), first locates a (not necessarily minimal) shattering set using a depth-first search strategy as follows. The procedure maintains a set $R \subseteq S$ that is initially $\emptyset$. It then repeatedly checks to see if R shatters $B'[\text{var}]$; if so, it terminates, otherwise, it adds a new element from S into R. The observations above guarantee that the above procedure will terminate after at most $|S|$ iterations. The second stage of the procedure then locates a minimal subset of the shattering set R returned by the first stage as follows. Each edge (except the last one added) is removed from R, and the set without this edge is checked for shattering. If the newly modified set R', consisting of R with this single edge removed, shatters $B'[\text{var}]$ then the edge is permanently removed from R; otherwise, the edge is left in R. When this procedure terminates the resulting value of R is guaranteed to be a minimal shattering subset of S.

6.5   Implementation and Evaluation

We have developed prototype implementations of the BFS and GSS algorithms. Kripke structures are read in as directed graph data containing node labels, and LTL formulas are represented as simple strings. As stated previously, the LTL3BA routine was used to generate Büchi query automata from LTL queries.

For a proof-of-concept assessment of the techniques we use a modified version of NuSMV to extract the explicit Kripke structures from a sample .smv model files included in the NuSMV distribution. For each choice of model used, we considered property queries that were conceivably of interest based upon grounded properties known to be true of the systems already. These always took one of the following forms: $\mathbf{G}\,a$, $\mathbf{G}\,\mathbf{F}\,a$ or $\mathbf{G}\,(a \to \mathbf{F}\,b)$. The models we considered in our evaluation are the following.

- Counter[k] - An implementation of a k-bit counter.
- Semaphore[k] - An implementation of a semaphore access control scheme for k different processes.
- Production cell - A production cell control model, first presented as an SMV model by Winter [20]. The original intent of this model concerned safety and liveness specifications.

Figure 2 contains relevant data about sizes of these models, and about the size of the Büchi query automata formed when composing the models with the query automaton $B_{\neg\,\mathbf{G}\,\mathrm{var}}$. For our purposes, the following measures are relevant: (1) number of states, (2) number of transitions, (3) number of atomic propositions in the Kripke structure, (4) number of transition labels containing variable labels in the composite automaton, and (5) number of unique transition labels.

Dataset	# States	# Transitions	$|\mathcal{A}|$	# var-present edges	# distinct edge labels
counter[3]	17	26	3	9	8
counter[4]	33	50	4	17	16
counter[5]	65	98	5	33	32
counter[10]	2049	3074	10	1025	1024
semaphore[2]	25	98	9	33	12
semaphore[3]	65	314	13	105	32
semaphore[4]	161	917	17	305	80
semaphore[5]	385	2498	21	833	192
semaphore[6]	897	6530	25	2177	448
semaphore[7]	2049	16514	29	5505	1024
production-cell	163	245	76	82	81

Fig. 2. Statistics for Büchi product query automata when composed with $\mathbf{G}(\mathrm{var})$.

Figure 3 contains performance data for both BFS and GSS. Algorithms were implemented in Java, and experiments were conducted on a single machine with a 3.5 GHz processor containing 32 GB of memory. Individual experiments were allowed to run for up to 2 h before being stopped and considered timed out. BFS yielded minimal success, as most datasets timed out. The GSS approach to find a single minimal shattering set proved much more effective.

Dataset	Time (s)	# Queries
counter[3]	0.2	257
counter[4]	7.2	65537
counter[5]	timeout	2^{32} (*)
counter[10]	timeout	2^{1024} (*)
semaphore[2]	1.3	4097
semaphore[3]	timeout	2^{32} (*)
semaphore[4]	timeout	2^{80} (*)
semaphore[5]	timeout	2^{192} (*)
semaphore[6]	timeout	2^{448} (*)
semaphore[7]	timeout	2^{1024} (*)
production-cell	timeout	2^{81} (*)

(a)

Dataset	Time (s)	# Queries
counter[3]	0.2	17
counter[4]	0.2	33
counter[5]	0.6	65
counter[10]	22.4	2049
semaphore[2]	0.2	25
semaphore[3]	0.4	65
semaphore[4]	1.4	161
semaphore[5]	6.9	385
semaphore[6]	44.1	897
semaphore[7]	296.9	2049
production-cell	1.3	163

(b)

Fig. 3. Timing results for finding (a) all shattering sets via breadth first search, and (b) one minimal shattering set via GREEDY SET SEARCH. The number of total shattering queries that are made for each experiment are also reported. Query counts marked with a (*) are estimates based on our understanding of the models.

7   Conclusions and Directions for Future Research

In this paper we have considered the problem of query checking for Linear Temporal Logic (LTL). An LTL query checker takes a query, or LTL formula with a missing propositional subformula, together with a Kripke structure and computes a solution for the missing subformula. We have shown how this problem may be solved using automata-theoretic techniques that rely on the use of Büchi automata and the computation of so-called shattering conditions that make the languages of these automata empty. An implementation and preliminary performance data are also given.

As future work, we intend to fully develop the implementation and extend the experimental results we have so far. We also would like to extend the results to handle queries involving multiple missing subformulas, as well as ones in which the missing subformula can appear both positively and negatively. Finally, we would like to leverage relationships between different edge labels containing variables, such as in cases where one label implies another.

References

1. Ackermann, C., Cleaveland, R., Huang, S., Ray, A., Shelton, C., Latronico, E.: Automatic requirement extraction from test cases. In: Barringer, H., et al. (eds.) RV 2010. LNCS, vol. 6418, pp. 1–15. Springer, Heidelberg (2010). doi:10.1007/978-3-642-16612-9_1
2. Armoni, R., et al.: The ForSpec temporal logic: a new temporal property-specification language. In: Katoen, J.-P., Stevens, P. (eds.) TACAS 2002. LNCS, vol. 2280, pp. 296–311. Springer, Heidelberg (2002). doi:10.1007/3-540-46002-0_21

3. Babiak, T., Křetínský, M., Řehák, V., Strejček, J.: LTL to Büchi automata translation: fast and more deterministic. In: Flanagan, C., König, B. (eds.) TACAS 2012. LNCS, vol. 7214, pp. 95–109. Springer, Heidelberg (2012). doi:10.1007/978-3-642-28756-5_8
4. Baier, C., Katoen, J.-P.: Principles of Model Checking. MIT Press, Cambridge (2008)
5. Bruns, G., Godefroid, P.: Temporal logic query checking. In: 16th Annual IEEE Symposium on Logic in Computer Science, pp. 409–417. IEEE, June 2001
6. Chan, W.: Temporal-logic queries. In: Emerson, E.A., Sistla, A.P. (eds.) CAV 2000. LNCS, vol. 1855, pp. 450–463. Springer, Heidelberg (2000). doi:10.1007/10722167_34
7. Chockler, H., Gurfinkel, A., Strichman, O.: Variants of LTL Query Checking. In: Barner, S., Harris, I., Kroening, D., Raz, O. (eds.) HVC 2010. LNCS, vol. 6504, pp. 76–92. Springer, Heidelberg (2011). doi:10.1007/978-3-642-19583-9_11
8. Clarke, E.M., Grumberg, O., Peled, D.: Model Checking. MIT Press, Cambridge (1999)
9. Emerson, E.A.: Temporal and modal logic. In: van Leeuwen, J. (ed.) Handbook of Theoretical Computer Science, vol. B, pp. 995–1072. MIT Press (1990)
10. Emerson, E.A., Halpern, J.Y.: "Sometimes" and "not never" revisited: On branching versus linear time temporal logic. JACM **33**(1), 151–178 (1986)
11. Ernst, M.D., Perkins, J.H., Guo, P.J., McCamant, S., Pacheco, C., Tschantz, M.S., Xiao, C.: The Daikon system for dynamic detection of likely invariants. Sci. Comput. Program. **69**(1–3), 35–45 (2007)
12. Etessami, K., Holzmann, G.J.: Optimizing Büchi automata. In: Palamidessi, C. (ed.) CONCUR 2000. LNCS, vol. 1877, pp. 153–168. Springer, Heidelberg (2000). doi:10.1007/3-540-44618-4_13
13. Gastin, P., Oddoux, D.: Fast LTL to Büchi automata translation. In: Berry, G., Comon, H., Finkel, A. (eds.) CAV 2001. LNCS, vol. 2102, pp. 53–65. Springer, Heidelberg (2001). doi:10.1007/3-540-44585-4_6
14. Giannakopoulou, D., Lerda, F.: From states to transitions: improving translation of LTL formulae to Büchi automata. In: Peled, D.A., Vardi, M.Y. (eds.) FORTE 2002. LNCS, vol. 2529, pp. 308–326. Springer, Heidelberg (2002). doi:10.1007/3-540-36135-9_20
15. Gurfinkel, A., Chechik, M., Devereux, B.: Temporal logic query checking: a tool for model exploration. IEEE Trans. Soft. Eng. **29**(10), 898–914 (2003)
16. Lemieux, C., Park, D., Beschastnikh, I.: General LTL specification mining. In: 30th IEEE/ACM International Conference on Automated Software Engineering, pp. 81–92. IEEE, Lincoln, November 2015
17. Li, W., Forin, A., Seshia, S.A.: Scalable specification mining for verification and diagnosis. In: 47th Design Automation Conference, pp. 755–760. ACM, Anaheim, June 2010
18. Shoham, S., Yahav, E., Fink, S.J., Pistoia, M.: Static specification mining using automata-based abstractions. IEEE Trans. Soft. Eng. **34**(5), 651–666 (2008)
19. Vardi, M.Y., Wolper, P.: An automata-theoretic approach to automatic program verification. In: First Symposium on Logic in Computer Science, pp. 322–331. IEEE Computer Society, Boston, June 1986
20. Winter, K.: Model checking for abstract state machines. J. Univ. Comput. Sci. **3**(5), 689–701 (1997)
21. Zhang, D., Cleaveland, R.: Efficient temporal-logic query checking for Presburger systems. In: 20th IEEE/ACM International Conference on Automated Software Engineering, pp. 24–33. ACM, Long Beach, November 2005

Testing and Scheduling

Automatic Conformance Testing of Safety Instrumented Systems for Offshore Oil Platforms

Hallan William Veiga[1]([envelope]), Max Hering de Queiroz[1]([envelope]),
Jean-Marie Farines[1]([envelope]), and Marcelo Lopes de Lima[2]([envelope])

[1] Departamento de Automação e Sistemas,
Universidade Federal de Santa Catarina, Florianópolis, Brazil
hallan.william@gmail.com, {max.queiroz,j.m.farines}@ufsc.br
[2] CENPES, Petrobras, Rio de Janeiro, Brazil
marceloll@petrobras.com.br

Abstract. Functional failures in Safety Instrumented System (SIS) of offshore platforms may have catastrophic consequences for the production, facility, environment and health. This work presents a method for automatic conformance testing of safety specifications represented in a Cause and Effect Matrix (CEM) for Programmable Logic Controllers (PLC) in charge of SIS. Test cases are automatically designed from the CEM using a CEG-BOR strategy to enhance coverage of black box test. Petri Net models support the automated oracle creation and test result evaluation. An experimental tool has been developed to edit the CEM, to generate and execute test cases on a PLC simulator, to generate and execute the Petri Net oracles and to present the verdict. The method has been applied to test the SIS of an offshore oil platform.

Keywords: Conformance test · Safety Instrumented Systems · Petri-nets · Automatic testing · Programmable Logic Controllers · Offshore platforms

1 Introduction

The operational safety of Oil and Gas Facilities currently relies on the existence of multiple independent layers of protection responsible for the prevention of accidents and, in the worst case, for the mitigation of damages. In this context, the Safety Instrumented System (SIS) is the last barrier for prevention of accidents. A SIS is an automatic system composed by a separate combination of sensors that can identify hazardous situations, a safety Programmable Logic Controller (PLC) and final elements that lead the process back to a safe state [1]. A SIS is therefore a critical system, whose design errors may have catastrophic consequences for the production, facility, environment and health. Moreover,

We thank CAPES and Petrobras for the financial support and the engineering team from Petrobras/UO-RIO for their valuable technical cooperation.

© Springer International Publishing AG 2017
L. Petrucci et al. (Eds.): FMICS-AVoCS 2017, LNCS 10471, pp. 51–65, 2017.
DOI: 10.1007/978-3-319-67113-0_4

programming errors in safety PLC may remain unknown for a long time until the SIS is demanded to act in a critical situation [2].

The IEC 61511 [3] standard presents good engineering practices for the life-cycle of SIS in the process industries. The design of hardware and software for SIS must follow rigorous development methodologies aiming to verify the functional specifications defined by risk analysis techniques. The regulatory agencies and standards demand the Conformance Testing to validate the PLC implementation.

Among the various methods for validation of PLC systems [4], conformance testing, or functional testing, is a black-box approach, which allows to verify that the system conforms to the specifications without the knowledge of the internal program. Basically, test cases are applied to the system inputs and the resulting outputs are compared to the expected behavior according to the specifications [5–7]. As combinatorial complexity makes it impossible to generate an exhaustive set of test cases for complex systems, the testing method cannot produce an absolute and positive verdict. Thus, in critical systems, conformance testing should be taken as a complementary technique aiming to reduce the number of undiagnosed failures. Consequently, the automation of test procedures is an important strategy to enhance test coverage, beyond reducing costs, time and human-errors of manual tests.

In addition to software testing methods, formal methods are suitable for synthesis and verification of safety PLC programs [9,10]. However, the hindrance of obtaining a correct mathematical model of a PLC program and the risk of state-space exponential growth of formal models render black box testing techniques more appealing approaches in practice for the validation of complex applications such as offshore oil platforms. Recent works in the literature apply formal methods to substantiate the automation of PLC testing. Provost, Roussel and Faure [11] propose a model based method [12] for conformance testing of a PLC and a Grafcet specification, which is modeled as a Mealy machine. Based on this model, an algorithm defines a test sequence with single input changes that allows to check the PLC behavior against the Grafcet by comparing the observed outputs with the expected output sequence. Meinke and Sindhu [13] have presented a tool for Learning Based Testing (LBT) that combines incremental learning with model checking for automatic generation and execution of test cases. The basic idea of LBT is to generate a model representing the behavior of the device from output data observation. Then this model is checked with the specification represented in temporal logic. The complexity of PLC code and the large number of safety requirements renders such model based methods nonviable for testing the SIS of offshore installations.

In a previous work [14] we present a method for automatic conformance test of PLC with focus on the cause-and-effect relationships specified in the CEM according to the standards of Oil and Gas Industry. Although it has simple syntax, the CEM specifies a large number of critical relationships between PLC inputs (causes) and outputs (effects), including logic operations, voting and delays. In the proposed method, test cases and Time Petri Nets are systematically derived from the CEM. Then, the test cases are used to command the PLC inputs and the generated Time Petri Nets are used as oracles, i.e., as processes that evaluates the test result according to the (timed) sequence of observed inputs and outputs. This paper presents the current state of the research, with improvements in both the test case generation technique and the oracle models. We also present a new prototype tool for editing the CEM and for automatic generation and execution of PLC tests, which is applied to test the safety specifications of the Fire and Gas System of an offshore platform.

The outline of this paper is the following. Next section presents the development methodology of safety PLC programs in the oil and gas industry. The proposed testing method is explained in Sect. 3. Section 4 presents the experimental tool for automatic testing and Sect. 5 shows the results of the real-world application.

2 Software Development for Safety PLC

Safety Instrumented Systems are composed by field devices (sensors and actuators) and a logic solver responsible for carrying the process to a safe state at the detection of a risk condition [1]. A Safety PLC is usually chosen as the logic solver for SIS of complex process in the oil and gas industry. Although the safety integrity level of the PLC hardware can be certified by the PLC vendors, the logic implemented in a Safety PLC must be individually validated for each SIS design.

There are two types of failures of SIS: dangerous failures occur if the correct actuator is not activated in the presence of a risky situation and safe failures occur when the actuator is activated unnecessarily. Since safe failures may result in needless plant shutdowns, operators tend to lose confidence in the SIS and may be dangerously tempted to bypass the SIS [1].

The development of PLC programs of offshore platforms follows a methodical process where a series of standardized documentation is generated and communicated among multiple engineering teams. In a simplified overview, the development process can be organized in three main stages: specification, planning and implementation. The specification stage follows a series of risk analysis methods and oil and gas industry standards. Piping and Instrumentation Diagram (P&ID) is a document created by process engineers that specifies the instrumentation and control loops for both the Basic Process Control System (BPCS) and the SIS. The specification of the safety logic relating the sensors and actuators in the P&ID is systematically presented in the form of a Cause and Effect Matrix (CEM). Complementary specifications mostly related to the BCPS such as start-up and shut-down sequences are documented in the Descriptive Memorial. In the second stage of design process the program specification and a testing plan for Safety PLC are documented by the Logic Diagram and the Factory Acceptance Test (FAT). Logic Diagram is a midfield document between the specification and the PLC programming that is normally implemented by an third-party company. The FAT plan defines a check-list and the corresponding procedures for testing the SIS. The final stage comprises PLC code implementation and test execution.

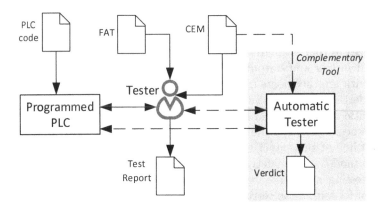

Fig. 1. Test of safety PLC programs

During test execution (Fig. 1), testers must perform a time-demanding list of manual procedures according to the FAT plan and the CEM. However, the FAT execution explores only a superficial number of existing test cases and requires agility because it is constrained by the delivery date. The coverage of tests can be augmented with the use of an automatic testing tool that interacts with the inputs and outputs of the Safety PLC to check if the implemented logic conforms to the CEM.

2.1 Cause and Effect Matrix

The SIS of a typical Offshore Platform comprises several hundred sensors and actuators, such as smoke detectors, high pressure sensors, emergency alarms and shutdown valves. The Cause and Effect Matrix is a document used by the process and control engineers throughout the SIS life-cycle to systematically specify the safety logic between the large number of sensors (causes) and actuators (effects). According to the Project Guidelines for Offshore Production Installation [15], each matrix has a maximum of 50 rows (causes) and 50 columns (effects), and the entries can be specified with the following symbols:

- X: The causes related to this entry are combined with OR logic to activate the corresponding effect.
- Ai: For $i = 1, 2, ...$, the causes related to an entry Ai are combined with a AND logic to activate the corresponding effect.
- Tx: The cause related to an entry Tx must be active for x seconds to activate the corresponding output.
- Xoo$Y$: The cause in the corresponding line of the CEM is the result of the voting X out of Y from a group of sensors.

For example, the small CEM in Table 1 defines the following safety specifications:

Table 1. Small Example of Cause & Effect Matrix

CAUSE Equip.	Voting	TAG	ESD-101 Emerg. Alarm	FD-101 Fire Detected	FC-102 Fire Confirmed
Flame Fire Detector	1oo3	UST-101001		A1	
Flame Fire Detector	2oo3	UST-101002			X
Flame Fire Detector		UST-101003			
Manual Fire Alarm		HSS-101100	X	A1	
Smoke Fire Detector		YST-101200	X	X	T10

- "ESD-101" must be activated when "HSS-101100" or "YST-101200"
- "FD-101" must be activated when "YST-101200" or "HSS-101100" and at least one input of the group { "UST-101001", "UST-101002", "UST-101003" } is active
- "FC-102" must be activated when "YST-101200" remains active for 10 s or at least two inputs of the group { "UST-101001", "UST-101002", "UST-101003" } are active.

3   A Method for Conformance Testing of PLC

Figure 1 shows how an Automatic Tester can be used as a complementary tool to improve the coverage of conformance test of safety PLC. The automatic testing method proposed in this work uses a black-box approach where the generation of test cases and evaluation of results are done directly from the CEM, without the need of a model of the PLC code. Figure 2 gives an overview of the testing method. Basically, the method has two main steps: test generation and test execution. The automatic test generation aims to define a sequence of causes combinations (test cases) from the safety specification of CEM, and a set of oracles in the form of Time Petri Nets. During the test execution, the test cases are transformed into commands to the PLC inputs and the resulting behavior is evaluated by the oracles in order to produce a verdict identifying the nonconformities between the PLC implementation and the CEM.

3.1   Generation of Test Cases

In order to check conformity of the safety PLC implementation with respect to the specifications in the CEM, it is necessary to define a sequence of signals to activate the PLC inputs. Each combination of PLC inputs is called a test case [5]. As the number of possible test cases grows exponentially to the number of inputs, and as outputs may also depend on the PLC memory and timers, the goal of test case generation in black-box testing is not to assure an exhaustive search of failures, but to increase the coverage of test.

In black-box testing, the tester does not consider the PLC program and the test cases are generated from the relations between inputs and outputs defined by the specification. Each test case consists in a combination of PLC inputs to be activated for a period of time. The exhaustive test is not feasible for complex systems such as offshore unit protection systems. For illustration, even for the small CEM in Table 1, it would be necessary to execute 32 tests only to cover all possible combinations of 5 boolean input. But still a failure depending on a specific sequence of inputs and delays could pass undetected. Notice that safety PLC of offshore platforms may easily have much more than 1000 inputs. The techniques to avoid combinatorial complexity in the generation of test cases include Equivalence Partitioning, Boundary Value Analysis and Cause and Effect Graph (CEG).

The CEG method provides a systematic way to obtain a set of test cases including combinations of inputs that allow an efficient coverage of failures [6,17]. The method consists of representing the specifications for the relations between inputs and outputs in the form of an acyclic Boolean logic network, from which a Limited Entry Decision Table (LEDT) is generated containing only the combinations of causes that effectively sensitize an effect, avoiding redundancies and ambiguities for fault detection. For example, when an effect must be activated by the logical relation AND of a set of causes, it is enough to test the case in which all

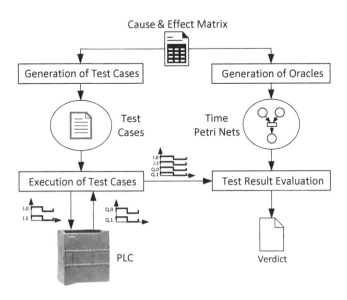

Fig. 2. Method overview

the causes are activated. For an OR logic, only those cases where only one cause is activated should be tested, preventing a cause from masking any failure in the path from another cause to the effect. Among the several methods for converting CEG to LEDT Table [6,17], the CEG-BOR Boolean operator-based method [18] calculates the smallest number of test cases to cover all requirements through a computationally efficient and appropriate to be automated algorithm [20]. The BOR algorithm is effective only for expressions that are singular, i.e., with only one occurrence of each constituent Boolean variable. Paradkar and Tai [19] combines the CEG-BOR strategy and Meaning Impact (MI) strategy to deal with non-singularities like, for example, in the Boolean expression of a 2oo3 voting.

The main advantage of the CEG-BOR and CEG-BOR-MI strategies is that the size of the set of test cases for an effect node is linear with the number of nodes linked with the effect in the CEG [18]. In this work, we have adapted these methods to generate test cases automatically from the Cause and Effect Matrix. Once we have the specification represented formally by a matrix it is not necessary to construct a graph and we can directly apply the BOR algorithm to define the test cases constraint. In short, the proposed strategy for test generation follows these rules:

Rule 1: For each column of the CEM a set of test cases is defined considering only the related causes. In case of a *singular* logic relating causes to an effect, the CEG-BOR strategy is used. In case of a non-singular logic (voting of multiple causes), the CEG-BOR-MI strategy is used.

Rule 2: For each test case, the causes not related to the corresponding effect are all set to true if the expected output is false, or to false if the expected output is true. In this way, the test cases remain efficient to detect safe-failure and dangerous-failure, respectively.

Rule 3: All the test cases defined are listed to form a LEDT Table, where duplicated tests are removed from this table.

3.2 Example

For the CEM example in Table 1, we compute a set of test cases for each effect: "ESD-101", "FD-101", "FC-102" (*Rule 1*). Applying the CEG-BOR algorithm to the logic of the Effect "ESD-101", we obtain the set of test cases defined by a vector in Table 2. Each vector contains the value for the five inputs in the CEM, which can be true (t), false (f) or don't care (x), when the input is not related to the effect. Note that, for the OR relation between "HSS-101100" and "YST-101200", the test case that set to true both inputs is not selected, since it could mask the dangerous failure when one input is problematic and the other still activates the effect (path sensitizing). As the remaining inputs are not related to "ESD-101", they are set to true when the expected output is false and false when the expected output is true (*Rule 2*).

Next we compute the set of test cases of the effect "FD-101", which are listed in Table 2. Since the voting 1oo3 among causes "UST-101001", "UST-101002"

Table 2. CEM test cases - Effects: "ESD-101", "FD-101", "FC-102"

CEG-BOR test cases	CEM test cases	ESD-101
(x, x, x, f, f)	(t, t, t, f, f)	f
(x, x, x, f, t)	(f, f, f, f, t)	t
(x, x, x, t, f)	(f, f, f, t, f)	t
CEG-BOR test cases	CEM test cases	FD-101
(f, f, f, t, f)	(f, f, f, t, f)	f
(t, f, f, f, f)	(t, f, f, f, f)	f
(t, f, f, t, f)	(t, f, f, t, f)	t
(f, t, f, t, f)	(f, t, f, t, f)	t
(f, f, t, t, f)	(f, f, t, t, f)	t
(f, f, f, t, t)	(f, f, f, t, t)	t
CEG-BOR-MI test cases	CEM test cases	FC-102
(t, f, f, x, f)	(t, f, f, t, f)	f
(f, t, f, x, f)	(f, t, f, t, f)	f
(f, f, t, x, f)	(f, f, t, t, f)	f
(t, t, f, x, f)	(t, t, f, f, f)	t
(f, t, t, x, f)	(f, t, t, f, f)	t
(t, f, t, x, f)	(t, f, t, f, f)	t
(t, f, f, x, t)	(t, f, f, f, t)	t

and "UST-101003" can be represented as a singular expression (OR), we can apply the CEG-BOR strategy.

The logic for the last column (FC-102 effect) includes non-singularities due to the voting 2oo3 of multiple causes. Thus, CEG-BOR-MI method is applied to obtain the test cases in Table 2. *Rule 2* is used to define the values of input "HSS-101100". Note that the "T10" entry logic respective to input "YST-101200" is considered as a simple OR. A sufficient delay to activate the effect by the corresponding test case will be assured by the oracle model to be presented in the next subsection.

Finally, all the test cases are joined to form the LEDT in Table 3, where duplicated tests ((f, f, f, t, f), (t, f, f, t, f), (f, t, f, t, f) and (f, f, t, t, f)) have been eliminated (*Rule 3*).

3.3 Generation of Oracles

The most important aspect of any testing situation is the determination of success or failure. An effective oracle can be used to automate this process executing the specification and comparing with the program output [8].

Some black-box testing strategies do not implement an oracle to evaluate the behaviour of the implementation. The diagnostic is made comparing the observed

Table 3. Decision table for the CEM example

CEM test cases	ESD-101	FD-101	FC-102
(t, t, t, f, f)	f	f	t
(f, f, f, f, t)	t	t	t
(f, f, f, t, f)	t	f	f
(t, f, f, f, f)	f	f	f
(t, f, f, t, f)	t	t	f
(f, t, f, t, f)	t	t	f
(f, f, t, t, f)	t	t	f
(f, f, f, t, t)	t	t	t
(t, t, f, f, f)	f	f	t
(f, t, t, f, f)	f	f	t
(t, f, t, f, f)	f	f	t
(t, f, f, f, t)	f	f	t

PLC outputs with the expected values determined by the LEDT Table. However, in this work the diagnostic must consider situations where a delay must be taken into account in order to activate an effect. To evaluate the results of test cases, the method proposed in this work uses oracles automatically generated from the CEM. Time Petri nets [21] are used for both modeling and execution of oracles, in order to ensure consistency and facilitate the automation of the test tool. Beyond the advantages of model-based software development [22], the use of a formal model allows the use of mathematical operations for the composition and analysis of oracles. Moreover Time Petri Nets are suitable for representing multiple timed specifications of concurrent PLC inputs.

The Petri Nets transitions are driven by the changes in the values of PLCs inputs and outputs, allowing to diagnose safe or dangerous failures according to the specifications in the CEM.

One oracle is created for each effect (column) of the CEM. The corresponding Time Petri Net model is organized in five main modules: input/output reading, delay, logic, control and diagnostic. Each module is defined separately according to the CEM entries in the corresponding column and then the composed model is computed by place fusion [21]. In this paper we present details about the diagnostic module (responsible to provide the verdict about the test cases) and a brief explanation about the other modules by means of an example.

In the diagnostic module (Fig. 3), a token in places PASS OK–, SAFE FAILURE, DANGEROUS FAILURE and PASS OK+ represents the corresponding test result. The place EFFECT has a token when the corresponding PLC output is active, during the test cases execution. The place CAUSE receives a token from the logic module when the observed combination of inputs is expected to activate the effect according to the CEM entries. The transitions are fired according to the relations in Table 4. A tolerance time T(greater than the PLC

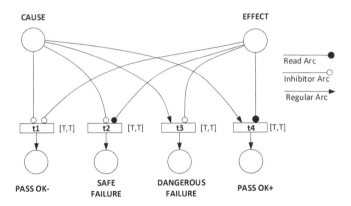

Fig. 3. Petri net observer - diagnostic module

scan cycle) is assigned to transitions t1, t2, t3 and t4 in order to assure that the
PLC has enough time to update the output (PLC scan cycle) before a verdict is
given. An inhibitor arc must also be linked from each delay module to transition
t1 in order to avoid a TEST OK– verdict before the specified activation time
of the corresponding input. For example, if the CAUSE and EFFECT places do
not have a token for [T] seconds and no delay module is counting, then transition
t1 is fired and PASS OK– place receives a token.

The diagnosis of failures in effect FC-102 is performed by the oracle of Fig. 4
represented with its five modules. The I/O module is responsible for observing
the input/outputs signals from PLC. For example, transition t19 is fired when the
inputs group satisfies the 2oo3 voting. By the CEM, FC-102 should be activated
if voting is true or if YST-101200 holds a true signal for 10 s. The delay module
treats this situation avoiding a diagnostic while the WAIT place has a token.
The logic module represents the Boolean operation OR. The control module is
responsible to enable the execution of a new test case only when the diagnostic
of the previous test case is finished.

Table 4. Oracle diagnostic

Cause (expected effect)	Observed effect	Diagnostic
False	False	Pass (OK –)
False	True	Safe failure
True	False	Dangerous failure
True	True	Pass (OK +)

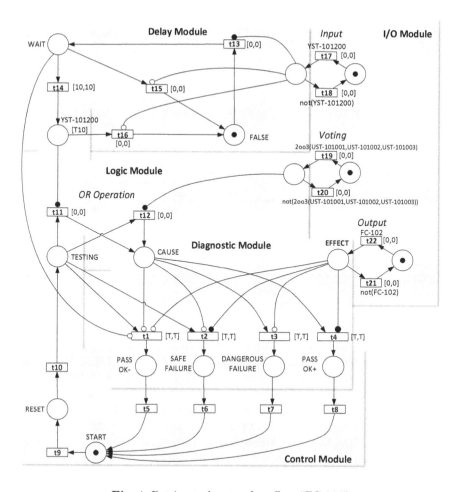

Fig. 4. Petri net observer for effect "FC-102"

4 Automatic Testing Tool

Figure 5 presents an overview of the proposed solution to automate the conformance test. An experimental tool has been developed in Python with two main modules: the Cause and Effect Matrix Editor and the Automatic Tester. Through the CEM Editor, the designer can build a standardized specification in a graphical interface that allows both the generation of PDF file for documentation and the storage of the data in a structured XML file that serves as input for the automatic tester. The graphical interface includes features that facilitate edition and visualization of large CEM for real-world platforms, such as: highlighting rows and columns to make it easier to view relationships, searching for TAGs, and checking for inconsistencies.

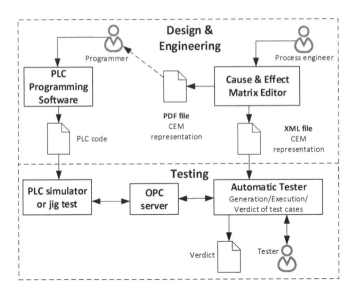

Fig. 5. The automatic conformance test

The Automatic Tester implements the method in Sect. 3, allowing to perform black-box testing directly from the XML file generated by the CEM Editor. Test cases can be automatically derived from the CEM using CEG-BOR-MI technique or random generation, or manually defined in a graphical interface. The CEM specifications are automatically transformed into oracles. The Python Snakes library [23] was used to create, compose and execute the Petri Net models. Through an OPC interface, the Automatic Tester activates the PLC inputs and reads the resulting outputs according to the test cases and executes the oracles concurrently in order to present a verdict for each test case and each effect in the CEM.

5 Application of the Proposed Method

We have applied the automatic tester to assist the preparation of the as-built CEM for the SIS of an offshore oil platform. The overall safety specification has 130 Cause and Effect Matrices of dimension 50×50, comprising several subsystems: electrical, shutdown, fire and gas (F&G), control, turret, and vessel subsystem. During the installation and start-up of systems as complex as oil platforms, small changes in the control and automation system are frequently made on the fly by engineers. However, each nonconformity between the current PLC implementation and the safety specifications in the original project must be identified and carefully analyzed.

Aiming to validate the experimental tool and the proposed method, we have tested the current safety PLC code against two Cause & Effect Matrices (representing different zones of the F&G subsystem). The relationships in these CEM include voting of sensor groups, Boolean logic and delays. The experiment has been executed in a 2.70 GHz PC where the Automatic Tester could interact via OPC with a PLC simulator running a copy of the safety PLC code in the platform. Table 5 shows the number of test cases generated to each CEM, the time spent to execute all test cases, and the number of conformities (OK+ or OK–) and nonconformities (SF or DF) diagnosed by the oracles. Note that the number of diagnoses must be equal to the product of the number of test cases and effects. In order to evaluate the effectiveness of the proposed test case generation strategy, we have also implemented an exhaustive testing that executes all combinations of PLC inputs.

Table 5. Testing results for the CEM of fire & gas system

CEM of F&G	Causes/ effects	Exhaustive testing			Proposed strategy		
		Test cases	Running time	OK+/OK–/SF/DF	Test cases	Running time	OK+/OK–/SF/DF
Zone A	8/4	256	523 s	942/82/0/0	24	66 s	74/22/0/0
Zone B	11/9	2048	1 h	11008/7424/0/0	28	92 s	123/129/0/0
Zone C	14/9	16384	>2 h	–	33	98 s	140/152/5/0
Zone D	24/2	16777216	>>2 h	–	40	104 s	51/29/0/0

For the CEM of Zone A, for example, the Automatic Tester has executed 24 test cases and evaluated 4 effects, totalizing 96 diagnoses (74 OK+, 22 OK–, 0 SF and 0 DF) in 66 s. The exhaustive testing executed all 256 combinations of causes for the CEM of Zone A, resulting in 1024 diagnoses (942 OK+, 82 OK–, 0 SF and 0 DF) after 523 s of automatic test.

For the CEM of Zone C, five test cases have been diagnosed as safe-failures by the automatic testing tool in two minutes. By running these test cases in the PLC simulator, we could observe that all these failures are due to a unique nonconformity: the safety PLC activates a shutdown device in Zone C by a sensor that is not related to this effect in the CEM. The exhaustive testing was aborted after 2 h of execution without diagnosing any additional nonconformity for this CEM.

We can observe that the number of test cases and the running time grow linearly with the number of causes for the proposed method, and exponentially for the exhaustive testing. During the whole experiment, it was possible to diagnose five safe-failures in six minutes of test execution. By focusing on these critical test-cases we could efficiently identify a nonconformity between the original project and the current SIS in the offshore platform that shall be the subject of a rigorous safety analysis.

6   Conclusion

This work has presented a method for automating conformity testing between the safety specifications of CEM and the PLC program, which is based on an adaptation of CEG-BOR-MI strategy for the generation of test cases and on the use of Time Petri Nets for the generation and execution of oracles. The CEG-BOR-MI technique guarantees an efficient coverage for the identification of failures avoiding the combinatorial complexity of an exhaustive test. The use of Time Petri Net as formal models to represent the CEM specifications facilitates the automation of oracle generation and improves the reliability of the test result evaluation process. Because Petri Nets are independent of the test case, the automatic tester allows diagnosing failures also by manually or randomly performing tests. More over, Time Petri Net could be easily adapted for diagnosing failures during online operation of the plant, if it could be interconnected to the process monitoring system.

The experimental tool for automatic testing has allowed to validate the proposed method by identifying nonconformities between the CEM of the fire and gas system and the PLC program installed on a real platform. The experimental results show that the method is efficient for real-world problems and may provide an important assistance to improve the safety of oil and gas facilities. Currently the tool is being improved for its use in practice, through functionalities to facilitate, for example, the configuration of the links between the causes and effects of the CEM and the corresponding PLC memory addresses.

References

1. Gruhn, P., Cheddie, H.: Safety Instrumented Systems - Design, Analysis, and Justification, 2nd edn. ISA: The Instrumentation, Systems, and Automation Society (2005)
2. Skogdalen, J.E., Smogeli, O.: Looking Forward-Reliability of Safety Critical Control Systems on Offshore Drilling Vessels. Working Paper, Deepwater Horizon Study Group (2011)
3. IEC 61511: Functional safety: safety instrumented systems for the process industry sector, part 1–3. International Electrotechnical Commission, Geneva (2003)
4. Gergely, E.I., Coroiu, L., Popentiu-Vladicescu, F.: Methods for validation of PLC systems. J. Comput. Sci. Control Syst. **4**, 47 (2011)
5. Jorgensen, P.: Software Testing: A Craftsman's Approach, 2nd edn. CRC Press, New York (2002)
6. Myers, G.J., Thomas, T.M., Sandler, C.: The Art of Software Testing, 3rd edn. Wiley, New York (2011)
7. Nidhra, S.: Black box and white box testing techniques - a literature review. Int. J. Embed. Syst. Appl. **2**, 29–50 (2012)
8. Hamlet, D.: Software Quality, Software Process, and Software Testing. In: Advances in Computers, pp. 41–191. Academic Press (1994)
9. Frey, G., Litz, L.: Formal methods in PLC programming. In: IEEE International Conference on Systems, Man and Cybernetics (2000)
10. Tretmans, G.J., Belinfante, A.: Automatic testing with formal methods. Technical report, Centre for Telematics and Information Technology University of Twente (1999)
11. Provost, J., Roussel, J.M., Faure, J.M.: Translating Grafcet specifications into Mealy machines for conformance test purposes. Control Engineering Practice (2011)

12. Utting, M., Legeard, B.: Software Testing: Practical Model-Based Testing: A Tools Approach, 2nd edn. Morgan Kaufmann Publishers Inc., San Francisco (2006)
13. Meinke, K., Sindhu, M.A.: LBTest: a learning-based testing tool for reactive systems. In: International Conference on Software Testing, Verification and Validation, ICST (2013)
14. Prati, T.J., Farines, J.M., Queiroz, M.H.: Automatic test of safety specifications for PLC programs in the oil and gas industry. In: Proceedings of the 2nd IFAC Workshop on Automatic Control in Offshore Oil and Gas Production, Florianópolis (2015)
15. ET-3000.00-1200-800-PGT-006: Project Guidelines for the Confection of Cause and Effect Matrixes and Logic Diagrams. Project Guidelines for Offshore Production Installation. Technical Specification, Petrobras (2000)
16. Howden, W.E.: Functional program testing. IEEE Trans. Softw. Eng. **6**, 162–169 (1980)
17. Elmendorf, W.R.: Automated design of program test libraries. IBM Technical report (1970)
18. Paradkar, A.M., Tai, K.-C., Vouk, M.A.: Specification-based testing using cause-effect graphs. Anna. Softw. Eng. **4**, 133–157 (1997)
19. Paradkar, A., Tai, K.-C.: Test generation for Boolean expressions. In: Proceedings of the Sixth International Symposium on Software Reliability Engineering. IEEE (1995)
20. Malekzadeh, M., Raja, N.A.: An automatic test case generator for testing safety-critical software systems. In: The 2nd International Conference on Computer and Automation Engineering (ICCAE), vol. 1. IEEE (2010)
21. Berthomieu, B., Diaz, M.: Modeling and verification of time dependent systems using time Petri nets. IEEE Trans. Softw. **17**, 259–273 (1991)
22. Selic, B.: What will it take? A view on adoption of model-based methods in practice. Softw. Syst. Model. 1–14 (2012)
23. Pommereau, F.: SNAKES: a flexible high-level petri nets library (tool paper). In: Devillers, R., Valmari, A. (eds.) PETRI NETS 2015. LNCS, vol. 9115, pp. 254–265. Springer, Cham (2015). doi:10.1007/978-3-319-19488-2_13

Model-Based Testing for Asynchronous Systems

Alexander Graf-Brill[(⊠)] and Holger Hermanns

Saarland University, Saarland Informatics Campus, Saarbrücken, Germany
grafbrill@depend.uni-saarland.de

Abstract. Model-based testing is a prominent validation technique, integrating well with other formal approaches to verification, such as model checking. Automated test derivation and execution approaches often struggle with asynchrony in communication between the implementation under test (IUT) and tester, a phenomenon present in most networked systems. Earlier attacks on this problem came with different restrictions on the specification model side. This paper presents a new and effective approach to model-based testing under asynchrony. By waiving the need to guess the possible output state of the IUT, we reduce the computational effort of the test generation algorithm while preserving soundness and conceptual completeness of the testing procedures. In addition, no restrictions on the specification model need to be imposed. We define a suitable conformance relation and we report on empirical results obtained from an industrial case study from the domain of electric mobility.

1 Introduction

Model-based testing is a validation technique where, based on a formal specification of a system, a suitable set of experiments (test suite) is generated in an automated manner and executed on the implementation of that system, so as to assert some notion of conformance between the implementation and its specification. In model-based testing it is common to use variants of input-output transitions systems (IOTS) as formal models to capture the system behaviour on the specification side. In IOTS, transitions between states have structured action labels: the name of a performed action and an identifier of its type, i.e. input (stimuli) to the implementation or output (response) of the implementation. By automated inspection of the possible inputs and outputs in the current states of a given specification model, a model-based testing tool can either provide one of these inputs to or records an output from the implementation under test (IUT). It then updates its knowledge of the current state in the specification model. Whenever an unexpected output of the IUT occurs, i.e. an output which is not considered possible according to the current state(s) of the specification model, the IUT is refused with a verdict "fail". Testing is usually employed for finding problems in an IUT, instead of for verifying the absence of any problems. Nevertheless it is theoretically appealing to discuss the size a complete test suite needs to have in order to be usable for such a verification. Finiteness of such a

© Springer International Publishing AG 2017
L. Petrucci et al. (Eds.): FMICS-AVoCS 2017, LNCS 10471, pp. 66–82, 2017.
DOI: 10.1007/978-3-319-67113-0_5

complete test suite however requires finite and acyclic behaviour, which is rarely the case for embedded systems, the class of systems we look at.

While the specification can be provided as a formal model, this is not naturally given for the IUT, which is most often a real physical object, or a piece of code. To enable a formal relation between the specification and the IUT, the so-called *testing hypothesis* or *test assumption*, is usually put in place, assuming the existence of an equivalent formal model of the IUT. It is common to use IOTS for both, the model of the specification and the IUT, as we do in the sequel.

The most prominent conformance relation in use is *input-output conformance* (**ioco**) [24]. It is defined for systems interacting *synchronously* with their environment, and especially with the model-based testing tool. Here "synchronously" means that each input to the IUT instantaneously leads to a state transition in the IUT, and each output of the IUT can be instantaneously processed by its environment. Model-based testing for synchronous communication has been extensively studied for decades [2,8–10,17–19,21–23], spanning varying conformance relations and modelling formalisms. IOTS may be nondeterministic in the sense that a state has several outgoing transitions with the same label, so as to support abstraction or implementation freedom w.r.t. certain system aspects.

In contrast to synchronous testing, where the exact state of an IUT on the specification side is known modulo non-determinism, this does not hold if testing systems communicating asynchronously, especially if being tested via one or more asynchronous channels. Rooted in possible message delays, it is then no longer guaranteed that inputs provided to and outputs received from an IUT are being processed in the order they appear to the tester.

Asynchronous communication can appear in different flavours, since buffering and delaying of messages may happen in various ways, depending on the characteristics of the channels connecting the two sides. Channels may only delay inputs w.r.t. outputs, or the other way around, they may allow arbitrary re-ordering of messages, for instance if separate channels for different inputs or outputs are in place. However, the most commonly assumed communication scenario is that of bidirectional FIFO (first-in-first-out) communication, effectuated by two independent FIFO channels, one for inputs, one for outputs.

The problem of asynchronous testing has received attention since the inception of model-based testing [22]. A conceptually pioneering approach [26,27] considers a so-called queue operator, which adds infinite queues for inputs and outputs, so as to model the entirety of the possible asynchrony in interaction between tester and IUT. Modelling these queues explicitly however is challenging because of their infinite size. Indeed, it is left unanswered how the presented theory could be implemented without the need for restrictions on the model to be taken into account. Additionally, the queue context may induce that the test case generation algorithm [27] produces irrelevant test cases. This is because the queue context is always ready to receive any input action, which includes inputs which are impossible according to the specification at the current state (and states reachable by a sequence of output actions of the system), thereby inspecting executions which are irrelevant for testing conformance.

A conceptually different approach [20] proposes to divide the tester into an input test process and an output test process, both operating with finite buffer. This approach comes with appropriate implementation relations and test derivation procedures which however require a fault model for the tester architecture, and focusses on input-enabled specifications, i.e. systems where in every state, every input action is enabled, and without output cycles. Under these assumptions, completeness relative to the fault model can be achieved by a finite suite. Subsequent work [16] considers a single interaction sequence derived from a specification to generate asynchronous test cases. By applying the delay operator [1], outputs of the system are shifted along the sequence to emulate asynchrony. This enables relaxations of several of the restrictions on the specification model imposed before. Test case generation is incomplete but driven by coverage criteria w.r.t. the specification model. The need for repeated delay operator constructions is costly, and the proposed algorithm is only applied to offline test generation.

Another approach [28] considers IUTs which are internal-choice IOTS. Internal-choice IOTS do only have inputs enabled in quiescent states, i.e. in states which do not possess output transitions. With this assumption in place for both, IUT and specification, asynchronous testing and synchronous testing are equivalent and standard test case generation algorithms can be used. If the specification is not an internal-choice IOTS, the methodology becomes incomplete.

Asynchronous test case generation from test purposes is considered in [7] for specifications and IUTs obeying certain restrictions. A test purpose describes a set of interaction sequences which are to be investigated at the IUT. By incorporating the asynchronous behaviour directly at the finite test purpose the approach ensures finiteness of the test suite. A comparison of the complexity of different asynchronous testing approaches can be found in [14], together with an overview of several implementation relations for testing through asynchronous channels [15].

All the approaches discussed above either impose restrictions on the specification, or sacrifice expressiveness of the generated test suite, or work with potentially unboundedly growing representations. In this paper we propose a methodology for model-based testing of asynchronous system which does not impose restrictions on the specification model, while preserving soundness and completeness. The method we are going to present is rooted in the theory of the delay operator, but derives the test cases directly from an IOTS using a single input queue, and executes them. The approach is effective and computationally affordable, and can be applied to generate a test suite offline, or to construct a test case online, i.e. incrementally during test execution. We thereby construct on-the-fly the asynchronous transition system of the specification, based on its input queue behaviour only. Our methodology is driven by the practical needs arising in the context of the ENERGYBUS specification [6] which aims at establishing a common basis for the interchange and interoperation of electric devices in the context of energy management systems (EMS).

2 Synchronous Input-Output Conformance Testing

The basis for model-based testing is a precise specification of the IUT which unambiguously describes what an implementation may do and what it may not do.

Input-Output Transition Systems. A common semantic model to describe the behaviour of a system are labeled transition systems (LTS). In the presence of inputs and outputs, a suitable variation is provided by *Input-Output Transition Systems* (IOTS).

Definition 1. *An input-output transition system is a 5-tuple* $\langle Q, L_?, L_!, T, q_0 \rangle$ *where*

- Q *is a countable, non-empty set of* states;
- $L_?$ *and* $L_!$ *are disjoint countable sets* $(L_? \cap L_! = \emptyset)$ *of* input labels *and* output labels, *respectively*;
- $T \subseteq Q \times (L \cup \{\tau\}) \times Q$, *with* $\tau \notin L$, *is the* transition relation, *where* $L = L_? \cup L_!$;
- q_0 *is the* initial state.

The class of input-output transition systems with inputs in $L_?$ *and outputs in* $L_!$ *is denoted by* $\mathcal{IOTS}(L_?, L_!)$.

As usual, τ represents an unobservable internal action of the system. We write $q \xrightarrow{\mu} q'$ if there is a transition labelled μ from state q to state q', i.e., $(q, \mu, q') \in T$. The composition of transitions $q_1 \xrightarrow{\mu_1 \cdot \mu_2 \cdot \ldots \cdot \mu_{n-1}} q_n$ expresses that the system, when in state q_1, may end in state q_n, after performing the sequence of actions $\mu_1 \cdot \mu_2 \cdot \ldots \cdot \mu_{n-1}$, i.e. $\exists (q_i, \mu_i, q_{i+1}) \in T, i \leq n - 1$. Due to non-determinism, it may be the case, that after performing the same sequence, the system may end in another state (or multiple such states): $q_1 \xrightarrow{\mu_1 \cdot \mu_2 \cdot \ldots \cdot \mu_{n-1}} q'_n$ with $q_n \neq q'_n$.

Traces and Derived Notions. Usually an IOTS can represent the entire behaviour of a system, including concrete interactions between system and environment. One such behaviour is represented by a so-called *trace*, of which we are only interested in its observable part, obtained by abstracting from internal actions of the system. Let $p = \langle Q, L_?, L_!, T, q_0 \rangle$ be an IOTS with $q, q' \in Q, L = L_? \cup L_!, a,$ $a_i \in L$, and $\sigma \in L^*$. We write $q \xRightarrow{\epsilon} q'$ to express that $q = q'$ or $q \xrightarrow{\tau \cdot \ldots \cdot \tau} q'. q \xRightarrow{a} q'$ denotes the fact that $\exists q_1, q_2 \in Q : q \xRightarrow{\epsilon} q_1 \xrightarrow{a} q_2 \xRightarrow{\epsilon} q'$. This can be extended for a sequence of actions $q \xRightarrow{a_1 \cdot \ldots \cdot a_n} q'$ s.t. $\exists q_0, ..., q_n \in Q : q = q_0 \xRightarrow{a_1} q_1 \xRightarrow{a_2} ... \xRightarrow{a_n} q_n = q'. q \xRightarrow{\sigma}$ and $q \not\xRightarrow{\sigma}$ are then defined as $\exists q' : q \xRightarrow{\sigma} q'$ and $\nexists q' : q \xRightarrow{\sigma} q'$, respectively.

Furthermore, $init(q)$ denotes the set of available transitions in a state q, i.e., $\{\mu \in L \cup \{\tau\} \mid q \xrightarrow{\mu}\}$. The set of traces starting in state q is then defined as $traces(q) =_{\text{def}} \{\sigma \in L^* \mid q \xRightarrow{\sigma}\}$. For a given trace σ, the set of reachable states is given by the definition $q \textbf{ after } \sigma =_{\text{def}} \{q' \mid q \xRightarrow{\sigma} q'\}$. The extension for starting in a set of states Q' is $Q' \textbf{ after } \sigma =_{\text{def}} \bigcup \{q \textbf{ after } \sigma \mid q \in Q'\}$. With $der(q)$ we denote the set of all reachable states from q, i.e., $\{q' \mid \exists \sigma \in L^* : q \xRightarrow{\sigma} q'\}$.

Definition 2. *Let $p = \langle Q, L_?, L_!, T, q_0 \rangle$ be an IOTS with $q, q_1, q_2 \in Q$, $a \in L_?$, and $\sigma \in L^*$.*

- q *is* input-enabled, *iff $\forall a \in L_?.q \xrightarrow{a}$.*
- q *is* input-progressive, *iff $\nexists \sigma \in L_!^+ : q \xRightarrow{\sigma} q \wedge \nexists q_1, q_2 : q \xRightarrow{\epsilon} q_1 \xrightarrow{\tau} q_2 \xRightarrow{\epsilon} q$*
- q *is* fully-specified, *iff $L_? \subseteq init(q) \vee init(q) \cap L_? = \emptyset$*

An IOTS p is input-enabled, or input-progressive, or fully-specified if and only if all its reachable states are input-enabled, or input-progressive, or fully-specified, respectively. It is common practice to work with specifications modelled as IOTS without further restrictions while IUTs are often assumed to be represented as input-enabled IOTS.

Input-Output Conformance and Quiescence. A specific conformance relation, input-out conformance (**ioco**) [24] dominates theoretical as well as practical work on model-based testing. It relates implementations with specifications with respect to the possible output behaviour observed after executing traces of the specification. In **ioco**, the output behaviour includes a designated output *quiescence*, abbreviated with the special label δ. *Quiescence* represents the situation when there is no output to observe at all. A state q is said to be quiescent, denoted by $\delta(q)$, iff $init(q) \cap L_! = \emptyset$, whereby $\delta \notin (L \cup \{\tau\})$. In this case we add the transition $q \xrightarrow{\delta} q$ for technical convenience. The set of possible outputs of a state q is then defined as $out(q) =_{\text{def}} \{a \in L_! \mid q \xrightarrow{a}\} \cup \{\delta \mid \delta(q)\}$, and this is lifted to sets of states P by $out(P) =_{\text{def}} \bigcup \{out(q) \mid q \in P\}$. Since quiescence is now interpreted as an additional observable output, we extend the definition for traces to *suspension traces*.

Definition 3. *Let $p = \langle Q, L_?, L_!, T, q_0 \rangle \in \mathcal{IOTS}(L_?, L_!)$. The suspension traces of p are given by $Straces(p) =_{\text{def}} \{\sigma \in (L \cup \{\delta\})^* \mid q_0 \xRightarrow{\sigma}\}$.*

The definition of **ioco** then looks as follows:

Definition 4. *Given a set of input labels $L_?$ and a set of output labels $L_!$, the relation* **ioco** $\subseteq \mathcal{IOTS}(L_?, L_!) \times \mathcal{IOTS}(L_?, L_!)$ *is defined for a specification s and an input-enabled implementation i as*

$$i \text{ } \mathbf{ioco} \text{ } s \Leftrightarrow_{\text{def}} \forall \sigma \in Straces(s) : out(i \text{ } \mathbf{after} \text{ } \sigma) \subseteq out(s \text{ } \mathbf{after} \text{ } \sigma).$$

Underspecification. Since **ioco** is defined for specifications without further restrictions and only takes suspension traces of the specification into account, the behaviour of an implementation after a trace not considered according to the specification is irrelevant for the relation. Figure 1 displays three IOTS (for readability we omitted the δ transitions as well as self-loops needed to ensure input-enabledness). The trace $x!b?$ is not in $Straces(s)$, i.e. it is *underspecified* w.r.t. s. So, any implementation of s is allowed to behave as it desires after that trace, and therefore i **ioco** s. In contrast, the trace $x!a?$ is in $Straces(s)$ and the allowed outputs after $x!a?$ are $\{y!\}$. Therefore, i' **ioco** s does not hold. However, s_1 **after** $x! = \{s_2, s_3\}$ and $a?$ is not specified in state s_2. Thus, one could argue

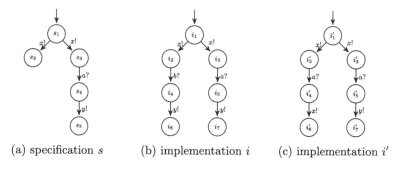

(a) specification s (b) implementation i (c) implementation i'

Fig. 1. Variants of underspecification

that the trace $x!a?$ actually constitutes a variant of underspecification, as well. This reasoning leads to the definition of **uioco** [24] which actually excludes such traces from consideration, and hence i' **uioco** s.

Test Generation and Execution. Based on the definition of **ioco**, test cases are generated and executed in interaction with the IUT. A test case $t = \langle Q_t, L_?, L_!, T_t, v, t_0 \rangle$ is an extension of IOTS s.t. $\langle Q_t, L_?, L_!, T_t, t_0 \rangle \in \mathcal{IOTS}(L_?, L_!)$. Q_t is a set of states of Q, i.e. $Q_t \subseteq \mathcal{P}(Q)$ and $T_t \subseteq Q_t \times (L_? \cup L_! \cup \{\theta\}) \times Q_t$, where $\theta \neq \tau \neq \delta$ and $\theta \notin (L_? \cup L_!)$ is a special label synchronising with δ to detect quiescence. The function $v \in Q_t \times V$ is the *verdict label function* which assigns to each state of the test case a verdict in the set $V = \{\text{none}, \textbf{pass}, \textbf{fail}\}$. A test case is then generated as follows: The initial state of a test case consists of the τ-closure of the initial state of the specification, i.e. the set of all states which are reachable by a sequence of τ transitions. Then, one of the following three options is chosen nondeterministically. Either the current state is marked in the verdict label function as **pass** and test case generation is stopped; or an input action which is enabled in one of the current states of the specification is chosen and a transition for this action is added to the test. The successor state than consists of all valid successor states for the chosen (weak) input action. In addition, to be prepared to perform any output action of the IUT which might interrupt the input, for all outputs in $L_!$ a transition is added to all corresponding successor states of the specification. If the output is not foreseen by the specification, the successor state is a new state labeled with **fail**. For all valid successor states the test case generation algorithm is called recursively. The third option is to wait for an output of the system. For all outputs in $L_!$ and quiescence a transition is added to all corresponding successor states of the specification. Again, if the output is not foreseen by the specification, the successor state is a new state labeled with **fail** and for all valid successor states the test case generation algorithm is called recursively. States which are neither labeled with **pass** nor **fail** are marked with "none" in the verdict label function.

An execution of a test case is then the parallel composition of the test case and the IUT. A *test run* is than any trace of the parallel composition which ends in a state which is labeled with **pass** or **fail**. An IUT then passes a test case if and only if all possible test runs lead to states labeled with **pass**. It fails the test case otherwise. By assuming some kind of fairness, an IUT will reveal sooner or later all its nondeterministic behaviour when executed with a test case.

3 Asynchronous Input-Output Conformance Testing

The traditional synchronous testing theory is not applicable when testing communication is asynchronous [27]. The implementation relations used for synchronous testing are not testable in an asynchronous context, and test cases derived from specifications to be used for synchronous testing do reject correct implementations when tested asynchronously. Therefore, the asynchronous communication behaviour needs to be directly taken into account within the conformance relation and the test case generation.

Queue Operator. One approach to include the asynchronous communication behaviour of a system applies the so-called queue operator [26]. This takes an IOTS s and yields an IOTS s' which behaves like s in the context of an input queue and an output queue, both with infinite capacity. The behaviour of $s \in \mathcal{IOTS}(L_?, L_!)$ in a queue context $[_{\sigma_!} \ll s \ll_{\sigma_?}]$ (abbreviated by $Q(s)$), where $\sigma_! \in L_!^*$ and $\sigma_? \in L_?^*$ represent the input and output queue state as words of arbitrary length over inputs, respectively outputs. It is derived by applying the following axioms and inference rules:

$$A1 \quad [_{\sigma_!} \ll s \ll_{\sigma_?}] \xrightarrow{a} [_{\sigma_!} \ll s \ll_{\sigma_? \cdot a}] \quad a \in L_? \qquad A2 \quad [_{x \cdot \sigma_!} \ll s \ll_{\sigma_?}] \xrightarrow{x} [_{\sigma_!} \ll s \ll_{\sigma_?}] \quad x \in L_!$$

$$I1 \quad \frac{s \xrightarrow{\tau} s'}{[_{\sigma_!} \ll s \ll_{\sigma_?}] \xrightarrow{\tau} [_{\sigma_!} \ll s' \ll_{\sigma_?}]} \qquad I2 \quad \frac{s \xrightarrow{a} s'}{[_{\sigma_!} \ll s \ll_{a \cdot \sigma_?}] \xrightarrow{\tau} [_{\sigma_!} \ll s' \ll_{\sigma_?}]} \quad a \in L_?$$

$$I3 \quad \frac{s \xrightarrow{x} s'}{[_{\sigma_!} \ll s \ll_{\sigma_?}] \xrightarrow{\tau} [_{\sigma_! \cdot x} \ll s' \ll_{\sigma_?}]} \quad x \in L_!$$

Obviously, the resulting state space of $Q(s)$ is infinite. Looking at the output queue, this infinity problem materialises for systems having at least one output action on a cycle, i.e. $\exists \sigma_1, \sigma_2 \in L^*, x \in L_!, q, q_1, q_2 \in der(s) : q \xRightarrow{\sigma_1} q_1 \xrightarrow{x} q_2 \xRightarrow{\sigma_2} q$. The state space however remains finite at any finite depth of the testing process, unless the system contains output loops. In the latter case, the weak trace construction in the testing theory leads to an immediate explosion, rooted in an infinite branching. This however can be prevented by putting restrictions on the specification, namely input-progressiveness. The input queue, in turn, is always ready to receive an input, thus, growing to unbounded size. In addition, the input capability of $Q(s)$ is in no sense related to the actual structure of the underlying system s. Thus, providing input actions which are not specified in s at the current state, may lead to the execution of underspecified traces w.r.t. s, which are being irrelevant for testing conformance. When only considering input-enabled or fully-specified specifications, this discrepancy is obviously not there. Therefore, using the queue operator as basis for asynchronous testing seems to be rather inconvenient.

Delay Operator. A conceptually different way of including asynchronous communication is the *delay* operator [1]. Instead of being directly applied to an IOTS,
the delay operator works on the traces of a system. For a set of action sequences,
e.g. traces, $E \subseteq L^*$ and a subset $L' \subseteq L$, the operator $delay[L'] : 2^{L^*} \to 2^{L^*}$
gives the smallest superset of E s.t. for $\sigma_1, \sigma_2 \in L^*$, any $a \in L \setminus L'$ and $a_1 \in L'$:

$$\sigma_1 a_1 a \sigma_2 \in delay[L'](E) \Rightarrow \sigma_1 a a_1 \sigma_2 \in delay[L'](E).$$

Given a set of traces E and a set of actions L', $delay[L'](E)$ calculates a set
of traces where actions in L' are shifted towards the end of a trace in E while
keeping the relative order of actions in $L \setminus L'$. For an IOTS $p = \langle Q, L_?, L_!, T, q_0 \rangle$,
the observable traces in a queue context can then be defined as $traces(Q(p)) =$
$pref(delay[L_!](traces(p)))$, where $pref(U)$ is the prefix closure of a set of traces
U. On the other hand, when a trace σ has been observed, p can have executed
any of the traces in $delay[L_?](\sigma L_!^*) \cap traces(p)$.

Since the delay operator directly operates on traces of a system, genuine
underspecified traces are excluded. However, due to delayed input actions, it is
still possibly that an execution is steered away from specified traces, which has to
be dealt with in the test case generation algorithm [16]. Again, this problem does
not arise when only considering input-enabled or fully-specified specifications. If
assuming input progressive specifications (as in [16]) the test algorithm can be
made to assign verdicts in quiescent states of an IUT only. But this assumption
is otherwise not needed for generating test cases from given traces, which are in
fact, finite. Nevertheless, the test generation algorithm is only suitable for offline
test case generation due to the need for repeated calculation of delayed traces
and their intersection with traces of the system.

Our Approach

The method we are going to present is a practical approach to deriving test
cases directly from an IOTS, offline or online, while theoretically being (almost)
equivalent to applying the delay operator to the specification traces. Notably, we
neither have to propose any restrictions on the specification, nor do we examine
underspecified traces of the system, nor can our tester become trapped in an
immediate growth of the state space due to infinite branching. At the same
time, the approach is effective and computationally affordable.

Input Queue Context. The starting point of our approach is the construction
of the *input queue context* of a system s which represents the asynchronous
communication behaviour of s in the presence of an infinite input queue.

Definition 5. *For an IOTS $s = \langle Q, L_?, L_!, T, q_0 \rangle$, the* input queue context *is the
smallest IOTS $s_\ll = \langle Q_\ll, L_?, L_!, T_\ll, q_{0\ll} \rangle$ where $Q_\ll \subseteq (Q \times L_?^*), \sigma \in L_?^*, \mu \in L \cup \{\tau\}$ s.t. :*

– $q_{0\ll} = (q_0, \epsilon)$ and $q_{0\ll} \in Q_\ll$

$$- \ T_{\ll} = \{((q,\sigma),\tau,(q',\sigma)) \mid q,q' \in Q, q \xrightarrow{\tau} q'\}$$
$$\cup \ \{((q,\sigma),a,(q,\sigma a)) \mid q \in Q, a \in L_?\}$$
$$\cup \ \{((q,a\sigma),\tau,(q',\sigma)) \mid q,q' \in Q, q \xrightarrow{a} q'\}$$
$$\cup \ \{((q,\sigma),x,(q',\sigma)) \mid q,q' \in Q, x \in L_!, q \xrightarrow{x} q'\}$$
$$- \ q \in Q_{\ll} \wedge (q,\mu,q') \in T_{\ll} \Rightarrow q' \in Q_{\ll}$$

The input queue context of a system behaves exactly as the queue context derived by the queue operator, but without applying the rules A2 and I3. Interestingly, despite the fact that for a system s, $s_{\ll}$ and $Q(s)$ are not isomorphic, the observable trace behaviour of both resulting systems is actually equivalent.

Proposition 1. *Let* $s \in \mathcal{IOTS}(L_?, L_!)$

1. $traces(Q(s)) = traces(s_{\ll})$
2. $Straces(Q(s)) = Straces(s_{\ll})$

This follows from the observation already mentioned when introducing the delay operator: $traces(Q(p)) = pref(delay[L_!](traces(p)))$.

Shifting Outputs. The core property exploited by our approach (already appearing above) is that the asynchronous behaviour can be modelled by only shifting one action set, i.e. outputs, w.r.t. the other action set. To establish this shift, it is actually irrelevant which set of actions is buffered. Notably, this means, that we could equally well model the same phenomena by an output queue context instead of an input queue context, but requiring input-enabled specifications. However, inputs are under full control of the tester while outputs are under the control of the IUT. So, with an output queue context we would still face the immediate explosion problem due to infinite branching in the test generation algorithm when dealing with output loops. This is not the case for the input queue context as defined above. Thus, the input queue context is computable using the standard test case generation algorithm proposed for synchronous communication.

Asynchronous Transition System. In comparison with the delay operator approach, we however still have the issue with unnecessarily testing underspecified traces. In order to remedy this, we define the *asynchronous transition system* on top of the input queue context.

Definition 6. *Given an IOTS* $s = \langle Q, L_?, L_!, T, q_0 \rangle$ *and its input queue context* $s_{\ll} = \langle Q_{\ll}, L_?, L_!, T_{\ll}, q_{0\ll} \rangle$, *the* asynchronous transition system *(ATS) is the smallest IOTS* $_{\ll}s_{\ll} = \langle _{\ll}Q_{\ll}, L_?, L_!, _{\ll}T_{\ll}, _{\ll}q_{0\ll} \rangle$ *where* $_{\ll}Q_{\ll} \subseteq \mathcal{P}(Q \times L_?^*)$, $a \in L_?, x \in L_!, \sigma, \sigma_1, \sigma_2 \in L^*, \mu \in L \cup \{\tau, \delta\}$ *s.t.* :

$$- \ _{\ll}q_{0\ll} = \{q_{0\ll}\} \cup q_{0\ll} \ \textbf{after} \ \epsilon$$
$$- \ _{\ll}T_{\ll} = \{(\hat{q}, a, \hat{q}') \mid \exists(q,\epsilon) \in \hat{q} : q \xrightarrow{a} \wedge \forall(q',\sigma_1) \in \hat{q} : (q',\sigma_1) \xRightarrow{a} (q'',\sigma_2) \implies (q'',\sigma_2) \in \hat{q}'\}$$
$$\cup \ \{(\hat{q}, x, \hat{q}') \mid \exists q \in \hat{q} : q \xrightarrow{x} \wedge \hat{q}' = \hat{q} \ \textbf{after} \ x\}$$
$$\cup \ \{(\hat{q}, \delta, \hat{q}') \mid \exists(q,\epsilon) \in \hat{q} : \delta(q) \wedge \hat{q}' = \{(q',\epsilon) \in \hat{q}\}\}$$

$$- q \in_{\ll} Q_{\ll} \wedge (q, \mu, q') \in_{\ll} T_{\ll} \Rightarrow q' \in_{\ll} Q_{\ll}$$

The initial state of the ATS is the τ-closure of the initial state of the underlying input queue context. Continuing from here, the ATS is further constructed by adding transitions for the asynchronous behaviour and by eliminating nondeterminism (putting all successor states together). A state in the ATS can receive an input action, iff there is one state in the input queue context which has an empty input queue. Then, the successor state consists of all the successor states of the input queue context after the corresponding input transition. By restricting the input functionality in this way, we make sure that we always follow specified traces of the system, i.e. we are not examining genuine underspecified traces. The ATS can issue an output action, again, iff there is a state in the input queue context which enables this output action. All states reachable by this output transition form the new successor state, including states reachable by successive τ transitions inherited from the underlying system or from the opportunity of the input queue context to process inputs present in the input queue. The last part of the definition of the above transition relation deals with our interpretation of quiescence in the asynchronous communication setting. When quiescence is observed, we do not only assume that the system is in no state which can produce an output, but we also assume the input queue to be as processed as possible. Thus, we only can observe quiescence in a state of an input queue context which is quiescent in the perspective of the underlying system and whose input queue is either empty, or the next input action in the queue is blocking w.r.t. the currently enabled input transitions. If the input queue is not empty, we can conclude that this state configuration represents an underspecified trace. Since it is quiescent, it can not evolve by further output and it does not have a suitable input action enabled w.r.t. the specification, thus it must be an underspecified trace. Therefore, we restrict quiescence further to only quiescent states with empty input queues.

Passing Underspecified Behaviour. Regarding unintended examination of underspecified traces due to the asynchronous communication, there is one situation left which we did not take care of so far. When receiving an output from the system, which is not foreseen in any of the current states, this is seen as an illegal output. However, when we already drifted in an underspecified trace, the reception of such an output should lead to the verdict "pass". Such a situation is identified by inspecting the input queues of the current states. If there is no state with an empty input queue, we know that there is no trace of the specification corresponding to the current execution. Note, a valid output in such a situation will be processed further, since we could still be on a valid trace with pending inputs not received so far by the IUT. Technically speaking, we observed a trace σ_1 s.t. $delay[L_?](\sigma_1) \cap traces(s) = \emptyset$, but their might be a sequence of output actions $\sigma_2 \in L_!^+$ s.t. $delay[L_?](\sigma_1 \sigma_2) \cap traces(s) \neq \emptyset$. Taking care of this situation is done during the test case generation.

Role of ATS. Since the asynchronous transition system directly takes all non-determinism and weak transitions in the input queue context into account, it represents an intermediate step to the *test graph* of our testing approach.

Test Generation Algorithm. Our test case generation algorithm is provided as Algorithm 1. Starting with an empty test case, we set the initial state to the τ-closure of the initial state of the system with empty input queues. Following the structure of the test case generation algorithm for synchronous communication, we then nondeterministically choose between ending with verdict **pass** (lines 11–14), providing an enabled input to the IUT and recursively construct the following subtree (lines 15–20), or add transitions for all outputs (including quiescence) (lines 21–52) and recursively construct the following subtree for valid outputs (lines 23–28 and 38–42). The provided algorithm is suitable for both, offline and online test case generation. For offline test case generation, it is common to only explore one subtree of valid outputs and stop with the verdict **pass** for the other output actions.

Asynchronous Input-Output Conformance. With the test case generation algorithm in place, what is missing is the definition of the actual conformance relation we are testing for, which we call **asy**nchronous **i**nput-**o**utput **co**nformance (**asyioco**). First, we need an additional definition.

Definition 7. *For a given IOTS $s \in \mathcal{IOTS}(L_?, L_!)$ and a suspension trace $\sigma \in Straces(s)$, the set of asynchronous trace executions is defined as the smallest subset of $Straces(s)$ s.t. for $\sigma_1, \sigma_2 \in (L_? \cup L_!)^*$, any $x \in L_!$ with $x \neq \delta$ and $a \in L_?$:*

$$\sigma \in asyexec_s(\sigma)$$
$$\sigma_1 a x \sigma_2 \in asyexec_s(\sigma) \implies (\sigma_1 x a \sigma_2 \in Straces(s) \implies \sigma_1 x a \sigma_2 \in asyexec_s(\sigma))$$

Here we directly encode the delay operator into the definition of asynchronous trace executions to point out, that input actions can not be shifted along quiescence.

Definition 8. *Given a set of input labels $L_?$ and a set of output labels $L_!$, the relation $\mathbf{asyioco} \subseteq \mathcal{IOTS}(L_?, L_!) \times \mathcal{IOTS}(L_?, L_!)$ is defined for a specification s and an input-enabled implementation i as:*

$$i \, \mathbf{asyioco} \, s \Leftrightarrow_{\text{def}} \forall \sigma \in Straces(s). \, out(i \, \mathbf{after} \, asyexec_s(\sigma)) \subseteq out(s \, \mathbf{after} \, asyexec_s(\sigma))$$

In words, this definition says that an IUT conforms to a specification, iff for each observable behaviour of the specification, the possible outputs of the IUT after asynchronously executing this trace w.r.t. the specified traces are foreseen by the specification after all possible asynchronous executions.

Proposition 2. *Let specification s and implementation $i \in \mathcal{IOTS}(L_?, L_!)$. The following holds for input-enabled i and for s being*

Algorithm 1. Test case generation algorithm for asynchronous communicating systems through queues

```
 1  Function TCG(s)
        Input  : IOTS s = ⟨Q, L_?, L_!, T, q_0⟩
        Output: Test case t = ⟨Q_t, L_!, L_?, T_t, v, t_0⟩
 2      t_0 ← (q_0, ε) after ε
 3      Q_t ← {t_0}
 4      T_t, v ← ∅
 5      ⟨Q_t, L_!, L_?, T_t, v, t'⟩ ← reTCG(s, ⟨Q_t, L_!, L_?, T_t, v, t_0⟩)
 6      return reTCG(s, ⟨Q_t, L_!, L_?, T_t, v, t_0⟩)
 7  end
 8
 9  Function reTCG(s, t)
        Input  : IOTS s = ⟨Q, L_?, L_!, T, q_0⟩,
                 Test case t = ⟨Q_t, L_!, L_?, T_t, v, t_0⟩
        Output: Test case t' = ⟨Q_t, L_!, L_?, T_t, v, t_0⟩
10      choice {pass, input, output} do
11          case pass
12              v ← v ∪ {(t_0, pass)}
13              return ⟨Q_t, L_!, L_?, T_t, v, t_0⟩
14          end
15          case input ∧ ∃a ∈ L_?, (q, ε) ∈ t_0. q --a-->
16              t' ← t_0 after a
17              Q_t ← Q_t ∪ {t'}
18              T_t ← T_t ∪ {(t_0, a, t')}
19              return reTCG(s, ⟨Q_t, L_!, L_?, T_t, v, t'⟩)
20          end
21          otherwise
22              v ← v ∪ {(t_0, none)}
23              for x ∈ L_! : ∃(q, σ) ∈ t_0 : q --x--> do
24                  t' ← t_0 after x
25                  Q_t ← Q_t ∪ {t'}
26                  T_t ← T_t ∪ {(t_0, x, t')}
27                  ⟨Q_t, L_!, L_?, T_t, v, t'⟩ ← reTCG(s, ⟨Q_t, L_!, L_?, T_t, v, t'⟩)
28              end
29              for x ∈ L_! : ∄(q, σ) ∈ t_0 : q --x--> do
30                  Q_t ← Q_t ∪ {t'}
31                  T_t ← T_t ∪ {(t_0, x, t')}
32                  if ∃(q, ε) ∈ t_0 then
33                      v ← v ∪ {(t', fail)}
34                  else
35                      v ← v ∪ {(t', pass)}
36                  end
37              end
38              if ∃(q, ε) ∈ t_0 : δ(q) then
39                  t' ← {(q, ε) ∈ t_0. δ(q)}
40                  Q_t ← Q_t ∪ {t'}
41                  T_t ← T_t ∪ {(t_0, δ, t')}
42                  ⟨Q_t, L_!, L_?, T_t, v, t'⟩ ← reTCG(s, ⟨Q_t, L_!, L_?, T_t, v, t'⟩)
43              else if ∃(q, ε) ∈ t_0 ∧ ∀(q', ε) ∈ t_0 : ¬δ(q') then
44                  Q_t ← Q_t ∪ {t'}
45                  T_t ← T_t ∪ {(t_0, δ, t')}
46                  v ← v ∪ {(t', fail)}
47              else
48                  Q_t ← Q_t ∪ {t'}
49                  T_t ← T_t ∪ {(t_0, δ, t')}
50                  v ← v ∪ {(t', pass)}
51              end
52          end
53      end
54      return ⟨Q_t, L_!, L_?, T_t, v, t_0⟩
55  end
```

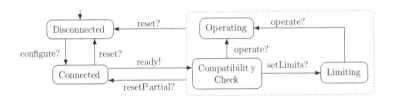

Fig. 2. EnergyBus energy management system FSA (simplified)

1. *input-enabled:* i **asyioco** $s \Leftrightarrow i \leq_{qcst} s \Leftrightarrow Q(i)$ **ioco** $Q(s)$
2. *fully-specified:* i **asyioco** $s \Leftarrow i \leq_{qcst} s \Leftrightarrow Q(i)$ **ioco** $Q(s)$
3. *partially-specified:* i **asyioco** $s \Leftarrow Q(i)$ **ioco** $Q(s) \wedge i \leq_{qcst} s \Leftarrow Q(i)$ **ioco** $Q(s)$

The definition of **asyioco** is similar to *queue-context suspension trace inclusion* ($\leq_{qcst}$) [16] if restricting to fully or partially specified IOTS. As already discussed, these settings either exclude the need to handle underspecification of the specification or they exclude underspecification in its entirety. The latter can thus be considered as an asynchronous version of **uioco** [24]. In contrast, **asyioco** follows the **ioco** philosophy and only exclude traces which in any case are underspecified. Therefore, we think **asyioco** is a more natural extension of **ioco** to asynchronous communication.

We claim that the test case generation algorithm we presented is sound and complete w.r.t. **asyioco**. The latter feature is of only a theoretical nature. Since completeness can only be achieved by generating an infinite amount of test cases, which can in practice not be executed in finite time.

4   EnergyBus Case Study

The ENERGYBUS specification [6] aims at establishing a common basis for the interchange and interoperation of electric devices in the context of energy management systems (EMS). The central and innovative role of ENERGYBUS is the transmission and management of electrical power: the purpose of its protocol suite is not just to transmit data, but in particular to manage the safe access to electricity and its distribution inside an ENERGYBUS network. Conceptually, ENERGYBUS extends the CANopen architecture in terms of *CANopen application profiles* endorsed by the CiA association [6]. Among these, the "Pedelec Profile 1" (PP1) is very elaborate, targeting a predominant business context, which is also at the centre of ongoing international standardisation efforts as part of IEC/IS/TC69/JPT61851-3.

Formal EnergyBus Specification. Since ENERGYBUS is defined as a layer on top of CANopen, ENERGYBUS documentation [6] as well as the CANopen documentation [4] have to be taken into account for formal modelling. Both specifications are provided as informal combinations of text, protocol flow charts, data tables, and finite state automata (FSA). The definitions include several data structures and various services for e.g. initial configuration, data exchange, and basic communication capability control. Figure 2 presents a simplified view on a core EnergyBus control functionality. Our formal model of ENERGYBUS uses the MODEST modelling language.

Aside from the basic control functionality, the ENERGYBUS protocol is all about data. To overcome the state space explosion problem, we applied several abstraction techniques to appropriate areas of our model, transferring the complexity from the MODEST model to the adapter component.

Results. Already during the model construction phase, our work [11] uncovered several issues concerning the (at that time current version of the) ENERGY-BUS specification documents. On the one hand there were gaps in the specification, preventing some parts of the services to be modelled to a reasonable extent; on the other hand there were ambiguities in some parts of the specification, possibly inducing non-interoperability. These have been reported so as to be corrected in standardisation. The actual test runs then revealed two different types of further errors. The first type were traditional implementation bugs of a non-severe nature. The second type of observed errors were intricately related to the hard- and software hierarchy of the test and IUT architecture, i.e. the CAN bus system. They can be viewed as spurious **fail** verdicts rooted in the fact that the different communication layers made the traditional model-based testing assumption of synchronous communication unsound. One of these spurious **fail** verdicts can be illustrated by means of Fig. 2. An already *configured* device can transit from state *Connected* to state *Compatibility Check* by announcing being *ready*, or it can be ordered to switch back to state *Disconnected* via a *reset*. One test execution trace we observed was *configure?.reset?.ready!*. In the synchronous testing approach this should end in a **fail** verdict, because after performing the prefix *configure?.reset?* the set of potential states where the IUT might be in is {*Disconnected*}, and *ready!* is not part of the *out* set of this state. However, the behaviour obviously represents the case where the device already switched to the state *Compatibility Check*, but the tester issued the *reset?* command before the *ready!* output arrived. In our asynchronous approach, the above prefix we would instead lead to the set {(*Disconnected, ϵ*), (*Connected, reset?*), (*Disconnected, configured?.reset?*)}. And since *ready!* is in the *out* set of *Connected*, this turns *ready!* into a valid output. We can thus conclude the test with a **pass** verdict, or, more importantly, we can continue testing from the set {(*Disconnected, ϵ*), (*CompatibilityCheck, reset?*)}.

The above asynchronicity phenomena indeed triggered the development and implementation of the asynchronous model-based testing method discussed here. New test runs with this improved methodology confirmed the already uncovered implementation bugs that have been reported and fixed. Since the spurious **fail** runs no longer appear, we have invested in a better analysis of the remaining errors. A newly identified type of error was rooted in two distinct interpretations of the ENERGYBUS basic device initialisation and the core ENERGYBUS device control leading to incompatible implementations. To pinpoint this, we developed two different models of the specification and continued testing with the respective version. In addition, we observed that some CAN implementations take the liberty to reorder messages within responses, so that consecutive messages passed by an IUT's application to its local CAN controller may be sent out in reverse order, which made manual inspection still be needed to definitely rule out spurious **fail** verdicts.

Asynchronous Testing with MOTEST. The presented approach is implemented in our model-based testing tool MOTEST, which is part of the MODEST TOOLSET [13]. The tool platform is based on the MODEST modelling language [12] and encompasses several tools for formal modelling, simulation and verification of systems. The MODEST TOOLSET is available at www.modestchecker.net.

Due to our tight interaction with the ENERGYBUS consortium we had the opportunity to apply MOTEST to a variety of prototypes and retail devices implementing ENERGYBUS as soon as those became available. Lately we went a step further, by making MOTEST together with the specification models available free-of-charge to the entirety of the EnergyBus e.V. association, so as to enable its direct use by association members as part of their in-house testing. The feedback collected is very encouraging.

5 Conclusion

This paper has discussed a novel, practical approach to model-based testing for asynchronous communicating systems. Test cases are generated directly on the model of the specification in a way that resembles the theory of the delay operator. We presented a pseudo-code algorithm together with the definition of **asyioco**, for which our algorithm produces sound and theoretically complete test suites. Our algorithm is implemented in the MOTEST tool as part of the MODEST TOOLSET. As we discussed, this tool is in use for model-based conformance testing of the ENERGYBUS standard over CAN.

Acknowledgments. This work is supported by the ERC Advanced Grant POWVER (695614) and the Sino-German project CAP (GZ 1023).

References

1. Balemi, S.: Control of discrete event systems: theory and application. Ph.D. thesis, Swiss Federal Institute of Technology, Zurich, Switzerland (1992)
2. Bernot, G., Gaudel, M.-C., Marre, B.: Software testing based on formal specifications: a theory and a tool. Softw. Eng. J. **6**(6), 387–405 (1991)
3. Bijl, M., Rensink, A., Tretmans, J.: Action refinement in conformance testing. In: Khendek, F., Dssouli, R. (eds.) TestCom 2005. LNCS, vol. 3502, pp. 81–96. Springer, Heidelberg (2005). doi:10.1007/11430230_7
4. CAN in Automation International Users and Manufacturers Group e.V.: CiA 301 CANopen Application Layer and Communication Profile, v. 4.2.0 (2011)

5. CAN in Automation International Users and Manufacturers Group e.V.: CiA 305 Layer setting services (LSS) and protocols, v. 3.0.0 (2013)
6. CAN in Automation International Users and Manufacturers Group e.V. and EnergyBus e.V.: CiA 454 Draft Standard Proposal Application profile for energy management systems - doc. series 1-14, v. 2.0.0 (2014)
7. da Silva Simão, A., Petrenko, A.: From test purposes to asynchronous test cases. In: ICST 2010 Workshops Proceedings, pp. 1–10. IEEE Computer Society (2010)
8. De Nicola, R.: Extensional equivalences for transition systems. Acta Inf. **24**(2), 211–237 (1987)
9. De Nicola, R., Hennessy, M.: Testing equivalences for processes. Theor. Comput. Sci. **34**, 83–133 (1984)
10. Gaudel, M.-C.: Testing can be formal, too. In: Mosses, P.D., Nielsen, M., Schwartzbach, M.I. (eds.) CAAP 1995. LNCS, vol. 915, pp. 82–96. Springer, Heidelberg (1995). doi:10.1007/3-540-59293-8_188
11. Graf-Brill, A., Hermanns, H., Garavel, H.: A model-based certification framework for the EnergyBus standard. In: Ábrahám, E., Palamidessi, C. (eds.) FORTE 2014. LNCS, vol. 8461, pp. 84–99. Springer, Heidelberg (2014). doi:10.1007/978-3-662-43613-4_6
12. Hahn, E.M., Hartmanns, A., Hermanns, H., Katoen, J.-P.: A compositional modelling and analysis framework for stochastic hybrid systems. Form. Methods Syst. Des. **43**(2), 191–232 (2013)
13. Hartmanns, A., Hermanns, H.: The modest toolset: an integrated environment for quantitative modelling and verification. In: Ábrahám, E., Havelund, K. (eds.) TACAS 2014. LNCS, vol. 8413, pp. 593–598. Springer, Heidelberg (2014). doi:10.1007/978-3-642-54862-8_51
14. Hierons, R.M.: The complexity of asynchronous model based testing. Theor. Comput. Sci. **451**, 70–82 (2012)
15. Hierons, R.M.: Implementation relations for testing through asynchronous channels. Comput. J. **56**(11), 1305–1319 (2013)
16. Huo, J., Petrenko, A.: On testing partially specified IOTS through lossless queues. In: Groz, R., Hierons, R.M. (eds.) TestCom 2004. LNCS, vol. 2978, pp. 76–94. Springer, Heidelberg (2004). doi:10.1007/978-3-540-24704-3_6
17. Jard, C., Jéron, T.: TGV: theory, principles and algorithms. STTT **7**(4), 297–315 (2005)
18. Langerak, R.: A testing theory for LOTOS using deadlock detection. In: PSTV 1989, North-Holland, pp. 87–98 (1989)
19. Petrenko, A.: Fault model-driven test derivation from finite state models: annotated bibliography. In: Cassez, F., Jard, C., Rozoy, B., Ryan, M.D. (eds.) MOVEP 2000. LNCS, vol. 2067, pp. 196–205. Springer, Heidelberg (2001). doi:10.1007/3-540-45510-8_10
20. Petrenko, A., Yevtushenko, N.: Queued testing of transition systems with inputs and outputs. In: Proceedings of FATES 2002, pp. 79–93 (2002)
21. Phillips, I.: Refusal testing. Theor. Comput. Sci. **50**, 241–284 (1987)
22. Tretmans, J.: A formal approach to conformance testing. Ph.D. thesis, University of Twente, Enschede (1992)
23. Tretmans, J.: Testing concurrent systems: a formal approach. In: Baeten, J.C.M., Mauw, S. (eds.) CONCUR 1999. LNCS, vol. 1664, pp. 46–65. Springer, Heidelberg (1999). doi:10.1007/3-540-48320-9_6
24. Tretmans, J.: Model based testing with labelled transition systems. In: Hierons, R.M., Bowen, J.P., Harman, M. (eds.) Formal Methods and Testing. LNCS, vol. 4949, pp. 1–38. Springer, Heidelberg (2008). doi:10.1007/978-3-540-78917-8_1

25. Tretmans, J., Brinksma, E.: TorX: Automated Model Based Testing - Côte de Resyste (2003)
26. Tretmans, J., Verhaard, L.: A queue model relating synchronous and asynchronous communication. In: PSTV 1992, North-Holland, pp. 131–145 (1992)
27. Verhaard, L., Tretmans, J., Kars, P., Brinksma, E.: On asynchronous testing. In: IWPTS 1992, North-Holland, pp. 55–66 (1992)
28. Weiglhofer, M., Wotawa, F.: Asynchronous input-output conformance testing. In: COMPSAC 2009, pp. 154–159. IEEE Computer Society (2009)

Information Leakage as a Scheduling Resource

Fabrizio Biondi[1], Mounir Chadli[2], Thomas Given-Wilson[2](✉), and Axel Legay[2]

[1] CentraleSupélec, Châtenay-Malabry, France
[2] Inria, Paris, France
thomas.given-wilson@inria.fr

Abstract. High-security processes have to load confidential information into shared resources as part of their operation. This confidential information may be leaked (directly or indirectly) to low-security processes via the shared resource. This paper considers leakage from high-security to low-security processes from the perspective of scheduling. The workflow model is here extended to support preemption, security levels, and leakage. Formalization of leakage properties is then built upon this extended model, allowing formal reasoning about the security of schedulers. Several heuristics are presented in the form of compositional preprocessors and postprocessors as part of a more general scheduling approach. The effectiveness of such heuristics are evaluated experimentally, showing them to achieve significantly better schedulability than the state of the art. Modeling of leakage from cache attacks is presented as a case study.

1 Introduction

This paper considers a shared resource system where processes are classified as either *high-security* or *low-security*. High-security processes work with confidential information that should not be leaked to low-security processes. Typically, this includes loading confidential information into memory for use within high-security processes. Examples of such confidential information include encryption keys, medical data, and bank details. This confidential information may be vital to the operation of the high-security processes, but must also be tightly controlled and not be leaked to low-security processes. For instance, in an embedded sensor, high-security encryption processes handle encryption keys that must not be leaked to low-security data compression processes.

However, high-security processes may not properly flush confidential information from the shared resource, or context switching may interrupt their execution before such flushing can be applied. Consequently, confidential information remaining in the shared resource becomes (directly or indirectly) available to low-security processes.

© Springer International Publishing AG 2017
L. Petrucci et al. (Eds.): FMICS-AVoCS 2017, LNCS 10471, pp. 83–99, 2017.
DOI: 10.1007/978-3-319-67113-0_6

Consider the small example in Fig. 1, written in Intel x86-64 assembly code for Linux compiled to ELF format[1]. There are two processes: Process 1 doing some (trivial) encryption operations, and Process 2 attempting to access the encryption key. Process 1 takes a *key* $KEY and a *message* $MSG then encrypts the message with the key using an exclusive or XOR operation. The result is then output to the disk (represented by $DISK1). Process 2 writes to a different disk location (represented by $DISK2) the content of register r13. It is clear that if Process 2 is executed after the first operation and before the fourth operation of Process 1, then the value of the key is directly leaked.

If a scheduler is aware of a process' access level, then the scheduler can take action to prevent confidential information being leaked to low-security processes. Recent work [15,17] has explored these kinds of problems in a real-time setting by scheduling a complete resource (memory) flush after any high-security process that is followed by a low-security process. However, this provides only limited options to the scheduler since such a complete resource flush is expensive and may prevent real-time tasks from meeting their deadlines. Further, when flushing is not possible, current approaches do not quantify the information leakage, simply considering any leakage unacceptable.

```
; Process 1:
  mov    r13,$KEY  ; load key to register r13
  mov    r14,$MSG  ; load message to register r14
  xor    r14,r13   ; encrypt message with key
                   ; using XOR, store result in r14
  xor    r13,r13   ; wipe value of key
  out    $DISK1,r14 ; output the ciphertext (r14)

; Process 2:
  out    $DISK2,r13 ; output r13 (may store the key)
```

Fig. 1. Example Processes with schedule-dependent confidential information leakage.

This paper proposes treating *confidentiality*, measured by the *resulting leakage* of secure information, as a quantitative resource that the scheduler can exploit. This allows for better quantification of the resulting leakage in different scenarios, as well as having a clear measure of the cost of different scheduling

---

[1] Technical details for X86-64 (https://software.intel.com/sites/default/files/article/402129/mpx-linux64-abi.pdf) and ELF initialization (http://lxr.linux.no/linux+v3.2.4/arch/ia64/include/asm/elf.h).

choices. Further, this allows for the creation of schedulers that can make better scheduling choices and also respect confidential information leakage constraints.

The paper builds upon the *workflow model* commonly used to represent real-time systems [3,9,26]. In the workflow model a set of *tasks* periodically produce *jobs* that have to be scheduled to complete before *deadlines*.

The workflow model is here extended by considering tasks to be composed of *steps*, each of which has an *execution time*, *leakage value*, and *security level*. Each one of these steps is implicitly an atomic sequence of actions that can be taken within a task without preemption by the scheduler. Thus a task consists of an ordered sequence of steps to be performed, that yields the total behavior of the task.

Using this extended workflow model, schedulers can operate upon steps rather than jobs, and so implement preemption while also being able to reason about leakage in a fine-grained manner. This supports offline schedulers in periodic systems that can plan an optimal strategy, as well as online schedulers that optimize using the knowledge available. (The focus in this paper is on the former.) Further, schedulers can be considered that operate over leakage thresholds or within quantified security constraints.

The approach in this paper easily captures prior work [15,17] by inserting a *flush* task that has a known runtime cost and ensures a complete resource (memory) wipe (and thus zero resulting leakage). When a high-security job would be followed by a low-security job, a flush is inserted between them. This enforces zero resulting leakage, but often results in poor schedulability due to the high cost of frequently flushing resources.

By considering the flush task to be always available (rather than at prescribed times), schedulers can add flushes when this reduces resulting leakage and still achieve schedulability. Indeed, it is often possible to achieve zero resulting leakage even when flushing after every high-security job is not possible. Thus, solutions can be found here that achieve zero leakage that could not be scheduled by the prior state-of-the-art.

More generally, this paper proposes heuristic algorithms to achieve efficient scheduling while reducing resulting leakage, i.e. the amount of confidential information that can be leaked to low-security jobs. Thus allowing for more flexibility in choices; a scheduling approach may allow a limited amount of leakage to achieve schedulability. The scheduling algorithms presented here produce a schedule for a set of tasks. Standard scheduling algorithms are extended with a *preprocessing* and a *postprocessing* phase. Preprocessing modifies the set of tasks to be scheduled, while postprocessing modifies the schedule produced by a scheduling algorithm to yield another schedule. Several pre- and postprocessors designed to reduce leakage are introduced in this paper.

Experimental results are presented that demonstrate the trade-off between leakage and schedulability. These show that this approach schedules, with good (or zero) resulting leakage, sets of tasks that are not schedulable by the state-of-the-art. Different pre- and postprocessors and their impact on the resulting leakage are evaluated. This clearly illustrates that there is a trade-off to be made between leakage and schedulability. Accepting some leakage can allow for schedulability when requiring zero leakage would fail to be schedulable. Further, experimental results here show that zero leakage can still be achieved in cases where the current state-of-the-art fails schedulability.

A case study demonstrates the flexibility of the model, by detailing how to represent cache attacks and their leakage using the extended workflow model. This demonstrates a different leakage model and alternative ways to exploit the model.

Key Contributions. The key contributions of this paper are as follows.

- A model to reason quantitatively on the amount of information leaked by scheduling tasks with different security levels on a shared resource system.
- A scheduling approach with compositional and specialized pre- and post-processors that schedule tasks while reducing the amount of confidential information leaked.
- Several heuristic pre- and postprocessing algorithms that can reduce leakage.
- Experimental evaluation of the combinations of the pre- and postprocessors, showing that the approach provides significantly better schedulability and lower information leakage than the state of the art.
- A case study showing how to adapt the model to other scenarios and kinds of leakage, demonstrated with cache attacks.

The structure of the paper is as follows. Section 2 recalls background information. Section 3 extends the workflow model. Section 4 presents our approach to scheduling used here, with algorithms for pre- and postprocessing. Section 5 highlights and discusses the experimental results. Section 6 presents a case study on adapting leakage for cache attacks. Section 7 discusses variations and extensions to the model and algorithms. Section 8 concludes and considers future work.

2 Background

Workflow Model. This section recalls the workflow model, a standard model for the scheduling of periodic tasks [3,9,26]. Section 3 extends the workflow model to account for the possible leakage of confidential information. Assume an infinite time divided into discrete time units indexed by natural numbers. Let Γ be a set of independent periodic *tasks* $\{\mathcal{T}_\alpha, \mathcal{T}_\beta, \dots\}$ with each task $\mathcal{T}_x \in \Gamma$ having a *period* P_x, an *execution time* E_x, and a *relative deadline* D_x. A *job* $\tau_{x,k}$ is produced by the activation of a task $\mathcal{T}_x \in \Gamma$ at *release time* $R_{x,k} = (k-1)P_x, \forall k \in \mathbb{N}_0$. Each job $\tau_{x,k}$ must be completed before its *absolute deadline* $A_{x,k} = R_{x,k} + D_x$. The *hyperperiod* H_Γ of a set of tasks Γ corresponds to the least common multiplier of the period P_x of each task $\mathcal{T}_x \in \Gamma$: $H_\Gamma = lcm\{P_x \mid \mathcal{T}_x \in \Gamma\}$.

Scheduling Algorithms. This paper uses two standard scheduling algorithms to schedule the jobs produced by sets of tasks: Earliest Deadline First (EDF) and Least Slack First (LSF). Both are simple and widely used offline scheduling algorithms based on dynamic priority of the jobs being scheduled. EDF determines the priority of jobs according to their absolute deadline. At any given point in time, out of the currently available jobs, the job with the earliest absolute deadline is scheduled first. LSF determines the priority of jobs according to their amount of *slack*. This slack is calculated for a job $\tau_{x,k}$ according to the formula $A_{x,k} - t - E_x$ where t is the current time. At any given point in time, out of the currently available jobs, the job with the least slack is scheduled first.

Information Leakage. *Information leakage* quantifies the amount of confidential information leaked by a system, and is widely used to measure of the (in)security of the system [1,2,4,12]. In this paper, leakage is used to measure the amount of confidential information that a high-level job leaves in the shared resource at different moments of its execution. The unit of measure of leakage is not relevant since it depends on the specific application. For instance, if the confidential information is a private key, leakage could measure the number of bits of the key that are leaked. Alternatively, leakage could measure the number of confidential packets leaked from a secure transmission. Therefore, the same leakage model can be used with different leakage measures, where zero leakage represents no loss of confidential information.

Related Work. Real-time systems need to communicate with the outside world, such as receiving data from sensors or communicating with other systems, sometimes over unsecured networks. This communication has allowed attacks against even air-gapped industrial control systems [8].

The real-time scheduling requirement itself can be exploited to generate additional vulnerabilities. For instance, a process can modulate its use of a resource to affect the scheduling of another process, and use this to covertly transmit information [20,21].

Further vulnerabilities can occur in any system with shared resources. When processes with different security levels share the same memory resources, it is possible for low-security processes to monitor the access to confidential information by high-security processes, causing information leakage [15]. Using separated memory for processes with different security levels is expensive, particularly if the system has more than two security levels. Mohan et al. [15] consider a shared memory scenario where low-security processes executing after high-security processes could access the high-security processes' memory space resulting in information leakage. To prevent this, they propose completely flushing the shared resource (memory) after the execution of high-security processes when followed by a low-security process. In [17], Pellizzoni et al. generalize this work by introducing a binary relation NO-LEAK on tasks, where NO-LEAK $(\mathcal{T}_x, \mathcal{T}_y)$ holds if no leakage can occur from $\mathcal{T}_x$ to $\mathcal{T}_y$. The authors also determine the number of resource (memory) flushes needed to enforce the NO-LEAK relation, and consequently construct a preemptivity-assignment scheduling algorithm. This work proposes a more fine-grained approach to confidentiality in similar scenarios.

Another less formal approach is that used in [24] where they limit the time between preemptions between virtual machines in an online scheduling scenario to prevent cache attacks. This can be represented using the approach here as a case study.

Intel propose the *Software Guard Extension* (SGX) architecture to prevent leakage through shared memory [7]. SGX aims to keep each process in a separate enclave, and keep these enclaves isolated from other processes (and flushing them upon exit). However, Schwarz et al. [19] demonstrate that SGX is not safe using cache attacks.

Formal analysis of scheduling system under resource constraints has been performed by Kim et al. [13,14]. The proposed approach can be extended to confidentiality as a resource using the model proposed in this paper.

3   Model

This section introduces the key concepts and model of the system being scheduled, and is based upon the workflow model recalled in Sect. 2. The extension here is to represent precise information about the internal operations and preemptivity of tasks by dividing them into *steps*. Steps include their own execution time (like a task or job), and are extended to include leakage value and security level. Special tasks are also added to model other operations of the system. The rest of this section details this extended model and presents illustrative examples that motivate the choices in this paper.

3.1   Concept

This section considers concepts and motivations for the model presented here; the division of tasks into steps, accounting for leakage, and justification for special tasks.

Steps. This model considers the possibility to divide tasks into fine-grained steps. A step represents an atomic sequence of operations that cannot be interrupted by preemption. The practical implementation of steps depends on the architecture and granularity of the scheduling system. The model is agnostic to step implementation details as long as an execution time, leakage value, and security level can be defined for each step. The most fine-grained approach would be to consider each CPU operation as a step. For instance, `Process 1` in Fig. 1 would be represented as a task divided into five steps. Thus, a task could be preempted after each CPU operation. Although very simple, in practice this approach is too fine-grained. In lightweight and embedded systems it is common to delegate part of the handling of preemption and atomicity to the programmer, so it is reasonable to consider that the programmer themself could define the steps.

Special Tasks. This paper considers two special tasks representing special system operations: *flush* and *wait*. The flush task flushes all confidential information from the shared resource, for instance by overwriting all shared memory with zeroes. This preserves compatibility with the state of the art [15,17] where flushing is used as the main tool to preserve confidentiality. The wait task represents idle processor time. Apart from the obvious use, scheduling of idle time can impact confidentiality of the system.

Leakage Values. The leakage value of a step represents the amount of confidential information that would be leaked to an attacker able to read the shared resource just after the steps' execution. The model does not constrain the way the leakage value is obtained: leakage can be added by the programmer as an annotation, computed by an automatic tool [5,6,23], or possibly both. For instance, the programmer could specify critical zones in which the program must not be interrupted, and the leakage values would be computed automatically by a tool (for both critical and non-critical zones). An alternative, variable-based approach would be to have the programmer annotate some variables as containing confidential information at a certain point (and as cleared of confidential information at a later point). Taint analysis can be used to identify which variables are tainted at each point. Information leakage quantification can be used to quantify leakage from the tainted variables.

3.2   Formal Model

Steps, Tasks and Jobs

Definition 1 (Step). *Formally, each* step *is a tuple* $S(E, L, X)$ *where* E *denotes the (worst case) execution time that the step takes to be completed,* L *denotes its (potential) leakage value, and* X *denotes its security level (either high* $\top$ *or low* $\bot$ *).*

The (potential) leakage value L of a step S is a measure of the amount of confidential information left in a shared resource at the completion of S. Here $\top$ indicates that the step contains confidential information and therefore is high-security. Similarly, $\bot$ indicates that the step should not have access to confidential information and therefore is low-security. Since $\top$ and $\bot$ are used to indicate whether the step has access to confidential information, $\bot$ steps typically have leakage zero. This is not a strict requirement, see Sect. 6. The choice of having two security levels here is to clearly illustrate the model, however the extension to any number of security levels is straightforward.

> For instance, consider `Process 1` in Fig. 1. Each assembly instruction can be represented by a single step with an execution time of one time unit and a security level of $\top$. The first three instructions have a leakage value of one, representing the fact that one word of confidential information (the key) is in the shared resource (in register `r13`). However, the remaining instructions have a leakage value of zero since the fourth instruction wipes `r13`.

The system operates with a set of *tasks* $\Gamma = \{\mathcal{T}_\alpha, \mathcal{T}_\beta, \ldots\}$.

Definition 2 (Task). *Each task* $\mathcal{T}_x \in \Gamma$ *is a tuple* $\mathcal{T}_x(P_x, D_x, \widehat{S_x})$ *where* P_x *is the* period *of the task,* D_x *is its* relative deadline, *and* $\widehat{S_x}$ *is a sequence of steps* $S_{xa}, S_{xb}, \ldots$ *making up the ordered actions of the task.*

Tasks are named with Greek letters, e.g. $\mathcal{T}_\beta$. Steps are named with the corresponding task's Greek letter and a Latin letter in alphabetical order, e.g. step $\mathcal{S}_{\beta c}$ represents the third step of task $\mathcal{T}_\beta$.

Observe that **Process 1** in Fig. 1 can be modeled by the following task:

$$\mathcal{T}_\alpha = \mathcal{T}(P_\alpha, D_\alpha, (\mathcal{S}_{\alpha a}(1,1,\top), \mathcal{S}_{\alpha b}(1,1,\top), \mathcal{S}_{\alpha c}(1,1,\top), \mathcal{S}_{\alpha d}(1,0,\top), \mathcal{S}_{\alpha e}(1,0,\top))).$$

Similarly, **Process 2** in Fig. 1 can be modeled by the following task:

$$\mathcal{T}_\beta = \mathcal{T}(P_\beta, D_\beta, \mathcal{S}_{\beta a}(1,0,\bot)).$$

Definition 3 (Job). *Each job $\tau_{x,k}$ is created by the activation of the task $\mathcal{T}_x$ at release time $R_{x,k} = (k-1)P_x$ for $k \in \mathbb{N}_0$, and is a tuple $\tau_{x,k}(R_{x,k}, A_{x,k}, \widehat{\mathcal{S}}_{x,k})$ where $A_{x,k} = R_{x,k} + D_x$ is the job's absolute deadline, and $\widehat{\mathcal{S}}_{x,k}$ is the sequence of steps inherited from task $\mathcal{T}_x$.*

Jobs are named with the corresponding task's Greek letter and the number k, so job $\tau_{\beta 4}$ is the fourth job generated by task $\mathcal{T}_\beta$ and step $\mathcal{S}_{\beta 4 c}$ is the third step of job $\tau_{\beta 4}$.

For simplicity, a task (resp. job) will be referred to as $\top$ or $\bot$ when all steps within that task (resp. job) are either $\top$ or $\bot$, respectively.

Flush and Wait. The model uses a task to represent complete flushing of the shared resource. The *flush* task is defined by $\mathcal{T}_\mathcal{F}(-, -, \mathcal{S}_\mathcal{F}(E_\mathcal{F}, 0, \top))$ where $E_\mathcal{F}$ is the execution time to completely flush the shared resource. Observe that *after flushing the shared resource the leakage is reduced to zero.* This is achieved by the single step $\mathcal{S}_\mathcal{F}(E_\mathcal{F}, 0, \top)$ that takes all the execution time of the flush task and has a zero leakage value. Since the flush task is always available to be scheduled, it has no defined period or deadline (denoted here as -), being able to scheduled (or not) at whim. The security level of flush is $\top$ since it is acceptable for flush to have access to confidential information, and for use in calculating the resulting leakage (see below). For simplicity and when no ambiguity may occur, $\mathcal{F}$ is used for the flush task or step.

To represent idle processor time, define the *wait* task as $\mathcal{T}_\mathcal{W}(-, -, \mathcal{S}_\mathcal{W}(1, *, *))$. Similar to flush, wait is always available to be scheduled and has no period or deadline (again denoted as -). Wait also has a single step that has the minimal runtime of one time unit. However, the leakage value of wait is here denoted by $*$ since waiting does not change the shared resource, instead the $*$ denotes that *the leakage value of a wait step is the same as the previous step.* Similarly, the security level is also represented by $*$ because it is the same as the previous step. Again for simplicity and where no ambiguity may occur, $\mathcal{W}$ may be used in place of the wait task or step.

Traces, Solutions, and Resulting Leakage

Definition 4 (Trace). *A trace $\widetilde{\mathcal{S}} = (\mathcal{S}_1(E_1, L_1, X_1), \mathcal{S}_2(E_2, L_2, X_2), \dots)$ is a (possibly infinite) sequence of $n \in \mathbb{N} \cup \{\infty\}$ steps that may come from any number of jobs.*

In a trace, Step S_1 starts execution at time $t_1 = 0$, and each step S_i for $i > 1$ starts execution at time $t_i = \sum_{j=1}^{i-1} E_j$ and terminates execution at time $t_i + E_i$. The notation $\widetilde{S_1} ++ \widetilde{S_2}$ is used to indicate concatenation of traces $\widetilde{S_1}$ and $\widetilde{S_2}$, and $\widetilde{S} \setminus S_1$ the removal of the step S_1 from the trace $\widetilde{S}$. The focus of this paper is upon *solutions*.

Definition 5 (Solution). *A trace $\widetilde{S}$ is a solution $\overline{S}$ if:*

1. *for each job $\tau(R, A, \widehat{S})$:*
   (a) *each step in $\widehat{S}$ appears in the trace $\widetilde{S}$ in the order that it appears in $\widehat{S}$;*
   (b) *the first step of $\widehat{S}$ does not start execution before R;*
   (c) *the last step of $\widehat{S}$ does not terminate execution after A;*
2. *each step that is not wait $\mathcal{W}$ or flush $\mathcal{F}$ appears exactly once in the trace $\widetilde{S}$.*

Given a set of tasks Γ, a solution $\overline{S}$ is a *solution for Γ*, written $\overline{S}_\Gamma$, iff $\forall \mathcal{T}_x \in \Gamma, \forall k \in \mathbb{N}_0$ then for each job $\tau_{x,k}(R_{x,k}, A_{x,k}, \widehat{S_{x,k}})$ it holds that every step in $\widehat{S_{x,k}}$ is in $\overline{S}$.

A solution $\overline{S}$ is *periodic* if it periodically repeats the same sequence of steps up to job indexing. For simplicity, a periodic solution may be represented by the periodically repeated sequence alone.

Given a trace $\widetilde{S}$ the *resulting leakage* $\mathscr{L}(\widetilde{S})$ of trace $\widetilde{S}$ represents the total amount of information leaked during the execution of the jobs scheduled according to $\widetilde{S}$.

Definition 6 (Resulting leakage). *Given a trace $\widetilde{S}$ composed of n steps with $n \in \mathbb{N} \cup \{\infty\}$, the* resulting leakage *$\mathscr{L}(\widetilde{S})$ of the trace $\widetilde{S}$ is defined inductively as follows:*

- *if $n \leq 1$, then $\mathscr{L}(\widetilde{S}) = 0$;*
- *if $n > 1$ and the second step S_2 of trace $\widetilde{S}$ is $\top$, then the resulting leakage is the leakage of the trace without the first step S_1: $\mathscr{L}(\widetilde{S}) = \mathscr{L}(\widetilde{S} \setminus S_1)$;*
- *if $n > 1$ and the second step S_2 of trace $\widetilde{S}$ is $\bot$, then the resulting leakage is the leakage of the trace without the first step $S_1 = S(E_1, L_1, X_1)$ plus the leakage value L_1 of the first step S_1: $\mathscr{L}(\widetilde{S}) = \mathscr{L}(\widetilde{S} \setminus S_1) + L_1$.*

Since every solution $\overline{S}$ is a trace $\widetilde{S}$, a solution's resulting leakage $\mathscr{L}(\overline{S})$ is defined in the same manner.

Recall the example from Fig. 1. The solution in Fig. 2a has resulting leakage one, since **Process 2** is executed when the key is in the shared resource and so the step $S_{\beta a}$ is able to access the key.

However, the solution in Fig. 2b has resulting leakage is zero, since **Process 2** is executed after the key has been wiped from the shared resource.

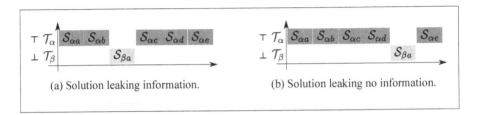

(a) Solution leaking information. (b) Solution leaking no information.

Fig. 2. Schedulings for the processes in Fig. 1.

If a solution is periodic, the *periodic leakage* can be calculated as follows. Given one instance of the periodically repeated sequence of steps $\tilde{S} = (S_1, S_2, \ldots, S_i)$, the periodic leakage is the resulting leakage of the sequence $\tilde{S} + S_1$.

4 Our Approach

The overarching goal of the approach proposed in this paper is to produce a solution with low resulting leakage for a given set of tasks. To achieve this, standard offline scheduling algorithms are extended with a *preprocessing* and a *postprocessing* phase. The preprocessing phase transforms a set of tasks Γ into a set of preprocessed tasks Γ'. Then scheduling is applied to Γ' obtaining a solution $\overline{S}'_{\Gamma'}$ for Γ'. Finally, the postprocessing phase transforms the solution $\overline{S}'_{\Gamma'}$ into a postprocessed solution $\overline{S}''_{\Gamma'}$. Both the pre- and postprocessing phases can affect the desired solution $\overline{S}''_{\Gamma'}$, here with the goal of reducing the resulting leakage. The rest of this section presents various heuristic algorithms used for the results (see Sect. 5). The scheduling algorithms considered are EDF and LSF. Note that EDF and LSF do no consider the security-level or leakage of the steps (for discussion of this see Sect. 7). The rest of this section focuses upon the pre- and postprocessors. The division in phases creates a modular and compositional approach, allowing for a better comparison of different pre- and postprocessors.

4.1 Preprocessing

Preprocessors are algorithms that take a set of tasks Γ and produce a set of tasks Γ' to be scheduled. This paper considers preprocessors that attempt to "merge" adjacent steps with the same security level within each task in Γ. The merged step has the sum of the execution times of the merged steps, the leakage value of the last merged step, and the same security level as the merged steps. For instance, the steps $S_{aa}(1, 0, \top)$ and $S_{ab}(1, 4, \top)$ could be merged producing the step $S_{aa'}(2, 4, \top)$. The rest of this section presents three preprocessing algorithms that exploit merging.

Total Merge. The Total Merge algorithm merges all the steps in a task into a single step. The merging is achieved by starting with a step that has execution time and leakage value zero. The execution time for each other step in the task is then added, and the leakage value from the last step being merged is preserved. The security level is set to that of the last step (this is reasonable here since all steps within a task share the same security level, for other approaches to this see Sect. 6). Finally, the processed task uses this single merged step as its only step.

One-Step Merge. The One-Step Merge algorithm attempts to merge pairs of adjacent steps. Adjacent pairs are merged iff the leakage of the former step is higher than the latter. This is achieved by iterating through the steps S_i of the task. If $L_i > L_{i+1}$, then the steps S_i and S_{i+1} are merged. Otherwise, S_i is maintained unchanged. This algorithm generates a new sequence of steps $\widehat{S'}$, that are then used in the processed task.

n-Step Merge. A straightforward extension to the One-Step Merge algorithm is to allow merging of any number of steps. This appears in the results as n-Step Merge.

4.2 Postprocessing

Postprocessing algorithms take one solution and produce another solution. This can be done by any possible manipulation of the steps within the original solution $\overline{S'}_\Gamma$ to produce the new solution $\overline{S''}_\Gamma$ that does not break the property of being a solution for Γ. The rest of this section presents four such postprocessors.

Add Flush. The Add Flush algorithm replaces sequences of $\mathcal{W}$ with $\mathcal{F}$ where possible. Add Flush operates by finding sequences of $\mathcal{W}$ whose length is greater than or equal the execution time of $\mathcal{F}$. If such a sequence is found, a $\mathcal{F}$ is added to the produced solution instead of the initial sequence of $\mathcal{W}$ with execution time equal to the $\mathcal{F}$. Any remaining $\mathcal{W}$ in the solution are maintained.

Swap. The Swap algorithm attempts to reduce the resulting leakage by swapping steps within the solution. Swap works by considering each step S_i. Then each possible swap $[S_i \leftrightarrow S_j]$ between the step S_i and a following step S_j is considered. If the trace with this swap applied has less resulting leakage and is still a solution, then this solution $[S_i \leftrightarrow S_j]\overline{S}$ is kept as the best possible solution so far. Finally, once all possible swaps have been considered, the best swap to the solution is applied and i is incremented.

Move. The Move algorithm moves one step to a new position in the solution. Move works in the same manner as the Swap postprocessor, except instead of swapping $[S_i \leftrightarrow S_j]\overline{S}$ the steps S_i and S_j, the move $[S_i \longrightarrow S_j]\overline{S}$ moves the step S_i to be after S_j. For example: $[S_1 \longrightarrow S_3]S_a, S_b, S_c = S_b, S_c, S_a$ where the first step S_a is moved to be after the third step S_c. The rest of the algorithm is the same as Swap, finding the best possible move and ensuring the trace after the move is a solution. The algorithm is identical to the Swap algorithm substituting $[S_i \leftrightarrow S_j]\overline{S}$ with $[S_i \longrightarrow S_j]\overline{S}$ in Line 4.

1-Swap. Observe that if only swapping or moving with the following step is considered, that is $[\mathcal{S}_i \leftrightarrow \mathcal{S}_{i+1}]$ or $[\mathcal{S}_i \longrightarrow \mathcal{S}_{i+1}]$, then the swap and move postprocessors coincide. This postprocessor is denoted as 1-Swap in the results.

5 Experimental Results

This section discusses the results obtained by running experiments with the preprocessing, scheduling, and postprocessing algorithms in this paper.

The experiments were conducted by using approximately 30,000 randomly generated sets of tasks[2], and then testing each possible combination of one preprocessing, one scheduling, and one postprocessing algorithm. Each set of tasks consists of 2 to 6 tasks with at least one $\top$ task and one $\bot$ task, with each task having 1 to 8 steps, and each step execution time from 1 to 5. Sets of tasks with a hyperperiod over 5000 have been discarded to reduce testing time. The code[3] to perform the tests and implement the preprocessing, scheduling, and postprocessing is written in Java 1.8, and all experiments conducted on a Linux 3.13 64-bit kernel on an Intel Core i7-3720QM 2.60 GHz CPU with 8 GB of RAM. A demo[4] is available that shows examples, and allows users to conduct their own GUI-based experiments. The rest of this section discusses experimental outcomes.

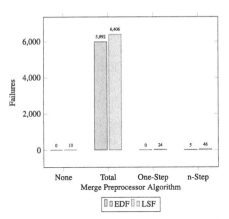
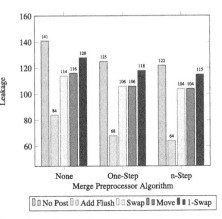

(a) Number of failures for each combination of preprocessor and scheduling algorithm, out of ~30,000 experiments. Note that Total Merge, corresponding to the state of the art [15, 17], fails ~20% of the time.

(b) Information leakage of the solutions for each combination of pre- and postprocessor (except Total Merge) using the EDF scheduling algorithm.

Fig. 3. Failures and leakage results for pre- and postprocessing.

---

[2] 30,000 sets of tasks were generated, 22 were discarded as unschedulable.

[3] Available via git from: https://scm.gforge.inria.fr/anonscm/git/secleakpublic/secleakpublic.git.

[4] Demo available via website at: http://secleakpublic.gforge.inria.fr/.

The first point of interest is the schedulability of the set of tasks used in each experiment. Merging task steps in a preprocessor can make a set of tasks unschedulable, and the EDF

Table 1. Average execution time (in ms) for each combination of pre- and postprocessor (except Total Merge) using the EDF scheduling algorithm.

Preprocessor Merge	Postprocessor				
	None	Add flush	Swap	Move	1-Swap
None	2	116	1919	1903	190
One-Step	1	93	1567	1489	149
n-Step	1	88	1486	1404	141

and LSF scheduling algorithms are not equally able to find solutions. The failure percentage for each combination of preprocessing and scheduling algorithm is shown in Fig. 3a.

Figure 3a clearly shows that greater merging of steps leads to more schedulability failures. In particular, indicating that Total Merge is not an effective algorithm to use in practice despite being considered the current state of the art [15,17]. This is a strong motivation for the approach presented in this work to consider fine-grained preprocessing and preemption of tasks. Due to its high failure rate, Total Merge will not be considered further in this paper.

Figure 3a also shows that, for all preprocessing algorithms, EDF performs better for schedulability than LSF. (This is expected since EDF is guaranteed to find a solution if the tasks are schedulable, while LSF is not.) The two scheduling algorithms produce almost the same results for every other measure tested, so the rest of this paper shall present only experimental results using the EDF scheduling algorithm.

Comparing the experimental results from postprocessing algorithms, the average resulting leakages for each combination of pre- and postprocessor is shown in Fig. 3b, while the average running times to generate a solution are shown in Table 1.

As expected, solutions without any postprocessing produce the highest resulting leakage. The best resulting leakage is obtained by the Add Flush algorithm. (This would correspond to the approach in [15,17] when combined with Total Merge, however as noted above this is often not schedulable.) Note that merging preprocessors reduce total time, since they reduce the number of steps that the scheduler has to schedule.

1-Swap slightly reduces the resulting leakage, however Table 1 shows that it is significantly more expensive than the scheduling operation, so 1-Swap could be applied after Add Flush only if the cost is acceptable. Swap and Move do not reduce the resulting leakage significantly more than 1-Swap and are significantly more expensive to compute. These indicate that there is a balance to be found depending on the scenario. Taking significant time to pre-compute an optimal scheduling strategy for a sensor or other real-time system prior to shipping could be worth the time cost. However, for online scheduling with limited (or no) ability to look ahead and consider such options, the cost of anything more complex than Add Flush or 1-Swap may be too much.

6   Case Study: Modeling Cache Attacks

This section demonstrates how to reason about cache attacks using the model presented in this paper, and how leakage can be used in different ways. This includes how to adapt resulting leakage to represent leakage via cache attacks, and how to exploit the general definition of the model to handle more complex notions of leakage.

In cache attacks, the shared resource is the cache itself. There are several approaches to gaining information from the cache (which is in general a form of side-channel attack) [10,18,22,25]. One such method is for the attacker to attempt to load code that uses the same cache lines as the program being attacked. When these load very quickly, then this indicates that the program being attacked has already loaded particular parts of the program, and from this the attacker can infer information about the program.

The main point in modeling cache attacks is that leakage is related to the cache lines, and there are many such lines in the cache. Thus, the measure of leakage is which lines of the cache are known to have been loaded by the attacker.

This can be modeled using the techniques in this paper, by exploiting the flexibility of the leakage representation as follows:

- The leakage value L of a step is represented by a bit-vector, with 1 bit for each cache line. Loading a cache line is represented by setting the bit in the bit-vector that represents that line of the cache to 1.
- When calculating leakage from a trace, the leakage is calculated by taking the bit-wise disjunction (represented as |) of the leakage bit-vectors. Observe that this automatically accounts for over-writing by newer lines.
- The leakage result from a high security step to a low security step can then be calculated over bit-vectors, e.g. by the bit-wise conjunction operation (represented as &). Recall that since the attacker loads cache lines to test if another process has accessed these lines, they will appear to have loaded these lines to another step.
- The flush step $\mathcal{F}$ is represented by setting the leakage vector to 0000.

For example, assume four cache lines, then leakage would be represented by bit-vectors of length four. A step that loads into the first cache line would have the leakage bit-vector 1000, and the step that loads into the third cache line would have the leakage bit-vector 0010. If these steps were executed sequentially, the leakage bit-vectors 1000 and 0010 bit-wise disjoined would yield 1000 | 0010 = 1010.

An attacker that attacks (by using) the first and second cache line would have a bit-vector 1100. If the leakage of the last high security step is 1010 and the attacker has leakage bit-vector 1100, then the attacker would gain information about the first cache line being used (since 1010 & 1100 = 1000), and the leakage would end up in the state 1110 (since 1010 | 1100 = 1110) since the attacker must access these cache lines to perform the attack.

The leakage value calculated from the cache attacks can also be more realistic. In practice certain cache lines yield more information. So if the cache attack is being modeled for an attack against the key of AES [16, 22], different lines can be given different values, thus allowing precise computation of key leakage. Indeed, works such as [11] could be used to determine the most appropriate leakage values to use.

Thus, the model presented in this paper already supports many interesting and real scenarios by instantiating the leakage in an appropriate manner. This has been kept simple earlier in the paper for illustration, but highly complex leakage models can easily be accounted for in the manner demonstrated above.

7 Discussion

On the Division of Scheduling into Three Phases. The division into three phases is to separate out distinct parts of an overall scheduling from tasks to a solution. This approach allows for separation conceptually of different phases, and also for composition of simple algorithms in the pre- and postprocessing phases. For example, a postprocessor could move steps in a solution around to maximize contiguous $\mathcal{W}$s and then be composed with the Add Flush postprocessor to improve the resulting leakage further. This also allows different strategies to be employed in different phases, including strategies with different goals. For example, processors for resulting leakage minimization and energy consumption could be combined during pre- or postprocessing (or both).

Online Scheduling. This paper considers offline scheduling, i.e. when the tasks to be scheduled are known beforehand. In most real cases the tasks appear at runtime, requiring online heuristics to decide the scheduling. The division in steps and the leakage model presented in this paper extend immediately to the online scenario. While the preprocessors and postprocessors do not, they provide insight that can be used to build online heuristics that reduce leakage. We consider this as future work.

Execution Time. This paper has considered the execution time to be essentially fixed for each step. Although formally the execution time is worst case, the scheduling here does not exploit when steps may terminate prior to their (worst case) execution time. This could naturally be incorporated into online scheduling (above), but even in a purely offline scheduling system this could be exploited. For example, consider the cache attack scenario, where flushing not only effects the leakage, but by flushing the cache the execution time will go up due to cache misses.

8 Conclusions and Future Work

In a system with shared resources, the security of confidential information is a major concern. This paper allows reasoning about leakage of confidential information by extending the workflow model to support fine-grained preemption and confidentiality. This allows confidentiality to be addressed by quantifying the amount of information leaked by the system, including different leakage models.

Scheduling in this new model is then considered using pre-and postprocessors. These can be compositonally combined for scheduling that exploits different techniques and approaches, including focusing on different aspects of the overall problem. Several pre- and postprocessing heuristic algorithms are presented that can operate on the model. These are focused upon improving resulting leakage, but the principles can be adapted to other areas as well. Experimental results evaluate the algorithms presented here, showing that the model and heuristics improve over the state of the art and show that even simple heuristics can be effective. The case demonstrates the flexibility of the model, and illustrates how to adapt to different kinds of leakage and scenarios.

Future work could generalise to multi-resource approaches, where scheduling considers confidentiality, energy consumption, schedulability, etc. Another direction would be to consider theoretical complexity, and optimal scheduling strategies.

References

1. Alvim, M.S., Chatzikokolakis, K., Palamidessi, C., Smith, G.: Measuring information leakage using generalized gain functions. In: Chong, S. (ed.) CSF. IEEE (2012)
2. Backes, M., Köpf, B., Rybalchenko, A.: Automatic discovery and quantification of information leaks. In: S&P, pp. 141–153. IEEE (2009)
3. Benoit, A., Çatalyürek, U.V., Robert, Y., Saule, E.: A survey of pipelined workflow scheduling: models and algorithms. ACM Comput. Surv. **45**(4), 50:1–50:36 (2013)
4. Biondi, F., Legay, A., Malacaria, P., Wasowski, A.: Quantifying information leakage of randomized protocols. Theor. Comput. Sci. **597**, 62–87 (2015)
5. Biondi, F., Legay, A., Traonouez, L.-M., Wąsowski, A.: QUAIL: a quantitative security analyzer for imperative code. In: Sharygina, N., Veith, H. (eds.) CAV 2013. LNCS, vol. 8044, pp. 702–707. Springer, Heidelberg (2013). doi:10.1007/978-3-642-39799-8_49
6. Chothia, T., Kawamoto, Y., Novakovic, C.: LeakWatch: estimating information leakage from java programs. In: Kutyłowski, M., Vaidya, J. (eds.) ESORICS 2014. LNCS, vol. 8713, pp. 219–236. Springer, Cham (2014). doi:10.1007/978-3-319-11212-1_13
7. Costan, V., Devadas, S.: Intel sgx explained. IACR ePrint Archive 2016, 86 (2016)
8. Falliere, N., Murchu, L.O., Chien, E.: W32.Stuxnet dossier (2011)
9. Graham, R.L.: Bounds for certain multiprocessing anomalies. Bell Syst. Tech. J. **45**(9), 1563–1581 (1966)
10. Gruss, D., Maurice, C., Wagner, K., Mangard, S.: Flush+Flush: a fast and stealthy cache attack. In: Caballero, J., Zurutuza, U., Rodríguez, R.J. (eds.) DIMVA 2016. LNCS, vol. 9721, pp. 279–299. Springer, Cham (2016). doi:10.1007/978-3-319-40667-1_14
11. Gruss, D., Spreitzer, R., Mangard, S.: Cache template attacks: automating attacks on inclusive last-level caches. In: Usenix Security 2015, pp. 897–912 (2015)

12. Heusser, J., Malacaria, P.: Quantifying information leaks in software. In: Gates, C., Franz, M., McDermott, J.P. (ed.) ACSAC, pp. 261–269. ACM (2010)
13. Kim, J.H., Legay, A., Larsen, K.G., Mikučionis, M., Nielsen, B.: Resource-parameterized timing analysis of real-time systems. In: Piterman, N. (ed.) HVC 2015. LNCS, vol. 9434, pp. 190–205. Springer, Cham (2015). doi:10.1007/978-3-319-26287-1_12
14. Kim, J.H., Legay, A., Traonouez, L., Boudjadar, A., Nyman, U., Larsen, K.G., Lee, I., Choi, J.: Optimizing the resource requirements of hierarchical scheduling systems. SIGBED Rev. **13**(3), 41–48 (2016)
15. Mohan, S., Yoon, M., Pellizzoni, R., Bobba, R.: Real-time systems security through scheduler constraints. In: ECRTS, pp. 129–140. IEEE Computer Society (2014)
16. Osvik, D.A., Shamir, A., Tromer, E.: Cache attacks and countermeasures: the case of AES. In: Pointcheval, D. (ed.) CT-RSA 2006. LNCS, vol. 3860, pp. 1–20. Springer, Heidelberg (2006). doi:10.1007/11605805_1
17. Pellizzoni, R., Paryab, N., Yoon, M., Bak, S., Mohan, S., Bobba, R.: A generalized model for preventing information leakage in hard real-time systems. In: RTAS. IEEE (2015)
18. Ristenpart, T., Tromer, E., Shacham, H., Savage, S.: Hey, you, get off of my cloud: exploring information leakage in third-party compute clouds. In: CCS 2009. ACM (2009)
19. Schwarz, M., Weiser, S., Gruss, D., Maurice, C., Mangard, S.: Malware guard extension: Using SGX to conceal cache attacks. arXiv preprint (2017). arXiv:1702.08719
20. Son, J., Alves-Foss, J.: Covert timing channel capacity of rate monotonic real-time scheduling algorithm in MLS systems. In: IASTED, pp. 13–18 (2006)
21. Son, S.H., Mukkamala, R., David, R.: Integrating security and real-time requirements using covert channel capacity. IEEE Trans. Knowl. Data Eng. **12**(6), 865–879 (2000)
22. Tromer, E., Osvik, D.A., Shamir, A.: Efficient cache attacks on AES, and countermeasures. J. Cryptol. **23**(1), 37–71 (2010)
23. Val, C.G., Enescu, M.A., Bayless, S., Aiello, W., Hu, A.J.: Precisely measuring quantitative information flow: 10k lines of code and beyond. In: Euro S&P. IEEE (2016)
24. Varadarajan, V., Ristenpart, T., Swift, M.M.: Scheduler-based defenses against cross-VM side-channels. In: Usenix Security, pp. 687–702 (2014)
25. Yarom, Y., Falkner, K.: FLUSH+RELOAD: a high resolution, low noise, L3 cache side-channel attack. In: USENIX Security, pp. 719–732 (2014)
26. Yoon, M.-K., Mohan, S., Chen, C.-Y., Sha, L.: Taskshuffler: a schedule randomization protocol for obfuscation against timing inference attacks in real-time systems. In: RTAS, pp. 1–12. IEEE (2016)

A Unified Formalism for Monoprocessor Schedulability Analysis Under Uncertainty

Étienne André[(✉)]

Université Paris 13, LIPN, CNRS, UMR 7030, 93430 Villetaneuse, France
eandre93430@lipn13.fr

Abstract. The schedulability analysis of real-time systems (even on a single processor) is a very difficult task, which becomes even more complex (or undecidable) when periods or deadlines become uncertain. In this work, we propose a unified formalism to model monoprocessor schedulability problems with several types of tasks (periodic, sporadic, or more complex), most types of schedulers (including EDF, FPS and SJF), with or without preemption, in the presence of uncertain timing constants. Although the general case is undecidable, we exhibit a large decidable subclass. We demonstrate the expressive power of our formalism on several examples, allowing also for robust schedulability.

Keywords: Schedulability analysis · Real-time systems · Timing parameters

1 Introduction

The schedulability problem for real-time systems consists in checking whether, for a given set of tasks bound by some constraints (precedence between tasks, periods ...) and for a given scheduler, all tasks can finish their computation before their relative deadline. This problem is a very delicate task, even on a single processor, and becomes even more complex (or undecidable) when periods or deadlines become unknown or subject to uncertainty.

Timed automata (TAs) [2] are a powerful formalism to model and verify timed concurrent systems, by extending finite-state automata with continuous variables ("clocks") that can be compared to constants in transitions ("guards") and locations ("invariants") or reset along transitions. Schedulability analysis with stopwatch automata (an extension of TAs) was proposed in [1]: although stopwatch automata are an undecidable formalism in general [10], job-shop scheduling using stopwatch automata is still possible [1].

Task automata (TaskA) were introduced in [17] as an extension of TAs where discrete transitions can be labeled with tasks, that can have a worst case execution time and a deadline. Thanks to the expressive power of TAs, this formalism

---

This work is partially supported by the ANR national research program PACS (ANR-14-CE28-0002).

L. Petrucci et al. (Eds.): FMICS-AVoCS 2017, LNCS 10471, pp. 100–115, 2017.
DOI: 10.1007/978-3-319-67113-0_7

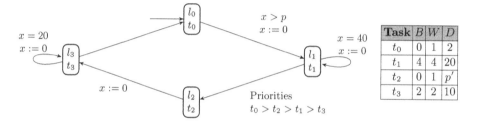

Fig. 1. Encoding semi-periodic and sporadic tasks using a PTaskA

is richer than the traditional periodic tasks (characterized by their period) or sporadic tasks (characterized only by their minimal inter-arrival time). In addition, the schedulability problem ("is the TaskA schedulable for a given strategy?") is decidable for non-preemptive strategies, i.e., without the ability of the scheduler to temporarily suspend a task for a more urgent one. This formalism is enriched and slightly modified in [13], where the tasks become associated with locations (instead of transitions) and are also characterized with a minimum execution time. Although the schedulability problem for task automata of [13] is undecidable in general (for some preemptive strategies), the decidable case is large, including all non-preemptive strategies, and all strategies without task feedback (i.e., the precise finishing time of a task influences the release of another one) or when best- and worst-case computation times of tasks are equal to each other.

Example 1. Consider the TaskA in Fig. 1 (from [13, Fig. 2b]) with two tasks t_1 and t_3 which are similar to periodic tasks, though they alternate between each other. D, B and W denote the deadline, the best and worst-case execution time of each task, respectively. In addition, two sporadic tasks (t_0 and t_2) are interleaved between t_1 and t_3. Every time location l_i is entered, an instance of t_i is created. For preemptive fixed priority scheduling (FPS), the tasks ordered by decreasing priority order are $t_0 > t_2 > t_1 > t_3$. TaskA can help to solve the schedulability problem: e.g., for $p = 10$ and $p' = 4$ and FPS strategy, is the system schedulable?

Contributions. Task automata cannot be used anymore if some of the timing constants are uncertain (for instance due to clock drift) or if they are unknown – which rules out the verification at early design stage. In this work, we extend task automata with timing parameters, i.e., unknown constants, as a unified formalism to model monoprocessor schedulability problems with several types of tasks (periodic, sporadic, or more complex). Most types of schedulers, including EDF (earliest-deadline first), FPS (fixed-priority) and SJF (shortest job first), with or without preemption, can be used. Most importantly, uncertain or unknown timing constants can be used thanks to timing parameters. Although the general case is undecidable, we exhibit a large decidable subclass. We then propose a method that, given a parametric task automaton and a scheduling strategy, synthesizes parameter valuations for which the system is schedulable. For example, for what valuations of p, p' is the PTaskA in Fig. 1 schedulable? We demonstrate the applicability of our formalism using the parametric real-time model-checker IMITATOR [5] augmented with an ad-hoc extension, and show that it can also address robust schedulability.

Related Work. Schedulability analysis under uncertainty, i.e., with uncertain or unknown parameters, attracted recent attention. In [11], parametric timed automata (PTAs) [3] are used to perform parametric schedulability analysis: whereas the general case is unsurprisingly undecidable, the authors exhibit a subclass for which the schedulability-synthesis (i.e., synthesizing all valuations for which the system is schedulable) can be performed exactly.

In [8] parametric interrupt timed automata are proposed: this class inspired by PTAs is such that, at any time, at most one clock is active. This class allows a kind of preemption, and the reachability-emptiness problem is decidable.

In [18], we used parametric stopwatch automata (PSwA) to analyze a distributed real-time system with a preemptive fixed-priority strategy; while the analytical methods are faster, they are often incomplete, while the PSwA method implemented in a former version of IMITATOR turns out to be exact (sound and complete) on a set of case studies. This justifies the use of parametric model checking techniques instead of analytical techniques in order to analyze real-time systems under uncertainty. Finally, in [6], IMITATOR was able to output the exact answer to an industrial challenge by Thales with uncertain periods, whereas other approaches were not able to compute this result (with the exception of one simulation-based approach, which did obtain the exact result without however the ability to assess its optimality).

Different from these previous works, are contribution aims at providing real-time system designers with a formalism natively including periods, deadlines and best- and worst-case computation times, and that also allows for uncertainty.

Outline. Section 2 recalls TaskA and introduces PTaskA. Section 3 studies the decidability of PTaskA. Section 4 introduces the modeling with PTaskA. Section 5 presents the practical translation into IMITATOR and Sect. 6 describes experiments. Section 7 concludes the paper.

2   Preliminaries: Task Automata

In this section, we mainly recall *task automata* from [13] (with some modifications in the syntax to fit our framework), and introduce our parametric extension.

2.1   Clocks, Parameters and Constraints

Let $\mathbb{N}$, $\mathbb{Z}$, $\mathbb{Q}_+$ and $\mathbb{R}_+$ denote the sets of non-negative integers, integers, non-negative rational and non-negative real numbers respectively.

Throughout this paper, we assume a set $\mathcal{X} = \{x_1, \ldots, x_H\}$ of *clocks*, i.e., real-valued variables that evolve at the same rate. A clock valuation is a function

$\mu : \mathcal{X} \rightarrow \mathbb{R}_+$. We write $\mathbf{0}$ for the clock valuation that assigns 0 to all clocks. Given $d \in \mathbb{R}_+$, $\mu + d$ denotes the valuation such that $(\mu + d)(x) = \mu(x) + d$, for all $x \in \mathcal{X}$. Given $R \subseteq \mathcal{X}$, we define the *reset* of a valuation μ, denoted by $[\mu]_R$, as follows: $[\mu]_R(x) = 0$ if $x \in R$, and $[\mu]_R(x) = \mu(x)$ otherwise.

We assume a set $\mathcal{P} = \{p_1, \ldots, p_M\}$ of *parameters*, i.e., unknown rational-valued constants. A parameter *valuation* v is a function $v : \mathcal{P} \rightarrow \mathbb{Q}_+$.

In the following, we assume $\lhd \in \{<, \leq\}$ and $\bowtie \in \{<, \leq, \geq, >\}$. A $\mathcal{P}$-*guard* is a constraint over $\mathcal{X} \cup \mathcal{P}$ defined by a conjunction of inequalities of the form $x \bowtie z$, where z is either a parameter or a constant in $\mathbb{Q}_+$. A non-parametric guard is a $\mathcal{P}$-guard over $\mathcal{X}$ only, i.e., defined by a conjunction of inequalities of the form $x \bowtie d$.

We may assume bounds on the parameters; a parameter p is *bounded* if its valuation domain is of the form $[a, \infty)$ or $[a, b]$ with $a, b \in \mathbb{N}$.

2.2   Tasks

Let $\mathcal{T} = \{t_1, t_2, \cdots\}$ be a set of tasks. Each task is characterized by three *timings*, i.e., constants in $\mathcal{P} \cup \mathbb{Q}_+$: *(i)* B: its best-case execution time, *(ii)* W: its worst-case execution time, and *(iii)* D: its relative deadline (i.e., the latest time after the release of the task by which it must be completed). Given a task t and a parameter valuation v, we denote by $v(t)$ the task where the parameters in the timings (i.e., B, W and D) are replaced with their value in v.

Each task can have several *instances*, i.e., copies of the same task. An instance of task t is written (t, b, w, d) where $b \in \mathbb{R}_+$ (resp. $w \in \mathbb{R}_+$) is the best-case (resp. worst-case) remaining computation time, and $d \in \mathbb{R}_+$ the remaining time before the deadline.

2.3   Parametric Task Automata

Let us define parametric task automata as an extension of task automata defined in [13], where we allow the use of parameters in guards and invariants.[1]

Definition 1 (PTaskA). *A parametric task automaton (hereafter PTaskA) is a tuple* $(\mathcal{T}, \Sigma, \mathcal{L}, l_0, \mathcal{X}, x_{done}, \mathcal{P}, I, T, E)$, *where: (i)* $\mathcal{T}$ *is a set of tasks, (ii)* Σ *is a set of actions, (iii)* $\mathcal{L}$ *is a finite set of locations, (iv)* $l_0 \in \mathcal{L}$ *is the initial location, (v)* $\mathcal{X}$ *is a finite set of clocks, (vi)* $x_{done} \in \mathcal{X}$ *is a special clock to be reset only when a task finishes, (vii)* $\mathcal{P}$ *is a finite set of parameters, (viii)* I *is the invariant, assigning to every* $l \in \mathcal{L}$ *a* $\mathcal{P}$-*guard* $I(l)$, *(ix)* $T : \mathcal{L} \rightharpoonup \mathcal{T}$ *is the partial task function, assigning to some locations a task, (x)* E *is a finite set of edges* $e = (l, g, a, R, l')$ *where* $l, l' \in \mathcal{L}$ *are the source and target locations,* $a \in \Sigma$, $R \subseteq \mathcal{X}$ *is a set of clocks to be reset, and* g *is a* $\mathcal{P}$-*guard.*

---

[1] As this definition is a contribution of this paper, it would better fit outside of the preliminaries section; however, it is convenient to define it first so as to then define task automata, and (parametric) timed automata in a straightforward manner.

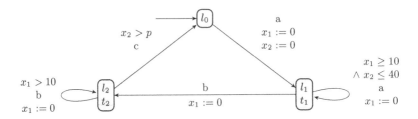

Fig. 2. An example of a PTaskA (inspired by [13, Fig. 1])

T is a partial function, and therefore some locations may be associated with no task. Also note that we define at most one task per location. Several tasks can be encoded in a straightforward manner by using several consecutive locations in 0-time. Also note that the parameters can be used both in the guards and invariants of the automaton, and/or in the task timings.

A PTaskA is said to have *no task feedback* if none of its guards and invariants contain x_{done}.

Given a PTaskA A and a parameter valuation v, we denote by $v(A)$ the non-parametric *task automaton* (TaskA) where all occurrences of a parameter p_i (in task timings, guards and invariants) have been replaced by $v(p_i)$. We will denote a TaskA using a tuple $(T, \Sigma, \mathcal{L}, l_0, \mathcal{X}, x_{done}, I, T, E)$, with all elements defined as Definition 1 except that guards and invariants are non-parametric guards, and that all B, W, and d in the tasks of T are non-parametric.

A TaskA is said to have *exact computation times* if $B = W$ for all tasks.

Example 2. Figure 2 describes a PTask with 2 clocks, and 2 tasks: t_1, an instance of which is activated every time the PTaskA enters l_1, and t_2 (in l_2). For t_1, we have $B = 1$, $W = 2$ and $D = 10$; for t_2, $B = 2$, $W = p'$ and $D = 8$. Note that our formalism allows one to define parameters both in the automaton (p) and the task timings (p'). This PTaskA has no task feedback (x_{done} is not used).

Basically, this PTaskA can create in l_1 between 1 and 5 instances of t_1 (but no more frequently than every 10 time units); then, it moves to l_2 where it can remain as long as wished, creating instances of t_2 (again no more frequently than every 10 time units). Eventually, the PTaskA can move back to the initial location no sooner than p time units since the entering of l_1.

Intuitively, this PTaskA will be schedulable only if p' (W of t_2) is not too large, and only when p is not too small (otherwise one may loop too fast through the automaton for all tasks to terminate before their deadline).

2.4   (Parametric) Timed and Stopwatch Automata

A parametric timed automaton (PTA) is a PTaskA for which $T = \emptyset$. Similarly, a timed automaton (TA) is a TaskA for which $T = \emptyset$.[2]

---

[2] In the literature, TAs are often defined using integer constants in guards and invariants; it is well-known that using rationals preserves decidability results, as rationals can be translated to integers using an appropriate constants rescaling.

Lower-bound/upper-bound parametric timed automata (L/U-PTAs), proposed in [14], restrict the use of parameters in the model. A parameter is said to be an *upper-bound parameter* if, whenever it is compared with a clock, it is necessarily compared as an upper bound, i.e., it only appears in inequalities of the form $x \lhd p$. Conversely, a parameter is a *lower-bound parameter* if it is only compared with clocks as a lower bound, i.e., of the form $p \lhd x$. An L/U-PTA is a PTA where the set of parameters is partitioned into upper-bound parameters and lower-bound parameters.

Finally, TAs can be extended into stopwatch automata with the additional ability to stop some clocks in selected locations [10]. Similarly, PTAs can be extended into parametric stopwatch automata (PSwAs) [18]. We assume that (P)SwAs are equipped with *diagonal constraints*, i.e., guards made of a conjunction of inequalities of the form $x_i - x_j \bowtie \sum_{1 \leq i \leq M} \alpha_i p_i + d$, with $\alpha_i, d \in \mathbb{Q}$.

2.5 Task Queue and Scheduling Strategy

A *task queue* is a sequence of instances of the form $\big((t_1, b_1, w_1, d_1), (t_2, b_2, w_2, d_2), \cdots \big)$. Given a non-parametric task set $\mathcal{T}$, let $\mathcal{Q}_\mathcal{T}$ denote all possible task queues. A *scheduling strategy* is a function $\mathsf{Sch} : \mathcal{T} \times \mathcal{Q}_\mathcal{T} \to \mathcal{Q}_\mathcal{T}$ that, given a task and a current task queue, inserts a new instance of this task into the task queue, while preserving the order of the other task instances in the queue. Famous scheduling strategies are EDF (earliest deadline first), FPS (fixed-priority scheduling) and SJF (shortest job first).

Definition 2. *A strategy is* non-preemptive *if it can never insert a new task instance as the first element of a non-empty queue. A strategy is* preemptive *if it can insert a new task instance as the first element of the queue, provided its task name is different from the name of every task in the queue, i.e., the current running task and all preempted tasks in the queue.*

Example 3. Let $q = \big((t_1, 1.4, 2.4, 3), (t_2, 2.5, 3.5, 4.2)\big)$. Assume a task t_3 where $B = 1$, $W = 1$ and $D = 10$. Then $\mathsf{EDF}(t_3, q) = \big((t_1, 1.4, 2.4, 3), (t_2, 2.5, 3.5, 4.2), (t_3, 1, 1, 10)\big)$, whereas preemptive $\mathsf{SJF}(t_3, q) = \big((t_3, 1, 1, 10), (t_1, 1.4, 2.4, 3), (t_2, 2.5, 3.5, 4.2)\big)$.

To be general enough, we only assume that schedulers must be encoded using a SwA. Also, the decision to insert a new task instance into the queue must be made only by comparing task timings of the new task instance with each of the existing instances (and possibly by looking at the discrete part of the queue, i.e., the ordering of the task names). This is not strong an assumption: for example, note that EDF, FPS and SJF (preemptive or not) all meet these criteria.

2.6 Semantics of Task Automata

A configuration is a triple (l, μ, q) for location l, clock valuation μ and queue q.

Definition 3 (Semantics of TaskA [13]). *Given a scheduling strategy* Sch, *the semantics of a TaskA* $A = (\mathcal{T}, \Sigma, \mathcal{L}, l_0, \mathcal{X}, x_{done}, I, T, E)$ *is a labeled transition system with initial state* $(l_0, \mathbf{0}, [])$ *and transitions defined as follows:*

- $(l, \mu, q) \xrightarrow{a}_{\mathsf{Sch}} (l', [\mu]_R, \mathsf{Sch}(T(l), q))$ *if* $(l, g, a, R, l') \in E$, $\mu \models g$ *and* $[\mu]_R \models I(l')$, *(⊨ denotes satisfiability)*
- $(l, \mu, []) \xrightarrow{\delta}_{\mathsf{Sch}} (l', \mu + \delta, [])$ *if* $\delta \in \mathbb{R}_+$ *and* $(\mu + \delta) \models I(l)$,
- $(l, \mu, (t, b, w, d) :: q) \xrightarrow{\delta}_{\mathsf{Sch}} (l', \mu + \delta, \mathsf{Run}((t, b, w, d) :: q, \delta))$ *if* $\delta \in \mathbb{R}_+$, $\delta \leq w$ *and* $(\mu + \delta) \models I(l)$, *and*
- $(l, \mu, (t, b, w, d) :: q) \xrightarrow{fin}_{\mathsf{Sch}} (l, [\mu]_{\{x_{done}\}}, q)$ *if* $b \leq 0 \leq w$ *and* $[\mu]_{\{x_{done}\}} \models I(l)$.

where [] *denotes the empty queue,* :: *is the list "cons" operator, and fin* $\notin \Sigma$ *is a fresh action name denoting task completion.*

The transition relation → is parameterized by the scheduler Sch, as the strategy impacts the choice of the insertion into the queue of a new task instance. The first rule defines a discrete transition. The second rule defines time elapsing for the empty queue. The third rule defines time elapsing for a non-empty queue; $\mathsf{Run}(q, \delta)$ decreases by δ the value of all d in q, as well as the b and w of its first element. The fourth rule defines the task completion, and resets x_{done} as this clock is reset iff a task has completed.

2.7   Decidability of Task Automata

A TaskA is *schedulable* for a given strategy if, for all possible executions of the TaskA, all task instances meet their deadlines, i.e., they finish before their deadline, for any computation time within $[B, W]$.

Let us recall the main results from [13].

Theorem 1 ([13, Theorems 1–4]). *The problem of checking schedulability is decidable when relative to: (i) a non-preemptive scheduling for TaskA; or (ii) a preemptive scheduling strategy for TaskA without task feedback or with exact computation times.*

The decidability is obtained by encoding the scheduler Sch for this decidable class into a timed automaton, or a timed automaton with bounded subtraction, denoted by $A_{enc}(\mathsf{Sch})$. Then, the synchronous product automaton $A \parallel A_{enc}(\mathsf{Sch})$ is constructed. Finally, it is shown that the system is schedulable iff a special location (which corresponds to a deadline miss) is not reachable in $A \parallel A_{enc}(\mathsf{Sch})$. The result follows from the decidability of the reachability in both timed automata [2] and timed automata with bounded subtraction [13].

Theorem 2 ([13, Theorems 5]). *The problem of checking schedulability is undecidable with (preemptive)* EDF, FPS, SJF.

3   Decidability and Undecidability

In this section, we address the following decision problem.

Schedulability-emptiness problem:
INPUT: A PTaskA A and a scheduling strategy Sch
PROBLEM: is the set of valuations v for which $v(A)$ is schedulable for strategy Sch empty?

3.1   Undecidability

The following undecidability results derive from two well-known results: *(i)* the reachability-emptiness problem is undecidable for PTAs with at least three parametric clocks (clocks that are indeed compared to a parameter somewhere in the model) and a single parameter [16]; and *(ii)* general schedulability analysis is undecidable for TaskA [13].

Theorem 3 (Undecidability). *The schedulability-emptiness problem is undecidable for PTaskA with at least three parametric clocks and a single timing parameter, whatever the scheduling strategy.*

The schedulability-emptiness problem is undecidable for general PTaskA.

Proof. It is known that reachability emptiness is undecidable with at least three parametric clocks and one parameter [16]. That is, we can encode a 2-counter machine using a PTA such that the machine halts iff a special location in the PTA is reachable. We reuse this construction by adding no task in the PTA, except to the special location, where we add two tasks with $B = W = D = 1$, activated in 0-time (adding two tasks requires a second additional location with an urgent transition). Now, if the special location is reachable, the system is necessarily non-schedulable (the first task will complete within 1 time unit, and the second one will immediately miss its deadline). Conversely, if the special location is unreachable, no task is ever activated and the system is necessarily schedulable. The result follows from the undecidability of the halting problem for 2-counter machines.

For the second part, it suffices to consider a PTaskA with a single parameter never used in the model, since non-parametric-schedulability analysis is already undecidable in general [13] (using possibly preemptive scheduling strategies). □

Remark 1. In the first part of Theorem 3, we require three parametric clocks in the model. Note that the scheduler translates itself into a PTA with several (possibly parametric) clocks; therefore, it is likely that the undecidability result holds for less clocks in the PTaskA. Exhibiting better bounds (which does not have huge practical applications though) is the subject of future work.

3.2   Decidability

In the non-parametric setting, the number of instances of a task t (with timings B, W, D) is intuitively bounded by $\lceil D/W \rceil$; indeed, when the number of instances exceeds this bound, the queue will be overflown in the sense that it will be impossible to finish that many instances before the deadline D. Therefore, as soon as the queue exceeds this value, the system is non-schedulable and therefore, it is sufficient to consider a bounded queue for schedulability analysis. However, this reasoning does not hold for general PTaskA, as W can be arbitrarily small, and D arbitrarily large. This motivates the following definition.

Definition 4. *A PTaskA has schedulable-bounded parameters if, for each task t, its worst-case execution time W is bounded in $[a, \infty)$ or $[a, b]$ with $a > 0$, and its deadline D is bounded in $[a, b]$, with $a, b \geq 0$.*

That is, the W cannot be 0, and the deadline cannot be infinite. Therefore, the maximum number of instances to be considered for a task is bounded by $\lceil \max(D)/\min(W) \rceil$, where max (resp. min) denotes the upper (resp. lower) bound of a parameter.

Example 4. Figure 2 trivially meets the schedulable-boundedness assumption, as necessarily $p' \geq B = 2 > 0$. In addition, the maximum number of instances necessary to check schedulability is $10/2 = 5$ for t_1 and $8/2 = 4$ for t_2.

We then slightly restrain the use of parameters in PTaskA in the following definition, following the similar restriction in L/U-PTAs.

Definition 5. *A PTaskA is an L/U-PTaskA if its parameters set is partitioned into lower-bound parameters and upper-bound parameters.*

Theorem 4 (Decidability). *The schedulability-emptiness problem is decidable for L/U-PTaskAs with schedulable-bounded parameters, for non-preemptive FPS and SJF, and non-preemptive EDF without parametric deadlines.*

Proof. Let us first show that Sch can be encoded into an L/U-PTA $A_{\mathsf{enc}}(\mathsf{Sch})$. Thanks to the restriction in Definition 4, we note that it is sufficient to consider a bounded number of instances for each task. Therefore, there is a bounded number of possible discrete queues. These combinations can be encoded using a finite number of locations in the L/U-PTA (more pragmatically, both in [13, 17] and in our implementation, we use shared global variables such as Booleans, integers, or lists, that act as syntactic sugar for extra locations). Whenever the queue exceeds its bounded size, we add a transition to a special error location.

Then, we follow the same encoding as in [13] for non-preemptive strategies: we create one clock per possible task instance (of which the number is bounded). Whenever $x > D \wedge x \leq W$, where x denotes a task instance in a given location encoding a queue where this instance is indeed active, we add a transition to the error location, as this task instance missed its deadline. For FPS, this encoding is such that D and B are always compared to clocks as lower-bounds, and are therefore lower-bound parameters, whereas W is an upper-bound parameter. This gives that $A_{enc}(\mathsf{Sch})$ is a (finite) L/U-PTA. For EDF, we need to compare expressions such as $D_i - x_i \bowtie D_j - x_j$; by forbidding parametric deadlines, the model remains again an L/U-PTA. Now, since A is itself an L/U-PTA, the product $A \parallel A_{enc}(\mathsf{Sch})$ is an L/U-PTA, where the error location is reachable for all valuations iff there exists no parameter valuation for which the system is schedulable. The result follows from the fact that the problem of knowing whether a location is reachable for all valuations is decidable for L/U-PTAs [4].

For SJF, we have to compare the B and W with each other, but that can be done "statically" by considering all possible orderings, which gives a finite union of L/U-PTAs; we can show using a monotonicity property that the universality of each of these constrained L/U-PTAs is decidable.   □

The class of PTaskA in Theorem 4 is large. Indeed, the assumption of schedulable-bounded parameters is more than reasonable: both an infinite deadline and a 0-time WCET seem doubtful cases. In addition, the L/U assumption is not much restrictive either: first note that any PTaskA with no parameter in the automaton (but with parametric timings in the tasks, except for deadlines for EDF) fits into this class. Second, this assumption mainly consists in disallowing equality with parameters in the PTaskA, which does not seem much a restriction. Both Fig. 1 (except for EDF, unless p' is valuated) and Fig. 2 (for all strategies) fit into this class.

Remark 2. The decidability of the schedulability-emptiness problem does not necessarily mean that one is able to *synthesize* all parameter valuations. In fact, it was shown in [15] that the synthesis is in general intractable for L/U-PTAs: more precisely, it is (in general) impossible to represent the set of valuations for which a given location is reachable in an L/U-PTA using a finite union of polyhedra. However, we can mitigate this in two ways. First, the non-emptiness is constructive: that is, if the set of valuations for which the system is schedulable is not empty, then one is certain to exhibit immediately a set of valuations (maybe incomplete though) using procedures from [14]. When synthesizing all valuations is out of reach, exhibiting at least some is also of interest. Second, we have in fact a more pragmatical goal, as the subject of the next section will be to synthesize valuations not only for this decidable subclass, but for the general class of PTaskA – maybe not all such valuations (due to Theorem 3) but as many as possible.

4 Schedulability Analysis for Parametric Task Automata

In this section, we adopt a more pragmatical view. Since we only constrain a scheduler to be encoded using a stopwatch automaton, we therefore directly translate any scheduler (preemptive or not) into a (parametric) stopwatch automaton. Even in the decidable cases (where we showed that stopwatches are not needed), we potentially use stopwatches.

As noted in [13], most scheduling strategies can fit into timed (or stopwatch) automata, and therefore fit into parametric stopwatch automata when extended with parameters.

However, the discrete part of the queue might require an unbounded number of locations. Whereas in the non-parametric case, a sufficient bound can be computed which is sufficient for schedulability, this does not hold anymore in the parametric case. Therefore, in the remainder of the paper, we always assume the mild assumption of schedulable-boundedness of Definition 4, and therefore we can infer a bound on the length of the tasks queue.

We do not go into full details for encoding strategies, as this was (partially) done in [13,17], and would require lengthy details; we however give the general idea below.

General Idea. We will consider the synchronous product of two PSwAs in parallel: the actual PTaskA A, and the translation of the scheduler Sch into a second PSwA $A_{enc}(Sch)$. As noted earlier, a PTaskA is just a PTA, where some locations activate task instances. Therefore, the PTaskA can be transformed into an almost-identical PSwA (without stopwatches), by labeling each edge going into a location where task t is activated by a fresh action Act_t. Then, the scheduler will synchronize on actions Act_t, and manage the tasks queue according to its strategy.

The locations of $A_{enc}(Sch)$ are all possible configurations of the discrete part of the tasks queue, of which there is a finite number thanks to the schedulable-boundedness assumption. At any time, if the size of the queue overflows the maximal queue size implied by the schedulable-boundedness assumption, $A_{enc}(Sch)$ will go to a special error location, which denotes that the system is non-schedulable.

We use the following clocks for $A_{enc}(Sch)$. First, for each task t_i, we use a unique clock (say x_i), that serves to measure the unique running instance; note that at most one task instance of task t_i has a non-zero time of already executed computation, from the definition of non-preemptive and preemptive strategies (from Definition 2). These task clocks may be stopped (which is why we require stopwatches): in fact, they will always be stopped, unless an instance of the current task is currently being executed. These task clocks are initially 0, run when an instance of the task is executed, and are reset when such an instance is completed.

Second, for each task instance, we create one clock. For example, clock x_i^j denotes the clock for the instance j of task t_i. Thanks to the schedulable-boundedness assumption, we know the maximum required number of instances per task. These task instance clocks are never stopped; whenever an instance j of task t_i is active, if this instance misses its deadline D_i (which can be tested using a guard $x_i^j > D_i$), $A_{enc}(Sch)$ is sent to a special error location.

We now briefly review the specificities of the three scheduling strategies.

EDF *scheduler.* In order to encode EDF, one must identify the task instance with an earliest deadline: for example, if $D_i - x_i^j < D_{i'} - x_{i'}^{j'}$, then instance j of task t_i

has an earlier deadline than instance j' of task $t_{i'}$ and should be executed first. This can be tested thanks to the diagonal constraints in PSwAs.

FPS *scheduler.* The fixed-priority scheduling is encoded directly on the discrete part of $A_{enc}(Sch)$. When a new instance of task t_i is activated (action Act_t), if that task has a higher priority than the task currently executed (say $t_{i'}$), then the scheduler temporarily stops $t_{i'}$ and starts executing t_i; otherwise, the scheduler keeps executing $t_{i'}$ and inserts a new instance of t_i into the queue.

SJF *scheduler.* In order to encode SJF, one must identify the task with the shortest job: for example, if $W_i - x_i < W_{i'} - x_{i'}$, then the running instance of task t_i has a shorter job than the running of $t_{i'}$ and should be executed first.

Using the above construction A_{enc}, we have:

Proposition 1. *Given a PTaskA A and strategy* Sch, *the system is schedulable for all valuations for which the error location is unreachable in $A \parallel A_{enc}(Sch)$.*

5   Parameter Synthesis for PTaskA Using **IMITATOR**

5.1   **IMITATOR**

IMITATOR [5] is a parametric model checker for networks of PSwAs extended with various features, including global variables, strong broadcast synchronization, and linear clock assignments (instead of being reset to 0, a clock x can also be set, e.g., to $x' + p$). The symbolic computations are performed using polyhedra [7]. IMITATOR implements various algorithms; the one used here is EFsynth ("reachability synthesis" [3,15]). EFsynth is in fact a semi-algorithm: it is not guaranteed to terminate but, if it does, then its result is exact.

5.2   Translation into Parametric Stopwatch Automata

In our translation of the scheduler into a PSwA, we extensively use stopwatches, even in the decidable cases. The reason is that, while the semantics of SwA cannot be encoded using Difference Bound Matrices (a popular data structure rendering TAs very efficient) in the non-parametric setting, however they come for free in the parametric setting (as stopwatches can be encoded into polyhedra, which usually encode the semantics of PTAs).

In order to reduce the state space, we also implemented several optimizations using the expressive power of IMITATOR: *(i)* The queue is not implemented into locations, but using a set of variables. In contrast to [17] where Booleans are used to denote whether a task instance is active or not, we use a single integer for each task t_i, that encodes the number of active instances for t_i. *(ii)* We also use stopwatches as much as possible: whenever a instance clock denotes an inactive instance, it is set to 0 and stopped so as to not create unnecessary diverging relations with the other clocks.

6 Experiments

As writing such a scheduler quickly becomes tedious and error-prone, we implemented an external program (650 lines of Python) that takes as input on the one hand a scheduling strategy Sch and on the other hand the list of tasks of the PTaskA A (with their timings, their priority (for FPS), their maximum number of instances ...), and automatically generates the corresponding PSwA $A_{enc}(Sch)$ in the IMITATOR input format. Then, it suffices to pass to IMITATOR the model made of A and $A_{enc}(Sch)$.

We used IMITATOR 2.9.1 for our experiments. All the subsequent analyses terminate in (at most) a few seconds on a MacBook Pro i7 2.67 GHz.[3]

In this section, we consider a preemptive FPS scheduler. All the results are exact – although the preemptive FPS scheduler is clearly beyond the decidable class of Theorem 4.

Non-parametric Analysis. Quite trivially, our framework allows for non-parametric analysis. Setting $p = 10$ and $p' = 4$, IMITATOR concludes that the PTaskA in Fig. 1 is schedulable for preemptive FPS. With priorities $t_0 > t_1 > t_2 > t_3$, the system becomes non-schedulable.

Mixing Parameters. Let us go back to Fig. 2. First, we set $p = 100$, and we obtain that the system is schedulable for $p' \in [2,3]$. Second, we set $p' = 3$, and we obtain that the system is schedulable for $p \geq 42$. This confirms both intuitions that p' should be not too large, and p large enough for the system to be schedulable. Finally, we run an analysis with both parameter dimensions, which gives:

$$p' \in [2,3] \wedge p \geq 42 \quad \vee \quad p' = 2 \wedge p \in [8,42) \quad \vee \quad p' > 2 \wedge p < 42 \wedge p \geq 36 + 2 \times p'$$

A graphical representation output by IMITATOR is given in Fig. 3a (where p100 stands for p and Q_WCET for p').

Concerning Fig. 1, setting $p' = 4$ yields $p \geq 9$, while a parametric schedulability analysis on both dimensions gives

$$p \geq 9 \wedge p' \geq 2 \wedge p + p' \geq 23 \quad \vee \quad p \geq 9 \wedge p' \geq 3 \wedge p + p' < 23$$

A graphical representation is given in Fig. 3a (where S_D stands for p').

Robustness Analysis. Finally, we can perform robustness analysis: often, TAs and their extension are not by default robust, i.e., they can require infinitely precise behaviors. It may happen that a property holds only if all timing constants are implemented exactly as they were specified. In contrast, robustness analysis (see, e. g., [9]) consists in checking whether there exists some $\epsilon > 0$ for which, when all guards may be enlarged by ϵ, the system still meets its property. To check whether Fig. 1 is robustly schedulable, we modify the system as

---

[3] Sources, binaries, models and results are available at imitator.fr/static/FMICS17.

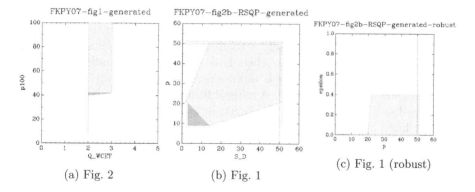

(a) Fig. 2   (b) Fig. 1   (c) Fig. 1 (robust)

Fig. 3. Visualization of parametric schedulability zones

follows: any constraint (in both A and $A_{enc}(Sch)$) of the form $x \leq z$, $x \geq z$, or $x = z$, where $z \in \mathbb{Q}_+ \cup \mathcal{P}$, is transformed into $x \leq z + \epsilon$, $x \geq z - \epsilon$, or $z - \epsilon \leq x \leq z + \epsilon$, respectively (and similarly for strict constraints). Applying this modification to Fig. 1 with $p = 10$ and $p' = 4$, by adding a fresh parameter ϵ, gives the constraint $\epsilon = 0$: that is, this system is *not* robustly schedulable. Any modification (even infinitesimal) of the timing constants may render the system non-schedulable.

We can combine parametric schedulability with robustness analysis: keeping both p and ϵ gives

$$p \geq 9 \quad \vee \quad \epsilon \leq \frac{2}{5} \wedge p \geq 20 + 5\epsilon \wedge p \geq 19 + 8\epsilon$$

That is, the system is not schedulable for $p < 9$, is schedulable but not robustly for $p \in [9, 20]$ and becomes robust from 20. Note that our constraint even gives by how much the guards can be enlarged (the value depends on p and never exceeds $\frac{2}{5}$). A graphical representation is given in Fig. 3c.

7   Conclusion

We introduced a unified and concise model for parametric schedulability analysis for (non-)preemptive strategies on a monoprocessor. While the general case is undecidable, we exhibited a decidable subclass, and our implementation terminates with an exact result on benchmarks even outside of the decidable class.

While formal methods with timing parameters might not scale to verify the schedulability of very large systems with all details, we believe they can provide designers with first schedulability results on subparts of the system, or to derive timing bounds on abstractions of it. Designing ad-hoc abstractions for our framework is on our agenda.

There is still some open space between our decidability result (Theorem 4) and our undecidability results (Theorem 3). A promising way to improve the knowledge of decidability would be to show that L/U-parametric timed automata with bounded subtractions are decidable, which would allow to extend our decidable subclass of PTaskA. Conversely, a good candidate for undecidability is non-preemptive strategies without the schedulable-boundedness assumption.

So far, whereas the scheduler is automatically generated, the PTaskA still needs to be manually constructed. A natural future work is therefore to propose on the one hand a library of patterns (periodic tasks, sporadic tasks ...), and on the other hand an automated translation from existing formalisms.

Of course, handling multiprocessor scheduling is on our agenda, as well as mixed-criticality scheduling. Finally, we would also like to consider a parameterization of a recent extension of TaskA [12].

References

1. Abdeddaïm, Y., Maler, O.: Preemptive job-shop scheduling using stopwatch automata. In: Katoen, J.-P., Stevens, P. (eds.) TACAS 2002. LNCS, vol. 2280, pp. 113–126. Springer, Heidelberg (2002). doi:10.1007/3-540-46002-0_9
2. Alur, R., Dill, D.L.: A theory of timed automata. Theor. Comput. Sci. **126**(2), 183–235 (1994)
3. Alur, R., Henzinger, T.A., Vardi, M.Y.: Parametric real-time reasoning. In: STOC, pp. 592–601. ACM (1993)
4. André, É.: What's decidable about parametric timed automata? In: Artho, C., Ölveczky, P.C. (eds.) FTSCS 2015. CCIS, vol. 596, pp. 52–68. Springer, Cham (2016). doi:10.1007/978-3-319-29510-7_3
5. André, É., Fribourg, L., Kühne, U., Soulat, R.: IMITATOR 2.5: a tool for analyzing robustness in scheduling problems. In: Giannakopoulou, D., Méry, D. (eds.) FM 2012. LNCS, vol. 7436, pp. 33–36. Springer, Heidelberg (2012). doi:10.1007/978-3-642-32759-9_6
6. André, É., Lipari, G., Sun, Y.: Verification of two real-time systems using parametric timed automata. In: WATERS (2015)
7. Bagnara, R., Hill, P.M., Zaffanella, E.: The parma polyhedra library: toward a complete set of numerical abstractions for the analysis and verification of hardware and software systems. Sci. Comput. Program. **72**(1–2), 3–21 (2008)
8. Bérard, B., Haddad, S., Jovanović, A., Lime, D.: Parametric interrupt timed automata. In: Abdulla, P.A., Potapov, I. (eds.) RP 2013. LNCS, vol. 8169, pp. 59–69. Springer, Heidelberg (2013). doi:10.1007/978-3-642-41036-9_7
9. Bouyer, P., Markey, N., Sankur, O.: Robustness in timed automata. In: Abdulla, P.A., Potapov, I. (eds.) RP 2013. LNCS, vol. 8169, pp. 1–18. Springer, Heidelberg (2013). doi:10.1007/978-3-642-41036-9_1
10. Cassez, F., Larsen, K.: The impressive power of stopwatches. In: Palamidessi, C. (ed.) CONCUR 2000. LNCS, vol. 1877, pp. 138–152. Springer, Heidelberg (2000). doi:10.1007/3-540-44618-4_12
11. Cimatti, A., Palopoli, L., Ramadian, Y.: Symbolic computation of schedulability regions using parametric timed automata. In: RTSS, pp. 80–89. IEEE Computer Society (2008)
12. Fang, B., Li, G., Sun, D., Cai, H.: Schedulability analysis of timed regular tasks by under-approximation on WCET. In: Fränzle, M., Kapur, D., Zhan, N. (eds.) SETTA 2016. LNCS, vol. 9984, pp. 147–162. Springer, Cham (2016). doi:10.1007/978-3-319-47677-3_10

13. Fersman, E., Krcál, P., Pettersson, P., Yi, W.: Task automata: schedulability, decidability and undecidability. Inf. Comput. **205**(8), 1149–1172 (2007)
14. Hune, T., Romijn, J., Stoelinga, M., Vaandrager, F.W.: Linear parametric model checking of timed automata. J. Logic Algebr. Program. **52–53**, 183–220 (2002)
15. Jovanović, A., Lime, D., Roux, O.H.: Integer parameter synthesis for timed automata. IEEE Trans. Softw. Eng. **41**(5), 445–461 (2015)
16. Miller, J.S.: Decidability and complexity results for timed automata and semilinear hybrid automata. In: Lynch, N., Krogh, B.H. (eds.) HSCC 2000. LNCS, vol. 1790, pp. 296–310. Springer, Heidelberg (2000). doi:10.1007/3-540-46430-1_26
17. Norström, C., Wall, A., Yi, W.: Timed automata as task models for event-driven systems. In: RTCSA, pp. 182–189. IEEE Computer Society (1999)
18. Sun, Y., Soulat, R., Lipari, G., André, É., Fribourg, L.: Parametric schedulability analysis of fixed priority real-time distributed systems. In: Artho, C., Ölveczky, P.C. (eds.) FTSCS 2013. CCIS, vol. 419, pp. 212–228. Springer, Cham (2014). doi:10.1007/978-3-319-05416-2_14

Special Track: Formal Methods for Mobile and Autonomous Robots

CRutoN: Automatic Verification of a Robotic Assistant's Behaviours

Paul Gainer[1]([⊠]), Clare Dixon[1], Kerstin Dautenhahn[2], Michael Fisher[1], Ullrich Hustadt[1], Joe Saunders[2], and Matt Webster[1]

[1] University of Liverpool, Liverpool, UK
{p.gainer,cldixon,mfisher,u.hustadt,matt}@liverpool.ac.uk
[2] University of Hertfordshire, Hatfield, UK
{k.dautenhahn,j.1.saunders}@herts.ac.uk

Abstract. The Care-O-bot is an autonomous robotic assistant that can support people in domestic and other environments. The behaviour of the robot can be defined by a set of high level control rules. The adoption and further development of such robotic assistants is inhibited by the absence of assurances about their safety. In previous work, formal models of the robot behaviour and its environment were constructed by hand and model checkers were then used to check whether desirable formal temporal properties were satisfied for all possible system behaviours. In this paper we describe the details of the software CRutoN, that provides an automatic translation from sets of robot control rules into input for the model checker NuSMV. We compare our work with previous attempts to formally verify the robot control rules, discuss the potential applications of the approach, and consider future directions of research.

1 Introduction

Robot assistants are autonomous robots that can help with home and work-oriented activities collaborating closely with humans. Personal care robots assist those who might be vulnerable due to illness, age or disability. In 2014 a new ISO safety standard for personal care robots was published, providing guidelines to manufacturers of personal care robots to ensure the safety of their design, construction and application [7]. However, the development and deployment of robotic assistants has been restricted by the lack of formal assurances of their safety.

Formal verification is the application of mathematical techniques to determine whether or not a system conforms exactly to its specification. These techniques are used in the development of software and hardware systems, notably in the development of critical systems where system failure can have drastic human or economic repercussions. Formal verification has already been applied

This work was supported by both the Sir Joseph Rotblat Alumni Scholarship at Liverpool and the EPSRC Research Programme EP/K006193/1 *Trustworthy Robotic Assistants*.

© Springer International Publishing AG 2017
L. Petrucci et al. (Eds.): FMICS-AVoCS 2017, LNCS 10471, pp. 119–133, 2017.
DOI: 10.1007/978-3-319-67113-0_8

to robotic systems, for instance, Cowley and Taylor [2] used linear logic and dependent-type theory to verify assembly robots. A different approach using hybrid automata and hybrid statecharts was employed by Mohammed et al. [10] to formally model and verify multirobot systems, and control algorithms for a surgical robot were verified by Kouskoulas et al. in [8]. Applying formal verification to the behaviours of robotic assistants can help to support their safety and trustworthiness by demonstrating that the robot always behaves in accordance with a set of formal requirements. We might, for instance, want to show that for all possible executions of robot behaviours the robot eventually performs some good action, or conversely that some bad action is never performed.

The Care-O-bot® is a robotic assistant that has been deployed in a domestic-style house at the University of Hertfordshire. The house is equipped with sensors which provide real-time information on the state of the house and its occupants. Studies have already been conducted to apply formal verification to the behaviours of the Care-O-bot in this environment. Model checking, an automated algorithmic verification technique, was applied in [3]. A model of the robot and its environment was manually constructed and the model checker NuSMV [1] was used to prove several properties relating to the priority and interruptibility of behaviours. Sensor data pertaining to the house was modelled by non-deterministically selecting one of several possible values for every sensor at any moment in time. In [17] algorithmic verification was again applied to the set of Care-O-bot behaviours. Here, models of the robot and its environment were manually constructed using the intelligent agent modelling and simulation language Brahms [15]. The *BrahmsToPromela* tool [16] was then used to automatically translate Brahms models into PROMELA, the input language for the model checker SPIN [6]. This approach differed from the first in that the model of sensor data was more restrictive. The non-deterministic choice of sensor values was constrained using data taken from an activity log for a real 6 h execution period of the robot.

These studies clearly demonstrated that the high level decision making of the Care-O-bot could indeed be verified using model checking, however both approaches had limiting factors. Firstly, effort was required to manually construct formal models for a fixed set of robot behaviours. Furthermore, a new set of control rules means the model needs to be constructed again. Secondly, in [3] the timing constraints in the control rules were dealt with in an ad-hoc manner. Additionally, the properties checked focused on the operation of the robot control rules rather than general requirements of the robot. In this paper we describe the software CRutoN[1], developed in [5], that proves to be an effective solution to the problem. CRutoN automates the generation of formal input models for the NuSMV model checker, and minimises the time needed to apply model checking to different sets of robot behaviours. Given a set of rules at the design stage, generated models could be used to find unexpected behaviour in the model. Less effort would then be required to refine the design since modification

---

[1] The software, sample output files, and input used in this paper, are available at https://github.com/PaulGainer/CRutoN.

of the formal model is automated. We show that the models generated using the software retain the same desirable properties as those constructed manually, and describe features of the software that facilitate modulation of the granularity of temporal aspects of the robot behaviours.

The Care-O-bot, the environment in which it operates, and the behaviours that determine the actions of the robot are introduced in Sect. 2. An overview of the CRutoN software, and the translation of control rules for the robot into an intermediate form representation are given in Sect. 3. In Sect. 4 we formalise the behaviour of the robot using linear time temporal logic, and we specify the expected behaviour of the robot in any generated formal model. Section 5 describes the translation from the intermediate form representation into input for the model checker NuSMV. In Sect. 6 the results of applying this translation to sets of control rules are presented, and we discuss the limitations of our approach. We give concluding remarks in Sect. 7 and outline some future work.

2 The Care-O-bot and the Robot House

The Robot House is a typical suburban house in Hertfordshire, UK. The house is appropriately furnished, and is equipped with a number of sensors. The sensors provide real time information about the state of the house and its occupants, for instance pressure sensors that detect when an occupant is seated, or electrical sensors indicating whether doors are open or closed [4,13].

The house provides a realistic setting in which experiments can be conducted using a number of robots, including the Care-O-bot (see Fig. 1). The Care-O-bot is a commercially available robot assistant developed at the Fraunhofer Institute for Manufacturing Engineering and Automation [12]. The robot has an articulated torso with a manipulator arm and tray, stereo optical sensors, LED lights, and appropriate sensors that provide information about its current state. The robot software is based on the Robot Operating System [11].

Control Rules and Behaviours. The high level decision making of the Care-O-bot is specified by a set of behaviours whose execution is controlled by a scheduler. Each *behaviour* consists of a sequence of atomic preconditions and a sequence of actions. Atomic preconditions and actions are also called *control rules*. *Actions* correspond to operations executed by the robot, including the setting of internal variables, implemented as ROS scripts. For instance, the robot may move to the living room and say "It's time for your medicine", or may turn its inbuilt lights to yellow. *Atomic preconditions* are propositional statements that check either the internal state of the robot or the state of the environment in which the robot operates. They may include an additional constraint requiring the condition to have remained *true* for some period of time, or requiring the condition to have been *true* at least once within some period of time.

The atomic preconditions of a behaviour are linked by Boolean operators into a propositional *precondition*. This precondition must evaluate to true for the behaviour to be scheduled for execution. If the sequence of atomic preconditions for a behaviour is empty then the associated propositional precondition,

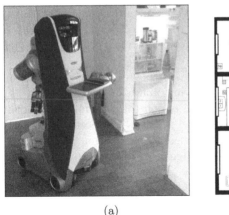

(a)   (b)

Fig. 1. The Care-O-bot (a) operating in the Robot House in Hertfordshire, and the floor plan of the house (b).

the empty conjunction, is always true. Behaviours without atomic preconditions can be declared to be *subroutines*. Subroutines cannot be picked by the scheduler for execution but can be executed directly by actions in other behaviours. Behaviours that are not subroutines are also called *schedulable*.

Behaviour Scheduling. The algorithm in Fig. 3 describes how the Care-O-bot schedules its behaviours. When all preconditions of a behaviour are true, then the behaviour can be selected by the scheduler for execution. Only one behaviour can be executed at a time and when a behaviour is executed, the robot will sequentially perform its sequence of actions. Each behaviour has a *priority*, given by a natural number, which is used by the scheduler to decide which behaviour to execute if the preconditions of several behaviour are true at the same time. Behaviours with higher priorities will be scheduled before those with lower priorities, and if more than one behaviour shares the highest priority then one of these will be non-deterministically selected for scheduling. A behaviour can be declared to be *interruptible*. The execution of the sequence of actions of an interruptible behaviour can be interrupted by another schedulable behaviour having a priority greater than the priority of the executing behaviour, if, and only if, the preconditions of the interrupting behaviour hold. Any remaining actions in the interrupted behaviour are lost, and the behaviour must again wait to be scheduled as usual. All subroutines are uninterruptible.

Figure 2 shows the control rules for the S1-Med-5PM-Remind behaviour. Rules 1 and 2 are atomic preconditions and rules 3–9 are actions. For each control rule in the database there is a flag indicating if that rule is a precondition or an action. These are omitted here for simplicity. Rule 1 requires the time to be after 5pm and rule 2 requires the robot's internal flag ::502::5PM-MedicineDue to be *true*. When both preconditions hold, and this behaviour is scheduled for execution, the robot will sequentially execute actions 3–9. It first turns its lights

1. Time is on or after 17:00:00
2. ::502::5PM-MedicineDue is true
3. Turn light on ::0::Care-O-Bot 3.2 to yellow
4. move ::0::Care-O-Bot 3.2 to ::14:: Living Room Sofa Area in the
   Living Room and wait for completion
5. Turn light on ::0::Care-O-Bot 3.2 to white and wait for completion
6. ::0::Care-O-Bot 3.2 says 'Its time for your medicine' and wait for
   completion
7. ::0::Care-O-Bot 3.2 GUI,S1-Set-GoToKitchen, S1-Set-ReturnHome,
   S1-Set-WaitHere
8. SET ::502::5PM-MedicineDue TO false
9. SET ::503::5PM-MedicineReminder TO true

Fig. 2. The S1-Med-5PM-Remind behaviour

to yellow, then moves to the living room, near the sofa and then turns its lights to white. The robot then tells the occupant "It's time to take your medicine", and displays some options on its GUI that allow the occupant to either send the robot to the kitchen, send the robot to its charging point, or instruct the robot to do nothing. The values of two internal variables are then set to *true* and *false* respectively.

3   Intermediate Form Translation

As a first step to the transformation of Care-O-bot control rules into input for NUSMV, we translate the extracted control rules into a succinct intermediate form representation that represents all of the information extracted from the control rules. This intermediate form facilitated the final translation into SMV. This was so that translations from the intermediate form into input for other model checkers could potentially be defined and implemented.

Precondition Classification. For the translation into intermediate form, we distinguish two categories of atomic preconditions: Value Check and Time Constraint. A Value Check checks the value of some variable corresponding to the internal state of the robot or the state of the environment. A Time Constraint requires the current time of day to be within some given time interval. Table 1 gives examples of preconditions for each of the two categories. The first Value Check checks the value of the Boolean variable ::502::5PM-MedicineDue, which equates to an internal variable of the robot, the second Value Check checks that the location of the robot is in the living room, and the two Time Constraints require the current time to be at or after 5pm, or between midnight and 5 pm.

Action Classification. We also distinguish four categories of actions: Value Assignment, Behaviour Execution, Behaviour Selection, and Delay. A Value Assignment assigns some value to a variable. This can represent a change in the internal state of the robot, or a change in the state of the environment. A Behaviour

Table 1. Precondition categories

Value Check	`::502::5PM-MedicineDue is true`
	`::0::Care-O-Bot 3.2 location is ::14::the Living Room`
Time Constraint	`Time is on or after 17:00:00`
	`Time is between 00:00:00 and 16:59:00`

Execution transfers control from some scheduled behaviour to another behaviour. A Behaviour Selection again transfers control to another behaviour, however, here a choice of possible behaviours is presented to the occupant of the house via the GUI of the Care-O-bot. A Delay instructs the robot to do nothing for a given number of seconds. Table 2 gives examples of actions for each of the four categories. The first Value Assignment assigns the value *true* to the internal variable `::503::5PM-MedicineReminder`, while the second Value Assignment selects a phrase to be vocalised by the robot. The Behaviour Execution executes the behaviour S1-sleep, and the Behaviour Selection allows the occupant to choose to execute one of the `S1-Set-GoToKitchen`, `S1-Set-ReturnHome`, and `S1-Set-WaitHere` behaviours. Finally, the Delay instructs the robot to do nothing for 1 s.

Parsing and Translation. As can be observed from the tables, the control rules can have a wide variety of syntactic forms. To ensure that future control rules that may use additional categories of preconditions or actions can be translated correctly, the parsing and extraction of information from the rules is not hard coded into the software. The translator takes as input a set of Grammar Rules defining the syntax of the control rules, and a set of Data Extraction Rules that define how information should be extracted from the control rules. The Grammar Rule for a new control rule allows an automaton to be constructed at run time that can be used to parse this new syntactic rule form. This Grammar Rule has a corresponding Data Extraction Rule that describes how meaningful information can be extracted from the text parsed by the automaton. The software has options that regulate the level of automation of the translation process and determine when a user should be prompted to disambiguate input if necessary.

Table 2. Action categories

Value Assignment	`SET ::503::5PM-MedicineReminder TO true`
	`::0::Care-O-Bot 3.2 says Its time for your medicine`
Behaviour Execution	`Execute sequence S1-sleep on ::0::Care-O-Bot 3.2`
Behaviour Selection	`::0::Care-O-Bot 3.2 GUI, S1-Set-GoToKitchen,`
	`S1-Set-ReturnHome, S1-Set-WaitHere`
Delay	`Wait for 1 seconds on ::0::Care-O-Bot 3.2`

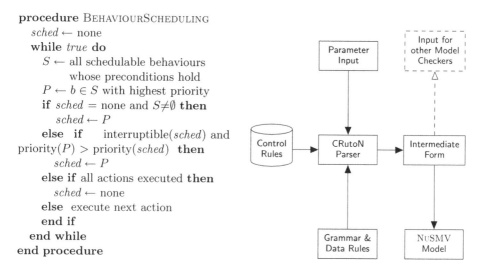

procedure BEHAVIOURSCHEDULING
   $sched \leftarrow$ none
  while *true* **do**
    $S \leftarrow$ all schedulable behaviours
      whose preconditions hold
    $P \leftarrow b \in S$ with highest priority
    if $sched =$ none and $S \neq \emptyset$ **then**
      $sched \leftarrow P$
    else if interruptible($sched$) and
priority(P) > priority($sched$) **then**
      $sched \leftarrow P$
    else if all actions executed **then**
      $sched \leftarrow$ none
    else execute next action
    end if
  end while
end procedure

Fig. 3. Care-O-bot behaviour scheduling.   **Fig. 4.** A system diagram of CRutoN.

Figure 4 shows a diagram of the system. Given a set of Care-O-bot behaviours $\mathcal{S}$, a set of Grammar Rules and Data Extraction Rules, and parameter input for the parser, we construct an intermediate form representation (IFR). The IFR of $\mathcal{S}$ is a tuple $I(\mathcal{S}) = \langle \Gamma, \Omega, f_{sch}, f_{int} \rangle$, where Γ is a set of behaviours in intermediate form, f_{sch} and f_{int} are predicates over Γ that are *true* if, and only if, a behaviour is respectively schedulable or interruptible, and Ω is a set of variables that represent the internal state of the robot and the state of the environment. A behaviour $\mathcal{B} \in \Gamma$ is a tuple $\mathcal{B} = \langle P, \mathcal{A}, \rho \rangle$, where P is a formula formed by combining the atomic preconditions of the behaviour, $\rho \in \mathbb{N}$ is the priority of the behaviour, and $\mathcal{A}$ is a sequence of actions. Each individual action $\alpha \in \mathcal{A}$ is a tuple of values. A Value Assignment is a pair (ω, ν), where $\omega \in \Omega$ is a variable and ν is a value from the domain of ω, a Behaviour Execution is a subroutine $\mathcal{B} \in \Gamma$, a Behaviour Selection is a set of subroutines $\mathfrak{B} \subseteq \Gamma$, and a Delay is a natural number D.

4 Property Specification

There was no available formal semantics specifying the behaviours of the Care-O-bot. An analysis of the set of control rules modelled in [3,17] and input from the development team led to the formulation of desirable properties that would be expected to hold in any model resulting from the translation into model checker input. Linear-time temporal logic (LTL) was used to specify these properties.

Linear Temporal Logic. In LTL the model of time is isomorphic to the natural numbers, and a model for a formula is a sequence of states $\Sigma = \sigma_0, \sigma_1, \ldots$ such that each state σ_i is a valuation for the set of variables $\mathcal{V}$ at the ith moment in time, and $\sigma_i(\omega)$ is finite for every $\omega \in \mathcal{V}$ and $i \geq 0$. The set of LTL formulae can be defined inductively as

$$\varphi{::} = \top \mid \bot \mid (\omega{=}\nu) \mid \neg\varphi \mid (\varphi\vee\psi) \mid (\varphi\wedge\psi) \mid (\varphi \implies \psi) \mid \bigcirc\varphi \mid \square\varphi \mid \lozenge\varphi$$

where $\omega \in \mathcal{V}$ and φ and ψ are LTL forumlae. If ω is a Boolean variable we will often use ω for $(\omega{=}true)$, and $\neg\omega$ for $(\omega{=}false)$. We can define $(\Sigma, i) \models \Phi$, the truth of a formula Φ in Σ at time i, as follows:

$$
\begin{aligned}
(\Sigma, i) &\models (\omega{=}\nu) & &\textbf{iff } \sigma_i(\omega){=}\nu \\
(\Sigma, i) &\models \bigcirc\Phi & &\textbf{iff } (\Sigma, i+1) \models \Phi \\
(\Sigma, i) &\models \lozenge\Phi & &\textbf{iff for some } k \in \mathbb{N}, (k \geq i) \text{ and } (\Sigma, k) \models \Phi \\
(\Sigma, i) &\models \square\Phi & &\textbf{iff for all } k \in \mathbb{N}, (k \geq i) \text{ implies } (\Sigma, k) \models \Phi.
\end{aligned}
$$

The semantics of propositional operators is defined as usual.

Formal Model of the System State. Given a set of Care-O-bot behaviours $\mathcal{S}$, and its intermediate form representation $\mathrm{I}(\mathcal{S}) = \langle \Gamma, \Omega, f_{sch}, f_{int} \rangle$, we define variables SCHED and STEP that are used to model the behaviour scheduling procedure of the robot. The scheduling variable SCHED ranges over the values $\{none\} \cup \{sched^{\mathcal{B}} \mid \mathcal{B} \in \Gamma\}$ and its value indicates the behaviour that is currently scheduled by the robot with *none* indicating that no behaviour is scheduled. The step variable STEP ranges over the values $\{none\} \cup \{step^1, \ldots, step^k\}$ where $k = \mathbf{max}\{|\mathcal{A}| \mid \langle P, \mathcal{A}, \rho \rangle \in \Gamma\}$, and its value indicates the index of an action that is being executed in the sequence of actions for a behaviour that is currently scheduled by the robot, with *none* indicating that no action is being executed. A model of our system is a sequence of states $\Sigma = \sigma_0, \sigma_1, \ldots$, and each state is a valuation for $\Omega \cup \{\text{SCHED}, \text{STEP}\}$.

Specification. We now formally express properties that we would expect to hold in any generated NuSMV model. The following schematic formulae intend to capture the behavioural semantics of the robot with regards to behaviour scheduling and action execution. Let $\Gamma^{sch} = \{\mathcal{B} \in \Gamma \mid f_{sch}(\mathcal{B})\}$ be the set of all behaviours that are schedulable, and let $\Gamma^{int} = \{\mathcal{B} \in \Gamma \mid f_{int}(\mathcal{B})\}$ be the set of all behaviours that are interruptible. For every $\mathcal{B} = \langle P, \mathcal{A}, \rho \rangle \in \Gamma$ we define $\triangle^{\mathcal{B}} = \{\langle P', \mathcal{A}', \rho' \rangle \in \Gamma \mid \rho' > \rho\}$ to be the set of all behaviours in Γ that have a higher priority than $\mathcal{B}$.

If the kth action of a scheduled behaviour $\mathcal{B}$ is the Value Assignment (ω, ν) and this action is executed, then the variable ω should have the value ν in the next moment in time.

$$\square\Big[\big(\text{SCHED} = sched^{\mathcal{B}} \wedge \text{STEP} = step^k\big) \implies \bigcirc\big[(\omega = \nu)\big]\Big] \tag{1}$$

Scheduling. If no behaviours are scheduled and the preconditions to at least one behaviour hold, then in the next moment in time a behaviour will be scheduled.

$$\square\left[\left(\begin{array}{c}\text{SCHED} = none \\ \wedge \bigvee_{\langle P, \mathcal{A}, \rho \rangle \in \Gamma^{sch}} P\end{array}\right) \implies \bigcirc\left[\begin{array}{c}\text{STEP} = step^1 \\ \wedge \bigvee_{\mathcal{B} \in \Gamma^{sch}} \text{SCHED} = sched^{\mathcal{B}}\end{array}\right]\right] \tag{2}$$

Termination. For any behaviour $\mathcal{B}$ that executes a Value Assignment or Delay as its kth action, and this is the last action of the behaviour, if the preconditions to no other schedulable behaviour hold then in the next moment in time no behaviour should be executing.

$$\Box \left[\left(\begin{array}{c} \text{SCHED} = sched^{\mathcal{B}} \wedge \text{STEP} = step^k \\ \wedge \bigwedge_{\langle P, \mathcal{A}, \rho \rangle \in \Gamma^{sch}} \neg P \end{array} \right) \implies \bigcirc \text{SCHED} = none \right] \qquad (3)$$

Prioritisation. If no behaviour is scheduled, and the preconditions to one or more behaviours hold, then in the next moment in time the schedulable behaviour with the highest priority will be executing its first action.

$$\Box \left[\begin{array}{c} \left(\text{SCHED} = none \wedge \bigvee_{\langle P, \mathcal{A}, \rho \rangle \in \Gamma^{sch}} P \right) \implies \\ \bigvee_{\mathcal{B} \in \Gamma^{sch}} \left(\begin{array}{c} \bigwedge_{\langle P', \mathcal{A}', \rho' \rangle \in \Delta^{\mathcal{B}} \cap \Gamma^{sch}} \neg P' \\ \wedge \bigcirc [\text{SCHED} = sched^{\mathcal{B}} \wedge \text{STEP} = step^1] \end{array} \right) \end{array} \right] \qquad (4)$$

Persistence. For every uninterruptible behaviour $\mathcal{B}$, if it has been scheduled and has an action sequence of length k, then it should always eventually execute its last (k^{th}) action.

$$\Box \left[\text{SCHED} = sched^{\mathcal{B}} \implies \Diamond (\text{SCHED} = sched^{\mathcal{B}} \wedge \text{STEP} = step^k) \right] \qquad (5)$$

Continuity. For any interruptible behaviour $\mathcal{B}$ that executes a Value Assignment or Delay as its kth action, where that action is not the last action, in the next moment in time the behaviour should be executing its $(k+1)^{th}$ action if no other behaviour can interrupt $\mathcal{B}$.

$$\Box \left[\begin{array}{c} (\text{SCHED} = sched^{\mathcal{B}} \wedge \text{STEP} = step^k \wedge \bigwedge_{\langle P, \mathcal{A}, \rho \rangle \in \Delta^{\mathcal{B}} \cap \Gamma^{sch}} \neg P) \\ \implies \bigcirc [\text{SCHED} = sched^{\mathcal{B}} \wedge \text{STEP} = step^{k+1}] \end{array} \right] \qquad (6)$$

Note that without the 3rd conjunct we can also show continuity for uninterruptible behaviours executing Value Assignment or Delay actions.

Discontinuity. For all interruptible behaviours it should be the case that if the behaviour can be interrupted in the next moment in time, the schedulable behaviour having the highest priority of all the behaviours that can interrupt should be executing its first action.

$$\bigwedge_{\mathcal{B} \in \Gamma^{int}} \Box \left[\bigvee_{\mathcal{B}' \in \Delta^{\mathcal{B}} \cap \Gamma^{sch}} \left(\begin{array}{c} \bigcirc [\text{SCHED} = sched^{\mathcal{B}'} \wedge \text{STEP} = step^1] \\ \wedge \bigwedge_{\langle P, \mathcal{A}, \rho \rangle \in \Delta^{\mathcal{B}'} \cap \Gamma^{sch}} \neg P \end{array} \right) \right] \qquad (7)$$

Delegation. For every behaviour $\mathcal{B}$ executing a Behaviour Execution, $\mathcal{B}_{ex}$, as its kth action, if $\mathcal{B}$ is not interrupted by another behaviour then in the next moment in time $\mathcal{B}_{ex}$ should be scheduled and executing its first action.

$$\Box \left[\left(\begin{array}{c} \text{SCHED} = sched^{\mathcal{B}} \wedge \text{STEP} = step^k \\ \wedge \bigwedge_{\langle P, \mathcal{A}, \rho \rangle \in \Delta^{\mathcal{B}} \cap \Gamma^{sch}} \neg P \end{array} \right) \implies \bigcirc \left[\begin{array}{c} \text{SCHED} = sched^{\mathcal{B}_{ex}} \\ \wedge \text{STEP} = step^1 \end{array} \right] \right] \qquad (8)$$

Resumption. For every behaviour $\mathcal{B}$ executing a Behaviour Execution $\mathcal{B}_{ex}$ as its kth action, where that action is not the last action, if $\mathcal{B}$ is not interrupted by another behaviour then at some time after that $\mathcal{B}_{ex}$ should have finished executing its actions, and the original behaviour should be executing its $(k+1)^{\text{th}}$ action.

$$\Box\left[\left(\begin{array}{c}\text{SCHED} = sched^{\mathcal{B}} \wedge \text{STEP} = step^k \\ \wedge \bigwedge_{\langle P,\mathcal{A},\rho\rangle \in \triangle^{\mathcal{B}} \cap \Gamma^{sch}} \neg P\end{array}\right) \implies \Diamond \left[\begin{array}{c}\text{SCHED} = sched^{\mathcal{B}} \\ \wedge \text{STEP} = step^{k+1}\end{array}\right]\right] \quad (9)$$

Selection. For every behaviour $\mathcal{B}$ executing a Behaviour Selection $\mathfrak{B}$ as its kth action, if $\mathcal{B}$ is not interrupted by another behaviour then in the next moment in time a behaviour in $\mathfrak{B}$ should be scheduled and executing its first action.

$$\Box\left[\left(\begin{array}{c}\text{SCHED} = sched^{\mathcal{B}} \\ \wedge \text{STEP} = step^k \\ \wedge \bigwedge_{\langle P,\mathcal{A},\rho\rangle \in \triangle^{\mathcal{B}} \cap \Gamma^{sch}} \neg P\end{array}\right) \implies \bigvee_{\mathcal{B}_{ex} \in \mathfrak{B}} \bigcirc \left[\begin{array}{c}\text{SCHED} = sched^{\mathcal{B}_{ex}} \\ \wedge \text{STEP} = step^1\end{array}\right]\right] \quad (10)$$

Selection Resumption. For every behaviour $\mathcal{B}$ executing a Behaviour Selection $\mathfrak{B}$ as its kth action, where that action is not the last action, if $\mathcal{B}$ is not interrupted by another behaviour then at some time after that any subroutine in $\mathfrak{B}$ should have finished executing its actions, and the original behaviour should be executing its $(k+1)^{\text{th}}$ action.

$$\Box\left[\left(\begin{array}{c}\text{SCHED} = sched^{\mathcal{B}} \\ \wedge \text{STEP} = step^k \\ \wedge \bigwedge_{\langle P,\mathcal{A},\rho\rangle \in \triangle^{\mathcal{B}} \cap \Gamma^{sch}} \neg P\end{array}\right) \implies \bigvee_{\mathcal{B}_{ex} \in \mathfrak{B}} \Diamond \left[\begin{array}{c}\text{SCHED} = sched^{\mathcal{B}} \\ \wedge \text{STEP} = step^{k+1}\end{array}\right]\right] \quad (11)$$

5 Translation into SMV

NuSMV [1] is a symbolic BDD-based model checker. The model checker accepts as input a finite state transition system defined using the modelling language SMV [9]. NuSMV input models can be decomposed into separate modules. Every model has at least one module, the main module, and some number of additional parameterisable modules. Each model consists of three sections: VAR, ASSIGN, and DEFINE. The VAR section defines variables and instances of modules; variables can be Booleans, symbolic enumerated types, or finitely bound integers. The global state of a NuSMV model is a valuation for all variables in the model. Initial states of the model and transitions between states are defined in the ASSIGN section. Finally, macro expressions can be defined in the DEFINE section.

Given a set of Care-O-bot behaviours $\mathcal{S}$, and its intermediate form representation $\text{I}(S) = \langle \Gamma, \Omega, f_{sch}, f_{int} \rangle$, we construct an input model for NuSMV as follows.

State Variables. For every $\omega \in \Omega$ there is a variable declaration in the VAR section of the main module. Variables are either Booleans or enumerated types – variables over a set of symbolic constants. Variables that correspond to internal flags of the robot are initialised to *false*, and initial values for variables corresponding to the environment are non-deterministically chosen by NuSMV in the initial state. Initial values for both types of variable can also be explicitly specified in the form of additional input to the software. As in Sect. 4 we also define the enumerated variables scheduled and step. Initially, both variables have the value *none*. The additional variable scheduled_last ranges over the same values as scheduled, and is used to record a behaviour that executes a Behaviour Execution or Behaviour Selection so that it can be rescheduled once the subroutine has executed all of its actions. The initial value of scheduled_last is *none*. Since we only use one variable to record behaviours that should be rescheduled, we can only construct models where the level of nesting of behaviour executions is at most 1. Introducing additional variables would allow us to extend the nesting level, at the expense of model size.

The time variable records the time of day in the Robot House. Values for time are defined by partitioning a 24 h period into intervals during which different subsets of the set of all Time Constraints in the model hold. The initial value of time is non-deterministically chosen in the initial state, and the value then remains constant throughout a run of the system. If desired, time can be set to an exact time of day using a parameter to the software, but still remains constant throughout. Note that this is a limitation relating to explicit time.

Behaviours. For every $\mathcal{B} = \langle P, \mathcal{A}, \rho \rangle \in \Gamma$ there is a corresponding macro expression for P in the main module; for non-schedulable behaviours this is simply *false*. In NuSMV a variable assignment occurs if some constraint holds. There is an ordering on variable assignments such that if the constraints hold for multiple assignments to a single variable then the assignment ordered first will be applied. We can exploit this to ensure that behaviours with higher priorities are scheduled before those with lower priorities i.e. scheduled is assigned a value corresponding to the behaviour having the highest priority of all those that can be scheduled. Assignments to scheduled are constrained by the expression corresponding to P, and by an interruptibility macro expression that evaluates to *true* if a behaviour with a lower priority is currently scheduled. For each Value Assignment in $\mathcal{A}$ there is a corresponding variable assignment, constrained by scheduled having a value corresponding to $\mathcal{B}$ and step having a value corresponding to the index of the action in $\mathcal{A}$. For each Behaviour Execution there is a corresponding assignment to scheduled_last of a value corresponding to $\mathcal{B}$, an assignment of 1 to step, and an assignment to scheduled of a value corresponding to that of the subroutine being executed. Additional variable assignments model the rescheduling of a behaviour that calls a subroutine, once the subroutine has executed all of its actions.

Temporal Constraints. Some Value Check rules have additional temporal constraints. There are two types of constraint, Been-In-State and Was-In-State, that require some variable $\omega \in \Omega$ to have respectively maintained some value ν during some previous period of time, or to have had the value ν at least once during some previous period of time. We model Been-In-State and Was-In-State constraints by introducing additional variables that record the number of

Table 3. Priorities and flags for Care-O-bot behaviours

Name	Pri	Int	Sch	Name	Pri	Int	Sch
S1-Med-5PM-Reset	90	0	1	S1-gotoTable	40	1	1
checkBell	80	0	1	S1-kitchenAwaitCmd	40	1	1
unCheckBell	80	0	1	Sw-sofaAwaitCmd	40	1	1
S1-remindFridgeDoor	80	0	1	S1-tableAwaitCmd	40	1	1
answerDoorBell	70	0	1	S1-WaitHere	40	1	1
S1-alertFridgeDoor	60	0	1	S1-ReturnHome	40	1	1
S1-Med5PM	50	1	1	S1-continueWatchTV	35	1	1
S1-Med5PM-Remind	50	1	1	S1-watchTV	30	1	1
S1-gotoKitchen	40	1	1	S1-sleep	10	1	1
S1-gotoSofa	40	1	1				

transitions of the model since a variable last had a value other than ν or since a variable last had the value ν respectively. We associate with each state of the model some fixed length of time in seconds (duration), and this determines the number of values over which these additional variables range. The software has a parameter determining the granularity of these temporal aspects of the model.

6   Results and Discussion

We focus on the complete set of 31 behaviours developed as part of the EU Accompany project[2] and available from the project's Git repository[3]. The priority (Pri), interruptibility (Int), and schedulability (Sch) of the 19 schedulable behaviours is given in Table 3. There were also 12 unschedulable subroutines all with Pri, Int, and Sch set to 0. For every behaviour, and every action in those behaviours, we instantiated the corresponding properties specified in Sect. 4. The full specification for the system was the conjunction of all of these individually instantiated properties. All models generated using all behaviours with different sets of parameter input for CRutoN satisfied their corresponding specification.

Generated models can be used to check properties pertaining to specific behaviours and robot actions. We might, for instance, want to check whether a behaviour will eventually be scheduled, or if the robot will eventually perform some action, given the current state of the robot and environment. We validated our model by checking properties that were originally specified in [3]. For example, *"is it always the case that if the fridge door is open and the robot has not already alerted the user, then at some point in the future the robot will alert the user?"* We found that for all generated models the verification results matched those obtained by checking the properties in the manually constructed model.

Recall that CRutoN accepts parameters to allow modulation of the temporal granularity of the model, and associates a fixed length of time (duration) in seconds with every state in the formal model. Table 4 shows the effect of temporal granularity on the size of the models, and the time taken to perform model

---
[2] http://accompanyproject.eu.
[3] https://github.com/uh-adapsys/accompany.

Table 4. Model size and model checking times for different temporal granularities.

Seconds per state	600	500	400	300	200	100	50
States	2^{49}	2^{49}	2^{49}	2^{50}	2^{51}	2^{53}	2^{56}
Reachable states	2^{22}	2^{22}	2^{23}	2^{23}	2^{24}	2^{26}	2^{28}
Model build time(s)	11.94	12.08	13.17	15.13	20.43	39.43	108.64
Model checking time(s)	0.73	0.82	0.99	1.16	1.75	3.77	8.95

checking. The results correspond to the initial set of 31 behaviours. We generated models for 7 different durations for each state. The model checking times indicate the time taken to check the property $\Box((\text{scheduled} = \text{S1-alertFridgeDoor} \wedge \text{step} = \text{step}^1) \implies \Diamond(\text{scheduled} = \text{S1-alertFridgeDoor} \wedge \text{step} = \text{step}^9))$, which was *true* in each model as it is always the case that if the behaviour S1-alertFridgeDoor is executing its first action then is should eventually execute its last (9th) action, since the behaviour is not interruptible. Note that this sample property was arbitrarily selected, and checking this property serves only to illustrate the effect of temporal granularity on model size, and hence model checking times. The results show that we can use a sensible duration of time for each state and still perform model checking within a reasonable amount of time. Using shorter durations per state would result in larger models, and hence longer model checking times. We can therefore extrapolate a trade-off between the time taken to perform model checking, and the time that would be required to manually extend existing formal models to include new behaviours.

For all investigated durations the corresponding model generated using CRutoN contains more reachable states than the manually constructed model described in [3]. One reason for this difference is that in the manual construction a distinction between value assignments to internal variables of the robot and all other actions was made. Only the latter result in a new state, the former do not. Whilst CRutoN currently does not make such a distinction and any action results in a new state, we could differentiate between value assignments and other actions (see Table 2) to group sequences of value assignments into one state.

It is clear that our modelling of temporal aspects is not ideal. Time Constraints are either always satisfied, or always not satisfied, along a run of the model, since the time of day is fixed for each path. Alternatively, we could allow the time of day to be non-deterministically chosen in each state, and then constrain that choice in the properties. We also note that it is sometimes difficult to determine a sensible value for the duration of time associated with a single state of the formal model, since setting this value too low can result in large models in which it is infeasible to check properties within a realistic amount of time, and setting this value to be too high results in unrealistic models where many of the constraints imposed by Been-In-State and Was-In-State conditions are not included in the model as the durations of time to which they refer are too small.

We also applied our automatic transformations to an extended set of Care-O-bot behaviours provided by the development team working with the robot. The original set of 31 behaviours with 156 control rules was extended to 88 behaviours with 324 control rules. Some rules had new syntactic forms, however the expressiveness of the Grammar Rules and Data Extraction Rules allowed the software to parse all control rules, and automatically generate a formal NuSMV model that satisfied its specification.

7   Conclusion

We have described a translation from a set of control rules defining the behaviour of the Care-O-bot into both an intermediate form representation, and furthermore into input for the model checker NuSMV. We presented the software CRutoN that automates these translation processes. Formal models that satisfy their specifications are automatically generated for different sets of input parameters to the software, and the complexity of the generated models was evaluated with regards to the granularity of the temporal aspects. We aim to generalise our approach so that formal models could be automatically generated for other robot systems using similar rule constructs.

The generated intermediate form representation for a set of control rules could be used to develop further translations into input for other model checkers. We could, for instance, extend our models to incorporate uncertainty arising from faulty sensors or actuators, or the unpredictable behaviour of a human in the Robot House, and develop a translation into a probabilistic model checker. In Sect. 6 we discussed the limitations of our model with regards to the temporal aspects of robot behaviours. Translations into input for verification tools for real-time systems could be developed to refine our model of time.

Recent work in the robot house has allowed users to add their own behaviours, built upon existing primitives, via the 'TeachMe' system [14]. We have carried out a static analysis on the priorities and preconditions of newly added behaviours to advise users of potential problems. For example, the added behaviour will never be executed because an existing behaviour with a higher priority has a subset of the preconditions of the added behaviour. Evaluations have shown that users find this helpful when adding behaviours. The tool accomplishes this using an intermediate form representation of the behaviours generated by the CRutoN parser.

The analysis of scheduling issues arising from the prioritisation of behaviours could be complemented by formalising a set of properties relating to changes in the state of the robot and its environment resulting from robot actions, and automatically checking that these hold in generated models. Properties to be checked could include safety properties that would require the robot to never perform a specific action when in proximity to a human. A further issue that could be addressed is how counterexamples, generated when requisite properties fail to hold in the model, could be presented to a user in a comprehensible form.

References

1. Cimatti, A., Clarke, E., Giunchiglia, E., Giunchiglia, F., Pistore, M., Roveri, M., Sebastiani, R., Tacchella, A.: NuSMV 2: an OpenSource tool for symbolic model checking. In: Brinksma, E., Larsen, K.G. (eds.) CAV 2002. LNCS, vol. 2404, pp. 359–364. Springer, Heidelberg (2002). doi:10.1007/3-540-45657-0_29

2. Cowley, A., Taylor, C.J.: Towards language-based verification of robot behaviors. In: Proceedings of IROS 2011, pp. 4776–4782. IEEE (2011)
3. Dixon, C., Webster, M., Saunders, J., Fisher, M., Dautenhahn, K.: "The fridge door is open"–temporal verification of a robotic assistant's behaviours. In: Mistry, M., Leonardis, A., Witkowski, M., Melhuish, C. (eds.) TAROS 2014. LNCS, vol. 8717, pp. 97–108. Springer, Cham (2014). doi:10.1007/978-3-319-10401-0_9
4. Duque, I., Dautenhahn, K., Koay, K.L., Willcock, L., Christianson, B.: Knowledge-driven user activity recognition for a smart house? Development and validation of a generic and low-cost, resource-efficient system. In: Proceedings of ACHI 2013. IARIA XPS Press (2013)
5. Gainer, P.: Verification for a robotic assistant. Technical report, ULCS-17-003, Department of Computer Science, University of Liverpool, Liverpool, UK (2017)
6. Holzmann, G.J.: The SPIN Model Checker: Primer and Reference Manual. Addison-Wesley, Reading (2004)
7. ISO: Robots and robotic devices - safety requirements for personal care robots. ISO 13482: 2014, International Organization for Standardization, Geneva, Switzerland (2014)
8. Kouskoulas, Y., Renshaw, D., Platzer, A., Kazanzides, P.: Certifying the safe design of a virtual fixture control algorithm for a surgical robot. In: Proceedings of HSCC 2013, pp. 263–272. ACM (2013)
9. McMillan, K.L.: The SMV language. Technical report, Cadence Berkeley Labs (1999)
10. Mohammed, A., Stolzenburg, F., Furbach, U.: Multi-robot systems: modeling, specification, and model checking. INTECH Open Access Publisher (2010)
11. Quigley, M., Conley, K., Gerkey, B., Faust, J., Foote, T., Leibs, J., Wheeler, R., Ng, A.Y.: ROS: an open-source robot operating system. In: Proceedings of the ICRA Workshop on Open Source Software in Robotics (2009)
12. Reiser, U., Connette, C., Fischer, J., Kubacki, J., Bubeck, A., Weisshardt, F., Jacobs, T., Parlitz, C., Hägele, M., Verl, A.: Care-o-bot® 3: creating a product vision for service robot applications by integrating design and technology. In: Proceedings of IROS 2009, pp. 1992–1998. IEEE (2009)
13. Saunders, J., Burke, N., Koay, K.L., Dautenhahn, K.: A user friendly robot architecture for re-ablement and co-learning in a sensorised home. In: Proceedings of AAATE 2013, pp. 49–58. IOS Press (2013)
14. Saunders, J., Syrdal, D.S., Koay, K.L., Burke, N., Dautenhahn, K.: "Teach Me-Show Me"—end-user personalization of a smart home and companion robot. IEEE Trans. Hum.-Mach. Syst. 46(1), 27–40 (2016)
15. Sierhuis, M., Clancey, W.J.: Modeling and simulating work practice: a method for work systems design. IEEE Intell. Syst. 17(5), 32–41 (2002)
16. Stocker, R., Dennis, L., Dixon, C., Fisher, M.: Verifying Brahms human-robot teamwork models. In: Cerro, L.F., Herzig, A., Mengin, J. (eds.) JELIA 2012. LNCS (LNAI), vol. 7519, pp. 385–397. Springer, Heidelberg (2012). doi:10.1007/978-3-642-33353-8_30
17. Webster, M., Dixon, C., Fisher, M., Salem, M., Saunders, J., Koay, K.L., Dautenhahn, K., Saez-Pons, J.: Toward reliable autonomous robotic assistants through formal verification: a case study. IEEE Trans. Hum.-Mach. Syst. 46(2), 186–196 (2016)

Sampling-Based Reactive Motion Planning with Temporal Logic Constraints and Imperfect State Information

Felipe J. Montana[1](✉), Jun Liu[2], and Tony J. Dodd[1]

[1] Department of Automatic Control and Systems Engineering,
University of Sheffield, Sheffield, UK
{fjmontanagonzalez1,t.j.dodd}@sheffield.ac.uk
[2] Department of Applied Mathematics, University of Waterloo, Waterloo, Canada
j.liu@uwaterloo.ca

Abstract. This paper presents a method that allows mobile systems with uncertainty in motion and sensing to react to unknown environments while high-level specifications are satisfied. Although previous works have addressed the problem of synthesising controllers under uncertainty constraints and temporal logic specifications, reaction to dynamic environments has not been considered under this scenario. The method uses feedback-based information roadmaps (FIRMs) to break the curse of history associated with partially observable systems. A transition system is incrementally constructed based on the idea of FIRMs by adding nodes on the belief space. Then, a policy is found in the product Markov decision process created between the transition system and a Rabin automaton representing a linear temporal logic formula. The proposed solution allows the system to react to previously unknown elements in the environment. To achieve fast reaction time, a FIRM considering the probability of violating the specification in each transition is used to drive the system towards local targets or to avoid obstacles. The method is demonstrated with an illustrative example.

1 Introduction

Efficient motion planning with imperfect state information is a desirable ability of systems operating in uncertain and dynamic environments. In these cases the system cannot decide the best actions based on a single deterministic state. Instead, a probability distribution over all possible states, called belief, is considered. This problem can be mathematically modelled as a partially observable Markov decision process (POMDP). Although several methods have adapted discrete POMDPs to motion planning, they have, in general, poor scalability

---

Felipe J. Montana is supported by the Mexican National Council of Science and Technology (CONACyT). Jun Liu is supported in part by the Natural Sciences and Engineering Research Council (NSERC) of Canada and the Canada Research Chairs (CRC) program.

L. Petrucci et al. (Eds.): FMICS-AVoCS 2017, LNCS 10471, pp. 134–149, 2017.
DOI: 10.1007/978-3-319-67113-0_9

with the number of states. This is caused by two main sources of complexity: (i) the so-called curse of dimensionality, for a system with n states, the belief space is an $(n-1)$-dimensional continuous space; and (ii) the curse of history [16], the number of distinct action-observation histories grows exponentially with the planning horizon. To alleviate this problem, sampling-based methods have been proposed, e.g., [1,5,17]. In these works, the objective is usually to optimally drive the system from an initial to a final state. Nevertheless, more complex objectives are required in some applications. This necessity has motivated the use of formal methods to automatically synthesise controllers for mobile systems such that high-level specifications are satisfied. Due to well-developed techniques in model checking using temporal logic, these specifications are commonly defined by linear temporal logic (LTL) formulae for robotic applications.

Using model checking techniques, several methods have been developed to solve the problem of control synthesis for stochastic systems with perfect state information, e.g., [9,15]. However, only few solutions have been presented for stochastic systems with partially observable states. Wongpiromsarn et al. [21] propose a method to compute policies that maximise the probability of satisfying an LTL specification for partially known environments. They assume that the environment can be in one of several modes, which are modelled as Markov chains. Although the system does not know exactly which is the current mode of the environment at each time, all the possible environment models are known by the system. This is a limitation since in many applications these models are not available. The policies are computed using a parallel composition between an MDP modelling the system and the set of Markov chains. Vasile et al. [20] propose a specification language, called Gaussian Distribution Temporal Logic (GDTL), that permits including noise mitigation in the specification. The work uses the idea of information feedback roadmaps to break the curse of history.

In contrast to the solution proposed in this paper, the approaches above do not consider dynamic environments. To deal with changing environments, reactive controllers have been proposed. Fu et al. [8] solve a two-player partially observable game with an adversarial environment, where the actions of the environment cannot be seen by the system. Although the system has incomplete information about the environment, the solution is computed based on a strategy using complete information. To reach states where a control is defined, the system uses a series of sensing actions to reduce the uncertainty until such states are reached. Chatterjee et al. [6] present finite-state controllers as a solution to POMDPs with parity objectives. To reduce the complexity, a series of heuristics are designed to find the solution. A practical case based on the results in [6] is presented in [18]. In this work a quadrotor performs a surveillance task while avoiding a ground vehicle. The motion of the quadrotor is considered deterministic as opposed to the stochastic motion considered in this paper.

To the best knowledge of the authors, we address for the first time the problem of computing optimal policies for mobile systems with uncertainty in motion and state information which follow temporal logic specifications and operate in dynamic environments. Rather than reacting to an adversarial environment as presented above, in the proposed method, the system reacts to static local targets and obstacles found during the execution of a plan such that the probability of satisfying an LTL specifications is maximised. Our method is based on the work in [20]. However, our solution permits the reaction of the system to local targets and obstacles unknown during the offline computation of the policy. To break the curse of history, we use feedback-based information roadmaps (FIRMs) to create a transition system by sampling the state space of the system. Based on results in probabilistic model checking, we find an optimal solution to the problem by constructing a product MDP with the transition system and a Rabin automaton representing the LTL specification. In order to permit a fast reaction to the environment, a FIRM with edge's cost equal to the probability of violating the LTL specification is computed offline. This computation is possible due to the property that the cost of the edges of the FIRM are independent of each other. This FIRM is then used to drive the system from its current state to a sensed local target or to avoid obstacles while the probability of violating the specification is minimised. Hence, the main contribution of this paper is a sampling-based framework that permits systems with imperfect state information and motion uncertainty to react to detected obstacles and local targets in real-time while a LTL specification is satisfied.

The rest of the paper is organised as follows. Section 2 presents definitions of formalisms used in the rest of the paper and the problem formulation. Section 3 explains in detail the proposed method. Finally, a numerical example and conclusions are shown in Sects. 4 and 5, respectively.

2   Preliminaries and Problem Definition

2.1   System Model

This paper focuses on dynamic systems with motion and sensing uncertainty that evolve according to the following system model:

$$x_{k+1} = f(x_k, u_k, w_k), \tag{1}$$

where $x \in X \subseteq \mathbb{R}^{d_x}$ is the system state, $u \in U \subseteq \mathbb{R}^{d_u}$ is the control input and w_k is the process noise at time k. We consider w_k as a zero-mean Gaussian noise with covariance Q_k. In partially observable systems, the system state is observed according to an observation model:

$$z_k = h(x_k, v_k), \tag{2}$$

where $z_k \in Z \subset \mathbb{R}^{d_z}$ denotes the observation and v_k is a zero-mean Gaussian noise with covariance R_k at time k.

2.2   Belief Space

Since the state of the system is only partially known due to sensing uncertainty, the information available at each time k is a distribution over the set of possible states [16]:

$$b_k = Pr(x_k | z_k, u_{k-1}, z_{k-1}, \ldots, u_1, z_1, u_0, b_0). \tag{3}$$

This distribution, called belief, compresses the history of observations $z_{0:k}$ and control actions $u_{0:k-1}$ taken from time 0 to time k and $k-1$, respectively. The updated belief for an applied control u_k and received observation z_{k+1} is given by:

$$b_{k+1} = \frac{Pr(z_{k+1}|x_{k+1})}{Pr(z_{k+1}|b_k, u_k)} \int_X b_k Pr(x_{k+1}|x_k, u_k) dx_k, \tag{4}$$

In a Gaussian belief space $\mathbb{B}$, the belief is characterised by the mean $\hat{x}$ and covariance P, i.e., $b_k = (\hat{x}_k, P_k) \in X \times \mathbb{S}_+^{d_x \times d_x}$, where $\mathbb{S}_+^{d_x \times d_x}$ represents the set of all possible positive semi-definite matrices with $d_x \times d_x$ entries.

2.3   Linear Temporal Logic

We use LTL to express system properties or desired behaviours. These properties are represented by a set Π of atomic propositions that indicate whether a property is true or false. A labelling function $L : x \to 2^\Pi$ maps the system state x to the set Π. Let $\boldsymbol{x} = x_0 x_1 \dots$ be a sequence of states describing the behaviour of the system (1). A word $\omega = L(x_0)L(x_1)\dots$ expresses this behaviour in terms of the atomic propositions.

Syntax: The syntax of LTL over Π is defined as follows:

$$\varphi := \pi|\neg\varphi|\varphi_1 \vee \varphi_2|\varphi_1 \wedge \varphi_2| \bigcirc \varphi|\varphi_1 \mathcal{U} \varphi_2,$$

where $\pi \in \Pi$ is an atomic proposition; and $\neg$, $\vee$, $\wedge$, $\bigcirc$ and $\mathcal{U}$ represent the operators *negation, disjunction, conjunction, next* and *until*, respectively. The temporal operators *eventually* and *always* are defined as $\Diamond\pi = True\,\mathcal{U}\,\pi$ and $\Box\pi = \neg\Diamond\neg\pi$, respectively.

Semantics: The semantic of LTL formulae are defined with respect to infinite words over Π. Given an LTL specification φ, a sequence $\boldsymbol{x}$, and the satisfaction relation $\models$, we define the semantics inductively as follows: (i) $x_i \models \pi$ iff $\pi \in L(x_i)$; (ii) $x_i \models \varphi_1 \wedge \varphi_2$ iff $x_i \models \varphi_1$ and $x_i \models \varphi_2$; (iii) $x_i \models \varphi_1 \vee \varphi_2$ iff $x_i \models \varphi_1$ or $x_i \models \varphi_2$; (iv) $x_i \models \bigcirc\varphi$ iff $x_{i+1} \models \varphi$; and (v) $x_i \models \varphi_1 \mathcal{U} \varphi_2$ iff $\exists j \geq i : x_j \models \varphi_2$ and $x_k \models \varphi_1, \forall i \leq k < j$.

2.4   Deterministic Rabin Automaton

An LTL specification can be represented by a deterministic Rabin automaton (DRA), which accepts only words ω that satisfy the specification. A DRA $\mathscr{R}$ is a tuple $\mathscr{R} = (\Sigma, Q, q_0, \delta_\mathscr{R}, F)$, where: $\Sigma = 2^\Pi$ is a finite alphabet, Q is a finite set of states, $q_0 \in Q$ is an initial state, $\delta_\mathscr{R} : Q \times \Sigma \to Q$ is a transition function and $F = \{(L_1, K_1), \dots, (L_r, K_r)\}$ is a set of pairs where $L_i, K_i \subseteq Q$ for all $i \in \{1, \dots, r\}$.

A run on $\mathscr{R}$, produced by a word ω over the alphabet Σ, is a sequence $\rho = q_0 q_1 \dots$ such that for every $i \geq 0$, there exists $\pi_i \in \Sigma$ and $\delta_\mathscr{R}(q_i, \pi_i) = q_{i+1}$. A run ρ is accepting if for a pair $(L_i, K_i) \in F$, the set L_i is intersected finitely many times while the set K_i is intersected infinitely many times. Figure 1 shows an example of a Rabin automaton.

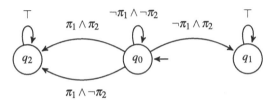

Fig. 1. Rabin automaton of LTL formula $\varphi = \neg\pi_2 \mathscr{U} \pi_1$, where $\pi_1, \pi_2 \in \Sigma$ are atomic propositions and $\mathscr{U}$ is the operator *until*. The formula indicates that the atomic proposition π_2 has to be avoided until π_1 is satisfied. The set F is formed by the pair $L = \{q_1\}$ and $K = \{q_2\}$. The arrow points to the initial state and $\top$ is unconditionally true.

2.5   Problem Formulation

Consider as an example a robot moving objects in a dynamically changing warehouse with two areas of interest, denoted by the atomic propositions π_1 and π_2, respectively. Using LTL, relevant behaviours can be specified. For example, the reachability formula $\Diamond\pi_1 \wedge \Diamond\pi_2$ can be used to indicate that the robot needs to eventually move an object to the areas π_1 and π_2. Safety formulae, e.g. $\Box\neg\pi_2$, indicates that certain properties remain invariant throughout the execution. In this work, we find a sequence of control inputs that maximises the probability of satisfying an LTL formula φ. Moreover, since the environment is dynamic, new local targets, e.g. objects in the warehouse, or obstacles can appear during the operation of the robot. Therefore, in addition to following the behaviour defined by φ, we allow the system to react to sensed local targets and obstacles in the environment while the probability of violating φ is minimised.

The labelling function L is used to identify the satisfaction of atomic propositions at each time k. That is, $L(x_k) = \pi_i$ if the system is in the region defined by π_i at time k. By labelling the system state at each time k, a word ω expressing the behaviour of the system in terms of the atomic propositions Π is obtained. Based on the definition of a Rabin automaton, a run $\boldsymbol{x} = x_0 x_1 \ldots$ of the system satisfies the specification φ if the word $\omega = L(x_0)L(x_1)\ldots$ is accepted by the Rabin automaton representing φ. Since the state is unknown in partially observable systems, instead of considering the state of the system to verify the satisfaction of the specification, we consider all the possible words generated during the transition between beliefs as presented in the next section. Now, we formally define the problem as follows.

Problem definition: Given a dynamic system with motion and sensing uncertainty of the form (1) and (2); and an LTL formula φ, compute a policy $\mu : \mathbb{B} \to U$ such that the probability of satisfying φ is maximised.

3   Solution

In this section, an overview of the proposed method is firstly presented followed by a detailed presentation. The main idea is to create a graph that represents the motion of the system in the environment. In this graph, vertices represent belief nodes and edges represent controllers that drive the system from one belief node to another, Fig. 2. The graph is initialised with a single vertex, the initial belief of the system. Then, the graph is incrementally expanded by adding a new vertex that represents a new belief created by randomly sampling the state space of the system. After each expansion, it is verified whether there is a path such that the LTL specification is satisfied. If such a path does not exist, a new belief is added to the graph and the process is repeated until a path is found. Section 3.1 presents the computation of belief nodes and controllers. The expansion of the graph and the search of a path that satisfies the specification are explained in Sects. 3.2, 3.3 and 3.4. Because a dynamically changing environment is considered, the system must be able to react to local targets and obstacles. To allow fast reaction time to sensed objects, we precompute another graph, called FIRM, assigning to each edge, as the cost, the probability of violating the LTL specification in the transition. This FIRM is used to guide the system to the local targets or to avoid obstacles while the probability of violating the LTL specification is minimised, see Sects. 3.5 and 3.6.

3.1 Feedback-Based Information Roadmap

The main difficulty of solving POMDPs is the so-called curse of dimensionality. To alleviate this problem, we use feedback-based information roadmaps (FIRMs) [1]. FIRMs generalise probabilistic roadmaps (PRMs) [12] to account for motion and sensing uncertainty. In most of the works considering PRM-based methods and imperfect state information, each edge of the graph depends on the path traveled by the system, i.e., actions and observations taken from the initial belief, and therefore recalculation is necessary when the initial belief changes. In contrast, in a FIRM, each edge is independent of the others as a consequence of feedback controllers used to guarantee the convergency of the belief to predefined belief nodes. We exploit this property to perform most of the computation offline.

Without loss of generality, we use SLQG-FIRMs [1], where stationary linear quadratic Gaussian (SLQG) controllers are used as belief stabilisers. Any other type of controller can be used provided that the reachability of a belief is guaranteed. To construct a FIRM, a PRM is first constructed by sampling the state space of the system. Let $G = (V, E)$ represent the PRM, where V is the set of vertices (sampled states) $\nu \in X$ and E is the set of edges connecting the elements of V. Each node ν of the PRM is used to create a FIRM node as follows. First the system model (1) and observation model (2) are linearised with respect to a node ν resulting in the linear models:

$$x_{k+1} = A_\nu x_k + B_\nu u_k + w_k, \tag{5}$$

$$z_{k+1} = H_\nu x_k + v_k, \tag{6}$$

where $A_\nu \in \mathbb{R}^{d_x \times d_x}$, $B_\nu \in \mathbb{R}^{d_x \times d_u}$ and $H_\nu \in \mathbb{R}^{d_z \times d_x}$ are obtained through Jacobian linearisation.

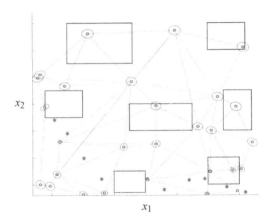

Fig. 2. FIRM created using a PRM on an environment in which the vertices represent the position (x_1, x_2) of the system. The grey rectangles and red stars are areas of interest and landmarks respectively. The landmarks are used by the system to localise itself. Hence, the uncertainty on the system state increases with the distance to the landmarks. The centre $b_\nu = (\nu, P_\nu)$ of the FIRM nodes is represented with a white disk and the 3σ ellipse (region where the true value lies with a probability of .988) of the associated covariances. The blue area around ν denotes the part of the node corresponding to the mean $\hat{x}$, i.e., $\{\hat{x} : \|\hat{x} - v\| < \varepsilon\}$, where ε is a constant. (Color figure online)

A SLQG controller is designed to maintain the system state x as close as possible to ν while a Kalman filter is used to estimate the belief. Under the assumption that the pairs (A, B) and (A, H) are controllable and observable, respectively, the SLQG controller stabilises the system to an expected belief $b_\nu = (\nu, P_\nu)$, where the covariance P_ν can be determined offline for each node ν [1]. Hence, a belief node is defined as $\mathfrak{b} = \{b : \|b - b_\nu\|_\mathfrak{b} < \varepsilon\}$, where $\|\cdot\|_\mathfrak{b}$ is a suitable norm in $\mathbb{B}$ and ε determines the size of the belief node. Each node is associated with its SLQG controller, denoted by $\mu_\mathfrak{b}$, as belief stabiliser. The edges in E of the PRM are used to design time-varying LQG controllers that drive the system to the proximity of the FIRM nodes where the stabilisers can maintain the system within the nodes. Therefore, an edge between two FIRM nodes $\mathfrak{b}$ and $\mathfrak{b}'$ is formed by the combination of the time-varying LQG and the stabiliser controller and is denoted by $\mu_{\mathfrak{b},\mathfrak{b}'}$. A FIRM can be presented as a graph $\mathcal{G} = (\mathcal{B}, \mathcal{E})$, where $\mathcal{B}$ is the set of FIRM nodes and $\mathcal{E}$ is the set of controllers used as edges, Fig. 2.

In the next subsection, we use the procedure for creating FIRM nodes and controllers to incrementally construct a transition system on which a path satisfying the LTL specification is sought.

Algorithm 1. Transition system expansion

1: $\mathcal{B}_{\mathcal{T}} \leftarrow b_0$
2: **while** φ not satisfied **do**
3:    $\mathcal{X} \leftarrow X, i \leftarrow 1$
4:    Get a new sample state $\nu_{\text{sample}} \in X$
5:    Create node $b_{\mathcal{T}}^{\text{new}}$ with centre $b_\nu = (\nu_{\text{sample}}, P_\nu)$
6:    **while** $\mathcal{B}_{\mathcal{T}} \cap \mathcal{X} \neq \emptyset$ **do**
7:       Find closest node $b_{\mathcal{T}}^{\text{near},i} \in \mathcal{B}$ to $b_{\mathcal{T}}^{\text{new}}$ such that $b_{\mathcal{T}}^{\text{near},i} \cap \mathcal{X}$
8:       $i \leftarrow i + 1$
9:       $\mathcal{X} \leftarrow \mathcal{X} \setminus H$, where H is the half-space containing $b_{\mathcal{T}}^{\text{near},i}$ but not $b_{\mathcal{T}}^{\text{new}}$
10:   $\mathcal{B}_{\mathcal{T}} \leftarrow \mathcal{B}_{\mathcal{T}} \cup b_{\mathcal{T}}^{\text{new}}$
11:   $\delta_{\mathcal{T}} \leftarrow \delta_{\mathcal{T}} \cup \mu_{b_{\mathcal{T}}^{\text{new}}, b_{\mathcal{T}}^{\text{near},j}} \cup \mu_{b_{\mathcal{T}}^{\text{near},j}, b_{\mathcal{T}}^{\text{new}}} \forall j \in \{1, \dots, i\}$

3.2   Incremental Transition System

Recall that using feedback controllers that guarantee the convergency of the belief to predefined belief nodes, the curse of dimensionality can be broken. Hence, we use the idea of FIRMs to create a transition system with the same property. In this subsection, an incremental construction of such a transition system is presented. A transition system is a tuple $\mathcal{T} = (\mathcal{B}_{\mathcal{T}}, b_0, \delta_{\mathcal{T}})$, where $\mathcal{B}_{\mathcal{T}}$ is a finite set of nodes $b_{\mathcal{T}}$, $b_0 \in \mathcal{B}_{\mathcal{T}}$ is an initial node and $\delta_{\mathcal{T}} \subseteq b_{\mathcal{T}} \times b'_{\mathcal{T}}$ is a transition relation.

Because the complexity of the problem depends on the number of nodes in the transition, the transition system is incrementally expanded by adding new nodes until the specification is satisfied. The transition system is constructed based on the idea of Rapidly-exploring Random Graphs (RRGs) [11] to allow satisfying words of infinite length and is constructed as follows, see Alg. 1. Initially, the transition system $\mathcal{T}$ includes only the initial node b_0 which contains the initial belief of the system. To add a new node, a state $\nu_{\text{sample}} \in X$ is sampled from the state space. This state is used to compute the FIRM node $b_{\mathcal{T}}^{\text{new}}$ including a belief stabiliser as presented in Sect. 3.1. Then, the closest node $b_{\mathcal{T}}^{\text{near}}$ in $\mathcal{B}_{\mathcal{T}}$ is sought. This process is repeated considering, in each iteration, the nearest nodes in $\mathcal{B}_{\mathcal{T}}$ in the half-space containing ν_{sample} but not the previously considered nearest nodes $b_{\mathcal{T}}^{\text{near}}$. Once no more nodes are available, the new node $b_{\mathcal{T}}^{\text{new}}$ is added to $\mathcal{T}$ with the transitions $(b_{\mathcal{T}}^{\text{new}}, b_{\mathcal{T}}^{\text{near},i})$ and $(b_{\mathcal{T}}^{\text{near},i}, b_{\mathcal{T}}^{\text{new}})$, where i is the index of the nearest nodes found in the process described above. For each transition $(b_{\mathcal{T}}, b'_{\mathcal{T}}) \in \delta_{\mathcal{T}}$, the edge controller $\mu_{b_{\mathcal{T}}, b'_{\mathcal{T}}}$ is computed. This process continues until a path that satisfies the LTL specification is found, see Sect. 3.4.

In order to reduce the number of nodes in $\mathcal{T}$ and at the same time cover most of the workspace, a coarse partition is computed over the workspace. A segment of partition is randomly selected based on the number of samples associated with this segment. Then, a state is sampled uniformly such that $\Gamma(\nu_{\text{sample}})$ is constrained by the selected segment, where $\Gamma : X \rightarrow \mathbb{R}^{d_r}$ is the projection of the system state to the workspace.

Based on results from probabilistic verification [3], the product MDP of the transition system $\mathscr{T}$ and the Rabin automaton representing the LTL specification is computed and used to find a path such that the LTL specification is satisfied. The computation of this product MDP is presented in the next subsection.

3.3   Product MDP

A product MDP $\mathscr{P} = \mathscr{T} \times \mathscr{R}$ is a tuple $\mathscr{P} = (S, s_0, A, P, F_{\mathscr{P}})$, where: $S = \mathscr{B}_{\mathscr{T}} \times Q$ is a finite set of states, $s_0 = (\mathfrak{b}_0, q_0)$ is an initial state, A is a finite set of actions, $P(\cdot|\cdot, \cdot) : S \times S \times A \to [0, 1]$ is the probability of transitioning to the state s' from the state s under action $a \in A$ and $F_{\mathscr{P}} = \{(L_1^{\mathscr{P}}, K_1^{\mathscr{P}}), \dots, (L_r^{\mathscr{P}}, K_r^{\mathscr{P}})\}$, where $L_i^{\mathscr{P}} = \mathscr{B}_{\mathscr{T}} \times L_i$ and $K_i^{\mathscr{P}} = \mathscr{B}_{\mathscr{T}} \times K_i$ for all $i \in \{1, \dots, r\}$.

A run on $\mathscr{P}$ is defined as a sequence $\rho_{\mathscr{P}} = s_0 s_1 \dots$, where $P(s_{i+1}|s_i, a) > 0$ for all $i \ge 0$. The set of actions A corresponds to the computed controllers associated with each transition in $\mathscr{T}$. Therefore, the set of actions available at state $s = (\mathfrak{b}_{\mathscr{T}}, q)$, denoted as $A(s)$, are the controllers computed for the transitions $(\mathfrak{b}_{\mathscr{T}}, \mathfrak{b}'_{\mathscr{T}}) \in \delta_{\mathscr{T}}$. The probability $P(s'|s, \mu_{\mathfrak{b}_{\mathscr{T}}, \mathfrak{b}'_{\mathscr{T}}})$, where $s = (\mathfrak{b}_{\mathscr{T}}, q)$ and $s' = (\mathfrak{b}'_{\mathscr{T}}, q')$, is the probability of ending on the DRA state q' starting from q when the transition $(\mathfrak{b}_{\mathscr{T}}, \mathfrak{b}'_{\mathscr{T}}) \in \delta_{\mathscr{T}}$ is performed using the control $\mu_{\mathfrak{b}, \mathfrak{b}'} \in A(s)$.

Let $\boldsymbol{b} = b_0 b_1 \dots b_n$ be the sequence of beliefs followed after applying $\mu_{\mathfrak{b}_{\mathscr{T}}, \mathfrak{b}'_{\mathscr{T}}}$, such that $b_0 \in \mathfrak{b}_{\mathscr{T}}$ and $b_n \in \mathfrak{b}'_{\mathscr{T}}$. To find the DRA state q' reached in $\mathscr{R}$ after the transition $(\mathfrak{b}_{\mathscr{T}}, \mathfrak{b}'_{\mathscr{T}}) \in \delta_{\mathscr{T}}$, the word ω produced by $\boldsymbol{b}$ is used as an input word in the DRA $\mathscr{R}$, starting from the state $q \in Q$. The last state of the run ρ on $\mathscr{R}$, produced by ω, is used as a state q' for the transition $s = (\mathfrak{b}_{\mathscr{T}}, q)$ to $s' = (\mathfrak{b}'_{\mathscr{T}}, q')$. As an example, consider the initial state q_0 of the Rabin automaton in Fig. 1 and assume that during the transition $(\mathfrak{b}_{\mathscr{T}}, \mathfrak{b}'_{\mathscr{T}})$ in $\mathscr{T}$ the words $\omega_1 = \{\neg \pi_1 \neg \pi_2\}\{\neg \pi_1 \neg \pi_2\}\{\pi_1\}$ and $\omega_2 = \{\neg \pi_1 \neg \pi_2\}\{\neg \pi_1 \neg \pi_2\}\{\pi_2\}$ are generated with probability 0.90 and 0.10, respectively. Therefore, the probability of transitioning from state $(\mathfrak{b}_{\mathscr{T}}, q_0)$ to $(\mathfrak{b}'_{\mathscr{T}}, q_2)$ is 0.90 and to $(\mathfrak{b}'_{\mathscr{T}}, q_1)$ is 0.10.

Recall that a specification is satisfied by the system if the word ω produces a run on $\mathscr{R}$ such that it visits finitely often times the set L_i and infinitely many times the set K_i, for $i \in \{1, \dots, r\}$. Because during the transition s to s' in $\mathscr{P}$, more than one DRA state can be reached, in order to find a run on $\mathscr{P}$ satisfying a specification, each transition in $\mathscr{P}$ is associated with a probability of visiting a state in a pair $(L_i, K_i) \in F$. These probabilities are denoted as $P_{s,s'}^{L_i}$ and $P_{s,s'}^{K_i}$, respectively.

Computing probabilities of transitioning from s to $s' \in S$ is computationally expensive [1]. In this work, we approximate them using particle-based methods. The probability $P((\mathfrak{b}'_{\mathscr{T}}, q')|(\mathfrak{b}_{\mathscr{T}}, q), \mu_{\mathfrak{b}_{\mathscr{T}}, \mathfrak{b}'_{\mathscr{T}}})$ is computed based on the number of particles that produced a word ω, during the transition $\mathfrak{b}_{\mathscr{T}}$ to $\mathfrak{b}'_{\mathscr{T}}$ under $\mu_{\mathfrak{b}_{\mathscr{T}}, \mathfrak{b}'_{\mathscr{T}}}$ and starting from q, finishing in q'. A similar procedure is used to calculate the probability of intersecting the pairs $(L_i, K_i) \in F$ during the transition from s to s'.

The product MDP $\mathscr{P}$ is updated with each new node $\mathfrak{b}_{\mathscr{T}}^{\text{new}}$ added to $\mathscr{T}$. After each update, it is checked whether the LTL specification can be satisfied. In the next subsection, the computation of a policy $\mu_{\mathscr{P}} : S \to A$ in $\mathscr{P}$ that satisfies the LTL specification is presented. Using $\mu_{\mathscr{P}}$, a policy $\mu : \mathbb{B} \to U$ that solves the formulated problem is finally obtained.

3.4   Optimal Policy Computation

This subsection presents the calculation of the policy that maximises the probability of satisfying a LTL specification φ. A run $\rho_{\mathscr{P}} = s_0 s_1 \ldots$ on $\mathscr{P}$ is accepting if there exists a pair $(L_i^{\mathscr{P}}, K_i^{\mathscr{P}}) \in F_{\mathscr{P}}$ such that $L_i^{\mathscr{P}}$ and $K_i^{\mathscr{P}}$ are visited finitely and infinitely many times, respectively. Thus, we define an accepting end component (AEC) as follows. An AEC of $\mathscr{P}$ for a pair $(L_i^{\mathscr{P}}, K_i^{\mathscr{P}}) \in F_{\mathscr{P}}$ is a subgraph of $\mathscr{P}$ where each state is reachable from every other state, $P_{s,s'}^{L_i} = 0$ for all transitions and there exists a transition with $P_{s,s'}^{K_i} > 0$. After each increment of the transition system $\mathscr{T}$, the existence of an AEC is checked. Once an AEC is found, an optimal policy is computed.

It has been shown in probabilistic model checking that maximising the probability of reaching an AEC is equivalent to maximising the probability of satisfying φ [3]. A policy $\mu_{\mathscr{P}}(s)$ on $\mathscr{P}$, where $s = (\flat_{\mathscr{T}}, q)$, induces a policy $\mu(\flat_{\mathscr{T}})$ on $\mathscr{T}$ by defining $\mu(\flat_{\mathscr{T}}) = \mu_{\mathscr{P}}(s)$. Hence, computing a policy on $\mathscr{P}$ that maximises the probability of reaching an AEC is equivalent to finding a policy on $\mathscr{T}$ that maximises the probability of satisfying the LTL specification. We use value iteration to compute the optimal policy by maximising the value function:

$$V(s) = \max_{a \in A(s)} \sum_{s' \in S} P(s'|s, a) V(s'), \tag{7}$$

$$\mu_{\mathscr{P}}(s) = \arg\max_{a \in A(s)} \sum_{s' \in S} P(s'|s, a) V(s'), \tag{8}$$

for all $s \notin$ AEC and $V(s) = 1$ for all $s \in$ AEC.

Since the product MDP is updated with each addition of nodes to $\mathscr{T}$, the end components of $\mathscr{P}$ must be maintained after each update. The complexity of maintaining the end components on $\mathscr{P}$ is $O(|F||S|^{\frac{3}{2}})$ [20], where the number of states in S is $|\mathscr{B}_{\mathscr{T}}| \times |Q|$. On the other hand, the running time of each iteration to find the optimal policy is $O(|S||A|^2)$ [14].

3.5   Local Targets

Approximating the probability of each transition on $\mathscr{P}$ using particle-based methods is in general a slow process [1,20]. The construction and computation of a policy for $\mathscr{T}$ is computed offline and hence this slow task can be tolerated. Nevertheless, for fast reactions to targets or obstacles sensed in real-time, this long time is restrictive. To solve this problem, an offline computation of a FIRM is performed. In addition to permitting reactions in a short period of time, PRM-like structures such as FIRM can present better performance than methods using RRG techniques on difficult scenarios [10].

To maximise the coverage of the workspace and to obtain a dynamic FIRM (see Sect. 3.6), an offline partition of the environment is first created. In our method we used a grid-based partition. Then, the process of selecting and sampling in cells is performed similar to the process presented in Sect. 3.2. After a minimum number of samples on each cell are obtained, a FIRM $\mathcal{G} = (\mathcal{B}, \mathcal{E})$ is created as presented in Sect. 3.1.

When a local target is sensed by the system at time k, the FIRM is used to drive the system from its current belief b_k to a predefined service region of the local target while the specification is satisfied. To use the transition system and the FIRM, three aspects have to be considered: (i) the connection of the current belief to a node in FIRM; (ii) the optimal path in the FIRM; and (iii) the reconnection to $\mathcal{T}$ after the local target has been attended. This procedure is presented in Algorithm 2.

Algorithm 2. Path to local target

1: $\mathcal{G}' = (\mathcal{B}', \mathcal{E}')$, where $\mathcal{B}' = \{b | b \in \mathcal{B}, \|\Gamma_b(b) - \Gamma_b(b_k)\| \leq r\}$, $\Gamma_b : \mathbb{B} \to \Gamma(\hat{x})$ and $\mathcal{E}' \subset \mathcal{E}$
2: $b_{\text{near}} \leftarrow \text{Nearest}(b_k, \mathcal{B}')$, $b_{\text{target}} \leftarrow \text{Nearest}(target, \mathcal{B}')$
3: Apply $\mu_{b_{\text{near}}}$
4: $path \leftarrow \text{OptimalPath}(b_{\text{near}}, b_{\text{target}})$
5: Follow $path$ applying edge controllers in $\mathcal{E}'$
6: $b_{\text{close}} \leftarrow \text{Nearest}(b_{\mathcal{T}}, \mathcal{B}')$, where $b_{\mathcal{T}} \in \mathcal{B}_{\mathcal{T}}$ and $V(s) > 0$ such that $s = (b_{\mathcal{T}}, q)$
7: $path \leftarrow \text{OptimalPath}(b_{\text{target}}, b_{\text{close}})$
8: Follow $path$ applying edge controllers in $\mathcal{E}'$
9: Apply $\mu_{b_{\mathcal{T}}}$

In the first step, when a local target is sensed by the system, a subgraph of the FIRM is created within the sensing area with radius r, Fig. 3(a). In this subgraph, the nearest FIRM node b_{near} to the current belief b_k is sought. Then, the local stabiliser of b_{near} is applied to drive the system to the FIRM node. Once the system is in the subgraph of the FIRM, an optimal path to the local target is computed. This path is optimal in terms of minimising the probability of violating the specification. To achieve this, it is necessary to verify which transitions of the FIRM do not violate the LTL specification. A similar problem has been solved in the literature for deterministic systems with perfect state information [2,19] using a monitor [4] which identifies if a specification has been satisfied or falsified as early as possible. In this work, since the state of the system is unknown, we use the Rabin automaton instead. Recall that in order to satisfy a specification, for a pair $(L_i, K_i) \in F$, the set L_i must be visited only finitely many times. Therefore, we calculate the probability of reaching states in L_i with a self transition, Fig. 1. Similar to the computation of $P_{s,s'}^{L_i}$ and $P_{s,s'}^{K_i}$ in $\mathcal{T}$, the probability of reaching such states starting in the Rabin state q during the transition from one node to another in the FIRM is computed during the FIRM construction. These probabilities are assigned as a weight on each transition on the FIRM. Since the probability of reaching a state L_i on a transition (b, b') depends on the DRA state q, the current DRA state is tracked all the time during the online operation. Because all the transitions are precomputed offline, the only computation online is a shortest path graph search on the subgraph using the weights according to the current DRA state q. This problem can be solved efficiently by methods such as Dijkstra's algorithm, which has a time complexity $O(|\mathscr{B}|^2)$ [7].

After the computed path is followed, the last FIRM node in the path has to be connected to the transition system $\mathscr{T}$ in order to continue with the specification. This is achieved by searching the closest node $\mathfrak{b}_{\mathscr{T}}$ in $\mathscr{T}$ such that $V(s) > 0$ and $s = (\mathfrak{b}_{\mathscr{T}}, q)$, where q is the current $\mathscr{R}$ state after following the path in the FIRM. Once this state has been found, the closest node $\mathfrak{b}_{\text{close}}$ of the FIRM to $\mathfrak{b}_{\mathscr{T}}$ is sought. Then, the path in the FIRM is computed between the current node and $\mathfrak{b}_{\text{close}}$. After following the path, the stabiliser of the node $\mathfrak{b}_{\mathscr{T}}$ is applied to make the connection.

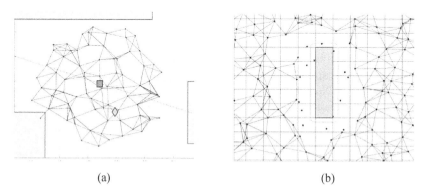

(a)   (b)

Fig. 3. FIRM used to drive the system close to local targets or to avoid obstacles. (a) Subgraph of the FIRM within the sensing area of the system. The offline path obtained by solving the product MDP $\mathscr{P}$ is shown as a blue dotted line. The current belief and local target are represented by a green rectangle and blue diamond, respectively. (b) Subgraph of the FIRM without transitions affected by the obstacle. The obstacle and estimated position of it are shown with a yellow and red rectangle, respectively. The cells (shown in blue) occupied by the obstacle determine the invalid nodes and transitions of the FIRM. (Color figure online)

3.6   Obstacle Avoidance

Similar to the local target case, the FIRM is used to avoid detected obstacles during the online operation. The main difference is that the presence of obstacles invalidates parts of the computed FIRM. Because edges of the FIRM are independent of each other, ideas from dynamic roadmaps [10,13] can be applied.

Recall that the environment is partitioned into cells. Each of these cells is associated with FIRM nodes and transitions as follows. During the computation of the probabilities from node $\mathfrak{b}$ to $\mathfrak{b}'$, see Sect. 3.5, the probability of visiting a cell c_i during a transition can be computed. Let $p_{0:T_k}^k$ be the sample path of the k-th particle p from $\mathfrak{b}$ at time zero to $\mathfrak{b}'$ at time T^k. The probability of the system reaching a state such that $\Gamma(x)$ is on the cell c_i during the transition from $\mathfrak{b}$ to $\mathfrak{b}'$ is approximated by:

$$Pr_{\mathfrak{b},\mathfrak{b}'}(c_i) \approx \sum_{k=1}^{K} w^k \mathbb{1}_{c_i}(p_{0:T_k}^k), \tag{9}$$

where w^k is a weight assigned to the particle p^k and $\mathbb{1}_{c_i}(\cdot)$ is an indicator that returns one, if a particle enters the cell c_i, and zero otherwise. Based on these probabilities, a cell is associated with the FIRM nodes $\mathfrak{b}, \mathfrak{b}'$ and its transition if $Pr_{\mathfrak{b},\mathfrak{b}'}(c_i) > 0$, Fig. 3(b).

When an obstacle is detected, the cells occupied by the obstacle are computed. Then, the nodes and transitions associated with these cells are invalidated from the FIRM. Since the current state of the system is uncertain, i.e., given by a mean and covariance over the belief space, the exact location of the obstacle cannot be determined by the system. To include the uncertainty on the obstacle's location, we compute the Minkowski sum of the detected obstacle and the contour of the 3σ ellipse of the current Gaussian. Assume that the system is transitioning between the nodes $\mathfrak{b}_{\mathscr{T}}$ and $\mathfrak{b}'_{\mathscr{T}}$ in $\mathscr{T}$ when an obstacle is detected. A subgraph of the FIRM is created within the sensing area as presented in Sect. 3.5. Note that this subgraph does not include any of the nodes affected by the estimation of the obstacle's location. In this subgraph, the closest node $\mathfrak{b}$ to the current belief b_k is sought. The stabiliser of $\mathfrak{b}$ is applied to drive the system to this node. Then, a path between $\mathfrak{b}$ and $\mathfrak{b}'$, the closest node to $\mathfrak{b}'_{\mathscr{T}}$, is computed using the weights as in the local target case. If, after applying the edge controllers of the computed path, the obstacle is still detected, a new subgraph is computed removing the invalid nodes. This process is repeated until the obstacle is not sensed. Then, the FIRM is connected to $\mathscr{T}$ as presented in Sect. 3.5. Algorithm 3 shows the procedure described above.

Algorithm 3. Obstacle avoidance

1: **while** obstacle detected **do**
2:     $obstacleposition \leftarrow$ EstimatedPosition($b_k, P_k, obstacle$)
3:     $C \leftarrow$ AffectedCells($obstacleposition$)
4:     $\mathscr{G}' = (\mathscr{B}', \mathscr{E}')$, where $\mathscr{B}' = \{\mathfrak{b}|\mathfrak{b} \in \mathscr{B}, \|\Gamma_b(b_k) - \Gamma_b(\mathfrak{b})\| \leq r\}$, $\Gamma_b : \mathbb{B} \rightarrow \Gamma(\hat{x})$,
5:     $\mathscr{E}' \subset \mathscr{E} \setminus \mathscr{E}''$ and $(\mathfrak{b}, \mathfrak{b}') \in \mathscr{E}''$ iff $\exists c \in C$ s.t. $Pr_{\mathfrak{b},\mathfrak{b}'}(c) > 0$
6:     $\mathfrak{b}_{near} \leftarrow$ Nearest($b_k, \mathscr{B}'$), $\mathfrak{b}_{target} \leftarrow$ Nearest($\mathfrak{b}'_{\mathscr{T}}, \mathscr{B}'$)
7:     $path \leftarrow$ OptimalPath($\mathfrak{b}_{near}, \mathfrak{b}_{target}$)
8:     Follow $path$ applying edge controllers in $\mathscr{E}'$
9: $\mathfrak{b}_{close} \leftarrow$ Nearest($\mathfrak{b}_{\mathscr{T}}, \mathscr{B}'$), where $\mathfrak{b}_{\mathscr{T}} \in \mathscr{B}_{\mathscr{T}}$ and $V(s) > 0$ such that $s = (\mathfrak{b}_{\mathscr{T}}, q)$
10: $path \leftarrow$ OptimalPath($\mathfrak{b}_{target}, \mathfrak{b}_{close}$)
11: Follow $path$ applying edge controllers in $\mathscr{E}'$
12: Apply $\mu_{\mathfrak{b}_{\mathscr{T}}}$

---

4   Example

In this section a numerical example is presented to illustrate the proposed method. We consider a robot in a workspace with 7 areas associated with the atomic propositions π_1, π_2, π_3 and π_4, Fig. 4. The mission of the robot is to visit the areas marked by the atomic proposition π_1, π_2 and π_3, in any order, while the areas marked with π_4 are avoided. Formally, this specification can be written as $\varphi = (\neg\pi_4\,\mathcal{U}\,\pi_1) \wedge (\neg\pi_4\,\mathcal{U}\,\pi_2) \wedge (\neg\pi_4\,\mathcal{U}\,\pi_3)$. The example is implemented in MATLAB on a computer with a 3.1 GHz i7 processor and 8 GB of RAM.

The three-wheel omnidirectional mobile robot model presented in [1] is considered. For this robot (1) becomes:

$$f = \begin{pmatrix} -\frac{2}{3}\sin(\theta) & -\frac{2}{3}\sin(\frac{\pi}{3} - \theta) & \frac{2}{3}\sin(\frac{\pi}{3} + \theta) \\ \frac{2}{3}\cos(\theta) & -\frac{2}{3}\cos(\frac{\pi}{3} - \theta) & -\frac{2}{3}\cos(\frac{\pi}{3} + \theta) \\ \frac{1}{3l} & \frac{1}{3l} & \frac{1}{3l} \end{pmatrix} u + w. \tag{10}$$

The state $x = [x_1, x_2, \theta]^T$ is composed of the robot position (x_1, x_2) and the orientation θ. The control input $u = [u_1, u_2, u_3]^T$ is formed of the linear velocities of each wheel. The distance of the wheels from the centre of the robot is denoted by l. The process noise w is a zero-mean Gaussian with covariance Q.

The robot uses landmarks, with known location on the workspace, to localise itself, Fig. 4. Let (LM_1^i, LM_2^i) denote the location of the i-th landmark; and η_r, σ_b^r, η_θ and σ_b^θ be constants. The observation model (2) with respect to the i-th landmark is expressed as:

$$z^i = [\|d^i\|, \operatorname{atan2}(d_2^i, d_1^i) - \theta]^T + v^i, \tag{11}$$

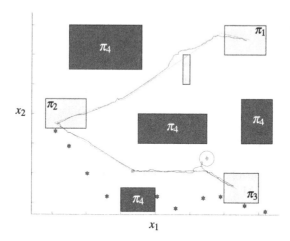

Fig. 4. Environment containing seven areas identified by the atomic proposition π_1, π_2, π_3 and π_4; a local target (blue diamond) with its service region (grey disk), an unknown obstacle (yellow rectangle) and ten landmarks (red stars). The objective of the robot is to visit the areas marked as π_1, π_2 and π_3 while areas π_4 have to be avoided. The grey line shows the path computed offline. The blue line shows a sample path of the system followed after detecting the local target and previously unknown obstacle. The initial position is marked by a red disk. (Color figure online)

where $d = [x_1, x_2] - [LM_1^i, LM_2^i]$ and v^i is zero-mean Gaussian noise with covariance R:

$$R^i = \text{diag}((\eta_r\|d^i\| + \sigma_b^r)^2, (\eta_\theta\|d^i\| + \sigma_b^\theta)^2). \tag{12}$$

The results presented below were obtained from 20 simulations, but for the purpose of clarity, only one run is presented in Fig. 4. In average (mean), the offline path is found in 82.46 s and the number of states in $\mathscr{T}$ and $\mathscr{P}$ are 31.61 and 284.5, respectively. The Rabin automaton $\mathscr{R}$ has 9 states and one pair (L, K) with $|L| = 1$ and $|K| = 1$. Computing the probability in each transition requires 0.536 s. The PRM used to create the FIRM has 1224 vertices, each vertex is connected to its seven nearest vertices. The FIRM requires on average 5022.61 s to be constructed. Since computing the probabilities for each edge of the FIRM is the most computationally demanding operation, the time to construct the FIRM could be reduced by limiting the number of edges on each vertex. Note that all the previous computations are performed offline. Finding a path in the FIRM, online, to reach the local target and to avoid the obstacle requires 0.097 and 0.698 s, respectively. Based on these results, it can be observed that computing a path in the FIRM to reach targets or avoid obstacles would require less time than expanding the transition system with the purpose of finding an alternative path.

5   Conclusions

In this paper we have introduced a new method to design control policies for mobile robots that can react to unknown environments under uncertainty in motion and sensing, while maximising the probability of satisfying high-level specifications. Although previous works have considered synthesis of controllers under uncertainty constraints and temporal logic specifications, reaction to unknown elements of the environment had not been considered under this scenario. An offline policy that maximises the probability of satisfying the specification is computed using an incrementally constructed transition system and a Rabin automaton. To achieve short reaction times, we precomputed a feedback-based information roadmap, considering the probability of violating the specification in each transition. Once the system finds an unknown element on the environment, the FIRM is used to reach or avoid this element. This task requires the connection of the current belief to the FIRM and the computation of a path that minimises the probability of violating the specification. Results show that using the FIRM requires less time than trying to find a path online by extending the transition system.

References

1. Agha-Mohammadi, A.A., Chakravorty, S., Amato, N.M.: FIRM: sampling-based feedback motion-planning under motion uncertainty and imperfect measurements. Int. J. Robot. Res. **33**(2), 268–304 (2014)

2. Ayala, A.M., Andersson, S.B., Belta, C.: Temporal logic motion planning in unknown environments. In: Proceedings of IROS, pp. 5279–5284. IEEE (2013)
3. Baier, C., Katoen, J.P.: Principles of Model Checking. MIT Press, Cambridge (2008)
4. Bauer, A., Leucker, M., Schallhart, C.: Runtime verification for LTL and TLTL. In: Proceedings of FSTTCS, vol. 20, pp. 1–68. ACM (2006)
5. Bry, A., Roy, N.: Rapidly-exploring random belief trees for motion planning under uncertainty. In: Proceedings of ICRA, pp. 723–730. IEEE (2011)
6. Chatterjee, K., Chmelík, M., Gupta, R., Kanodia, A.: Qualitative analysis of POMDPs with temporal logic specifications for robotics applications. In: Proceedings of ICRA, pp. 325–330. IEEE (2015)
7. Cormen, T.H.: Introduction to Algorithms. MIT press, Cambridge (2009)
8. Fu, J., Topcu, U.: Integrating active sensing into reactive synthesis with temporal logic constraints under partial observations. In: Proceedings of ACC, pp. 2408–2413. IEEE (2015)
9. Horowitz, M.B., Wolff, E.M., Murray, R.M.: A compositional approach to stochastic optimal control with co-safe temporal logic specifications. In: Proceedings of IROS, pp. 1466–1473. IEEE (2014)
10. Kallman, M., Mataric, M.: Motion planning using dynamic roadmaps. In: Proceedings of ICRA, vol. 5, pp. 4399–4404. IEEE (2004)
11. Karaman, S., Frazzoli, E.: Sampling-based motion planning with deterministic μ-calculus specifications. In: Proceedings of CDC/CCC, pp. 2222–2229. IEEE (2009)
12. Kavraki, L.E., Svestka, P., Latombe, J.C., Overmars, M.H.: Probabilistic roadmaps for path planning in high-dimensional configuration spaces. IEEE Trans. Robot. Autom. 12(4), 566–580 (1996)
13. Leven, P., Hutchinson, S.: Toward real-time path planning in changing environments. In: Algorithmic and Computational Robotics: New Directions, pp. 363–376. A K Peters (2000)
14. Littman, M.L., Dean, T.L., Kaelbling, L.P.: On the complexity of solvingMarkov decision problems. In: Proceedings of UAI, pp. 394–402. Morgan Kaufmann Publishers Inc. (1995)
15. Montana, F.J., Liu, J., Dodd, T.J.: Sampling-based stochastic optimal control with metric interval temporal logic specifications. In: Proceedings of CCA, pp. 767–773. IEEE (2016)
16. Pineau, J., Gordon, G., Thrun, S., et al.: Point-based value iteration: An anytime algorithm for POMDPs. In: Proceedings of IJCAI, vol. 3, pp. 1025–1032 (2003)
17. Prentice, S., Roy, N.: The belief roadmap: efficient planning in linear POMDPs by factoring the covariance. In: Kaneko, M., Nakamura, Y. (eds.) Robotics Research, pp. 293–305. Springer, Heidelberg (2010). doi:10.1007/978-3-642-14743-2_25
18. Svoreňová, M., Chmelík, M., Leahy, K., Eniser, H.F., Chatterjee, K., Černá, I., Belta, C.: Temporal logic motion planning using POMDPs with parity objectives: case study paper. In: Proceedings of HSCC, pp. 233–238. ACM (2015)
19. Vasile, C.I., Belta, C.: Reactive sampling-based temporal logic path planning. In: Proceedings of ICRA, pp. 4310–4315. IEEE (2014)
20. Vasile, C.I., Leahy, K., Cristofalo, E., Jones, A., Schwager, M., Belta, C.: Control in belief space with temporal logic specifications. In: Proceedings of CDC, pp. 7419–7424. IEEE (2016)
21. Wongpiromsarn, T., Frazzoli, E.: Control of probabilistic systems under dynamic, partially known environments with temporal logic specifications. In: Proceedings of CDC, pp. 7644–7651. IEEE (2012)

Sampling-Based Path Planning for Multi-robot Systems with Co-Safe Linear Temporal Logic Specifications

Felipe J. Montana[1(✉)], Jun Liu[2], and Tony J. Dodd[1]

[1] Department of Automatic Control and Systems Engineering,
University of Sheffield, Sheffield, UK
{fjmontanagonzalez1,t.j.dodd}@sheffield.ac.uk
[2] Department of Applied Mathematics, University of Waterloo, Waterloo, Canada
j.liu@uwaterloo.ca

Abstract. This paper addresses the problem of path planning for multiple robots under high-level specifications given as syntactically co-safe linear temporal logic formulae. Most of the existing solutions use the notion of abstraction to obtain a discrete transition system that simulates the dynamics of the robot. Nevertheless, these solutions have poor scalability with the dimension of the configuration space of the robots. For problems with a single robot, sampling-based methods have been presented as a solution to alleviate this limitation. The proposed solution extends the idea of sampling methods to the multiple robot case. The method samples the configuration space of the robots to incrementally constructs a transition system that models the motion of all the robots as a group. This transition system is then combined with a Büchi automaton, representing the specification, in a Cartesian product. The product is updated with each expansion of the transition system until a solution is found. We also present a new algorithm that improves the performance of the proposed method by guiding the expansion of the transition system. The method is demonstrated with examples considering different number of robots and specifications.

1 Introduction

Motion planning based on high-level temporal specifications has become an important area of research. Several methods have been developed for single robots, e.g., [5,15,18,22]; and for multiple robots, e.g., [2,6,19]. The multi-robot path planning problem with linear temporal logic (LTL) specifications can be categorised into two areas depending on the final goal: (i) each robot has its own task, or (ii) all the robots act as a team trying to accomplish a global specification. In general, to find a path that satisfies an LTL specification, most of

F.J. Montana is supported by the Mexican National Council of Science and Technology (CONACyT). Jun Liu is supported in part by the Natural Sciences and Engineering Research Council (NSERC) of Canada and the Canada Research Chairs (CRC) program.

© Springer International Publishing AG 2017
L. Petrucci et al. (Eds.): FMICS-AVoCS 2017, LNCS 10471, pp. 150–164, 2017.
DOI: 10.1007/978-3-319-67113-0_10

the methods use the notion of equivalent abstraction [1] to create a finite transition system that models the motion of the robot. Then, a product automaton is created using this transition system and a Büchi automaton that represents the LTL specification. In this product automaton, a graph search is performed to find a path satisfying the specification. When a single task has to be completed by all the robots, a parallel composition of the individual transition systems can be created to model the motion of all the robots as a group. Then, this composition is used to create a product automaton with the Büchi automaton as in the single robot case. Although this method can find a solution, it is computationally expensive and scales poorly with the number of robots [10].

To avoid the parallel composition, in [2], the authors present a method to decompose the global specification into local specifications. Then, individual strategies are computed for the robots. Using a similar approach, in [12], the problem of gathering information from an environment while the motion of the robots is constrained by a temporal logic specification is solved. Distributability has been also used to find robust paths when the travelling time of the robots is uncertain [20] and for nonholonomic robots [23]. Although these methods avoid the parallel composition by decomposing the specification, the approaches fail to find a solution, even if one exists, when the global specification is not distributable among the robots.

A common similarity of the works aforementioned is the assumption of a transition system obtained by the process of abstraction described above. A limitation of this approach is its complexity. They scale at least exponentially with the dimension of the configuration space of the robots [21]. Using sampling-based methods, this problem has been addressed by sampling the continuous configuration space and incrementally constructing a transition system until the specified task can be accomplished. In [8], the authors use an incremental model checking method to solve the problem when μ-calculus formulae are used to express the specifications. In [21], a method that uses a sparse sampling to reduce the number of states in the transition system is presented. These methods scale well since all the operations performed to find a path increment only with the number of samples. The previous methods only consider a single robot. For the multi-robot problem, in [7], a sampling-based method is used to create a tree that approximates the product automaton. This approximation permits to solve large problems, in terms of the number of states in the product automaton, that are not solvable considering the product automaton itself. Nevertheless, in contrast to the solution proposed in this paper, they sample states from a transition system representing regions of the environment and not from the configuration space of the robots.

In this paper we present a sampling-based method that explores the configuration space of a group of robots to find a path such that a global specification is satisfied. The proposed method explores an implicit representation of a composite roadmap that models the motion of all the robots as a group. During the exploration, a transition system is incrementally expanded by adding new states from individual roadmaps. With each expansion, the product automaton of the transition system and a Büchi automaton is updated. Although a solution can be found by naively exploring the composite roadmap, this process could require long time. To improve this time, we also present an algorithm that uses the Büchi automaton of the specification to guide the exploration of the composition. The main contribution of this paper is a novel method that combines a sampling-based method for multiple robots with a new algorithm that allows fast computation of solutions.

The rest of the paper is organised as follows. Preliminaries and a formal definition of the problem addressed are presented in Sect. 2. A detailed presentation of the proposed method is found in Sect. 3. The method is demonstrated with three examples in Sect. 4 and the conclusion is presented in Sect. 5.

2 Preliminaries and Problem Definition

2.1 Deterministic Transition System

A deterministic transition system is a tuple $\mathcal{T} = (S, s_0, \delta_{\mathcal{T}}, \Pi, L)$, where:

- S is a finite set of states,
- $s_0 \in S$ is an initial state,
- $\delta_{\mathcal{T}} \subseteq S \times S$ is a transition relation,
- Π is a finite set of atomic propositions,
- $L : S \to 2^{\Pi}$ is a labelling function.

A run on $\mathcal{T}$ is a sequence $\sigma = s_0 s_1 \ldots$ such that for every $i \geq 0$, $(s_i, s_{i+1}) \in \delta_{\mathcal{T}}$. The trace of a run σ, $\omega = L(s_0)L(s_1)\ldots$, is a word over the power set of Π that defines the atomic propositions that evaluate true in the states of the run.

2.2 Linear Temporal Logic

We use a segment of LTL, called syntactically co-safe LTL (sc-LTL) [11], to express the desired system behaviour. LTL formulae are built from atomic propositions $\pi \in \Pi$ that indicate whether a property of the system is true or false.

Syntax: The syntax of sc-LTL over Π is defined as follows:

$$\varphi := \pi \mid \neg\pi \mid \varphi_1 \vee \varphi_2 \mid \varphi_1 \wedge \varphi_2 \mid \bigcirc \varphi \mid \varphi_1 \mathcal{U} \varphi_2 \ ,$$

where $\pi \in \Pi$ is an atomic proposition, φ is a sc-LTL formula; and $\neg$, $\vee$, $\wedge$, $\bigcirc$ and $\mathcal{U}$ represent the operators *negation*, *disjunction*, *conjunction*, *next* and *until*, respectively. Other operators such as the temporal operator *eventually*, $\Diamond\pi = True\,\mathcal{U}\,\pi$, can be derived from the operators presented above.

Semantics: The semantics of LTL are defined over words ω. Given an LTL specification φ, a run $\sigma = s_i s_{i+1} \ldots$, and the satisfaction relation $\models$, the semantics are defined inductively as follows:

$$s_i \models \pi \text{ iff } \pi \in L(s_i),$$
$$s_i \models \varphi_1 \wedge \varphi_2 \text{ iff } s_i \models \varphi_1 \text{ and } s_i \models \varphi_2,$$
$$s_i \models \varphi_1 \vee \varphi_2 \text{ iff } s_i \models \varphi_1 \text{ or } s_i \models \varphi_2,$$
$$s_i \models \bigcirc\varphi \text{ iff } s_{i+1} \models \varphi,$$
$$s_i \models \varphi_1 \mathscr{U} \varphi_2 \text{ iff } \exists j \geq i : s_j \models \varphi_2 \text{ and } s_k \models \varphi_1, \forall i \leq k < j.$$

LTL formulae in positive normal form, where negations only occur in front of atomic propositions, and which only use the operators $\bigcirc$, $\mathscr{U}$ and $\Diamond$, are co-safe formulae [11].

2.3 Büchi Automaton

Given an LTL specification, it is possible to construct a Büchi automaton, which accepts only words ω that satisfy the specification. A Büchi automaton $\mathscr{B}$ is a tuple $\mathscr{B} = (\Sigma, Q, q_0, \delta_\mathscr{B}, Q_F)$, where:

- $\Sigma = 2^\Pi$ is a finite alphabet,
- Q is a finite set of states,
- $q_0 \in Q$ is an initial state,
- $\delta_\mathscr{B} : Q \times \Sigma \to Q$ is a transition function,
- $Q_F \subseteq Q$ is a set of accepting states.

A run on $\mathscr{B}$, produced by a word ω over the alphabet Σ, is a sequence $\rho = q_0 q_1 \ldots$ such that for every $i \geq 0$, there exists $\pi_i \in \Sigma$ and $\delta_\mathscr{B}(q_i, \pi_i) = q_{i+1}$. For sc-LTL formulae, an infinite word ω is accepted if it starts with a prefix such that the produced run ρ reaches the set Q_F of final states. An example of a specification and its Büchi automaton is shown in Fig. 1.

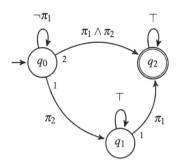

Fig. 1. Büchi automaton of formula $\varphi = (\neg\pi_1 \mathscr{U} \pi_2) \wedge \Diamond\pi_1$, where $\pi_1, \pi_2 \in \Sigma$ are atomic propositions, $\top$ is unconditionally true and $\mathscr{U}$, $\Diamond$ are the operator *until* and *eventually*, respectively. The formula indicates that the atomic propositions π_2 and π_1 have to be satisfied in that specific order or at the same time. The small numbers on the edges are used to identify each transition (see Sect. 3.4). The initial and final states, q_0 and q_2, are indicated with an arrow and a double circle, respectively.

Given a Büchi automaton $\mathscr{B} = (\Sigma, Q, q_0, \delta_{\mathscr{B}}, Q_F)$, let $|Q|$, $|q|$ and $AP(q, q')$ denote the cardinality of Q, the number non self-transitions from state q and the set of atomic propositions required for a transition from q to q', i.e., $AP(q, q') = \pi$ if $\delta_{\mathscr{B}}(q, \pi) = q'$.

2.4   Product Automaton

Given a transition system $\mathscr{T}$ and a Büchi automaton $\mathscr{B}$, the product automaton $\mathscr{P} = \mathscr{T} \times \mathscr{B}$ is defined by the tuple $\mathscr{P} = (S_{\mathscr{P}}, s_{\mathscr{P},0}, \delta_{\mathscr{P}}, S_{\mathscr{P},F})$, where:

- $S_{\mathscr{P}} = S \times Q$ is a finite set of states,
- $s_{\mathscr{P},0} = s_0 \times q_0$ is an initial state,
- $\delta_{\mathscr{P}} \subseteq S_{\mathscr{P}} \times S_{\mathscr{P}}$ is a transition relation, where $((s, q), (s', q')) \in \delta_{\mathscr{P}}$ iff $(s, s') \in \delta_{\mathscr{T}}$ and $\delta_{\mathscr{B}}(q, L(s')) = q'$,
- $S_{\mathscr{P},F} = S \times Q_F$ is a set of accepting states.

2.5   Problem Formulation

We consider R robots operating in a workspace containing obstacles and areas of interest, defined by disjoint regions, that are associated with atomic propositions. These atomic propositions are used to define sc-LTL formulae such as $\varphi_1 = \Diamond \pi_1$ or $\varphi_2 = \neg(\pi_1 \vee \pi_2)\,\mathscr{U}\,(\pi_1 \wedge \pi_2)$. Formula φ_1 indicates that a robot has to visit the area associated with the atomic proposition π_1 while the formula φ_2 indicates that the areas π_1 and π_2 cannot be visited until they are reached at the same time step. Let $X^i \subset \mathbb{R}^n$ be a compact set defining the configuration space of a robot i, where i is an element of the set $\Re = \{1, \ldots, R\}$ that indexes the robots and $\mathbb{R}^n$ is the n-dimensional Euclidean space. Each robot has an obstacle-free configuration space X_{free}^i. The configuration space of the full system is denoted as $X = \prod_{i \in \Re} X^i$. The obstacle-free space $X_{\text{free}} = \prod_{i \in \Re} X_{\text{free}}^i$ does not include states where collision between robots occurs. Let $\boldsymbol{x} = x_0 x_1 \ldots$, where $x_j = (x_j^1, \ldots, x_j^R)$ for all $j \geq 0$, be a sequence of configurations describing a path followed by the full system. A path is collision free if $x_j \in X_{\text{free}}$ for all $j \geq 0$. To interpret atomic propositions over the configuration space X, let $L : X \to 2^{\Pi}$ be a function that maps a configuration x to the atomic propositions satisfied by the configuration. Hence, a word $\omega = L(x_0)L(x_1) \ldots$ expresses a path $\boldsymbol{x}$ in terms of the atomic propositions. We say that the path $\boldsymbol{x}$ satisfies the sc-LTL specification φ if the word ω, produced by $\boldsymbol{x}$, is accepted by the Büchi automaton that accepts words satisfying φ.

Problem definition: Given a group of R robots with initial configuration x_0^i for $i \in \Re$ and a sc-LTL specification φ, find a collision-free path $\boldsymbol{x}$ such that φ is satisfied.

3   Solution

This section firstly presents an overview of the proposed method followed by a detailed explanation. The main idea of the method is to create a graph, called transition system, modelling the motion of all the robots as a single system. Each vertex of the graph represents a combination of single configurations of all the robots. Edges represent collision-free paths between these configurations. Initially, the graph contains only one vertex, the initial configuration of all the robots. Then, this graph is incrementally expanded by adding a new vertex and transitions. To obtain the new vertex, individual graphs, called roadmaps, that model the motion of each robot are used. The process of expanding the graph is repeated until the specification can be satisfied by a path in the graph. To improve the required time to find a solution, the method uses an algorithm that guides the expansion of the graph. Section 3.1 explains the creation of the individual roadmaps. In Sects. 3.2 and 3.3, the incremental construction of the transition system and the search for a path satisfying the specification are presented. In Sect. 3.4, the algorithm that guides the expansion is explained in detail. Finally, illustrative examples and conclusions are presented in Sect. 4 and 5, respectively.

3.1 Probabilistic Roadmap

The first step of the proposed method consists of creating probabilistic roadmaps [9] for each robot $i \in \Re$. A roadmap of a robot i models a subset of the possible trajectories of the robot and is formed by a set of sampled configurations $x \in X_{\text{free}}^i$ connected by collision-free paths. A graph $G^i = (V^i, E^i)$ is used to represent the roadmap of the robot i. Each vertex $v \in V^i$ is associated with an unique robot configuration $x \in X_{\text{free}}^i$. This association is given by the function $\chi : V^i \to X^i$. Connectivity between two configurations is represented by an edge $(v, v') \in E^i$. We refer to all the vertices v' that share an edge with v as neighbours of v. To verify the satisfaction of a specification using only the atomic propositions that are true in each state of the transition system, see Sect. 3.3, we limit the edges between vertices to those edges that intersect the boundary of a region in the workspace at most once [21]. Moreover, we reduce the size of the roadmaps by constructing sparse roadmaps [4]. Since each vertex $v \in V^i$ is associated with a configuration $x \in X_{\text{free}}^i$, with abuse of notation, we use $L(v)$ to denote the atomic propositions satisfied by $\chi(v)$. The set of vertices on a roadmap G^i that satisfy an atomic proposition $\pi \in \Pi$ is denoted by $[\![\pi]\!]_i$.

To consider the configuration of all the robots, a composite roadmap [17] $\mathbb{G} = (\mathbb{V}, \mathbb{E})$ is constructed as the tensor product of the individual roadmaps $\{G^i\}_{i=1}^R$. Formally, $\nu = (v^1, \dots, v^R)$ is a vertex of $\mathbb{G}$ if $v^i \in V^i$ for all $i \in \Re$ and $\chi(\nu) \in X_{\text{free}}$. Let $\nu = (v^1, \dots, v^R)$ and $\nu' = (v'^1, \dots, v'^R)$ be two vertices in $\mathbb{G}$. In a tensor product, an edge $(\nu, \nu') \in \mathbb{E}$ is defined if for every $i \in \Re$, $(v^i, v'^i) \in E^i$. The projection of a composite vertex $\nu \in \mathbb{V}$ onto the vertex $v^i \in V^i$ of robot i is denoted by $\nu \downarrow_i$, i.e., $\nu \downarrow_i = v^i$. The atomic propositions satisfied by a vertex $\nu = (v^1, \dots, v^R)$ is the union of the atomic propositions satisfied by the individual vertices forming ν, i.e., $L(\nu) = \cup_{i=1}^R L(v^i)$, where $v^i = \nu \downarrow_i$.

As explained in Sect. 1, it is possible to find a path for each robot satisfying a specification by creating a product automaton of the composite roadmap $\mathbb{G}$ and the Büchi automaton $\mathscr{B}$ of the specification φ. Nevertheless, this procedure is only applicable for small problems due to its poor scalability; the number of

---

Algorithm 1. IncrementalExpansion ($\{G^i\}_{i=1}^R, \mathscr{B}$)

1: $S \leftarrow s_0 = (v_0^1, v_0^2, \ldots, v_0^R)$
2: $\mathscr{P} = \mathscr{T} \times \mathscr{B}$
3: **while** $s_{\mathscr{P}} = (s, q) \notin S_{\mathscr{P}} : q \in Q_F$ **do**
4:    $\mathscr{T} \leftarrow \text{Explore}(\{G^i\}_{i=1}^R, \mathscr{T})$
5:    $\mathscr{P}, S'_{\mathscr{P}} \leftarrow \text{Update}(\mathscr{P}, \mathscr{B}, \mathscr{T})$
6:    $\mathscr{T} \leftarrow \text{LocalConnector}(\{G^i\}_{i=1}^R, \mathscr{B}, \mathscr{T}, S'_{\mathscr{P}})$
7:    **while** new connection **do**
8:       $\mathscr{P}, S'_{\mathscr{P}} \leftarrow \text{Update}(\mathscr{P}, \mathscr{B}, \mathscr{T})$
9:       $\mathscr{T} \leftarrow \text{LocalConnector}(\{G^i\}_{i=1}^R, \mathscr{B}, \mathscr{T}, S'_{\mathscr{P}})$

---

vertices in $\mathbb{G}$ is $|V|^R$. Instead, we implicitly represent $\mathbb{G}$ and perform a sampling of it until a solution is found. Algorithm 1, explained in the rest of Sect. 3, shows this procedure.

3.2   Composite Roadmap Exploration

In this subsection, the incremental exploration of the composite configuration space $\mathbb{G}$ is presented. First, a transition system $\mathscr{T}$ is initialised with only the vertex corresponding to the initial configuration of all robots, i.e., $s_0 = \nu_0 = (v_0^1, v_0^2, \ldots, v_0^R)$, where $\chi(v_0^i) = x_0^i \ \forall i \in \Re$ (Algorithm 1, line 1). Vertices ν added to the transition system are represented as s. In each iteration of Algorithm 1, a new state is added to $\mathscr{T}$ using the idea of discrete rapidly-exploring random trees [16] as follows (Algorithm 1, line 4).

Unless some conditions, explained in Sect. 3.4, are satisfied, a state $s = (v^1, \ldots, v^R) \in S$ is randomly selected from the transition system $\mathscr{T}$. Consider a single vertex v^i forming s and recall that $v^{i,j}$ is a neighbour of v^i in G^i if $(v^i, v^{i,j}) \in E^i$. The rays $\rho_{v^i, v^{i,j}}$, for all $j \in \{1, \ldots, l\}$, that start from v^i and pass through the l neighbours of v^i are computed. Then, a configuration x_{sample} is sampled from X_{free}^i and the ray $\rho_{v^i, x_{\text{sample}}}$ is calculated. To choose a neighbour of v^i in direction of x_{sample}, the angles between the ray $\rho_{v^i, x_{\text{sample}}}$ and each of the rays $\rho_{v^i, v^{i,j}}$ are computed. The neighbour vertex that generates the ray with the smallest angle is selected and denoted as v_{new}^i, Fig. 2. This process is repeated for all the vertices forming s, resulting in a candidate state $s_{\text{new}} = (v_{\text{new}}^1, \ldots, v_{\text{new}}^R)$.

Before adding s_{new} to $\mathscr{T}$, it is verified whether collision between robots exists. To avoid collisions during the transitions (v^i, v_{new}^i) for all $i \in \Re$, priorities are assigned to each robot according to the following rules [3]: (i) if robot i, transitioning from v^i to v_{new}^i, causes a collision with robot j, located in v_{new}^j, the robot i receives higher priority than j; (ii) if robot i collides with robot j placed in v^j during the transition (v^i, v_{new}^i), then, robot i receives lower priority than j. The state s_{new} is discarded if there is no ordering such that collisions are avoided. Otherwise, the state is added to $\mathscr{T}$ with the transitions (s, s_{new}) and (s_{new}, s). Note that by choosing only neighbours of each individual vertex v^i, $(v_{\text{new}}^1, \ldots, v_{\text{new}}^R)$ is an element of the composite roadmap $\mathbb{G}$. Intuitively, the transition system $\mathscr{T}$

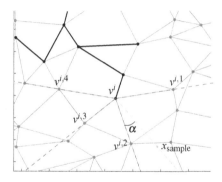

Fig. 2. Selection of vertex and edge in roadmap G^i. The states and transitions in $\mathcal{T}$ are illustrated with black vertices and edges. The roadmap G^i is shown in grey. To choose which neighbour $\{v^{i,j}\}_{j=1}^{4}$ of v^i is added to the $\mathcal{T}$, a configuration x_{sample} is randomly sampled from X_{free}^i. The rays starting from v^i and passing through x_{sample} and the neighbours are shown as red and blue dotted lines, respectively. The angles between the ray of the sample and the rest of the rays are computed. The smallest angle, α in the figure, determines which neighbour and edge are added to $\mathcal{T}$, neighbour $v^{i,2}$ in this example. (Color figure online)

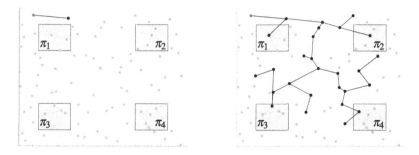

Fig. 3. Incremental construction of a transition system. The roadmap of the robot is shown in grey. The transition system, representing the explored part of the roadmap, is shown in black. The green areas, identified by the atomic propositions π_1, π_2, π_3 and π_4, are regions of interest. The proposed method iteratively adds vertices and edges from the roadmap to the transition system until the specifications can be satisfied. In this example, the specification is to visit the four green areas. The initial configuration of the robot is shown as a red vertex. (Color figure online)

represents the explored part of $\mathbb{G}$. An example of such exploration, for the case $R = 1$, is shown in Fig. 3.

Since each vertex ν of $\mathbb{G}$ is associated with a configuration $x \in X_{\text{free}}$, a run $\sigma = s_0 s_1 \ldots$ on $\mathcal{T}$ represents a path of the full system in the configuration space X_{free}. Hence, this exploration continues until a path that satisfies the specification φ is found. The procedure to determine whether the current transition system contains such a path is presented in the next subsection.

3.3   Product Automaton Update

Based on model checking techniques, the verification of a run σ satisfying the sc-LTL specification φ is made on the Cartesian product $\mathscr{P} = (S_{\mathscr{P}}, s_{\mathscr{P},0}, \delta_{\mathscr{P}}, S_{\mathscr{P},F})$ of $\mathscr{T}$ and the Büchi automaton $\mathscr{B}$ obtained from φ. States $s_{\mathscr{P}} \in S_{\mathscr{P}}$ are formed by pairs (s, q), where $s = (v^1, \ldots, v^R) \in S$ is a state of $\mathscr{T}$ and $q \in Q$ is a state of $\mathscr{B}$.

The product automaton $\mathscr{P}$ is firstly created when the transition system contains only the initial state s_0 (Algorithm 1, line 2). Since the transition system $\mathscr{T}$ changes with each new state s_{new}, the product $\mathscr{P}$ requires to be updated (Algorithm 1, line 5). The procedure to incrementally update $\mathscr{P}$ [21] and to search for a path satisfying φ is now presented.

When a new state s_{new} is added to $\mathscr{T}$ with the transition (s, s_{new}) and (s_{new}, s), the set $S'_{\mathscr{P}}$ of states $s'_{\mathscr{P}} = (s_{\text{new}}, q')$, such that $\delta_{\mathscr{B}}(q, L(s_{\text{new}})) = q'$ and $(s, q) \in S_{\mathscr{P}}$, is computed. Then, for each state $s'_{\mathscr{P}} \in S'_{\mathscr{P}}$, it is verified if $s'_{\mathscr{P}}$ is already in $S_{\mathscr{P}}$. If that is not the case, the state is added to $\mathscr{P}$ and is removed from $S'_{\mathscr{P}}$. Moreover, the set of states $s''_{\mathscr{P}} = (s', q'')$, such that $(s_{\text{new}}, s') \in \delta_{\mathscr{T}}$ and $\delta_{\mathscr{B}}(q', L(s')) = q''$, is computed. If a state $s''_{\mathscr{P}}$ is not already in $S_{\mathscr{P}}$, $s''_{\mathscr{P}}$ is added to $S_{\mathscr{P}}$ and to $S'_{\mathscr{P}}$. This recursive procedure continues until the set $S'_{\mathscr{P}}$ is empty.

By construction, if a run on $\mathscr{P}$, starting from $s_{\mathscr{P},0}$, reaches the set $S_{\mathscr{P},F}$ of accepting states, the language produced by the run σ on $\mathscr{T}$ generates a word ω that is accepted by the Büchi automaton $\mathscr{B}$ computed from the sc-LTL formula. In other words, a run σ on $\mathscr{T}$ satisfies the specification if a run on $\mathscr{P}$ reaches the set of accepting states. Hence, the process of exploring $\mathscr{B}$ and updating $\mathscr{P}$ continues until a state $s_{\mathscr{P}} = (s, q)$ is added to $\mathscr{P}$ such that $q \in Q_F$ (Algorithm 1, line 3).

A solution to the problem defined in Sect. 2.5 would be eventually found by repeating the process described above. Nevertheless, depending on the number of robots and the specification, this process could take an impractical amount of time. In the next subsection, an algorithm that improves the required time by guiding the exploration of $\mathbb{G}$ is presented.

3.4   Guided Expansion

In this subsection, we present a new algorithm, called local connector, which selects the states in $\mathscr{T}$ that must be expanded in order to satisfy the sc-LTL specification. The main idea is to find the shortest path, in terms of transitions, in the Büchi automaton to an accepting state and to search for vertices in the individual roadmaps $\{G^i\}_{i=1}^R$ satisfying the atomic propositions required to progress in such a path.

Before explaining the algorithm, some concepts and notation are introduced. The algorithm monitors which transitions of the Büchi automaton have been satisfied by the current transition system. To achieve this, each state and non-self transition of the Büchi automaton are identified by an index, Fig. 1. When one of the $|q_i|$ outgoing transitions from state $q_i \in Q$ is satisfied, the index that

Algorithm 2. LocalConnector ($\{G_i\}_{i=1}^R, \mathscr{B}, \mathscr{T}, S'_{\mathscr{P}}$)

```
 1: g_i ← {s : (s, q_i) ∈ S'_𝒫, ∀i ∈ {1,...,|Q|}}
 2: for i ∈ sorted(q_i) : i ∈ {1,...,|Q|}, g_i ≠ ∅ and i ∉ D_q} do
 3:   for j ∈ {ℜ : j ∉ W_R} do
 4:     for n = 1 → |g_i| do
 5:       v_s = s_n ↓_j , s_n ∈ g_i                                   ▷ Vertex to be connected
 6:       for k ∈ sorted(δ_𝓑(q_i, ·)) : k ∈ {1,...,|q_i|, W_δ ≠ ∅ → k ∈ W_δ and k ∉ D_δ^i} do
 7:         Π_req = AP(q_i, q_k)                                      ▷ Set of AP required
 8:         for m ∈ {1,...,|Π_req|} : m ∉ D_Π} do
 9:           for h = 1 → |[[π_m]]_j| do
10:             v_t = v_h, v_h ∈ [[π_m]]_j                            ▷ Target vertex
11:             if Connect (v_s, v_t) then
12:               if |Π_req| = 1 then
13:                 s_new = s , s ∈ g_i
14:                 s_new ↓_j= v_t                                    ▷ New state of 𝒯
15:                 D_δ^i ← D_δ^i ∪ k
16:               else if |D_Π| < |Π_req| − 1 then
17:                 W_R ← W_R ∪ j                                     ▷ robot j can satisfy π_m
18:                 W_q ← W_q ∪ i
19:                 W_δ ← W_δ ∪ k
20:                 D_Π ← D_Π ∪ m
21:                 v_{j,next} = v_t                                  ▷ Vertex satisfying π_m
22:               else if |D_Π| = |Π_req| − 1 then
23:                 s_new = s , s ∈ g_i
24:                 s_new ↓_p= v_{p,next} , ∀p ∈ W_R
25:                 s_new ↓_j= v_t                                    ▷ New state of 𝒯
26:                 D_δ^i ← D_δ^i ∪ k
27:                 W_R = ∅, W_q = ∅, W_δ = ∅, D_Π = ∅
```

identifies the transition is added to the set D_δ^i. Once all the outgoing transitions of a state $q_i \in Q$ are satisfied, i.e., $|D_\delta^i| = |q_i|$, the index i is added to the set D_q.

Depending on the transition, one or more atomic propositions have to be satisfied at the same time. Since each robot can satisfy one atomic proposition at a time, when more than one proposition is required, collaboration between robots is needed. Consider the transition (q_0, q_2) in the Büchi automaton shown in Fig. 1 as an example. To make this transition, the atomic propositions π_1 and π_2 have to be satisfied, i.e., $AP(q_0, q_2) = \{\pi_1, \pi_2\}$. The algorithm verifies if a robot i is able to satisfy any of the propositions by finding a local path from its current configuration to a configuration in G^i satisfying one of the atomic propositions. If, for instance, a path exists to a vertex $v \in V^i$ satisfying π_1, i.e., $v \in [[\pi_1]]_i$, the atomic proposition π_1 is added to the set D_Π and the index that identifies the robot is added to the set W_R. The set W_R identifies the robots that are waiting for other robots to satisfy the remaining atomic propositions required to make the transition in the Büchi automaton. Moreover, this set is used to guide the expansion of $\mathscr{T}$ as presented below. To identify which transition is tried to be satisfied when a robot is added to W_R, the index identifying the state q and its outgoing transition are added to the sets W_q and W_δ, respectively. We now explain the algorithm in detail, see Algorithm 2.

The algorithm receives as input the Büchi automaton $\mathscr{B}$ and the set $S'_{\mathscr{P}}$ of states added to the product automaton $\mathscr{P}$ after the last update. These states have the form (s, q), where $s = (v^1, \ldots, v^R) \in S$ and $q \in Q$. The states are divided into different groups depending on their Büchi state component (Algorithm 2, line 1). In other words, for each state q_i in the Büchi automaton, a group g_i containing states $s = (v^1, \ldots, v^R)$ such that $s_{\mathscr{P}} = (s, q_i) \in S'_{\mathscr{P}}$ is created. The algorithm eliminates the group g_i if there is no remaining outgoing transitions from the Büchi state q_i to be satisfied, i.e., $i \in D_q$. Then, the algorithm sorts, from shortest to longest, the different paths from the initial state $q_0 \in Q$ to the closest accepting state $q \in Q_F$ in the Büchi automaton $\mathscr{B}$.

Using these sorted paths, the algorithm tries to reach atomic propositions required in the paths, starting from the shortest path (Algorithm 2, line 2). An exception to the order is made when of one the robots is waiting for another atomic proposition to be satisfied, i.e., $W_R \neq \emptyset$. In this case, all the Büchi states are ignored except the states in the set W_q.

For each state s in g_i, the individual vertices of non-waiting robots forming s, i.e., $s \downarrow_j$ for $j \in \Re \setminus W_R$, are considered to be connected to vertices in G^j satisfying the required atomic propositions in the Büchi automaton transition. An individual vertex, denoted as v_s, is considered for connection in each iteration (Algorithm 2, lines 3–5). If a robot is waiting, all the transitions are ignored except the transition indicated by the set W_δ. Otherwise, the transition is selected based on the sorted paths (Algorithm 2, line 6). The required atomic propositions in the transition are assigned to the set Π_{req} (Algorithm 2, line 7). Then, all the vertices in the roadmap G^j that satisfy an atomic proposition that cannot be satisfied by a waiting robot, i.e., $\pi_m \in \Pi_{\mathrm{req}} \setminus D_\Pi$, are assigned as a target of the connection and are denoted as v_t (Algorithm 2, lines 8–10). The algorithm then tries to find a path between the vertices v_s and v_t. By connecting the transition system to vertices satisfying atomic propositions required for the specification, the time needed to solve the proposed problem is reduced.

In order to find a path between the vertices v_s and v_t any method can be used. However, because this process is constantly repeated, a method that sacrifices completeness for speed is preferred. In this work, the algorithm attempts to connect two vertices if the Euclidean distance between them is less than a pre-established value. If the path, given by a line between the vertices, is collision free, the connection is considered successful (Algorithm 2, line 11). Depending on the number of atomic propositions in the selected transition in $\mathscr{B}$, three different situations can occur:

Case 1: Only one atomic proposition is required in the transition, i.e., $|\Pi_{\mathrm{req}}| = 1$ (Algorithm 2, lines 12–15). In this case, if robot j can satisfy the required atomic proposition through the connection, a new state $s_{\mathrm{new}} = (v^1, \ldots, v^R)$, where $v^i = s \downarrow_i$ for $i \in \{\Re : i \neq j\}$ and v_t otherwise, is created. Intuitively, the new state has the same components as the composite state s, except the element of robot j that is replaced by v_s. If the new state is not in the transition system $\mathscr{T}$, the state is added with the transitions (s, s_{new}) and (s_{new}, s). Finally, the index k of the satisfied transition is added to D_δ^i indicating that the transition k from state q_i has been satisfied.

Case 2: More than one atomic proposition is required and at least one more is still required after the connection (Algorithm 2, lines 16–21). When a robot j can satisfy one of the required atomic propositions but at least another is needed for the transition in the Büchi automaton, the robot stays in the vertex v_s waiting for the remaining robots to satisfy the other atomic propositions. To indicate that the robot is waiting, the index j is added to the set W_R. The set W_R restricts the states that can be selected in the exploration of $\mathbb{G}$. The selected state in the exploration must be formed by the vertices v^i, where $i \in W_R$. Moreover, the next state s_{new} to be added to the transition system must have the same vertices. After adding the index j of the robot to the set W_R, the vertex that can be reached, i.e., v_t, is saved in $v_{j,\text{next}}$ to be used once all the atomic propositions of the transition are satisfied. Then, the index m of the atomic proposition that can be satisfied is added to the set D_Π to skip this atomic proposition the next iteration of Algorithm 2. Note that the restriction explained above guides the sampling process of $\mathbb{G}$.

Case 3: The last required atomic proposition is satisfied with the connection (Algorithm 2, lines 22–27). Similar to case 1, when a robot j can satisfy the last required atomic proposition, a new state s_{new} is created with the saved states $v_{i,\text{next}}$, i.e., $s_{\text{new}} \downarrow_i = v_{i,\text{next}}$ for all $i \in W_R$, v_t for $i = j$ and $s \downarrow_i$ otherwise. This state is added to $\mathscr{T}$ with the transitions (s, s_{new}) and (s_{new}, s). The index k of the satisfied transition is added to D_δ^i and the sets W_R, W_q and W_δ and D_Π become empty indicating that all the robots can move again and any non-satisfied state and transition in the Büchi automaton can be selected.

Every time a new state s_{new} is added to $\mathscr{T}$, the product automaton $\mathscr{P}$ is update (Algorithm 1, lines 7–9) and the process is repeated. As mentioned in Sect. 3.3, Algorithm 1 stops once a product state with a final state $q \in Q_F$ is added to $\mathscr{P}$.

3.5 Implementation

This subsection presents how a solution is obtained from $\mathscr{P}$ and the implementation of it in the robots. Once the condition to stop Algorithm 1 is satisfied, the shortest path $\sigma = s_{\mathscr{P},0} \ldots s_{\mathscr{P},n}$ on $\mathscr{P}$, where $s_{\mathscr{P},n} \in S_{\mathscr{P},F}$, is sought. Since a state $s_{\mathscr{P}}$ is formed by the pair (s, q), only the first element of each state is considered to create the path $\boldsymbol{x}$ that satisfies the sc-LTL specification. The function χ is used to define the configurations in X that defines $\boldsymbol{x}$. Finally, each configuration in $\boldsymbol{x}$ is projected to the individual configuration spaces X^i to define a path for each robot.

To execute the path, each robot stores a list of the vertices to visit in its roadmap G^i together with the configurations where the robot has to wait for other robots before performing a transition. When a robot finishes a transition, it broadcasts a unique identifier number and a signal indicating that the transition has been completed. If a robot needs to wait for other robots, the transition is

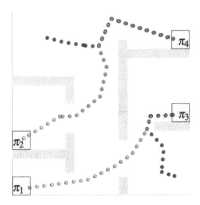

Fig. 4. Illustration of the path followed by two robots satisfying the specification $\varphi = \Diamond(\pi_1 \wedge \pi_2) \wedge \Diamond(\pi_3 \wedge \pi_4)$. This sc-LTL specification requires the robots to visit areas marked as π_1 and π_2 at the same time and the areas π_3 and π_4 with the same restriction. The colour of the robots changes, from darker to lighter blue, over time to show that the atomic propositions are satisfied at the same time step. (Color figure online)

not performed until the robot receives the signal of all the robots with higher priority.

4 Examples

The proposed method is illustrated with different sc-LTL specifications and number of robots. We consider a differential wheeled robot, called e-puck [14], in a workspace with 4 areas associated with the atomic propositions π_1, π_2, π_3 and π_4, Fig. 4. The computation of the path is implemented in MATLAB on a computer with a 3.1 GHz i7 processor and 8GB of RAM. The dynamics of the e-pucks are simulated using Enki [13].

We present three examples, considering two, three and four robots, respectively:

1. Regions π_1, π_2 have to be visited at the same time as well as π_3, π_4 with the same restriction, Fig. 4.
2. Regions π_1, π_2 and π_3 must be visited in the presented order.
3. Regions π_1, π_2, π_3 and π_4 cannot be visited until all of them are visited at the same time.

Recall that the number of vertices in $\mathbb{G}$ is equal to $|V|^R$, where $|V|$ is the number of vertices in the roadmap and R is the number of robots. In the example with four robots, the parallel composition $\mathbb{G}$ has more than 96 million vertices. Nevertheless, Table 1 shows that only a small portion of $\mathbb{G}$ is explored before finding a solution. This result can be attributed to the guided search performed by the local connector algorithm. For comparison, we compute a solution to the first specification without Algorithm 2. That is, we only expand the transition

Table 1. Average number of states in $\mathscr{T}$ and required time to solve the problem over 20 different runs.

Specification	Robots	States in $\mathscr{T}$	Time (seconds)
$\Diamond(\pi_1 \wedge \pi_2) \wedge \Diamond(\pi_3 \wedge \pi_4)$	2	278.55	6.30
$\Diamond(\pi_1 \wedge \bigcirc\Diamond(\pi_2 \wedge \bigcirc\Diamond(\pi_3)))$	3	6457.9	372.37
$\neg(\pi_1 \vee \pi_2 \vee \pi_3 \vee \pi_4)\mathscr{U}(\pi_1 \wedge \pi_2 \wedge \pi_3 \wedge \pi_4)$	4	270.4	7.48

system using the idea presented in Sect. 3.2. In average, the solution is found in 1057.91 s and require the exploration of 7242.43 vertices. This comparison shows that Algorithm 2 reduces the exploration or $\mathbb{G}$ and, as a consequence, the required time to find a solution. A direct comparison with other sampling-based methods for multiple robots, e.g., [7], is not possible because our method samples the continuous configuration space instead of a discrete representation of the robots mobility.

5   Conclusions

In this paper, we have introduced a new method to find collision-free paths for a multi-robot system that satisfy syntactically co-safe linear temporal logic formulae. Most of the work in the literature consider methods with low scalability with respect to the dimension of the robot's configuration space. We extend sampling-based methods, previously proposed to alleviate the scalability problem, to multi-robot systems. The proposed method explores a composite roadmap modelling the possible behaviour of all the robots. This exploration stops when a path satisfying the specification is found. Additionally, we have presented a new algorithm that guides the exploration to reduce the time required to find a solution. Numerical results show that only a small portion of the composite roadmap is explored as a result of using this algorithm. The proposed method is focused on obtaining a result in the shortest possible period of time regardless of its optimality. Hence, a possible direction for future work is the inclusion of a cost function to find optimal paths.

References

1. Alur, R., Henzinger, T.A., Lafferriere, G., Pappas, G.J.: Discrete abstractions of hybrid systems. Proc. IEEE **88**(7), 971–984 (2000)
2. Chen, Y., Ding, X.C., Belta, C.: Synthesis of distributed control and communication schemes from global LTL specifications. In: Proceedings of CDC-ECC, pp. 2718–2723. IEEE (2011)
3. van Den Berg, J., Snoeyink, J., Lin, M.C., Manocha, D.: Centralized path planning for multiple robots: optimal decoupling into sequential plans. In: Robotics: Science and Systems, vol. 2, pp. 2–3 (2009)
4. Dobson, A., Bekris, K.E.: Sparse roadmap spanners for asymptotically near-optimal motion planning. Int. J. Robot. Res. **33**(1), 18–47 (2014)

5. Fainekos, G.E., Girard, A., Kress-Gazit, H., Pappas, G.J.: Temporal logic motion planning for dynamic robots. Automatica **45**(2), 343–352 (2009)
6. Guo, M., Dimarogonas, D.V.: Multi-agent plan reconfiguration under local LTL specifications. Int. J. Robot. Res. **34**(2), 218–235 (2015)
7. Kantaros, Y., Zavlanos, M.M.: Sampling-based control synthesis for multi-robot systems under global temporal specifications. In: Proceedings of ICCPS, pp. 3–13. ACM (2017)
8. Karaman, S., Frazzoli, E.: Sampling-based motion planning with deterministic μ-calculus specifications. In: Proceedings of CDC/CCC, pp. 2222–2229. IEEE (2009)
9. Kavraki, L.E., Svestka, P., Latombe, J.C., Overmars, M.H.: Probabilistic roadmaps for path planning in high-dimensional configuration spaces. IEEE Trans. Robot. Autom. **12**(4), 566–580 (1996)
10. Kloetzer, M., Belta, C.: Automatic deployment of distributed teams of robots from temporal logic motion specifications. IEEE Trans. Rob. **26**(1), 48–61 (2010)
11. Kupferman, O., Vardi, M.Y.: Model checking of safety properties. Formal Meth. Syst. Des. **19**(3), 291–314 (2001)
12. Leahy, K., Jones, A., Schwager, M., Belta, C.: Distributed information gathering policies under temporal logic constraints. In: Proceedings of CDC, pp. 6803–6808. IEEE (2015)
13. Magnenat, S., Waibel, M., Beyeler, A.: Enki: the fast 2D robot simulator (2011). http://home.gna.org/enki
14. Mondada, F., Bonani, M., Raemy, X., Pugh, J., Cianci, C., Klaptocz, A., Magnenat, S., Zufferey, J.C., Floreano, D., Martinoli, A.: The e-puck, a robot designed for education in engineering. In: Proceedings of ICARSC, pp. 59–65. IPCB (2009)
15. Montana, F.J., Liu, J., Dodd, T.J.: Sampling-based stochastic optimal control with metric interval temporal logic specifications. In: Proceedings of CCA, pp. 767–773. IEEE (2016)
16. Solovey, K., Salzman, O., Halperin, D.: Finding a needle in an exponential haystack: Discrete RRT for exploration of implicit roadmaps in multi-robot motion planning. Int. J. Robot. Res. **35**(5), 501–513 (2016)
17. Švestka, P., Overmars, M.H.: Coordinated path planning for multiple robots. Rob. Auton. Syst. **23**(3), 125–152 (1998)
18. Svoreňová, M., Křetínský, J., Chmelík, M., Chatterjee, K., Černá, I., Belta, C.: Temporal logic control for stochastic linear systems using abstraction refinement of probabilistic games. In: Proceedings of HSCC, pp. 259–268. ACM (2015)
19. Tumová, J., Dimarogonas, D.V.: A receding horizon approach to multi-agent planning from local LTL specifications. In: Proceedings of ACC, pp. 1775–1780. IEEE (2014)
20. Ulusoy, A., Smith, S.L., Ding, X.C., Belta, C., Rus, D.: Optimality and robustness in multi-robot path planning with temporal logic constraints. Int. J. Robot. Res. **32**(8), 889–911 (2013)
21. Vasile, C.I., Belta, C.: Sampling-based temporal logic path planning. In: Proceedings of IROS, pp. 4817–4822. IEEE (2013)
22. Wolff, E.M., Topcu, U., Murray, R.M.: Optimal control of non-deterministic systems for a computationally efficient fragment of temporal logic. In: Proceedings of CDC, pp. 3197–3204. IEEE (2013)
23. Zhang, Z., Cowlagi, R.V.: Motion-planning with global temporal logic specifications for multiple nonholonomic robotic vehicles. In: Proceedings of ACC, pp. 7098–7103. IEEE (2016)

Certified Gathering of Oblivious Mobile Robots: Survey of Recent Results and Open Problems

Thibaut Balabonski[6], Pierre Courtieu[1], Lionel Rieg[2],
Sébastien Tixeuil[4,5], and Xavier Urbain[3]($\boxtimes$)

[1] CÉDRIC, Conservatoire National des Arts et Métiers, Paris, France
[2] Yale University, New Haven, USA
[3] Université de Lyon, Université Claude Bernard Lyon 1,
CNRS, LIRIS UMR 5205, Lyon, France
Xavier.Urbain@liris.cnrs.fr
[4] UPMC Sorbonne Universités, LIP6-CNRS 7606, Paris, France
[5] Institut Universitaire de France, Paris, France
[6] Université Paris-Sud, LRI, CNRS UMR 8623, Université Paris-Saclay, Paris, France

Abstract. Swarms of mobile robots have recently attracted the focus of the Distributed Computing community. One of the fundamental problems in this context is that of gathering the robots: the robots must meet at a common location, not known beforehand. Despite its apparent simplicity, this problem proved quite hard to characterise fully, due to many model variants, leading to informal error-prone reasoning.

Over the past few years, a significant effort has resulted in the set up of a formal framework, relying on the Coq proof assistant, that was used to provide certified results related to the gathering problem. We survey the main abstractions that permit to reason about oblivious mobile robots that evolve in a bidimensional Euclidean space, the distributed executions they can perform, and the variants of the gathering problem they can solve, while certifying all obtained results. We also describe the remaining steps to obtain a certified full characterisation of the problem.

1 Introduction

1.1 Oblivious Mobile Robots

We consider sets of mobile oblivious robots evolving in a bidimensional continuous Euclidean space. Robots follow the seminal model by Suzuki and Yamashita [24]: they do not remember their past actions, they cannot communicate explicitly, and they are disoriented: they do not agree on a common frame of reference (i.e., shared "North" direction, handedness or notion of distance). Note that obliviousness implies that the frame of reference of a single robot is not guaranteed to stay the same during execution.

This work was partially funded by the CNRS PEPS OCAAA 2017 project CYBORG and the Université Claude Bernard Lyon 1 BQR 2017 project PREFER.

The original version of this chapter was revised. The author corrections were updated. The erratum to this chapter is available at https://doi.org/10.1007/978-3-319-67113-0_15

L. Petrucci et al. (Eds.): FMICS-AVoCS 2017, LNCS 10471, pp. 165–181, 2017.
DOI: 10.1007/978-3-319-67113-0_11

However, they can sense their environment and detect the positions of the other robots according to their egocentered view of their surroundings. If several robots share the same position in space (forming a *tower*, or multiplicity point), other robots may or may not detect the tower. If robots have *weak* multiplicity detection, they are assumed to sense a tower on a position, but are not able to count the actual number of robots in this tower. With *strong* multiplicity detection, they are able to count the exact number of robots on a given position. Without multiplicity detection, robots simply detect occupied positions.

Robots are anonymous and execute the same deterministic algorithm to achieve together a given objective. Each robot behaves according to the following look-compute-move cycle: it takes a snapshot of its environment, it then computes its next move (either stay idle or move to a different position), and at the end of the cycle, it moves according to its computation. Since robots cannot rely on a common sense of direction, directions that are computed in the compute phase are only *relative* to the robot.

Existing execution models consider different types of synchronisation for the robots: in the fully synchronous model (FSYNC), all robots evolve simultaneously and complete full look-compute-move cycles at the same time. The semi-synchronous model (SSYNC) considers runs that evolve in phases: at each phase, an arbitrary subset of the robots is scheduled for a full look-compute-move cycle, which is executed simultaneously by all robots of the subset. Finally, in the asynchronous model (ASYNC), robots evolve freely at their own pace. In particular, a robot can move according to a computation based on an obsolete observation of its environment, as other robots may have moved in between.

The core problem to solve in the context of mobile robot networks is *pattern formation*, introduced in the seminal paper by Suzuki and Yamashita [24]. It turns out that a deterministic solution to construct general patterns in the SSYNC model can be devised, with the added assumption that robots have access to an infinite non-volatile memory (that is, robots are *not* oblivious). The construction was later refined for the ASYNC model by Bouzid et al. [7], still using a finite number of infinite precision variables. The search for an oblivious solution to general pattern formation proved difficult [19]. For oblivious deterministic robots to be able to construct any general pattern, it is required that they share a common "North" (that is, a common direction and orientation) but also a common "Right" (i.e. handedness, aka chirality), so that robots get to all agree on a common coordinate system. If only a "North" (and implicitly if only a "Right") is available, then some patterns involving an even number of robots cannot be formed.

Relaxing the common coordinate system condition led to a characterisation of the patterns that can be formed by deterministic oblivious robots [20,25,26]. The best deterministic algorithm so far in the ASYNC model without a common coordinate system [26] proves the following: If ρ denotes the number of geometric symmetries of a robot configuration, and I and P denote the initial and target configurations, respectively, then P can be formed if and only if $\rho(I)$ divides $\rho(P)$. Intuitively, this result says that we cannot break existing symmetries, so that any symmetry of the starting configuration must be present in the target configuration. A direct consequence of this result is that the only patterns that can possibly be formed from arbitrary initial positions are the regular polygons and the point. Forming a point as the target pattern is known as *gathering*.

1.2 The Gathering Problem

Despite its apparent simplicity, the solvability of gathering has received a considerable amount of attention [18]. A foundational result [13,24] shows that in the FSYNC or SSYNC models, no oblivious deterministic algorithm can solve gathering for two robots (without additional assumptions). The main argument for establishing this impossibility is the observation that robots can have symmetric coordinate systems and retain symmetry forever. This result can be extended [13] to the bivalent case, that is, when an even number of robots is initially evenly split in exactly two positions. This result was significantly extended by Prencipe [22]: in SSYNC, with $n > 2$ robots starting from initially distinct positions, no oblivious deterministic protocol can solve without additional assumptions, such as multiplicity detection. On the other hand, it is possible to solve gathering without additional assumptions in the FSYNC model [3]. In the ASYNC model, gathering is possible if $n > 2$ robots start from initially distinct positions and robots are endowed with weak multiplicity detection [10].

Gathering was further studied for hostile environments, where robots become likely to fail. So far, three kinds of failures were considered in the context of deterministic gathering [1,6,8,16]:

1. *Transient faults*: as robots are oblivious (they do not remember their past actions), they are naturally resilient to transient faults that corrupt their memory. However, if the transient fault consequence was to place the robots in some forbidden configuration (*e.g.* a bivalent configuration), some algorithms may not recover. Algorithms can thus be sorted according to the set of admissible initial configurations.
2. *Crash faults*: when robots may stop executing their algorithm unexpectedly (and correct robots are not able to distinguish a correct robot from a crashed one at first sight), guaranteeing that correct robots still gather in finite time is a challenge. Algorithms can thus be sorted according to the number of admissible crashed robots.
3. *Byzantine faults*: when robots may have completely random (and possibly malicious) behaviour, there exists no deterministic gathering protocol in the SSYNC model even assuming that at most one robot may be Byzantine [1].

The positive deterministic results so far in a fault tolerant context are as follows. With strong multiplicity detection, and restricting the set of admissible initial configurations to distinct configurations (that is, configurations where at most one robot occupies a particular position), gathering is feasible in the SSYNC model with one crash fault [1]. If only transient faults are considered, strong multiplicity detection (that is, being able to sense the exact number of robots at any particular position) permits to extend the set of initial configurations to those that include multiplicity points [16] (however, only the case with an odd number of robots is considered). When a common chirality is available, it becomes possible to tolerate up to $n - 1$ (n being the number of robots) crash faults [6], further expanding the set of initial configurations to those that are not bivalent (so all feasible initial configurations in a deterministic context are considered). This result was improved by Bramas *et al.* [8], as they present a deterministic gathering protocol that can start from any non-bivalent configuration (the largest possible set in the classical model), yet does not assume that all robots share a common direction, nor a common chirality (as in [6]). The protocol retains the ability to tolerate up to $n - 1$ crash faults.

1.3   Contributions and Outline of the Paper

In Sect. 2, we revisit the oblivious mobile robot model of Suzuki and Yamashita [24] under the prism of formal methods, and present the Pactole framework that we use throughout the paper. Section 3 surveys the core results related to mobile robot gathering, how they can be expressed using the Pactole framework, describes in detail key certified results obtained so far, and conclude of the benefits of using the Pactole framework. Finally, we present in Sect. 4 the next steps to obtain a complete certification of gathering-related results.

2   Formal Models of Oblivious Mobile Robots

2.1   Related Work/Overview

Designing and proving mobile robot protocols is notoriously difficult. Formal methods encompass a long-lasting path of research that is meant to overcome errors of human origin. Unsurprisingly, this mechanised approach to protocol correctness was successively used in the context of mobile robots [2–5, 9, 13, 15, 21, 23].

   In the discrete setting (that is, when the movements of the robots are restricted according to a pre-existing graph), model-checking proved useful to find bugs in existing literature [4, 17] and formally check the correctness of published algorithms [4, 15, 23]. Automatic program synthesis (for the problem of perpetual exclusive exploration in a discrete ring) is due to Bonnet *et al.* [5], and can be used to obtain automatically algorithms that are "correct-by-design". The approach was refined by Millet *et al.* [21] for the problem of gathering in a discrete ring network. Recently, Aminof *et al.* [23] presented a general framework for verifying properties about mobile robots evolving on graphs, where the graphs are a parameter of the problem. As all aforementioned approaches are designed for a discrete setting, they cannot permit to establish results that are valid for a continuous Euclidean space such as the one we consider in this paper.

When robots are *not* constrained to evolve on a particular topology but instead move freely in a bidimensional Euclidian space, to the best of our knowledge the only formal framework available is the Pactole framework.[1] Pactole enabled the use of higher-order logic to certify impossibility results for the problem of convergence [2]: robots are required to reach positions that are arbitrarily close to each other. Another classical impossibility result that was certified with Pactole is the impossibility of gathering starting from a *bivalent* configuration [13], that is, a configuration with exactly two distinct towers, each consisting of half the robots. Recently, positive certified results for SSYNC gathering with multiplicity detection [14], and for FSYNC gathering without multiplicity detection [3] were provided.

2.2   The Pactole Framework

Developed for the coq proof assistant,[2] the Pactole framework allows for formal specification, and proofs of both correctness [3,14] and impossibility [2,13] results, in the context of autonomous mobile robots.

The design of the formal platform is driven by two objectives. The first one is to provide means to specify problems, protocols, and properties in a relatively *easy* way, that is, without requiring the user to be a long time expert in formal proof. As a matter of fact, specifications are rather short, very close to mathematical statements as found in papers, and expressed in quite a readable functional programming language. We would like to stress that developing *proofs* is a completely different task, which does require expertise.

The second objective is to capture as many variations in the model as possible. The framework is highly generic and may be instantiated in numerous ways. This allows for each result to be proven with the appropriate minimal hypotheses, and then to be used in any setting where these hypotheses hold. For example, if a problem is proved to be impossible in the fully synchronous model then it is also impossible in the asynchronous model. Indeed, being more powerful, an ASYNC demon can simulate the FSYNC setting and reproduce the impossibility proof.

High-Level Description. In the current core of the framework, as in the original model of [24], robots are considered point-like and they all execute the same program. For the sake of genericity, positions are just elements of some arbitrary space (with a decidable equality). A robot is simply an identifier, and a configuration: a function mapping an identifier to the relevant information (position, state, etc.); an execution is an infinite sequence of configurations. The program embedded in all robots is a function that takes a perception of the environment as an input and returns a target destination.

---

[1] http://pactole.lri.fr.
[2] http://coq.inria.fr.

Perception of robots. To ensure that the program does not use more information than what is provided by the perceptions of robots, it must fulfil a compatibility constraint saying that equivalent perceptions lead to equivalent destinations; this is stated as an additional property. The definitions of "equivalent" for both perceptions and positions is a parameter of the framework. This modularity allows us maximum flexibility in the definition of robot perceptions, but comes at the burden of these extra compatibility proofs. We do not impose the use of Coq's equality (which would remove the need for the compatibility proofs) because on some datatypes equality is too fine grained, and we would like to use a coarser relation instead. A simple example of this phenomenon is Coq's sets library: they are represented by balanced trees, and different trees may represent the same set. Nevertheless, when these equivalences are actually Coq's equality, these compatibility proofs are trivial. The pair function/property is called a *robogram*. Perceptions of the environment are called *spectra* of the actual configuration, the definition and computation of which are defined by the user when the generic model is instantiated. For example, the provided function may then hide or show identifiers or multiplicity, it may limit the vision to some radius, etc. This flexibility allows the user to represent any kind of sensors.

Demons. Finally, demons are infinite sequences (stream) of actions, each of those activating a set of robots and giving to each one its current local coordinate system. The way activated sets of robots are selected depends on the instantiation: all robots for a fully synchronous scheme, subsets for semi-synchronous schemes, etc. Additional properties like *fairness*-related constraints (fair, unfair, k-fair,[3] etc.) are expressed as logical propositions on demons. This allows for the encoding of many types of demons, and for their theoretical formal study. The relevant library includes inclusions and equivalence theorems about demons, for example that a fully-synchronous demon is semi-synchronous, or that a k-fair demon is also $(k+1)$-fair.

We also define the usual temporal operators $\Diamond$, $\circ$, and $\Box$ to help expressing temporal properties about executions, written respectively stream.eventually, stream.next, and stream.forever in our formalisation. Yet, the logic of Coq is much more expressive and one can define new temporal operators or new properties directly on an execution.

Executions. We can generate an execution from a robogram and a demon by executing successively the robogram against the demonic action described by the demon for each round. To this end, the round function computes the configuration obtained after one round of executing a robogram against a demonic action da starting from a configuration. This is done in the following consecutive steps for each robot identifier id:

---

[3] A demon is *k-fair* when any robot is activated within k consecutive activations of any other robot.

1. If the robot `id` is not activated, return the same position.
2. If `id` is a byzantine robot, it is relocated by the demonic action `da`.
3. Use the local frame of reference provided by `da` to compute the local configuration.
4. Transform this local configuration into a spectrum.
5. Apply the robogram on this spectrum.
6. If moves are flexible, compute new position of `id` using the ratio given by `da`.
7. Convert the new position from the local frame to the global one.

In a discrete setting, the steps would be the same except for the local frame of reference which does not contain a zoom factor.

All the developments related to the results we survey in this article are available from http://pactole.lri.fr.

Description of the Coq Libraries. The Pactole framework contains a core part which is common to all settings and several libraries accommodating all supported variants for the model. The following table describes them with their sizes, as given by `coqwc`. Statements of intermediate lemmas in proofs are counted as specifications.

Component	Spec	Proof	Total
Instances of several Euclidian spaces with geometrical constructs (barycentres, smallest enclosing circles and their properties, etc.)	864	2708	3572
Formalism for rigid or flexible moves (i.e. robots cannot/can be interrupted before they reach the destination they computed), SSYNC/FSYNC, with various properties on demons (most notably flavours of fairness)	481	649	1130
Equivalence between rigid moves and flexible moves with ratio 1	63	86	149
Most common spectra to express perception capabilities of robots	217	280	497
Implementation and properties of multisets relevant to our context to deal with and to ease proof over some spectra	1786	4162	5948
Several case studies, in particular for gathering and convergence	1398	5638	7036
Total for Pactole	**5643**	**15264**	**20907**

2.3   Specifying in Pactole

We emphasise that the task of specifying the problem and its components, and the task of proving the various claims and statements are two separate activities. While the latter is more the work of an expert in formal proof, the former *has to* be accessible and manageable by every user and developer of distributed protocols for mobile robots. The language of Coq (Gallina) and the Pactole framework allow the user to characterise properties and contexts without a too cumbersome verbosity or intricacy. Due to the high parametricity of Pactole and the set of lemmas and definitions it comes with, specifying a gathering protocol in $\mathbb{R}^2$ can be as short as providing the code itself. Of course, if the robots enjoy capabilities that are not yet in the libraries, the user will have to define a function that takes a configuration and returns a spectrum; a special synchronicity may have to be defined by providing a property on demons (usually expressed with the help of the operators on streams), etc., but overall the framework helps to keep limited the amount of technical expertise in this phase, and allows for focusing on the crucial parts described as univocal statements.

3 A Formal Study of Gathering with Pactole

3.1 Formal Definitions in Pactole

Most of the formal definitions about the gathering problem are common to all results, ensuring on the one hand that we always consider the same problem in the various settings, and on the other hand that there is no gap between the impossibility result and the algorithms we design.

All these formal definitions do not make any assumption on the type of space in which robots evolve, abstracted as `Loc.t`. Thus, they are used in both $\mathbb{R}$ and $\mathbb{R}^2$.

Gathering. A general description on how to characterise a solution to the problem of gathering has been given in [13]; we briefly recall how it is specified, using 3 definitions which exactly reflect the mathematical description of the problem.

The first one characterises a configuration `config` in which all robots inhabit the very same position `pt`:

Definition gathered_at (pt : Loc.t) (config : Config.t) :=
  ∀ g : Names.G, Loc.eq (config (Good g)) pt.

The second one states that all robots inhabit forever the same position `pt` along a given execution `e`. This is the execution we expect after a successful gathering.

Definition Gather (pt: Loc.t) (e : execution) : **Prop** :=
  Stream.forever (Streams.instant (gathered_at pt)) e.

Finally, the last property means that robots will all reach the same position `pt` in finite time, and stay there forever.In other words, property `Gather` will hold eventually.

Definition WillGather (pt : Loc.t) (e : execution) : **Prop** :=
  Stream.eventually (Gather pt) e.

A robogram achieving gathering under a demon d without any additional initial condition fulfils `FullSolGathering`.

Definition FullSolGathering (r : robogram) (d : demon) :=
  ∀ config, ∃ pt : Loc.t, WillGather pt (execute r d config).

If any condition on the initial configuration is required, the relevant property is `ValidSolGathering`.

Definition ValidSolGathering (r : robogram) (d : demon) :=
  ∀ config,
    ¬invalid config → ∃ pt : Loc.t, WillGather pt (execute r d config).

Note that this is just the addition of a condition ¬invalid `config` over the starting configuration in the expression of `FullSolGathering`, which expresses that the starting configuration is not invalid.

3.2   Robot Models Considered in This Study

Synchrony. The model is instantiated for semi-synchronous demons. In this case, a demon is a stream of *demonic actions* which associate to each of the robots an *option* value: either `None` meaning that the robot is not activated, or a value `Some` carrying the new frame of reference of the (hence activated) robot. Fully synchronous demons are obtained as the particular case in which the value `None` is never used. Note that Obliviousness is achieved by providing a new frame at each activation.

Different notions of fairness are provided (demons may be fair, unfair, k-fair, etc.), and are to be used as assumptions in theorems if needed.

Multiplicity. As a robogram must compute the destination based only on the information available to robots, we have to select a suitable spectrum, containing only the information observable by the robots. When the considered capability is strong global multiplicity, the robots have access to the number of robots located at each point in space, that is: positions holding robots *with their respective multiplicities*. A suitable spectrum to compute from is thus the *multiset* of inhabited positions, available in our libraries with relevant functions and properties. With no multiplicity detection, we use instead the *set* of inhabited position.

3.3   SSYNC, Detection of Multiplicity, Rigid Movements

Impossibility: Theorem and Proof. Impossibility of Gathering for two robots was established by Suzuki and Yamashita in their seminal paper [24]. A recent work [13] shows that by following almost exactly the steps of their proof, we can establish a slightly stronger result: we relax the usual constraint that initial configurations should have all their robots at distinct positions, and we show impossibility for any positive even number of robots.

So as to keep the statement of the main theorem short, we state as parameter that the number of robots `N.nG` is even.

```
Parameter N.nG : nat.          (* number of robots *)
Hypothesis even_nG : Nat.Even N.nG.  (* assumed to be even *)
```

We prove that no matter what the algorithm does, we can build a demon such that starting from an invalid position, the execution resulting from the algorithm and the demon always stays invalid, hence the algorithm fails.

```
Definition Always_invalid (e : execution) :=
  Streams.forever (Streams.instant invalid) e.
```

```
Theorem different_no_gathering : ∀ (e : execution),
N.nG ≠ 0 → Always_invalid e → ∀ pt, ¬WillGather pt e.
```

Using similarities to convert from the global frame of reference to the local one, we can ensure that robots not located on the same position are always at (local) position 1, hence both towers of robots always perform the same actions. As in the original proof, we consider two cases, whether the algorithm sends one tower of robots on top of the other or not. In the first case, the demon activates all robots and they swap positions; after two rounds we are back to the starting configuration. Notice that in this case, the demon is actually fully synchronous, so in particular 1-fair.

In the second case, the demon only activates one tower of robots. After one round, the robots may be closer to each other in the global frame but with a similarity, the demon can scale this back to a unit distance for the next round. Therefore, activated in the next round, the other tower will perform the same move and both towers of robots will still be apart. Notice that in this case, the demon is 1-fair. The final theorem we prove expresses that for all robograms r, all integers $k \geq 1$, r does not solve gathering against all k-fair demons d.

Theorem noGathering:
    $\forall$ r k, $(1 \leq k) \rightarrow \neg (\forall$ d, kFair k d $\rightarrow$ FullSolGathering r d).

This is a universal quantification over protocols.

Note that we use FullSolGathering, hence we put no restriction on the initial configuration. The extension to k-fair demons (with $k \geq 1$) comes from a theorem in our formal library stating that any k-fair demon is also k'-fair for any $k' \geq k$.

Correctness: Theorem and Proof. The previous impossibility result is based on the fact that we cannot break the symmetry between two towers of robots. Thus, these *bivalent* configurations are exactly the ones we want to avoid for our algorithms. We thus define invalid configurations to be the ones with exactly two distinct towers, each consisting of half the robots.

Definition invalid (config : Config.t) :=
    Nat.Even N.nG $\wedge$ N.nG >=2
    $\wedge$ **let** m := Spect.from_config(config) in
        $\exists$ pt1 pt2, $\neg$Loc.eq pt1 pt2
                    $\wedge$ m[pt1] = Nat.div2 N.nG
                    $\wedge$ m[pt2] = Nat.div2 N.nG.

We initially designed an algorithm for $\mathbb{R}$ [12] and later extended it for $\mathbb{R}^2$ [14]. As the former can be seen as a particular case of the latter case, we focus our presentation on $\mathbb{R}^2$.

The full algorithm is described in Fig. 1. It proceeds by computing a target that only depends on "clean" robots, i.e. located on the smallest enclosing circle (SEC). Robots that are not clean are allowed to move first, so that the target does not change during their gathering. Then clean robots can move and modify the SEC and hence the target. Its translation in Gallina is about 20 lines long for the protocol itself, with an additional dozen of lines for properties over constituents (essentially equivalences of results when provided equivalent entries). This count does not include the geometrical characterisations for triangles, barycentres, etc. We refer to [14] for further details.

The three main difficulties in the design of the algorithm are: first avoiding the invalid configuration at all costs; second ensuring that all robots are in the same phase of the algorithm; third ensuring that all robots compute the same destination in the global frame. Avoiding the invalid configuration is done by testing the existence of a unique tower of maximal height and moving towards

Protocol gatherR2 (s:Spect.t) **returns** (dest:$\mathbb{R}^2$) :=
if max(s) = { p } **then** dest := p   (∗ *one max tower* ∗)
else begin
(∗ *Compute target* ∗)
  if support(s) ∩ SEC(s) = { p1,p2,p3 } **then**   (∗ *triangle cases* ∗)
    if equilateral(p1,p2,p3) **then** target := barycenter(p1,p2,p3)
      else if isosceles(p1,p2,p3) **then** target := opposite of base(p1,p2,p3)
      else target := opposite of longest(p1,p2,p3)
    else target := center(SEC(s)) **;**   (∗ *other cases* ∗)
(∗ *only dirty robots move to target, if any, otherwise clean robots can move* ∗)
  if ∀p ∈ s, p ∈ SEC(s) or p = target **then** dest := target
  else if (0,0)∈ SEC(s) or (0,0) = target **then** dest := (0,0)
end

Fig. 1. Gathering Protocol for $\mathbb{R}^2$. dest is the target position computed by the protocol. The spectrum s is a multiset of positions, support(s) and max(s) denote respectively the support set and set of maximal multiplicity elements of s. SEC(s) denotes the smallest enclosing circle of positions in s.

it if it exists: we then prove that starting from a non invalid configuration, an invalid one can never appear.

Theorem never_invalid :
  ∀ da config, ¬invalid config → ¬invalid (round gatherR2 da config).

It is interesting to notice that the proof of this theorem in $\mathbb{R}^2$ has been reused from the $\mathbb{R}$ case as it is *exactly* the same.

To solve the second and third difficulty, we only use geometric properties and shapes that are invariant by (conjugating by) similarities, in particular the smallest enclosing circle (SEC). Thus, we ensure that all robots see the same shape and compute the same position in the global frame, the center of the SEC. The actual algorithm must take into account some corner cases where the SEC changes, in particular when there are 3 or fewer robots on the SEC. Overall, we get the following key property stating that all moving robots compute the same target.

Lemma same_destination: ∀ da config id1 id2,
  In id1 (moving gatherR2 da config) → In id2 (moving gatherR2 da config)
  → round gatherR2 da config id1 = round gatherR2 da config id2.

The most intricate part of the proof of the algorithm is not its partial correctness but its termination. To prove it, we analyse the possible transitions between all phases of the algorithm, and design a measure lt_config which decreases each time a robot moves.

Theorem round_lt_config: ∀ da conf,
  ¬invalid conf → moving gatherR2 da conf ≠ nil
  → lt_config (round gatherR2 da conf) conf.

The main theorem states that for any fair demon, the robogram gatherR2 achieves gathering *provided that* the initial configuration is valid, i.e., not bivalent in this case. Hence we use the ValidSolGathering expression of the wanted property.

Theorem `Gathering_in_R2`: $\forall$ `d, Fair d` $\rightarrow$ `ValidSolGathering gatherR2 d`.

It is proven by well-founded induction on the measure `lt_config` and by case analysis.

3.4   FSYNC, No Detection of Multiplicity, Flexible Movements

When movements are not rigid but, on the contrary, are *flexible*, robots can be interrupted before they reach the destination they computed. In order to prevent Zenon-based counterexamples, it is assumed that the length of any non-conclusive movement is at least δ, an absolute distance that is unknown to robots. In other words, robots either reach their goal when it is at most at a certain absolute distance δ, or travel at least δ towards it, stopping to an arbitrary position (possibly the computed goal).

Cohen and Peleg [11] proposed that robots aim for the position that is the barycenter of all observed robots for the purpose of convergence (a weaker requirement than gathering, which mandates robots to reach positions that are arbitrarily close to one another) in the SSYNC model. They demonstrate that for the FSYNC model, robots actually solve gathering since they eventually all become closer than δ from the barycenter, and hence all reach it in the next round.

However, this centre of gravity algorithm does not prevent more than one robot to occupy the exact same position before gathering, even if they start from distinct positions. For example, consider two robots r_1 and r_2 aligned toward the barycenter at some round, at distances d_1 and d_2 ($d_1 < d_2$) that are both greater than δ, respectively. Then, the demon stops r_1 after δ and r_2 at the same position. Robots r_1 and r_2 now occupy the same position. From this observation is it clear that in the next round, to compute the barycenter, observing robots must take into account both r_1 and r_2. In other words, robots running this algorithm must be able to detect how many robots occupy simultaneously a given position, that is, make use of *strong multiplicity detection*. The question of gathering feasibility in FSYNC without multiplicity detection (nor any other additional assumption) has been solved using Pactole in [3].

Formal Specification and Certification. Switching from SSYNC to FSYNC is easy as the demon just has now to activate the whole set of robots at each round. The main changes in the setup lie in multiplicity detection, and movements that can be interrupted.

Multiplicity. In the case where multiplicity is *not* to be considered, the robots *cannot* receive any information about it. Thus a suitable definition of the spectrum they consider is to be devised. As the robograms can only rely on the knowledge of a position in space being inhabited or not, it is sufficient to represent the environment as the set of inhabited positions (and not a multiset as previously done). To this goal, we use the set-based spectra of our development.

Flexible Movements. Flexible demons of our framework are streams of 'flexible' demonic actions, which in turn provide each of the (activated) robots with both its new frame of reference *and* the ratio of its actual movement over its computed destination. Demonic actions also contain the same well-defined logical properties as before (for example ensuring that new frames of reference make sense), and the additional property that the provided ratio belongs to the $[0,1]$ interval. To avoid irrelevant details in rigid developments, and to allow for the reuse of proofs and theorems, our demon libraries come with theorems stating equivalence between flexible movements with ratio 1 and rigid movements.

Gathering in the Flexible Context. The formal definitions of the framework for the flexible move setting only require very minor changes: demonic actions now have an additional ratio (and proof of its bound) which is used in the round function computing the next configuration, together with the δ parameter to ensure that robots move a correct distance. This δ is only used in round, which in turn requires to add it as an extra parameter to the function execute that generates an execution from a demon and a robogram (by invoking repeatedly round), and to the definition of Gathering (which uses execute). As gathered_at, Gather, and WillGather stay exactly the same, the characterisation of a solution to Gathering in the flexible context is simply:

Definition FullSolGathering (r : robogram) (d : demon) δ :=
   $\forall$ config, $\exists$ pt : Loc.t, WillGather pt (execute δ r d config).

Theorem and Proof. The solution proposed in [3] does not rely on the centre of gravity of robots, but on the centre of gravity of *inhabited positions*. Remember that the spectrum in this context is just the set of inhabited positions. Bringing all robots to the centre of gravity of inhabited positions thus consists in bringing them to the barycentre of the spectrum.

Definition ffgatherR2_pgm (s : Spect.t) : R2.t :=
   barycenter (Spect.M.elements s).

From this code and the relevant properties (equivalence for equivalent perceptions) we can build Robogram ffgatherR2.

The main difficulty is to establish that after a finite number of steps, no robot will change its position. This amounts to finding a measure that decreases for a well founded ordering along with the execution. To this goal, we consider for a configuration C the maximal distance $dm(C)$ between any two robots, denoted by measure hereafter. Similarly to Sect. 3.3, we define a well-founded ordering that decreases by at least δ for each new obtained configuration (unless the distance is less than δ, in which case gathering is achieved in the next step).

Theorem round_lt_config:
   $\forall$ d conf δ, $\delta > 0 \rightarrow$ FullySynchronous d $\rightarrow$ $\delta \leq$ measure conf
   $\rightarrow$ measure(round δ ffgatherR2 (Streams.hd d) conf) $\leq$ measure conf - δ.

The main statement, establishing correctness, is the following:

Theorem FSGathering_in_R2:
   $\forall$ δ d, $\delta > 0 \rightarrow$ FullySynchronous d $\rightarrow$ FullSolGathering ffgatherR2 d δ.

Here again we are using `FullSolGathering`, hence we do not make any assumptions on the starting configuration.

This theorem is proven via well-founded induction over the ordering, and by case analysis: if the robots are already gathered or will be gathered at the next step then we are done, else we use `round_lt_config`.

3.5   Conclusion of This Study

We emphasise that the use of the Pactole framework allows for easy to write and human readable definitions and specifications for programs and properties in the context of oblivious mobile robots. During that phase, establishing the compatibility property of the robogram is the only technical requirement. It is however a composition of the compatibility proofs on the robogram's constituents.

The common framework encompasses many models (FSYNC/SSYNC, rigid/flexible moves, etc.), and allows for both impossibility results and proofs of correctness. It thus permits to share definitions, and ensures consistency in the notions and properties involved. It also prevents any shifting of models between statements of theorems, their proofs, and their applications, hence providing strong guarantees.

From a proving perspective, every time we follow the same methodology: after defining and specifying the robogram, we provide a global description of the execution of the robogram that does not make any reference to the local frame of reference, and prove that it is sufficient. This allows us to perform reasoning on the execution of the robogram in the global frame of reference, which we always do intuitively on paper but requires a formal proof. This relies crucially on the fact that computations performed by the robogram are invariant by similarities. From this point on, partial correctness is usually easy to establish. Proving termination is much harder, with arguments that are specific to each situation. Most of the work is devoted to geometrical properties: either invariants or transitions between given states of the algorithm.

4   Roadmap to a Complete Certified Characterisation

We summarise in Table 1 the certification progress for gathering and convergence in oblivious mobile robot problems. Results in bold face are certified using the Pactole framework. Extending the results will require to further develop the framework along the following roadmap:

1. **Impossibility of SSYNC n-gathering (with $n \geq 3$) without multiplicity detection.** An important (uncertified) impossibility result is due to Prencipe [22]: for any number of robots that is greater to 3, it is impossible to solve gathering without additional assumptions (*e.g.* multiplicity detection, agreement on direction, etc.). Prencipe's proof argument is based on an adaptive scheduling of robots: if the robots' algorithm is to gather them, then the scheduler only activates a subset of the robots to make the algorithm fail

Table 1. Oblivious robot gathering certification progresses. Bold entries are formally certified.

	2-gathering	n-gathering $(n \geq 3)$	n-gathering $(n \geq 3)$ w. multiplicity detection	wait-free n-gathering $(n \geq 3)$ w. multiplicity detection
FSYNC	Yes	Yes	Yes	Yes
SSYNC	No	No	Yes	Yes
ASYNC	No	No	Yes	?

at each step. The certification of Prencipe's proof thus requires the ability to express such adaptive schedules in the Pactole framework, remaining agnostic of the actual protocol that is executed by all robots. This would also certify the impossibility for the ASYNC model.

2. **Wait-freedom.** As explained in Sect. 1.2 when robots may stop executing their algorithm unexpectedly, guaranteeing that correct robots still gather in finite time is a challenge. Wait-freedom refers to the fact that no robot "waits" to observe the move of another robot before moving itself (hence, every correct robot always moves until completion of the algorithm): otherwise a crashed robot could prevent other correct robots from gathering. Certifying state of the art results [8] in this context requires defining wait-freedom as a property of the robots' algorithm, and its integration in the relevant lemmas and theorems.

3. **ASYNC certification.** To date, the only certified result in the ASYNC model is the impossibility of gathering when started from a bivalent configuration, as the impossibility proof for the SSYNC model naturally extends to the ASYNC model. For positive results, we focused on the atomic FSYNC and SSYNC models. Breaking the atomicity of the individual Look-Compute-Move cycles (that is, considering algorithm certification for the ASYNC model [18], or writing impossibility results that are specific to that model) implies that robots cannot maintain a current global view of the system (their own view may be outdated), nor be aware of the view of other robots (that may be outdated as well). The modelling of ASYNC is feasible in a proof assistant, and should not bring any additional difficulties in the specification of properties in that context. However, it would have a significant cost in terms of intricacy of the associated proofs. A really manageable formal development in an ASYNC model requires more automation at the proof level.

When both wait-freedom and ASYNC issues are resolved, we will have all required ingredients to tackle the currently open issue of the existence of wait-free algorithms for gathering in the ASYNC model.

References

1. Agmon, N., Peleg, D.: Fault-tolerant gathering algorithms for autonomous mobile robots. SIAM J. Comput. **36**(1), 56–82 (2006)

2. Auger, C., Bouzid, Z., Courtieu, P., Tixeuil, S., Urbain, X.: Certified impossibility results for byzantine-tolerant mobile robots. In: Higashino, T., Katayama, Y., Masuzawa, T., Potop-Butucaru, M., Yamashita, M. (eds.) SSS 2013. LNCS, vol. 8255, pp. 178–190. Springer, Cham (2013). doi:10.1007/978-3-319-03089-0_13

3. Balabonski, T., Delga, A., Rieg, L., Tixeuil, S., Urbain, X.: Synchronous gathering without multiplicity detection: a certified algorithm. In: Bonakdarpour, B., Petit, F. (eds.) SSS 2016. LNCS, vol. 10083, pp. 7–19. Springer, Cham (2016). doi:10.1007/978-3-319-49259-9_2

4. Bérard, B., Lafourcade, P., Millet, L., Potop-Butucaru, M., Thierry-Mieg, Y., Tixeuil, S.: Formal verification of mobile robot protocols. Dis. Comput. **29**(6), 459–487 (2016)

5. Bonnet, F., Défago, X., Petit, F., Potop-Butucaru, M., Tixeuil, S.: Discovering and assessing fine-grained metrics in robot networks protocols. In: SRDS Workshops 2014, pp. 50–59. IEEE (2014)

6. Bouzid, Z., Das, S., Tixeuil, S.: Gathering of mobile robots tolerating multiple crash faults. In: ICDCS, pp. 337–346. IEEE Computer Society (2013)

7. Bouzid, Z., Dolev, S., Potop-Butucaru, M., Tixeuil, S.: Robocast: asynchronous communication in robot networks. In: Lu, C., Masuzawa, T., Mosbah, M. (eds.) OPODIS 2010. LNCS, vol. 6490, pp. 16–31. Springer, Heidelberg (2010). doi:10.1007/978-3-642-17653-1_2

8. Bramas, Q., Tixeuil, S.: Wait-free gathering without chirality. In: Scheideler, C. (ed.) Structural Information and Communication Complexity. LNCS, vol. 9439, pp. 313–327. Springer, Cham (2015). doi:10.1007/978-3-319-25258-2_22

9. Bérard, B., Courtieu, P., Millet, L., Potop-Butucaru, M., Rieg, L., Sznajder, N., Tixeuil, S., Urbain, X.: Formal methods for mobile robots: current results and open problems. Int. J. Inform. Soc. **7**(3), 101–114 (2015). Invited Paper

10. Cieliebak, M., Flocchini, P., Prencipe, G., Santoro, N.: Distributed computing by mobile robots: Gathering. SIAM J. Comput. **41**(4), 829–879 (2012)

11. Cohen, R., Peleg, D.: Convergence properties of the gravitational algorithm in asynchronous robot systems. SIAM J. Comput. **34**(6), 1516–1528 (2005)

12. Courtieu, P., Rieg, L., Tixeuil, S., Urbain, X.: A certified universal gathering algorithm for oblivious mobile robots. CoRR, abs/1506.01603 (2015)

13. Courtieu, P., Rieg, L., Tixeuil, S., Urbain, X.: Impossibility of gathering, a Certification. Inf. Process. Lett. **115**, 447–452 (2015)

14. Courtieu, P., Rieg, L., Tixeuil, S., Urbain, X.: Certified universal gathering in $\mathbb{R}^2$ for oblivious mobile robots. In: Gavoille, C., Ilcinkas, D. (eds.) DISC 2016. LNCS, vol. 9888, pp. 187–200. Springer, Heidelberg (2016). doi:10.1007/978-3-662-53426-7_14

15. Devismes, S., Lamani, A., Petit, F., Raymond, P., Tixeuil, S.: Optimal grid exploration by asynchronous oblivious robots. In: Richa, A.W., Scheideler, C. (eds.) SSS 2012. LNCS, vol. 7596, pp. 64–76. Springer, Heidelberg (2012). doi:10.1007/978-3-642-33536-5_7

16. Dieudonné, Y., Petit, F.: Self-stabilizing gathering with strong multiplicity detection. Theoret. Comput. Sci. **428**, 47–57 (2012)

17. Doan, H.T.T., Bonnet, F., Ogata, K.: Model checking of a mobile robots perpetual exploration algorithm. In: Liu, S., Duan, Z., Tian, C., Nagoya, F. (eds.) SOFL+MSVL 2016. LNCS, vol. 10189, pp. 201–219. Springer, Cham (2017). doi:10.1007/978-3-319-57708-1_12

18. Flocchini, P., Prencipe, G., Santoro, N.: Distributed Computing by Oblivious Mobile Robots. Synthesis lectures on distributed computing theory. Morgan & Claypool Publishers, San Rafael (2012)

19. Flocchini, P., Prencipe, G., Santoro, N., Widmayer, P.: Arbitrary pattern formation by asynchronous, anonymous, oblivious robots. Theor. Comput. Sci. **407**(1–3), 412–447 (2008)

20. Fujinaga, N., Yamauchi, Y., Kijima, S., Yamashita, M.: Asynchronous pattern formation by anonymous oblivious mobile robots. In: Aguilera, M.K. (ed.) DISC 2012. LNCS, vol. 7611, pp. 312–325. Springer, Heidelberg (2012). doi:10.1007/978-3-642-33651-5_22

21. Millet, L., Potop-Butucaru, M., Sznajder, N., Tixeuil, S.: On the synthesis of mobile robots algorithms: the case of ring gathering. In: Felber, P., Garg, V. (eds.) SSS 2014. LNCS, vol. 8756, pp. 237–251. Springer, Cham (2014). doi:10.1007/978-3-319-11764-5_17

22. Prencipe, G.: Impossibility of gathering by a set of autonomous mobile robots. Theoret. Comput. Sci. **384**(2–3), 222–231 (2007)

23. Aminof, B., Murano, A., Rubin, S., Zuleger, F.: Verification of asynchronous mobile-robots in partially-known environments. In: Chen, Q., Torroni, P., Villata, S., Hsu, J., Omicini, A. (eds.) PRIMA 2015. LNCS (LNAI), vol. 9387, pp. 185–200. Springer, Cham (2015). doi:10.1007/978-3-319-25524-8_12

24. Suzuki, I., Yamashita, M.: Distributed anonymous mobile robots: formation of geometric patterns. SIAM J. Comput. **28**(4), 1347–1363 (1999)

25. Yamashita, M., Suzuki, I.: Characterizing geometric patterns formable by oblivious anonymous mobile robots. Theor. Comput. Sci. **411**(26–28), 2433–2453 (2010)

26. Yamauchi, Y., Yamashita, M.: Pattern formation by mobile robots with limited visibility. In: Moscibroda, T., Rescigno, A.A. (eds.) SIROCCO 2013. LNCS, vol. 8179, pp. 201–212. Springer, Cham (2013). doi:10.1007/978-3-319-03578-9_17

Modeling and Analysis Techniques

Learning-Based Testing the Sliding Window Behavior of TCP Implementations

Paul Fiterău-Broştean[1(✉)] and Falk Howar[2]

[1] Institute for Computing and Information Sciences,
Radboud University, Nijmegen, The Netherlands
fiteraup@yahoo.com
[2] Institute for Applied Software Systems Engineering,
Clausthal University of Technology, Clausthal-Zellerfeld, Germany

Abstract. We develop a learning-based testing framework for register automaton models that can express the windowing behavior of TCP, thereby presenting the first significant application of register automata learning to realistic software for a class of automata with Boolean-arithmetic constraints over data values. We have applied our framework to TCP implementations belonging to different operating systems and have found a violation of the TCP specification in Linux and Windows. The violation has been confirmed by Linux developers.

1 Introduction

Automata provide both formal and intuitive means of specifying the behavior for a wide range of applications, in particular network protocols. Unfortunately, protocol specifications often are textual and rarely include state machine models. Without such models, it is difficult to test if an application behaves as expected. Manual construction of models is a laborious and error-prone process and models become outdated as soon as the specification changes. Learning-based testing, as sketched in Fig. 1, alleviates this problem by generating models while testing a system. These models cannot serve as specifications but can be used to check desired properties, which are usually easier to formalize and maintain than complete behavioral models.

Integrating model learning, model-based testing, and model checking allows a tester to automatically obtain a model for a system under test. For a set of test inputs, model learning runs a series of tests on the system until, eventually, it will produce a conjectured model of the system's behavior. This model is used as the basis for model-based testing. Testing can discover counterexamples, which indicate incorrectness of the model. In such case, model learning is restarted, being provided with the counterexample. Once no counterexample is found, the model can be used for checking properties. The output of learning-based testing is threefold: model learning produces a conformance test suite for the model [4],

P. Fiterău-Broştean—Supported by NWO project 612.001.216, Active Learning of Security Protocols (ALSEP).

© Springer International Publishing AG 2017
L. Petrucci et al. (Eds.): FMICS-AVoCS 2017, LNCS 10471, pp. 185–200, 2017.
DOI: 10.1007/978-3-319-67113-0_12

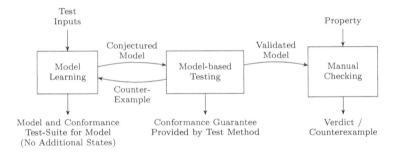

Fig. 1. Learning-based testing with additional checking of properties.

checking of properties can produce examples that document the violation of a specification, and in case no violation is found, testing can yields a conformance guarantee.

In order to instantiate learning-based testing for a certain class of models, one needs a learning algorithm and a testing algorithm for this class of models. In this paper, we present a learning-based testing framework for a class of register automata that can express the windowing behavior of TCP. Our framework utilizes the SL^* learning algorithm for register automata [6] and a random walk testing algorithm for such register automaton models. The testing algorithm ensures approximate correctness of models with a high confidence. We manually inspect models and find a violation of the TCP specification in Linux and Windows implementations.

Our work is the first significant application of register automata learning to realistic software for a class of automata with Boolean-arithmetic constraints over data values. Our results show that, on the one hand, learning more expressive models can ease the burden of manually constructed sophisticated test harnesses. On the other hand, experiments show that model learning for more expressive models is very expensive. Future work will focus on scaling learning-based testing to industrial applications as well as on integrating automated model checking into our approach.

Related Work. Learning-based testing in the form that we present here is based on the observation that model learning and model-based testing are merely two sides of the same coin [16]. The term has been introduced in [12] for a combination of model learning, model checking, and random testing. In contrast to our work, the approach is based on finite state models. On the other hand, model checking is automated and feed the model learning algorithm with counterexamples, leading to higher degree of automation.

Learning-based techniques have been steadily gaining traction for more than a decade, after pioneering work on learning and testing CTI systems [10] and learning and checking systems [13]. Previous applications of learning-based testing or checking have lead to the discovery of flaws in TLS implementations [15] and of various forms of specification non-compliance in TCP [7,8] and SSH [9]

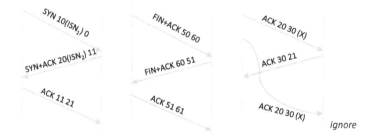

Fig. 2. TCP handshake, connection closure, and data transfer with re-transmission. Labels show flags, sequence and acknowledgment numbers. 1 byte of payload marked by (X). Initial Sequence Numbers marked by (ISN).

implementations. What all these case studies have in common, is the difficulty of manually constructing a sophisticated test harness for the system. This is in large part caused by the need to abstract away from system functionality, so that the functionality seen by the learner fits within the less expressive formalism the learner can infer, typically mealy machines or DFAs. Our learning setup can infer more expressive register automata, and requires no form of abstraction other than a general one for handling fresh values.

Outline. We provide a brief introduction to TCP in the next section before presenting our learning-based testing framework in Sect. 3. We discuss application of our framework on real TCP implementations in Sect. 4, before concluding in Sect. 5.

2   The Sliding Window Behavior of TCP

The Transport Control Protocol (TCP) is a widely used transport layer protocol of the TCP/IP stack, with implementations provided by all operating systems. TCP ensures reliable data transfer between parties. In order to communicate, a TCP client and server application must first establish a TCP connection, which is done by way of a handshake. They can then exchange data over the established connection until one of the parties decides to terminate the connection. A closure procedure ensues, which ultimately removes the connection. In all stages of the protocol, interaction is done by exchanging *TCP segments*. These segments are often the result of calls on the socket interface, which is available to each side and provides access to TCP services. Moreover, each side keeps track of the state of the connection. TCP uses sequence numbers and a sliding receive window to keep track of which segments have been received and acknowledged by the other party. This helps compensate for a potentially lossy communication channel in which reordering of segments can occur (e.g., due to changing routing of segments).

For the sake of exposition, let us assume a setting in which all segments are 1 byte in size. As sequence numbers encode the relative position of a segment in a byte stream, this assumption allows us to confuse the relative position segment in a sequence of segments with its position in a byte stream.

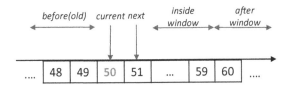

Fig. 3. Relevant relations of Sequence Numbers in TCP.

Sequence Numbers. To achieve reliable data transfer, TCP uses sequence and acknowledgement numbers, and flags which are included in the header of all TCP segments. In a stream of segments from a sender to a receiver, the *sequence number* encodes the relative number of a segment in such a stream. The receiver acknowledges a received segment by responding with a segment including as *acknowledgement number* the next expected sequence number. Sequence numbers are generated relative to an Initial Sequence Number (ISN), so the first segment has sequence number ISN, the second ISN+1... As data is sent, the sequence number increases, as does the acknowledgement number in responses.

Receive Window. Segments received with a sequence number greater than the one expected fall in two categories: those whose sequence number falls within a *receive window* of that expected and those whose sequence number falls outside of the receive window. The former should be processed by the receiver, the latter should be treated as invalid. As a concrete example, only reset segments (segments with the RST flag enabled) with the sequence number within the receive window are processed, and may reset the connection, those whose number lies outside should be ignored. The receive window is included in the TCP header and its value is communicated in each TCP segment a side sends.

Sliding Windows. Once a received segment is successfully processed, the receive window can be moved forward: if a sequence number of a received segment is equal to the sequence number expected, the expected sequence number is increased. If not equal, the expected sequence number is left unchanged. Acknowledgement numbers are also checked. Those equal to the last sequence number sent acknowledge all segments up to this last one. Those greater are unacceptable as they acknowledge segments not yet sent. Those smaller than the last sequence number sent are old acknowledgements. Segments with unacceptable or old acknowledgement numbers are generally discarded.

As stated above, sequence numbers and receive windows are used, among other things, to deal with reordering of routed segments and to prevent the processing of (bytes in) old segments, which are segments carrying already seen data with sequence numbers smaller than the those expected. Old segments are often the result of re-transmissions, which happen when a timeout for receiving an acknowledgement has expired. TCP is full duplex, which means communicating sides maintain two byte streams, one for each direction. Each side keeps track of the next sequence number to be sent, as well as the sequence number expected from the other side. To open (via handshake), maintain and close the two byte

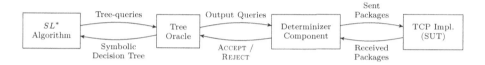

Fig. 4. Learning register automaton models from tests.

streams, TCP uses control flags. The SYN flag, for example, marks the beginning of a byte stream, whereas the FIN flag marks the end. Figure 2 gives sequence diagrams for typical TCP scenarios.

The description so far assumed that all segments were 1 byte in size. In actuality, the size of a segment is the size of the payload carried, plus 1 if either SYN or FIN flags are enabled, or 0 otherwise. We restrict the learning setting to one where segments carry no payload (thus segments are either of size 0 or 1).

Figure 3 depicts the relevant relations sequence numbers may have relative to a current sequence number, in line with our earlier description. These relations are equality and inequality over the current sequence number, and over its summation to one (for segments including either FIN or SYN), and to the receive window size.

3 Instantiating Learning-Based Testing for TCP

In order to apply learning-based testing to the windowing behavior of TCP, we instantiate the components of the framework that were sketched in Sect. 1. We use the SL^* active learning algorithm for learning register automaton models [6]. Active learning algorithms rely on the existence of a minimally adequate teacher (cf. [3]) that answers two kinds of queries for the learning algorithm: *output queries* (i.e., execution of tests) and *equivalence queries*. The learning algorithm submits a conjectured model to an equivalence oracle and expects a counterexample to the model (if one exists). In our scenario, we implement this oracle by performing model-based testing on the model.

The SL^* algorithm additionally assumes the existence of a *tree oracle*. A tree oracle produces register automata fragments that encode the relevant data relations for a sequence of actions on a SUT. The resulting setup is shown in Fig. 4. In order to infer symbolic transitions, e.g., for input $ACK(p_1, p_2)$ with two data parameters p_1 and p_2 from a state that is reached in the protocol by sending a message $SYN(10, 0)$ and receiving message $SYN+ACK(20, 11)$, the SL^* algorithm will perform a tree query for prefix $SYN(10, 0)$ and suffix ACK. The tree oracle will generate output queries for all relevant concrete instances of ACK messages capturing possible relations between values of p_1, p_2 and data values in the prefix (e.g., equality, being a sequence number, or being in a window). The determinizer component will test if output queries are valid traces of a TCP implementation by exchanging actual TCP packages with a system under testing (SUT). The tree oracle encodes the observed behavior and relevant relations as a symbolic decision tree.

In the remainder of this section, we present register automata for the windowing behavior of TCP, tree queries that capture all relevant data relations, and use the presented ideas as a basis for instantiating model-based testing in our framework.

3.1   Register Automata

We assume a set Σ of *actions*, each with an arity that determines how many values from $\mathbb{N}$ it takes as parameters (e.g., ACK takes two data values). To simplify presentation, we assume that all actions have arity 1, but it is straightforward to extend to the case where actions have arbitrary arity. A *data symbol* is a term of form $\alpha(d)$, where α is an action and $d \in \mathbb{N}$ is a data value. A *data word* is a sequence of data symbols. The concatenation of two data words w and w' is denoted ww'. In this context, we often refer to w as a *prefix* and w' as a *suffix*. For a data word $w = \alpha_1(d_1) \ldots \alpha_n(d_n)$, let $Acts(w)$ denote its sequence of actions $\alpha_1 \ldots \alpha_n$, and $Vals(w)$ its sequence of data values $d_1 \ldots d_n$. Let $|w|$ denote the number of symbols in w.

While there are infinitely many data words for every sequence of actions with data parameters, many of these data words are equivalent when considering only relations between data values (e.g., equality, being a sequence number, or being in a window). For a set of relations $\mathcal{R}$, data words $w = \alpha_1(d_1) \ldots \alpha_n(d_n)$ and $w' = \alpha_1(d_1') \ldots \alpha_n(d_n')$ are $\mathcal{R}$-*indistinguishable*, denoted $w \approx_{\mathcal{R}} w'$, if $R(d_{i_1}, \ldots, d_{i_j})$ iff $R(d_{i_1}', \ldots, d_{i_j}')$ whenever R is a relation in $\mathcal{R}$ and $i_1, \cdots, i_j$ are indices among $1 \ldots n$. We use $[w]_{\mathcal{R}}$ to denote the set of words that are $\mathcal{R}$-indistinguishable from w. A *data language* $\mathcal{L}$ is a set of data words that respects $\mathcal{R}$ in the sense that $w \approx_{\mathcal{R}} w'$ implies $w \in \mathcal{L} \leftrightarrow w' \in \mathcal{L}$.

In order to capture the windowing behavior of TCP, we define the set of relations $\mathcal{R} = \{R_{\otimes,c} \ : \ \otimes \in \{<, \leq, =, \geq, >\} \ \wedge \ c \in \{0, 1, 100\}\}$, and relation $R_{\otimes,c} \subset \mathbb{N} \times \mathbb{N}$ such that $x R_{\otimes,c} y$ iff $x + c \otimes y$. Relations $R_{\otimes,0}$ encode equality and an order on the sets of sequence numbers. Relations in $R_{\otimes,1}$ encode the successor relation between sequence numbers and $R_{\otimes,100}$ describes windows (of size 100).

We assume a set of *registers* $x_1, x_2, \ldots$ that can store data values of data words. A *parameterized symbol* is a term of form $\alpha(p)$, where α is an action and p a formal parameter. An *atomic guard* g over p is a logic formula of form $(x_i + c \otimes p)$ with $\otimes \in \{<, \leq, =, \geq, >\}$ and $c \in \{0, 1, 100\}$. We allow for aggregation of atomic guards into *intervals* of form $(g_1 \wedge g_2)$, where atomic guards g_1 and g_2 specify a lower and an upper bound on p, respectively. A valuation $\nu : \{p, x_1, x_2, \ldots\} \mapsto \mathbb{N}$ satisfies a guard g if $g[\nu] = g[\nu(p)/p][\nu(x_1)/x_1][\ldots]$ is true and we write $\nu \models g$ in this case.

An *assignment* is a simple parallel update of registers with values from registers or the formal parameter p. We represent an assignment which updates the registers $x_{i_1}, \ldots, x_{i_m}$ with values from the registers $x_{j_1}, \ldots, x_{j_n}$ or p as a mapping π from $\{x_{i_1}, \ldots, x_{i_m}\}$ to $\{x_{j_1}, \ldots, x_{j_n}\} \cup \{p\}$, meaning that the value of the register or parameter $\pi(x_{i_k})$ is assigned to the register x_{i_k}, for $k = 1, \ldots, m$.

Definition 1 (Register automaton). *A register automaton (RA) is a tuple* $\mathcal{A} = (L, l_0, \mathcal{X}, \Gamma, \lambda)$, *where*

- *L is a finite set of locations, with $l_0 \in L$ as the initial location,*
- *$\mathcal{X}$ maps each location $l \in L$ to a finite set $\mathcal{X}(l)$ of registers, and*
- *Γ is a finite set of transitions, each of form $\langle l, \alpha(p), g, \pi, l' \rangle$, where*
    - *$l \in L$ is a source location,*
    - *$l' \in L$ is a target location,*
    - *$\alpha(p)$ is a parameterized symbol,*
    - *g is a guard over p and $\mathcal{X}(l)$, and*
    - *π (the assignment) is a mapping from $\mathcal{X}(l')$ to $\mathcal{X}(l) \cup \{p\}$, and*
- *λ maps each $l \in L$ to $\{+, -\}$.* □

We require register automata to have no initial registers (i.e., $\mathcal{X}(l_0) = \emptyset$) and to be *completely specified* in the sense that for each location $l \in L$ and action α, the disjunction of the guards on the α-transitions from l is equivalent to *true*.

RA Semantics. Let us formalize the semantics of RAs. A *state* of an RA $\mathcal{A} = (L, l_0, \mathcal{X}, \Gamma, \lambda)$ is a pair $\langle l, \nu \rangle$ where $l \in L$ and ν is a valuation over $\mathcal{X}(l)$, i.e., a mapping from $\mathcal{X}(l)$ to $\mathcal{D}$. A *step* of $\mathcal{A}$, denoted $\langle l, \nu \rangle \xrightarrow{\alpha(d)} \langle l', \nu' \rangle$, transfers $\mathcal{A}$ from $\langle l, \nu \rangle$ to $\langle l', \nu' \rangle$ on input of the data symbol $\alpha(d)$ if there is a transition $\langle l, \alpha(p), g, \pi, l' \rangle \in \Gamma$ with

- $\nu \models g[d/p]$, i.e., d satisfies the guard g under the valuation ν, and
- ν' is the updated valuation with $\nu'(x_i) = \nu(x_j)$ if $\pi(x_i) = x_j$, otherwise $\nu'(x_i) = d$ if $\pi(x_i) = p$.

A *run* of $\mathcal{A}$ over a data word $w = \alpha(d_1) \ldots \alpha(d_n)$ is a sequence of steps of $\mathcal{A}$

$$\langle l_0, \nu_0 \rangle \xrightarrow{\alpha_1(d_1)} \langle l_1, \nu_1 \rangle \quad \ldots \quad \langle l_{n-1}, \nu_{n-1} \rangle \xrightarrow{\alpha_n(d_n)} \langle l_n, \nu_n \rangle$$

for some initial valuation ν_0. The run is *accepting* if $\lambda(l_n) = +$ and *rejecting* if $\lambda(l_n) = -$. The word w is *accepted (rejected)* by $\mathcal{A}$ under ν_0 if $\mathcal{A}$ has an accepting (rejecting) run over w which starts in $\langle l_0, \nu_0 \rangle$. An RA is *determinate* if there is no data word over which it has both accepting and rejecting runs. In this case we interpret an RA $\mathcal{A}$ as a mapping from the set of data words to $\{+, -\}$, where $+$ stands for ACCEPT and $-$ for REJECT. When using register automata as models for reactive system, we refine the set of actions into inputs and outputs (cf. [5]).

3.2 Tree Queries

For a data language $\mathcal{L}$, a data word u with $Vals(u) = d_1, \ldots, d_k$, and a set V of sequences of actions (so-called abstract suffixes), a (u, V)-*tree* is a decision tree (a tree-shaped RA) $\mathcal{T} = (L, l_0, \mathcal{X}, \Gamma, \lambda)$ with root l_0 and $\mathcal{X}(l_0) \subseteq \{x_1, \ldots, x_k\}$ that (1) has runs over exactly all data words v with $Acts(v) \in V$ and that (2) accepts a data word v from $\langle l_0, \nu_u \rangle$ iff $uv \in \mathcal{L}$. Please note, that we do not require $\mathcal{X}(l_0)$ to be empty for decision trees and let ν_u such that $\nu_u(x_i) = d_i$ for $x_i \in \mathcal{X}(l_0)$ and d_i the i-th data value of u.

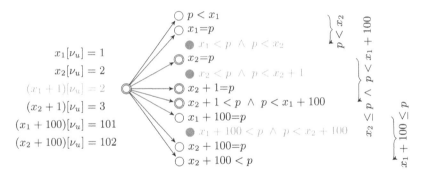

Fig. 5. Potential (left), maximally refined $(u, \hat{v})$-tree (center), and canonic guards (right) for u with $\nu_u = \{x_1 \mapsto 1, x_2 \mapsto 2\}$ and $\hat{v}$ with $|\hat{v}| = 1$. Actions omitted.

A tree oracle for $\mathcal{L}$ is a function $\mathcal{O}$ that for any prefix u and set of abstract suffixes V constructs a (u, V)-tree $\mathcal{O}(u, V)$. The SL^* algorithm combines multiple symbolic decision trees (SDTs) into a conjectured model. We can implement a tree oracle by starting with a maximally refined symbolic decision tree that has one unique sequence of transitions for every $\mathcal{R}$-indistinguishable class of words $[uv]_{\mathcal{R}}$ with $Acts(v) \in V$ and then compute a more concise tree by iteratively merging equivalent subtrees.

Maximally refined SDTs. For simplicity, we describe the generation of a maximally refined symbolic decision tree for a prefix u and a single abstract suffix $\hat{v}$. This allows us to omit actions from the presentation. For $|Vals(u)| = k$, the *potential of u* is the set of terms $(x_i + c)$ with $1 \leq i \leq k$ and $c \in \{0, 1, 100\}$ that can appear in guards after u. The valuation ν_u (with $\nu_u(x_i) = d_i$ for $d_i \in Vals(u)$) induces an order on the terms in the potential. An example of this order is shown on the left of Fig. 5 for a word u with two data values.

Omitting the trivial case of the empty sequence, let $|\hat{v}| = 1$ for the moment. We generate guards for cases p smaller than the smallest term in the potential of u, p equal to one of the terms, p in the interval between two successive terms, and p greater than any term in the potential of u. These guards are maximally refined: each (satisfiable) guard describes one class $[uv]_{\mathcal{R}}$ of $\mathcal{R}$-indistinguishable words. We instantiate each guard with the help of a constraint solver and use an output query to determine if $uv \in \mathcal{L}$. Figure 5 (middle) exemplifies the construction. As indicated by gray lines on the left of the figure, some terms in the potential are equal. For these cases we pick one of the equal terms as the basis for guards. Gray colored guards cannot be instantiated and are omitted.

In the general case of $|\hat{v}| > 1$, we apply the above technique iteratively, generating sequences of guards and transitions for the parameters of $\hat{v}$. We maintain data values of the suffix symbolically during sequence generation and only instantiate complete sequences of guards. The approach scales to sets of suffix sequences as we construct maximally refined paths: paths of suffixes with common prefixes will have common guards for those prefixes and can be expressed as trees.

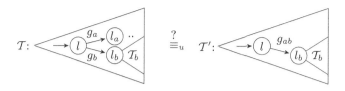

Fig. 6. Merging sub-trees of an SDT.

Maximally abstract SDTs and Monotonicity. In order to guarantee convergence of learning on a canonical automaton, the SL^* makes some monotonicity requirements on tree oracles [6]. For growing sets of abstract suffixes V, V', ... with $V \subset V'$, it has to be shown that $\mathcal{O}(u, V')$ refines $\mathcal{O}(u, V)$ by only adding registers to $\mathcal{X}(l_0)$, and only refining guards of transitions. Additionally, if decision trees $\mathcal{O}(u, V)$ and $\mathcal{O}(u', V)$ cannot be made equal under some renaming of registers from $\mathcal{X}(l_0)$ in one tree, trees $\mathcal{O}(u, V')$ and $\mathcal{O}(u', V')$ cannot become equal either by such a renaming. These conditions trivially hold on maximally refined SDTs. Unfortunately, however, maximally refined SDTs do not lead to finite models during learning as the shape of a tree depends on the length of the prefix. We transform maximally refined SDTs into more abstract trees by merging transitions and equivalent sub-trees (akin to BDD minimization), thereby hiding irrelevant structural differences between trees.

The essential idea is that two (u, V)-trees $\mathcal{T}$ and $\mathcal{T}'$ are semantically equivalent after u, denoted by $\mathcal{T} \equiv_u \mathcal{T}'$, if both trees accept the same set of suffixes under initial valuation ν_u with $\nu_u(x_i) = d_i$ for $d_i \in Vals(u)$. We can check semantic equivalence with finitely many test runs (i.e., one for each path in a maximally refined SDT for V). Let now l be a location in $\mathcal{T}$ with outgoing transitions to l_a and l_b, guarded by g_a and g_b, respectively, as sketched in Fig. 6. For some new guard g_{ab}, equivalent to $(g_a \vee g_b)$, we construct $\mathcal{T}'$ from $\mathcal{T}$ w.l.o.g. by removing the transition from l to l_a and the sub-tree rooted at l_a. On the transition from l to l_b, we replace g_b by g_{ab} (cf. right part of the figure). We abstract g_a and g_b into g_{ab} if $\mathcal{T} \equiv_u \mathcal{T}'$.

In order to arrive at a canonical representation, we perform merging in a fixed order: we always merge guards for the smallest possible terms with respect to the order on the potential (cf. maximally refined trees). This ensures that merging always results in intervals. An example is shown on the right of Fig. 5. Merged guards are obtained from top (smaller terms) to bottom (greater terms).

Our semantic merging process satisfies all three requirements: Adding more suffixes (and hence paths) cannot lead to merging subtrees that could not be merged before. Guards are refined into finer intervals. Since the original boundaries will be maintained, monotonic growth of registers follows. Finally, since abstract trees are semantically equivalent to maximally refined trees, differences between trees are preserved when adding suffixes.

Output queries observe the behavior of the SUT on a sequence of test inputs. In learning-based testing, these queries are computed by executing tests on the actual system under test.

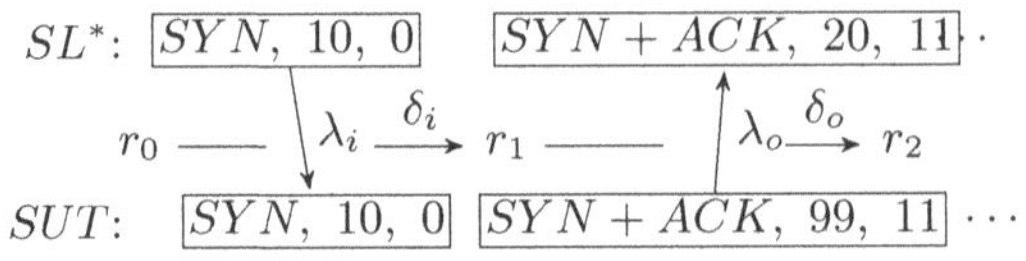

$$SL^*: \boxed{SYN,\ 10,\ 0} \quad \boxed{SYN + ACK,\ 20,\ 11}\cdot$$

$$SUT: \boxed{SYN,\ 10,\ 0}\ \boxed{SYN + ACK,\ 99,\ 11}\ \cdots$$

Fig. 7. Translation between Neat Trace and SUT Trace.

Testing has to be done in an adaptive fashion, synchronizing data values that are used in test inputs by the learning algorithm and those used in actual tests as the SUT may introduce new sequence numbers during tests. As an example, the learning algorithm may assume to receive a message $SYN+ACK$ with (new) sequence number 1. Then, in the actual communication the SUT sends a random new sequence number.

To tackle this problem, the work [2] introduces a determinizer component, placed between the *learner* and the SUT. This component provides the learner with a deterministic, or 'neat' view of the SUT, by constructing and applying a 1 to 1 mapping from regular values to *neat values*. This mapping transforms all relation equivalent traces (input/output sequences) encountered to a single neat trace. The learner then infers the SUT only in terms of its neat traces.

Output Queries. We extend the determinizer concept to a setting with inequalities and sums. Our definition focuses on data values and ignores actions, which are invariant under mapping. The determinizer is the mapper $\mathcal{D} = \langle R, r_0, \delta_i, \delta_o, \lambda_i, \lambda_o \rangle$ over states $R = \{r \subseteq \mathbb{N} \times \mathbb{N} \mid r \text{ finite and one-to-one}\}$ with initial state $r_0 = \emptyset$. Value transformations (λ) and mapper updates (δ) are defined for $c \in 0, 1, 100$ and $x, y, n, m \in \mathbb{N}$ as follows.

$$\lambda_i(r, n) = \begin{cases} x + c & \text{if } m + c = n \text{ for some } (x, m) \in r \\ \mathsf{smaller}(\mathsf{dom}(r)) & \text{if } m + c > n \text{ for all } (\cdot, m) \in r \\ \mathsf{fresh}(\mathsf{dom}(r)) & \text{if } m + c < n \text{ for all } (\cdot, m) \in r \\ (x + y)/2 & \text{else; for } (x - c_1, m_l - c_1), (y - c_2, m_u - c_2) \in r \\ & \text{s.t. } (m_l < n < m_u) \text{ and } (m_u - m_l) \text{ minimal} \end{cases}$$

$$\lambda_o(r, x) = \begin{cases} n + c & \text{if } y + c = x \text{ for some } (y, n) \in r \\ \mathsf{fresh}(\mathsf{ran}(r)) & \text{otherwise} \end{cases}$$

$$\delta_i(r, n) = \begin{cases} r & \text{if } (\cdot, n) \in r \\ r \cup \{ (\lambda_i(r, n), n) \} & \text{otherwise} \end{cases}$$

$$\delta_o(r, x) = \begin{cases} r & \text{if } (x, \cdot) \in r \\ r \cup \{ (x, \lambda_o(r, x)) \} & \text{otherwise} \end{cases}$$

There, dom and ran denote domain and image of a function. Functions fresh : $\mathbb{N}^* \to \mathbb{N}$ and smaller : $\mathbb{N}^* \to \mathbb{N}$ generate fresh values and smaller values. For $X \subset \mathbb{N}$ we use the concrete functions $\mathsf{fresh}(X) := (\lfloor max(X) \rfloor \div s_u \rfloor + 1) \times s_u$ and $\mathsf{smaller}(X) := (\lfloor \min(X) \div s_l \rfloor - 1) \times s_l$. Step sizes s_u and s_l are fixed big enough to avoid collisions (accidental relations between data values) during experiments.

Figure 7 shows an example application of the mapper, producing a neat trace from Fig. 2. Whenever the system generates an output, the determinizer processes it by replacing the output values with neat values before delivering the output to the learner . Conversely, on generating a concrete input, the learner passes it to the determinizer which replaces neat input values with regular values, and sends the resulting input to the SUT. Every time it processes a value, the determinizer updates its state.

3.3 Model-Based Testing

We instantiate the testing part of our framework with a relative simple adaptation of a random algorithm to the scenario of register automaton models. For a register automaton model $\mathcal{A}$, each test run begins by traversing the model to a randomly selected location of $\mathcal{A}$ and is continued by a random sequence of inputs until either a discrepancy is discovered between model and system under test, or until the run terminates and a new run starts.

Our extension consists in selecting data values for inputs. For a run with current prefix w and next input α, we use the machinery introduced above (the potential of a word, and symbolic guards that describe classes $[w\alpha(d)]_{\mathcal{R}}$ of data words) as a basis for computing a pool of data values for α. The pool contains one data value d for each $\mathcal{R}$-indistinguishable class $[w\alpha(d)]_{\mathcal{R}}$ of data words. We add a bias to the selection of data values, so that values in or related to those stored in registers in $\mathcal{A}$ after running over w are more likely to be picked.

We can easily obtain a PAC-inspired conformance guarantee (cf. [17]) with this testing method for the probability distribution on the set of data words induced by a model $\mathcal{A}$ and the above strategy for selecting tests. With respect to this distribution, $\mathcal{A}$ is an ϵ-approximation of SUT if $\sum_{w \in S} Pr(w) \leq \epsilon$ for the symmetric difference S of sets of words accepted by $\mathcal{A}$ and SUT. The probability of $\mathcal{A}$ not being an ϵ-approximation of the SUT after performing k independent test runs is at most $(1 - \epsilon)^k$. For some confidence value δ, we simply choose k such that $(1 - \epsilon)^k < \delta$ (i.e., such that $k > ln(\delta)/ln(1 - \epsilon)$).

4   Testing TCP Implementations

We have implemented the theories introduced earlier into RaLib [5]. We then set up an experimental setup through which we could connect RaLib to various TCP clients. RaLib inferred models, which we checked manually for conformance with the specification.

4.1 Experimental Setup

The experimental setup used to learn TCP is similar to the setup used in [7,8]. As in those works, the alphabet used to learn TCP defines two types of inputs. The first type is *packet inputs*, used to describe TCP segments sent to the system. These inputs are parameterized by TCP flag combinations, sequence and

Table 1. Learning Statistics. BASE stands for Baseline. [T] marks Use of Typing.

SUL	Alpha.	Term.	Inp. Loc.	Num. Hyp.	Learning		Testing	
					Inputs	Resets	Inputs	Resets
Linux 3.19	[T]BASE	yes	6	15	4,311	947	113,921	11,720
	BASE	yes	6	15	9,930	2,168	116,479	12,339
	[T]BASE+ACK	yes	8	21	77,922	13,414	119,768	12,289
FreeBSD 11.0	[T]BASE	yes	6	16	4,239	933	113,953	11,708
	BASE	yes	6	16	9,958	2,152	116,446	12,333
	[T]BASE+ACK	no	8	21	418,977	80,200	81,024	8,367
Windows 10	BASE-CLOSE	no	6	14	193,712	24,848	119,768	12,289

acknowledgement numbers. The second type of inputs is *socket inputs* such as connect and close, referring to the methods defined by the socket interface. Outputs defined are *packet outputs*, which bear the same structure as packet inputs and describe TCP segments generated by the system, and *timeouts*, which suggest that no output was generated by the system. For model learning, we use the SL^* algorithm with the theory and optimizations discussed earlier. Additionally, we used techniques for reducing the size of counterexamples as shorter counterexamples tend to lead to shorter suffixes, which greatly decreases the number of inputs needed to run. For sample techniques and a corresponding discussion we refer to [11]. Finally, to speed up learning, we used multiple systems under learning in parallel. Model-based testing was done using the algorithm described in the previous section.

4.2   Experiments and Results

We attempted to learn TCP client implementations of Linux, FreeBSD and Windows. We chose clients, since they are simpler to learn and contain less redundancy compared to servers (cf. [8]). In terms of the configurations used, we disabled adaptive receive windows (or window scale), so that receive windows remain fixed over the course of each test. Moreover, in the segments sent to the SUT we advertise the same receive window as that of the SUT. Doing so we avoid having to include an additional sum constant for our own receive window.

Our baseline alphabet consists of the connect, SYN+ACK, ACK+RST, RST and close inputs. This alphabet covers several states in the specification. The alphabet should also reveal how SUTs in these states react to RST segments. These segments are generated in cases where one side abruptly terminates a connection and should be processed only if their sequence numbers are in window of the expected. We have also extended the alphabet with the ACK input if learning with the baseline was successful. To obtain models in an adequate time, we do not explore data relations between all formal parameters in some experiments. This optimization has been introduced as *typing* of symbolic parameters in [5].

Once a hypothesis was constructed, we tested it using the algorithm presented earlier. We have set the size of the random sequence to 10 (sufficient for exploring

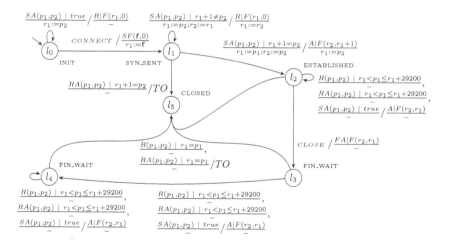

Fig. 8. Model of Linux Client. Flags are replaced by their starting characters (i.e. FIN by F, SYN by S). We group inputs with guards soliciting the same output and assignment over registers and use input/output notation. Inputs have guards over parameters. In outputs, parameters are instantiated.

the behavior we are interested in) and ran 15,000 tests on the final hypothesis. Using the confidence metric from the previous section, this yields a confidence of more than 99,9% that a model is an 0.05%-approximation of the SUT for data words up to a length of 10 — relative to the probability distribution our randomized testing algorithm generates over the set of data words.

Table 1 reports the setting, termination status and learning statistics for all experiments done. The setting indicates the concrete SUT, the alphabet relative to the baseline and whether typing was used. Successful experiments took at most two days to complete, the determining factors being the size in parameters of the suffixes and the 0.3 s wait time used for each response before concluding a timeout. We automatically terminated experiments still unresolved after 500,000 inputs. For these experiments, we still display the last hypothesis and learning numbers at the point of termination. Results are available on RaLib 's website.[1]

Using both un-typed and typed baseline alphabets we inferred models for Linux and FreeBSD. We inferred a model for Linux using the ACK-extended typed alphabet, but not for BSD. Learning FreeBSD for this setting followed a similar course to learning Linux, leading to a similar hypothesis. Testing generated a counterexample, whose processing resulted in a long new suffix. The suffix proved too expensive for tree queries to terminate within the input bounds set.

We couldn't learn Windows models even after removing the CLOSE input. Analysis of the last conjectured model and the generated tests revealed behavior inconsistent with the specification: Windows accepts sequence numbers up to and including window size plus one in the ESTABLISHED state for RST inputs.

---

[1] See: https://goo.gl/23VNfv.

```
#define after(seq2, seq1)  before(seq1, seq2)
static inline bool before(__u32 seq1, __u32 seq2) {
        return (__s32)(seq1-seq2) < 0;
}
static inline bool tcp_sequence(
    const struct tcp_sock *tp, u32 seq, u32 end_seq) {
    return !before(end_seq, tp->rcv_wup) &&
        !after(seq, tp->rcv_nxt + tcp_receive_window(tp));
}
```

Listing 9. Relevant Code of TCP Implementation in Linux Kernel.

This helps demonstrate a limitation of our approach: relevant data relations $\mathcal{R}$ are an input to learning and convergence is guaranteed only for systems that respect $\mathcal{R}$ (cf. Sect. 3.1).

4.3   Analysis of Conformance to RFC

Figure 8 presents the model learned for Linux using the baseline alphabet. The models learned for FreeBSD and Linux are near identical with one exception. Linux defines an in-window sequence number as a value up to and including $rcv.nxt + win$ (for a next expected sequence number $rcv.nxt$). FreeBSD excludes the higher bound. Windows, on the other hand, even seems to include $rcv.nxt + win + 1$. The RFC 793 [14, p. 26] specifies a closed upper bound. Thus, FreeBSD conforms to the upper bound requirement whereas Linux and Windows do not. For Linux, we trace this violation to code in the most recent kernel, v4.11.[2] Listing 9 shows the relevant code snippets. To check whether a sequence number is not after the window, they use the $!(seq > rcv.nxt + win)$ conjunct, allowing $rcv.nxt + win$ to be within the window. We inquired Linux developers about this issue and they confirmed it and said they would issue a fix for it. During our experiments, we have uncovered a different, unrelated, bug relating to faulty re-transmissions for which a fix has been issued.

Aside from that, reset processing seems to be implemented as stated in the RFC with the remark that both systems implement the 'Blind Reset Attack Using RST Bit' safe guard introduced in RFC 5961 [1, p. 7], by which only RST segments with the sequence number equal to the expected sequence number cause the termination of a connection. RST segments whose sequence number is in window but not equal to the expected sequence number prompt a 'challenge ACK response'. We can verify that this is the case by analyzing the Linux model's responses to RST segments in the ESTABLISHED and FIN_WAIT1 states. As a note, RFC 5961 might have been the cause of the inconsistency remarked previously. As of this writing, RFC 5961 gives a wrong description of the within/outside window conditions of RFC 793. The error had been reported in 2016 and is included in the RFC errata[3].

---

[2] See: https://goo.gl/9A8ZYM.
[3] See: https://www.rfc-editor.org/errata/rfc5961.

5 Conclusion

Our work introduces the first application of register automata learning to real networked systems, in the form of TCP clients. To that end, we have developed the theories needed to learn TCP into the learning framework of [6]. We implemented heuristics that improve scalability of learning and developed a component that deals with non-determinism in fresh data values. The application of our learning-based testing setup resulted in models for TCP client implementations of Linux and FreeBSD. Our setup helped reveal violation of the RFC 793 standard [14] in Linux and Windows. In Linux we identified the root cause for the violation in the Kernel code.

In a next step, we plan to produce models for extended sets of inputs and models of TCP servers. Despite the optimizations used, we eventually faced combinatorial blow up in the number of required tests. Combining learning with static or symbolic analysis methods may help reducing this blow up by identifying more precisely the relations one should test for. This will also address the limitation of fixed relations that prevented us from learning a model for Windows.

References

1. Stewart, R., Ramaiah, A., Dalal, M.: Improving TCP's Robustness to Blind In-Window Attacks. RFC 5961, August 2010
2. Aarts, F., Fiterau-Brostean, P., Kuppens, H., Vaandrager, F.: Learning register automata with fresh value generation. In: Leucker, M., Rueda, C., Valencia, F.D. (eds.) ICTAC 2015. LNCS, vol. 9399, pp. 165–183. Springer, Cham (2015). doi:10.1007/978-3-319-25150-9_11
3. Angluin, D.: Learning regular sets from queries and counterexamples. Inf. Comput. **75**(2), 87–106 (1987)
4. Berg, T., Grinchtein, O., Jonsson, B., Leucker, M., Raffelt, H., Steffen, B.: On the correspondence between conformance testing and regular inference. In: Cerioli, M. (ed.) FASE 2005. LNCS, vol. 3442, pp. 175–189. Springer, Heidelberg (2005). doi:10.1007/978-3-540-31984-9_14
5. Cassel, S., Howar, F., Jonsson, B.: RALib: a LearnLib extension for inferring EFSMs. In: DIFTS 2015 (2015)
6. Cassel, S., Howar, F., Jonsson, B., Steffen, B.: Active learning for extended finite state machines. Formal Aspects Comput. **28**(2), 233–263 (2016)
7. Fiterău-Broştean, P., Janssen, R., Vaandrager, F.: Learning fragments of the TCP network protocol. In: Lang, F., Flammini, F. (eds.) FMICS 2014. LNCS, vol. 8718, pp. 78–93. Springer, Cham (2014). doi:10.1007/978-3-319-10702-8_6
8. Fiterău-Broştean, P., Janssen, R., Vaandrager, F.: Combining model learning and model checking to analyze TCP implementations. In: Chaudhuri, S., Farzan, A. (eds.) CAV 2016. LNCS, vol. 9780, pp. 454–471. Springer, Cham (2016). doi:10.1007/978-3-319-41540-6_25
9. Fiterău-Broştean, P., Lenaerts, T., de Ruiter, J., Poll, E., Vaandrager, F.W., Verleg, P.: Model learning and model checking of SSH implementations. In: SPIN Symposium (2017, to appear)

10. Hagerer, A., Hungar, H., Niese, O., Steffen, B.: Model generation by moderated regular extrapolation. In: Kutsche, R.-D., Weber, H. (eds.) FASE 2002. LNCS, vol. 2306, pp. 80–95. Springer, Heidelberg (2002). doi:10.1007/3-540-45923-5_6

11. Koopman, P., Achten, P., Plasmeijer, R.: Model-based shrinking for state-based testing. In: McCarthy, J. (ed.) TFP 2013. LNCS, vol. 8322, pp. 107–124. Springer, Heidelberg (2014). doi:10.1007/978-3-642-45340-3_7

12. Meinke, K., Sindhu, M.A.: Lbtest: a learning-based testing tool for reactive systems. In: ICST 2013, pp. 447–454. IEEE Computer Society (2013)

13. Peled, D., Vardi, M.Y., Yannakakis, M.: Black box checking. J. Autom. Lang. Comb. **7**(2), 225–246 (2001)

14. Postel, J.: Transmission Control Protocol. RFC 793, September 1981

15. de Ruiter, J., Poll, E.: Protocol state fuzzing of TLS implementations. In: USENIX Security, pp. 193–206. USENIX Association, Washington, D.C. (2015)

16. Tretmans, J.: Model-based testing and some steps towards test-based modelling. In: Bernardo, M., Issarny, V. (eds.) SFM 2011. LNCS, vol. 6659, pp. 297–326. Springer, Heidelberg (2011). doi:10.1007/978-3-642-21455-4_9

17. Valiant, L.G.: A theory of the learnable. Commun. ACM **27**(11), 1134–1142 (1984)

Optimizing Feature Interaction Detection

Alessandro Fantechi[1,2], Stefania Gnesi[2], and Laura Semini[2,3(✉)]

[1] Dip. di Ing. Dell'Informazione, Università di Firenze, Firenze, Italy
[2] ISTI-CNR, Pisa, Italy
[3] Dipartimento di Informatica, Università di Pisa, Pisa, Italy
`semini@di.unipi.it`

Abstract. The feature interaction problem has been recognized as a general problem of software engineering. The problem appears when a combination of features interacts generating a conflict, exhibiting a behaviour that is unexpected for the features considered in isolation, possibly resulting in some critical safety violation. Verification of absence of critical feature interactions has been the subject of several studies. In this paper, we focus on functional interactions and we address the problem of the 3-way feature interactions, i.e. interactions that occur only when three features are all included in the system, but not when only two of them are. In this setting, we define a widely applicable definition framework, within which we show that a 3 (or greater)-way interaction is always caused by a 2-way interaction, i.e. that pairwise sampling is complete, hence reducing to quadratic the complexity of automatic detection of incorrect interaction.

1 Introduction

The specification of a complex software system may be simplified by decomposing the system into *features* that identify units of functionality. Feature-oriented software development of safety critical systems can simplify the configuration of large systems, as well as their verification and certification, by concentrating the verification efforts on single features, rather than on the whole system. But this happens only if a high degree of independence between features can be assumed, while frequently instead the *feature interaction* problem can be encountered, a problem which occurs when the concurrent composition of two (or more) features generates an unexpected behaviour.

The feature interaction problem has indeed been recognized as a general problem of software engineering in all those contexts where *features* are the basic functionality units that are composed to build up complex software systems [1,9,25,31], as also recently advocated in [2]. In particular, if a feature interaction affects critical systems, it may cause safety requirements violation; hence verification of the absence of feature interactions becomes a very important aspect of safety certification. The question is how many features are required to generate an interaction, two or more than two. In this paper, we concentrate on the so-called "3-way interaction". The problem was first discussed in the feature

© Springer International Publishing AG 2017
L. Petrucci et al. (Eds.): FMICS-AVoCS 2017, LNCS 10471, pp. 201–216, 2017.
DOI: 10.1007/978-3-319-67113-0_13

interaction detection contest at [18], where the community suggested that there are two types of 3-way interaction: those reducible to an interaction between a pair of features and those where the interaction only exists if all three features are present. The latter were termed "true" 3-way interactions.

The very existence of such cases is still under discussion, in the sense that there does not seem to be a consensus on the definition of the problem itself. For example, in [17,18] the existence of 3-way interactions is negated but with no proof. On the other end, in [3] an example of 3-way interaction is reported. The question is quite important for the verification of safety critical systems that are built by feature-oriented development: if we can limit the definition of features to a framework where "true" 3-way feature interactions do not exist, then the problem of checking for feature interactions can be reduced to checking features pairwise, hence with reduced (quadratic) verification complexity. In order to give a contribution to the New Feature Interaction Challenge [2], this paper offers a framework of feature definition by condition-action rules and interleaved composition, and presents a definition of a feature interaction as when the execution of one feature disallows the execution of another or when the two possible results of the interleaved execution of two features are inconsistent with each other. In this framework we then prove that any 3-way interaction is due to a 2-way interaction. In regards to verification, this amounts to say that checking by *pairwise sampling* [20,21,26] the combinations of features is complete with respect to feature interaction detection.

The proposed framework is contrasted with cases reported in the literature of 3-way interactions and discusses why these are not considered true 3-way interactions according to our behavioural interpretation of composition and interaction.

In the following, we define a running example: the features of a metro train (Sect. 2), and the formalisation of features and feature composition (Sect. 3). We then prove that the interactions among three features can always be revealed by checking for the 2-way interactions, therefore reducing the complexity of the verification problem (Sect. 4). A section on related work concludes the paper.

2   Running Example

As an example, we consider a control system composed by the following features, each feature devoted to the actuation of a separate requirement over safety-related behaviour of a metro train, regarding the usage of emergency brakes and the opening of doors, in normal situations or when a smoke sensor detects a fire. The train can be travelling in a tunnel, in which case safety regulations require that the train cannot be stopped even in case of fire. On the other hand, doors, normally opened only at stations, cannot be opened, even in emergency situations, when the train is running. If not in a tunnel, the train can normally be running in the open air or at standstill in a station. We assume that there are smoke sensors and that whether the train is running in a tunnel or at standstill in a station or elsewhere is known to the system through proper positioning sensors.

SD Station & Doors:	If the train is at a station, the doors are opened
DS Danger in Station:	If the train is at a station and there is a danger in the station, doors are closed and the train leaves the station
EH Emergency Handle:	If the emergency handle is pulled, actuate the emergency brake
TB Tunnel & Brake:	If the train is in a tunnel, disable the emergency brake
FA Fire alarm:	Raise a fire alarm when smoke is sensed
FB Fire alarm & Brake:	If fire alarm is raised and the train is running, actuate the emergency brake
FE Fire alarm & Escape:	If fire alarm is raised, open the doors

It is easy to note that, due to some interactions between the above features, we may have interacting behaviours. It is also apparent that, in order to provide a safe global behaviour, some form of conflict resolution is needed, possibly prioritizing some features with respect to others.

Below, we discuss all the possible interactions between the metro features and address their detection.

For instance, *EH* interferes with *TB* since, if applied concurrently, i.e. when the emergency handle is pulled and the train is in a tunnel, their actions conflict.

A 3-way interaction refers to those cases in which the interaction is generated by the composition of three features. Apparently, in the metro example there is a 3-way interaction among *FA*, *FB*, and *TB*. Assume that smoke is sensed while the train is in a tunnel, *FA* and *FB* are applied in sequence:

$$smoke\_sensed \xrightarrow{FA} fire\_alarm\_raised \xrightarrow{FB} emergency\_brake$$

and interact with *TB* disabling the emergency brake. In the paper we will provide a constructive technique to detect these interactions with pairwise analysis: such a technique will detect that the interaction is between *FB* and *TB*.

3 Formalisation of Features and Feature Interaction

Feature interaction is due to a mutual interference resulting in an unexpected behaviour. The most common way to define a feature interaction is based on behaviours:

"A feature interaction occurs when the behavior of one feature is affected by the presence of another feature" [1].

"A feature interaction is some way in which a feature or features modify or influence another feature in defining overall system behavior" [32].

Similar definitions can be found e.g. in [11,23,27]. This mutual influence of features is often described in an action oriented way, by listing the pairs of conflicting actions, and then deriving possible interactions between features including these actions. In a complementary way, we consider a state-based approach [24] and look at the effect of the features on a shared state. Indeed, any time two features F and F' access a shared state, and at least one of the accesses updates it, there might be an interaction.

The main purpose of this paper is to prove that, in the considered framework, the behavioural interactions between three features are always due to the interaction between two of the three considered features, therefore reducing the complexity of the verification problem to look for pairwise interaction. To do this we need to perform an analysis of the functional behaviour of feature combinations.

Without loss of generality, we define a framework in which features are described as condition-action rules and systems behave as the parallel composition of features [23,30]. In this framework, inspired by the *action systems* [5], if the action part of a condition-action rule of a feature is executed, it changes the state of the system: the state of a system is seen as a set of predicates that hold on some global, shared variables. A feature is said to be *enabled* when its condition is satisfied by the current state of the system. The application of the feature can occur only when it is enabled, having the effect of changing the state of the system according to its action. The computation of the system is given by a sequence of feature applications. When two or more features are enabled, one is selected non-deterministically.

In this section, we define a formalisation for the computation state and give the semantics of features in terms of transition systems.

3.1 Semantics of a Feature

Definition 1. *Let $\mathcal{S}$ be a finite set of states. Given a set AP of atomic propositions, with p ranging in AP, a **computation state** $s \in \mathcal{S}$ is defined as a conjunction of literals:*

$$s ::= \bot \,|\, p \,|\, \sim p \,|\, s \wedge s$$

where $\bot$ is the empty state, in which nothing is said on any atomic proposition.

Example 1. *Examples of computation states are: $s_1 = doors\_open$, $s_2 = tunnel \wedge \sim doors\_open$, $s_3 = \sim tunnel \wedge doors\_open \wedge smoke\_sensed$.*

We include negative atoms for convenience. An alternative modeling would have been defining states as conjunctions of atomic propositions, in a closed world assumption.

We assume the set of actions to be in correspondence with the set of predicates, i.e. each action α has an effect on the truth value of a predicate p: α can make p true or make p false.

Definition 2. *A **feature** is defined by a pair:* $F = \langle C, [A] \rangle$, *where C is a boolean condition to be evaluated on the current state, and $[A]$ is an (atomic) sequence of actions on the state.*

Example 2. *The features of our running metro example can be specified as:*
$SD = \langle station, [open\_doors] \rangle$
$DS = \langle station \wedge danger, [close\_doors, leave\_station] \rangle$
$EH = \langle ehpulled, [activate\_emergency\_brake] \rangle$
$TB = \langle tunnel, [disable\_emergency\_brake] \rangle$
$FA = \langle smoke\_sensed, [raise\_fire\_alarm] \rangle$
$FB = \langle fire\_alarm\_raised \wedge running, [activate\_emergency\_brake] \rangle$
$FE = \langle fire\_alarm\_raised, [open\_doors] \rangle$

An action α transforms a state s in a state $\alpha(s)$.

Definition 3. *We say that action α **writes** p when α makes p true, i.e. $\alpha(\bot) = p$ and that α **writes** $\sim p$ when α falsifies p, i.e. $\alpha(\bot) =\sim p$.*

For instance, action *open_doors* writes *doors_open*, *disable_emergency_brake* writes $\sim emergency\_brake$, and *leave_station* writes $\sim station$. We define now the effect of an action on a general state.

Definition 4. *Given a state s, and a literal p, we say that $s \models p$ when p occurs as a literal in the conjunction of literals representing s.*

Definition 5. *Let s be a state, p a predicate, and α an action writing p, we define the effect of the application of α in s, $\alpha(s)$ by cases:*

$$\alpha(s) = \begin{cases} s \wedge p \ if \ s \not\models p \ and \ s \not\models\sim p \\ s \quad if \ s \models p \\ \hat{s} \wedge p \ if \ s \models\sim p, \ i.e. \ s \ can \ be \ written \ as \ \hat{s}\wedge \sim p \end{cases}$$

We have a symmetric definition when α writes $\sim p$. For instance, let s be a state not telling whether the doors are open or not, then:

$$close\_doors(s) = s\wedge \sim doors\_open$$

Therefore, action *close_doors* is the identity when applied on a state with doors already closed, and changes the truth value of *doors_open* when initially true, i.e.:

$$close\_doors(s\wedge \sim doors\_open) = s\wedge \sim doors\_open$$
$$close\_doors(s \wedge doors\_open) = s\wedge \sim doors\_open$$

To define the semantics of a feature, we model the effect on a state of a sequence of actions as an atomic transition.

Definition 6. *Let A be a sequence of actions $\alpha_1, \ldots, \alpha_n$, we say $s \xrightarrow{A} s'$ when $s' = \alpha_n(\alpha_{n-1}(\ldots\alpha_1(s)\ldots))$.*

Definition 7. *We say that a feature* $F = \langle C, [A] \rangle$ *is* **enabled** *in a state s when* $s \models C$.

Definition 8. *The* **semantics of feature** $F = \langle C, [A] \rangle$ *is the set of all pairs of states* $(s, s') \in \mathcal{S} \times \mathcal{S}$ *such that* F *is enabled in s and* $s \xrightarrow{A} s'$.

In such a case, we also write $s \xrightarrow{F} s'$.

Example 3. *As an example, consider feature* FA, *and a state* s *satisfying* $smoke\_sensed$. *For simplicity we take* $s = smoke\_sensed$. *We have:*

$$smoke\_sensed \xrightarrow{FA} smoke\_sensed \wedge fire\_alarm\_raised$$

3.2   Composition of Features

Definition 9. *A* **software system** *is specified as the parallel composition of features:* $F_1 || \dots || F_n$.

Example 4. *The metro system can be specified as :* $SD || DS || EH || TB || FA || FB || FE$.

The **semantics of a software system** composed of features is given as a labeled transition system $(\mathcal{S}, \mathcal{S}_0, \mathcal{F}, \rightarrow)$ where: $\mathcal{S}$ is the set of states, $\mathcal{S}_0 \subseteq \mathcal{S}$ is a set of initial states, $\mathcal{F}$ is the set of features, and $\rightarrow \subseteq \mathcal{S} \times \mathcal{F} \times \mathcal{S}$ is a transition relation, whose elements, written $s \xrightarrow{F} s'$, are given by all the pairs of states s, s' of the semantics of each feature F, according to Definition 8.

Definition 10. *According to an interleaving semantics of the parallel composition, the* **semantics of a software system** $F_1 || F_2$, *with* $F_1 = \langle C_1, A_1 \rangle$ *and* $F_2 = \langle C_2, A_2 \rangle$, *is given by the labeled transition system* $(\mathcal{S}, \mathcal{S}_0, \mathcal{F}, \rightarrow)$, *generated by the alternative sequences of transitions possible from any initial state in* $\mathcal{S}_0$, *applying one of the features, followed by the other one.*

Hence, the application of features $F_1 || F_2$ *to an initial state* s *generates the following transitions:*

$- s \xrightarrow{F_1} s' \xrightarrow{F_2} s''$ *if* $s \models C_1$ *and* $s' \models C_2$
$- s \xrightarrow{F_2} s' \xrightarrow{F_1} s''$ *if* $s \models C_2$ *and* $s' \models C_1$
$- s \xrightarrow{F_1} s'$ \qquad *if* $s \models C_1$ *and* $s' \not\models C_2$
$- s \xrightarrow{F_2} s'$ \qquad *if* $s \models C_2$ *and* $s' \not\models C_1$

We write:

$$s \xrightarrow{F_1 || F_2} s'$$

as a shorthand for any sequence of transitions from s *to* s' *applying the features in the parallel composition.*

Definition 10 easily extends to the parallel composition of n features: $F_1||\ldots||F_n$:

$$s \xRightarrow{F_1||\ldots||F_n} s'$$

is the result of applying, in any possible ordering, the features $F_1, \ldots F_n$.

Example 5. *Let us consider* $F_1||F_2$, *where:* $F_1 = \langle p, [\alpha_1] \rangle$, $F_2 = \langle p, [\alpha_2] \rangle$, α_1 *writes* r, *and* α_2 *writes* q. *We have:*

$$p \xrightarrow{F_1} p \wedge r \xrightarrow{F_2} p \wedge r \wedge q \quad and \quad p \xrightarrow{F_2} p \wedge q \xrightarrow{F_1} p \wedge r \wedge q$$

i.e. $p \xRightarrow{F_1||F_2} p \wedge r \wedge q$ *and we have two traces from* p *to* $p \wedge r \wedge q$.

It is not guaranteed that all traces of $F_1||F_2$ from s converge in a unique state: it can happen that $s \xRightarrow{F_1||F_2} s'$ and $s \xRightarrow{F_1||F_2} s''$ with $s' \neq s''$, as in the following example.

Example 6. *Now consider* $F_1||F_3$ *where* F_1 *is as above,* $F_3 = \langle p, [\alpha_3] \rangle$, *and* α_3 *writes* $\sim r$. *We have:*

$$p \xrightarrow{F_1} p \wedge r \xrightarrow{F_3} p \wedge \sim r \quad and \quad p \xrightarrow{F_3} p \wedge \sim r \xrightarrow{F_1} p \wedge r$$

i.e. $p \xRightarrow{F_1||F_3} p \wedge r$ *and* $p \xRightarrow{F_1||F_3} p \wedge \sim r$

Example 6 introduces a feature interaction: feature F_1 interacts with F_3 since $F_1||F_3$ can lead to different states, depending on the order of feature application. In Sect. 3.3, we formalise the concept of interaction.

3.3   Formalisation of Interaction

We now give a formal definition of interaction between pairs of features.

Definition 11. *There is an* **interaction** *in* $F_1||F_2$, *where* $F_1 = \langle C_1, [A_1] \rangle$ *and* $F_2 = \langle C_2, [A_2] \rangle$, *when, given a state* s *enabling both, i.e. such that* $s \models C_1 \wedge C_2$, *one of the following two situations occurs:*

1. $s \xrightarrow{F_1} s_a$, *and* $s_a \not\models C_2$, *or* $s \xrightarrow{F_2} s_b$ *and* $s_b \not\models C_1$, *or both, i.e.:*

2. $s \xRightarrow{F_1||F_2} s_c$, $s \xRightarrow{F_1||F_2} s_d$ *and* s_c, s_d *are inconsistent (that is,* $s_c \wedge s_d = false$)

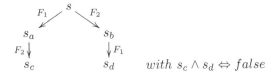

$$\text{with } s_c \wedge s_d \Leftrightarrow false$$

Example 7. *There is an interaction of the first kind in $SD\|DS$. In fact, in case of danger, if DS is applied first, it takes to a state that satisfies the condition: $\sim$ station and where SD is no longer enabled.*
There is an interaction of the second kind in $EH\|TB$ since they both can be applied if the condition ehpulled$\wedge$tunnel holds, and their executions go to inconsistent states.

Dually, according to Definition 11, the system $F_1\|F_2$ is *interaction free* either if the features can never be applied in the same state ($C_1 \wedge C_2 \Leftrightarrow false$) or if the execution of any of them does not falsify the condition of the other and the order of execution is irrelevant, i.e. the diagram commutes:

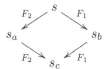

Definition 11 is extended straightforwardly to the parallel composition of **three features**: the features interact when there exists a state s enabling all of them, and the paths of the transition system rooted in s do not converge in a common final state. This happens, for instance, in $FA\|FB\|TB$, taking $s = smoke\_sensed \wedge tunnel$.

We also consider a second form of 3-way interaction arising in a situation where such a state cannot be built. This happens when a feature is enabled by p and another by $\sim p$, for some p, and a third feature writes $\sim p$ (p resp.). As the most general case, consider $F_1\|F_2\|F_3$, where:

$$F_1 = \langle p, [writes\ r] \rangle \qquad F_2 = \langle \sim p, [writes\ s] \rangle \qquad F_3 = \langle q, [writes \sim p] \rangle$$

In this case the three features are not enabled together in any state, but the triggering of F_3 enables F_2 as well, so that starting from a state in which F_1 and F_3 are enabled, we can derive the following diagram, rooted in $p \wedge q$, which does not converge to a unique state. Actually, this 3-way interaction is due to a pairwise interaction in the subsystem $F_1\|F_3$:

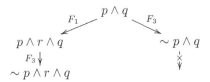

4   No True 3-Way Interaction

Now, we can address the main point of the paper and prove that, under our definition of feature interaction, any 3-way interaction is due to the interaction between two of the considered features. We first observe that there is a constructive way to find a (minimal) state enabling two (or more) features: it is sufficient to take the conjunction of their conditions.

Proposition 1. *Let F_1, F_2, and F_3 be a triple of interacting features, then there is an interaction between at least a pair of them.*

Proof. The 3-way interaction means that for some s satisfying the conditions of the three features we have one of the following cases:

Case 1.   It is not possible to complete all the possible sequences of transitions for $s \xrightarrow{F_1 || F_2 || F_3} s'$, i.e. one of the six sequences

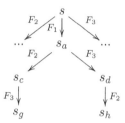

stops either after one step or two steps, because the conditions of the remaining feature(s) are not satisfied.

– *Case 1a.* (one step). Let a $s \xrightarrow{F_1} s_a$ with s_a not satisfying the condition of F_2 (resp. F_3),

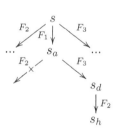

then F_1 interacts with F_2 (resp.F_3).

– *Case 1b.* (two steps). Let the subtree rooted in s_a be incomplete, e.g.

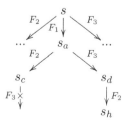

in this case, F_2 interacts with F_3.

Case 2. In the semantics of $F_1||F_2||F_3$, there are (at least) two sequences of transitions rooted in a common state and reaching two states which are inconsistent, i.e., for some s:

$$s \xRightarrow{F_1||F_2||F_3} s' \quad \text{and} \quad s \xRightarrow{F_1||F_2||F_3} s''$$

and $s' \wedge s'' = false$. We build the following tree and reason by cases. The tree is partial since it is sufficient to find two sequences. We can assume that none of them has F_3 at the first step (the general result is obtained with a label switching).

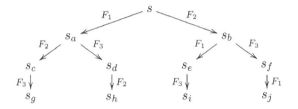

- *Case 2a.* s_g, s_h are inconsistent (similar reasoning for s_i, s_j): in this case the subtree rooted in s_a leads to inconsistent states, hence there is an interaction in $F_2||F_3$.
- *Case 2b.* s_g, s_i are inconsistent. Both s_g and s_i are the result of the application of F_3. This means that already s_c, s_e were inconsistent, hence the interaction is in $F_1||F_2$.
- *Case 2c.* s_h, s_j are inconsistent. This entails that there is a predicate p true in s_h and false in s_j (or vice-versa). We restrict our attention to the interested tree fragment.

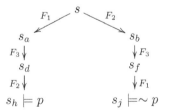

Assume p was false in s (similar reasoning with p true in s). Predicate p can be true in s_h only if there is a feature F_i writing p. As a consequence there is another feature F_j writing $\sim p$ (otherwise, since F_i is also in the right path, p would be true in s_j). We can say that $F_i \neq F_1$, since F_1 makes the last step before s_j. Similarly, we can say that $F_j \neq F_2$.

We are thus left with three cases:

(2.c.1) F_2 writes p and F_1 writes $\sim p$

(2.c.2) F_2 writes p and F_3 writes $\sim p$

(2.c.3) F_3 writes p and F_1 writes $\sim p$

We only show the proof of the first one, since the other cases use the same reasoning. Let F_2 write p and F_1 write $\sim p$. We consider the tree rooted in the subset of s satisfying $C_1 \wedge C_2$ (we recall that, for the initial hypothesis of the proposition, s satisfies $C_1 \wedge C_2 \wedge C_3$). Either one path is blocked after one step, or the tree is the following:

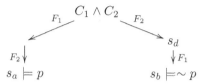

In both cases there is an interaction between F_1 and F_2.

– *Case 2d.* s_h, s_i are inconsistent (Similar reasoning for s_g, s_j).

We redraw the interested fragment of the initial tree:

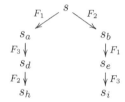

As discussed above, there must be:

– a predicate p with $s_h \models p$ and $s_i \models \sim p$;
– a feature writing p and a feature writing $\sim p$.

One of these features must be F_3, otherwise there is an inconsistency at the first step proving the interaction between F_1 and F_2.

State $s_i \models \sim p$ implies that F_3 writes $\sim p$.

If F_1 writes p we consider the tree rooted in $C_1 \wedge C_3$ and prove the interaction between F_1 and F_3. Otherwise, F_2 writes p, we derive the interaction between F_2 and F_3.   □

5   Related Work

Li et al. [19] define a technique for the analysis of feature interactions where features are complex state machines and the paper defines how to abstract their behaviour in a compact model. Abstraction makes analysis of the composition of the models much simpler, though sound and complete, with respect to the analysis of the composition of the base machines. The approach for analysing the composition of the models is not far from the one proposed in this paper for analysing the pairwise composition of features (in our setting features are already abstract).

Previous work on feature interactions addressed logical inconsistencies between features, due to conflicting actions, nondeterminism, deadlock, invariant violation, or unsatisfiability, as reported in [4]: that paper presents a method for measuring the degree to which features interact in feature-oriented software development, extending the notion of simulation between transition systems to a similarity measure and lifting it to compute a behavioural interaction score in featured transition systems.

In [29] a more general definition of feature interaction, in terms of a feature that is developed and verified to be correct in isolation but found to behave differently when combined with other features, has been presented showing how such behavioral interactions could be detected as a violation of a bisimulation [22].

In the action-based way to analyse features to detect interactions, pairs of actions are typically defined to be conflicting in the domain description by an expert. An interaction arises when, as a result of the features application, two actions are executed, which were defined as conflicting in the domain description. In this setting a true 3-way interaction is possible only if a triple of conflicting actions exists in the domain, and no combination of two of them does. This is an expert evaluation and we can rely on the results of feature interaction detection contest at FIW2000 [17,18] where no such an example was found.

The state-based approach addressed in this paper analyses interacting features (and their actions) looking at their effect on a shared state. In this line there is the abstract semantics given in [24], where the state is a set of resources and the operations on the shared state are abstracted to consider only their access mode, namely *read* or *write* to some resources. Then features interact when one of them accesses in write mode a resource accessed also by the other, in any mode. The results presented in Sect. 4 can be extended to this semantics, which is indeed not far from the one presented here.

An alternative formalisation of the same problem can be obtained using contextual Petri Nets with inhibitor arcs [6,7]. Indeed, the read-only arcs of the contextual nets permit to model a (positive) condition which is not overwritten, and the inhibitor arcs permit to model the negative conditions. A result similar to ours – reduction of all triples of conflicting transitions to the conflict of a pair of them – exists for regular Petri Nets, while, to the best of our knowledge, nothing has been proved yet for the enriched ones.

In case of an interaction, some conflict resolution strategy should be applied, and several resolution techniques are proposed in the literature [3,8,10,14,15,24].

5.1   Different Computational Models and Non-functional Interactions

In order to discuss feature interactions, we have assumed that features are computational bricks that are independently developed and can freely be composed to achieve the desired functionality, possibly in an incremental development. In

```
 1  class Stack {                          23  #ifdef UNDO
 2                                          24    boolean undo() {
 3    boolean push(Object o) {             25  #ifdef LOCKING
 4  #ifdef LOCKING                          26      Lock lock = lock ();
 5    Lock lock = lock ();                  27      if(lock == null) {
 6    if(lock == null) {                    28  #ifdef LOGGING
 7  #ifdef LOGGING                          29        log("undo-lock failed");
 8      log("lock failed for: " + o);       30  #endif
 9  #endif                                  31        return false;
10      return false;                       32      }
11    }                                     33  #endif
12  #endif                                  34      restoreValue();
13  #ifdef UNDO                             35      / * ... * /
14      rememberValue();                    36  #ifdef LOGGING
15  #endif                                  37      log("undone.");
16      elementData[size++] = o;            38  #endif
17      / * ... * /                         39    }
18    }                                     40
19                                          41    void rememberValue(); { / * ... * / }
20  #ifdef LOGGING                          42    void restoreValue(); { / * ... * / }
21    void log(String msg) { / * ... * / }  43  #endif
22  #endif                                  44 }
```

Fig. 1. This example appears in Sect. 9.1.1 "Higher-order Iterations" of [3],

this setting, feature interactions resemble the classic notion of *race condition* in multithreaded environments.

There are other ways to look at the feature interaction problem, either because features are used to choose between alternative control flows or because their composition is subject to non-functional constraints posed by available resources. In both these views irreducible 3-way (or n-way) interactions can be observed.

Features and Conditional Compilation. Within the *Software Product Line* discipline, features are considered as units of functionality that may be present or not in different products of the same family. According to our approach, this can be obtained by composing or not certain features. An alternative common way to achieve variability in product lines is by referring to *presence conditions*, which tell which parts of a software component have to be included if a certain feature is present.

In Apel et al. [3], presence conditions are configuration tags that drive conditional compilation in a Java-like program including all the features. The example reported in [3], which we reproduce in Fig. 1, is presented as a case of interaction that occurs only if all three features are selected, and does not occur if only two are. Indeed, the usage of conditional compilation directives makes line 29 executable only if all the three features UNDO, LOGGING and LOCKING are selected. If line 29 contains an error (e.g. a null pointer access), this error occurs only in products that include all the three features, and not in products that include only two of them.

This case cannot be considered a 3-ways interaction according to our definition, since it is not an interaction error possibly occurring at run-time, but rather an error that is present in the code anyway and is activated only if at the level of feature selection the proper feature combination is selected: in this way it is not different from a similar error inside a single #ifdef, that is activated just by selecting a single feature. For the detection of such an error it is not necessary to recur to behavioral analysis, but for example a static analysis of the "150% model", that is, the code obtained by switching all the features on, can be able to detect it.

Notice that the use of presence conditions reported in [3] is not amenable to incremental development, as the code of each feature is intertwined with that of the other features. A situation of this kind may occur also when delta-oriented programming or modelling [28] is adopted, in which a new feature may be defined as a set of changes to an existing program, or model. In this case, if a nested delta contains an error (similarly to the null pointer access in line 29 in the example above) this could be activated only if more features are included; again, a similar error could be detected with proper static analysis techniques run on the deltas. Notice also that similarly to this example, examples of interactions triggered by the selection of n features but not triggered by the selection of $n - 1$ features can be easily built for any n, as well as examples of interactions triggered only by some particular set of selections of features.

Although presence conditions are of common use in product line development, we tend to believe that in the case of incremental development of safety-critical systems, even when configuration of different products is needed, the entangled appearance of resulting code, as the one in Fig. 1, makes verification and certification of software more difficult. A development approach in which features are separately implemented and verified and then composed appears to be more suitable for this class of systems, and our results indicate that only pairwise verification of possible interactions is needed.

Non-functional Interactions. Even if features are properly composed so that they do not produce undesired functional feature interactions, non functional ones can occur when features have to compete for the usage of shared (physical) resources, other than shared variables. Typical cases are memory space and computation time. The usage of such resources typically sums up, and if a maximum usage threshold is globally reached, unexpected behaviour may occur. Hence, we could have the case in which two out of three features do not exhaust available memory, but all three of them do, or the case of a real-time system in which running only two out of three features satisfy real-time requirements, while running all three does not.

In general, exceeding a resource usage threshold may be triggered by the selection of n features but not triggered by the selection of $n - 1$ features for any given n, or may be triggered only by some particular set of selections of features.

6   Conclusions

We have addressed the problem of 3-way functional feature interactions, by giving a widely applicable definition framework within which we show that such cases can be always reduced to 2-way interactions, hence reducing the complexity of automatic verification of incorrect interactions. We believe that other definition frameworks based on feature composition concepts share the same property. However, we have also pointed out at different definitions of feature interactions which admit "true" 3-way interactions, either because they define features through presence conditions scattered in different software artifacts, or because non functional feature interactions are considered.

Acknowledgements. This work has been partially supported by the Tuscany Region project POR FESR 2014-2020 SISTER and the H2020 Shift2rail project ASTRail.

References

1. Feature Interactions: The Next Generation (Dagstuhl Seminar 14281), Dagstuhl Reports, vol. 4, n.7. pp. 1–24. Schloss Dagstuhl-Leibniz-Zentrum fuer Informatik, Dagstuhl, Germany (2014)
2. Apel, S.: The new feature interaction challenge. In: Proceedings of the Eleventh International Workshop on Variability Modelling of Software-intensive Systems, VAMOS 2017, p. 1. ACM, New York (2017)
3. Apel, S., Batory, D., Kästner, C., Saake, G.: Feature-Oriented Software Product Lines: Concepts and Implementation. Springer, Heidelberg (2013). doi:10.1007/978-3-642-37521-7
4. Atlee, J.M., Fahrenberg, U., Legay, A.: Measuring behaviour interactions between product-line features. In: Gnesi, S., Plat, N. (eds.) 3rd IEEE/ACM FME Workshop on Formal Methods in Software Engineering, FormaliSE 2015, Florence, Italy, May 18, 2015, pp. 20–25. IEEE Computer Society (2015)
5. Back, R.-J., Kurki-Suonio, R.: Distributed cooperation with action systems. ACM Trans. Program. Lang. Syst. **10**(4), 513–554 (1988)
6. Baldan, P., Busi, N., Corradini, A., Pinna, G.M.: Domain and event structure semantics for Petri Nets with read and inhibitor arcs. Theor. Comput. Sci. **323**(1–3), 129–189 (2004)
7. Baldan, P., Corradini, A., Montanari, U.: Contextual Petri Nets, asymmetric event structures, and processes. Inf. Comput. **171**(1), 1–49 (2001)
8. Boström, M., Engstedt, M.: Feature interaction detection and resolution in the Delphi framework. In: [13], pp. 157–172, October 1995
9. Bruns, G.: Foundations for features. In: Reiff-Marganiec, S., Ryan, M. (eds.) Feature Interactions in Telecommunications and Software Systems VIII, pp. 3–11. IOS Press, Amsterdam (2005)
10. Buhr, R.J.A., Amyot, D., Elammari, M., Quesnel, D., Gray, T., Mankovski, S.: Feature-interaction visualization and resolution in an agent environment. In: [16], pp. 135–149, September 1998
11. Calder, M., Kolberg, M., Magill, E.H., Reiff-Marganiec, S.: Feature interaction: a critical review and considered forecast. Comput. Netw. **41**, 115–141 (2001)
12. Calder, M., Magill, E. (eds.): Feature Interactions in Telecommunications and Software Systems VI. IOS Press, Amsterdam (2000)
13. Cheng, K.E., Ohta, T. (eds.): Feature Interactions in Telecommunications Systems III. IOS Press, Amsterdam (1995)

14. Danelutto, M., Kilpatrick, P., Montangero, C., Semini, L.: Model checking support for conflict resolution in multiple non-functional concern management. In: Alexander, M., D'Ambra, P., Belloum, A., Bosilca, G., Cannataro, M., Danelutto, M., Martino, B., Gerndt, M., Jeannot, E., Namyst, R., Roman, J., Scott, S.L., Traff, J.L., Vallée, G., Weidendorfer, J. (eds.) Euro-Par 2011. LNCS, vol. 7155, pp. 128–138. Springer, Heidelberg (2012). doi:10.1007/978-3-642-29737-3_16

15. Dunlop, N., Indulska, J., Raymond, K.: Methods for conflict resolution in policy-based management systems. In: Enterprise Distributed Object Computing Conference, pp. 15–26. IEEE Computer Society (2002)

16. Kimbler, K., Bouma, L.G. (eds.): Feature Interactions in Telecommunications and Software Systems V. IOS Press, Amsterdam (1998)

17. Kolberg, M., Magill, E.H., Marples, D., Reiff, S.: Results of the second feature interaction contest. In: [12], pp. 311–325 (2000)

18. Kolberg, M., Magill, E.H., Marples, D., Reiff, S.: Second feature interaction contest. In: [12], pp. 293–310, May 2000

19. Li, H., Krishnamurthi, S., Fisler, K.: Verifying cross-cutting features as open systems. SIGSOFT Softw. Eng. Notes **27**(6), 89–98 (2002)

20. Marijan, D., Gotlieb, A., Sen, S., Hervieu, A.: Practical pairwise testing for software product lines. In: Proceedings of the 17th International Software Product Line Conference, SPLC 2013, pp. 227–235. ACM, New York (2013)

21. Medeiros, F., Kästner, C., Ribeiro, M., Gheyi, R., Apel, S.: A comparison of 10 sampling algorithms for configurable systems. In: Proceedings of the 38th International Conference on Software Engineering, ICSE 2016, pp. 643–654. ACM, New York (2016)

22. Milner, R.: Communication and Concurrency. International Series in Computer Science. Prentice Hall, New York (1989)

23. Montangero, C., Reiff-Marganiec, S., Semini, L.: Logic-based conflict detection for distributed policies. Fundamenta Informaticae **89**(4), 511–538 (2008)

24. Montangero, C., Semini, L.: Detection and resolution of feature interactions, the early light way. Int. J. Adv. Syst. Measurements **8**(34), 210–220 (2015)

25. Nhlabatsi, A., Laney, R., Nuseibeh, B.: Feature interaction: the security threat from within software systems. Prog. Inform. **5**, 75–89 (2008)

26. Oster, S., Markert, F., Ritter, P.: Automated incremental pairwise testing of software product lines. In: Bosch, J., Lee, J. (eds.) SPLC 2010. LNCS, vol. 6287, pp. 196–210. Springer, Heidelberg (2010). doi:10.1007/978-3-642-15579-6_14

27. Reiff-Marganiec, S., Turner, K.J.: Feature interaction in policies. Comput. Networks **45**(5), 569–584 (2004)

28. Schaefer, I., Bettini, L., Bono, V., Damiani, F., Tanzarella, N.: Delta-oriented programming of software product lines. In: Bosch, J., Lee, J. (eds.) SPLC 2010. LNCS, vol. 6287, pp. 77–91. Springer, Heidelberg (2010). doi:10.1007/978-3-642-15579-6_6

29. Shaker, P., Atlee, J.M.: Behaviour interactions among product-line features. In: Gnesi, S., Fantechi, A., Heymans, P., Rubin, J., Czarnecki, K., Dhungana, D. (eds.) 18th International Software Product Line Conference, SPLC 2014, Florence, Italy, September 15–19, 2014, pp. 242–246. ACM (2014)

30. Turner, K.J., Reiff-Marganiec, S., Blair, L., Pang, J., Gray, T., Perry, P., Ireland, J.: Policy support for call control. Comput. Stand. Inter. **28**(6), 635–649 (2006)

31. Various Editors. Series of International Conferences on Feature Interactions in Software and Communication Systems (ICFI). IOS Press (1994–2009)

32. Zave, P.: An experiment in feature engineering. In: Morgan, C., McIver, A. (eds.) Programming Methodology, pp. 353–377. Springer, New York (2003). doi:10.1007/978-0-387-21798-7_17

Formalising the Dezyne Modelling Language in mCRL2

Rutger van Beusekom[2], Jan Friso Groote[1], Paul Hoogendijk[2], Robert Howe[2], Wieger Wesselink[1], Rob Wieringa[2], and Tim A.C. Willemse[1($\boxtimes$)]

[1] Eindhoven University of Technology, Eindhoven, The Netherlands
t.a.c.willemse@tue.nl
[2] Verum Software Tools B.V., Waalre, The Netherlands

Abstract. DEZYNE is an industrial language with an associated set of tools, allowing users to model interface behaviours and implementations of reactive components and generate executable code from these. The tool and language succeed the successful ASD:Suite tool set, which, in addition to modelling reactive components, offers a set of verification capabilities allowing users to check the conformance of implementations to their interfaces. In this paper, we describe the DEZYNE language and a model transformation to the mCRL2 language, providing users access to advanced model checking capabilities and refinement checks of the mCRL2 tool set.

1 Introduction

Companies increasingly rely on model-driven engineering for developing their (software) systems. The benefit of this approach, in which a high-level (often domain-specific) modelling language is used for designing systems, is that it raises the level of abstraction, resulting in an increased productivity and higher dependability of the developed artefacts. Formal verification of the models may help to further reduce development costs by detecting issues early and by further increasing the overall reliability of the system. However, the success of formal verification is directly linked to the maturity of the tooling used for performing the analysis. Most of the available tooling requires highly skilled and experienced verification engineers to tackle complex industrial problems.

The company Verum has created the ASD:Suite tool suite in the past, in an attempt to shield the system designer from the complexity of the verification language and technology by offering an intuitive integrated development environment for specifying complex, concurrent, industrial systems. This tool suite relies on a proprietary design language and associated development methodology. The latter is built on top of the verification technology offered by the FDR tool suite [4], which offers facilities for checking deadlock, livelock and refinement. While ASD:Suite is easy to use for both novice and experienced system designers, it limits more experienced designers in constructing more complex models and accessing the full power of formal verification.

© Springer International Publishing AG 2017
L. Petrucci et al. (Eds.): FMICS-AVoCS 2017, LNCS 10471, pp. 217–233, 2017.
DOI: 10.1007/978-3-319-67113-0_14

In an effort to move beyond these limitations, Verum has designed a new, open modelling language called DEZYNE[1], that, compared to ASD, is richer in terms of constructs and facilities. FDR still is the *de facto* back-end for conducting verifications, through a non-documented proprietary translation of DEZYNE models to FDR models, but the open nature of the language enables offering alternative verification technology through other back-ends. This will allow Verum and others to offer new services for expert users.

In this paper, we provide an encoding of the DEZYNE modelling language in the mCRL2 process algebra [5], thus giving a formal semantics to DEZYNE models. We address issues such as the transformation of DEZYNE models to mCRL2 process expressions, which we describe as formal as possible without going into unnecessary detail. Moreover, we also discuss the technology that we used to program the transformation between DEZYNE and mCRL2, and illustrate how the connection to mCRL2 and its analysis tool set [3] can be used as the basis for future verification services that can check for a much wider range of user-specific safety and liveness properties, and to offer advanced behavioural visualisation tooling to end-users.

The work we report on has been conducted in the context of the FP7 TTP VICTORIA. It took over 1 man-year of effort, of which a large portion was spent on uncovering details about DEZYNE's (execution) semantics, but also on improving the transformation to mCRL2 so that it yields mCRL2 models for which verification scales well. Moreover, our efforts led to a few improvements in the existing FDR translation, but also to some improvements and enhancements in the mCRL2 tool set.

Structure of the Paper. We introduce the DEZYNE language in Sect. 2 and our mCRL2 encoding of DEZYNE in Sect. 3. In Sect. 4, we discuss improvements in the mCRL2 tool set that were a direct result of the project and in Sect. 5 we discuss experiments using two versions of our translation and we illustrate some of the technology that becomes available through our translation. Section 6 finishes with closing remarks.

2   DEZYNE

DEZYNE is a language and design methodology for specifying the behaviours of *interfaces* and *components* and checking the compliance between these. The language constructs for describing interfaces are, save some small details, identical to the language constructs available for describing components, and take cues from the theory of Mealy machines and borrow concepts from process algebras. DEZYNE offers rudimentary facilities for using data variables of Boolean, (bounded) integer or user-defined enumerated types.

Components specified in DEZYNE assume a specific execution model, in which a component deals with inputs one at a time. That is, in standard practice a

---

[1] See https://www.verum.com; accessed 21 May 2017.

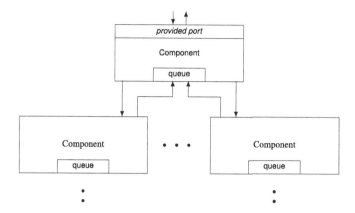

Fig. 1. Typical architecture in DEZYNE. Components interact with other components through ports. Components interact with other components in a hierarchical fashion. Each component has an interface specification which formalises how its behaviour at the provided port is *expected* to behave. A compliance check verifies whether a component *actually* respects its interface.

single-threaded *run-to-completion* semantics is employed. A 'user' of a component can interact with the component by sending events to it; these events are handled *synchronously* in the sense that the component essentially will remain blocked for unsolicited events from lower-level components (which run concurrently with the component) until the user receives a *reply* from the component, while solicited events from lower-level components are buffered and dealt with one at a time. Unsolicited events emitted by lower-level components are dealt with in a similar fashion; such events may result in 'spontaneous' outputs emitted asynchronously by the component.

The design methodology and system architecture implemented in DEZYNE is illustrated in Fig. 1. As a designer employing the DEZYNE language and methodology, one is only concerned with specifying the behaviour of interfaces and components. Subsequent checks compute whether the behaviour of a component as observed at its *provided* port (*i.e.* as seen by the 'user' of the component), when interacting with components through its *required* ports (*i.e.* the low-level components), formally complies with the behaviour as specified by its interface. This way one obtains a modular, hierarchical design of a software system. The modular design and compliance check are pivotal for designing large systems that are correct-by-design.

The essential part of the grammar of DEZYNE is depicted in Table 1; we have omitted those parts that are required for describing a *system*; the latter is essentially a collection of components and a static description of how they are connected. DEZYNE's static semantics excludes models in which there are obvious naming conflicts and consistency issues (*e.g.* multiple interface specifications with the same name are not permitted; events can be declared at most once in an interface, *etcetera*). Some constraints are there to enforce the typical

Table 1. EBNF for (the essential part of) the DEZYNE language. Terminal symbols are typeset in bold. For brevity, optional productions are enclosed within parentheses and a question mark (_)? whereas repetition, resp. positive repetition of productions are enclosed within (_)*, resp. (_)+. Nonterminal ID represents the identifiers that can be generated using standard ASCII characters; Expr represents typical expressions built from operations on data types, function calls, *etcetera*.

Model	::= (InterfaceDecl | ComponentDecl)*
InterfaceDecl	::= **interface** ID { (EventDir ID ID ;)* (Behaviour)? }
ComponentDecl	::= **component** ID { (InterfaceDir compoundName ID ;)* (Behaviour)? }
EventDir	::= **in** | **out**
InterfaceDir	::= **provides** | **requires**
Behaviour	::= **behaviour** (ID)? { (TypeDecl)* (VarDecl)* (FuncDecl)* (BehaviourStmt)* }
TypeDecl	::= **enum** ID { ID (, ID)* };
VarDecl	::= ID ID = Expr ;
FuncDecl	::= ID ID ((ID ID)?){ (BehaviourStmt)* }
BehaviourStmt	::= GuardedStmt | CompoundBehaviourStmt | OnEventStmt | ReplyStmt | IllegalStmt | AssignmentBehaviourStmt | ActionStmt | ReturnStmt ConditionalStmt
GuardedStmt	::= **[** Guard **]** BehaviourStmt
Guard	::= Expr | **otherwise**
ConditionalStmt	::= **if** Guard **then** BehaviourStmt **else** BehaviourStmt ;
CompoundBehaviourStmt	::= **{** (BehaviourStmt)* **}**
OnEventStmt	::= **on** OnTrigger : BehaviourStmt
ReplyStmt	::= **reply** ((Expr))? ;
OnTrigger	::= (EventInstance)+ | **optional** | **inevitable**
EventInstance	::= ID | ID.ID
IllegalStmt	::= **illegal;**
AssignmentBehaviourStmt	::= ID = Expr ;
ActionStmt	::= EventInstance ;
ReturnStmt	::= **return** (Expr)? ;

tree-like architectural design pattern of Fig. 1, used in DEZYNE (*e.g.* each component has at most one provided port). Most importantly for our exposition is the fact that correct interface specifications, components and recursive functions can be rewritten to a normal form where the behaviour can be represented by the following production rules:

BehaviourStmt	::= **[** Guard **]** OnEventStmt
...	
FuncDecl	::= ID ID ((ID ID)?) { (ImperativeStmt)* }
...	
OnEventStmt	::= **on** OnTrigger : ImperativeStmt
ImperativeStmt	::= CompoundImperativeStmt | ReplyStmt | IllegalStmt AssignmentBehaviourStmt | ActionStmt | ReturnStmt | ConditionalStmt
CompoundImperativeStmt	::= **{** (ImperativeStmt)* **}**
ConditionalStmt	::= **if** Guard **then** ImperativeStmt **else** ImperativeStmt ;

In essence, this means that each interface and component specifies a sequence of responses and assignments for each event stimulating the interface or component.

Example 1. Consider the description of a controller described in DEZYNE, given in Fig. 2(left). Its interface specification (not depicted here), describing the external behaviour the component must comply with, is described by specification IController, as indicated by the provides keyword; it communicates with the 'outside world' via the port called controller. The requires keyword indicates that the controller communicates with a lower-level component, via a port named

```
component Controller
{
    provides IController controller;
    requires IActuator actuator;
    behaviour
    {
        enum State { Off, Init };
        State s = State.Off;
        [s.Off]
        {
            on controller.start(): { actuator.start(); s = State.Init; }
            on controller.shutdown(), actuator.fail(): illegal;
        }
        [s.Init]
        {
            on controller.start(), controller.shutdown(): illegal;
            on actuator.fail(): { controller.failed(); s = State.Off; }
        }
    }
}
```

```
...
bool b = true;
subint CounterType 0..2;
void f()
{
    i.on(); g(2);
    i.on(); g(2);
}
void g(CounterType c)
{
    if (c == 2 && b){ i.run(); b = false; g(c); }
    else if (c == 0) { i.stop(); }
    else { i.standby(); g(c-1); }
}
...
```

Fig. 2. Left: a DEZYNE model describing a very simple controller. Right: a snippet of a recursive function in DEZYNE; i is a port over which events such as start, stop, on, run and standby are sent.

actuator, behaving in line with the IActuator interface. Events can be received via, or sent via the ports. The behaviour section prescribes the behaviour of the component, indicating, *e.g.* that when s.Off holds (which is shorthand for s == Off) and a start event occurs at port controller (indicated by the on keyword), the component invokes a start event on port actuator, assigns variable s the value State.Init and subsequently returns control via an implicit reply message via the controller port. Also, when s.Off holds, neither a shutdown event via port controller, nor a fail event via port actuator, are permitted; this is indicated by the illegal keyword.   □

Using (mutually) recursive functions, one can specify a finite or infinite sequence of statements to be executed upon receiving an event. Recursion is limited to tail recursion [2], allowing for predictable and effective implementations of DEZYNE models in standard programming languages such as C and C++. A typical excerpt of a recursive function is given in Fig. 2(right).

DEZYNE allows its users to read and update the values of the variables declared in the variable section of a behaviour in recursive functions. Such manipulations offer a high degree of flexibility to the modeller and are appealing to those accustomed to using iteration rather than recursion. As a consequence, the function g in Fig. 2(right) sets Boolean b to false so that the second time g is called from f, no run event is emitted from port i. Another way for functions to save part of their computation is to explicitly return a value via a return keyword.

3   An mCRL2 Semantics for DEZYNE

Our formalisation of the DEZYNE methodology includes both a transformation of the core language constructs of DEZYNE to mCRL2, and a sketch of our formalisation of the underlying execution semantics which is used to analyse the compliance of a component to its interface. We first give a cursory overview of the mCRL2 language in Sect. 3.1, followed by the formalisation of the DEZYNE language in Sect. 3.2 and its execution semantics in Sect. 3.3. The implementation and validation of our transformation is briefly discussed in Sect. 3.4.

3.1   The Process Algebra mCRL2

The mCRL2 language is a process algebra in the lineage of the *Algebra of Communicating Processes* [1]. It consists of a data language for describing data transformations and data types, and a process language for specifying system behaviours. The semantics of mCRL2 processes is given both axiomatically and operationally, associating a labelled transition system to process expressions. For a comprehensive overview of the language, we refer to [5]; for the associated tool set, we refer to [3]; due to page limits, we only informally explain the constructs essential for understanding our work.

The data language includes built-in definitions for most of the commonly used data types, such as Booleans, integers, natural numbers, *etcetera*. In addition, container sorts, such as *lists*, *sets* and *bags* are available. Users can specify their own data sorts using a basic equational data type specification mechanism.

The process specification language of mCRL2 consists of a relatively small number of basic operators and primitives. Since we are concerned with only a fragment of the language we focus on the intuition behind those operators and constructs that are essential for the current exposition. The basic observable events are modelled by parameterised (multi-)actions. Unobservable events are modelled by the constant τ, and the constant δ represents *inaction* (the process that performs no action, colloquially referred to as the deadlock process). Processes are constructed compositionally: the non-deterministic choice between processes p and q is denoted p+q; their sequential composition is denoted p·q, and their parallel composition is denoted p∥q. A parallel composition of processes may give rise to *multi-actions*: actions that occur simultaneously. A *communication operator* $\Gamma_C(\mathsf{p})$ can map such multi-actions to new actions when their parameters coincide, thus modelling the synchronisation of actions. Using an abstraction operator $\tau_H(\mathsf{p})$, one can turn observable actions into unobservable actions. An *allow operator* $\nabla_A(\mathsf{p})$ can be used to only allow (multi-)actions of the set A that occur in process p.

Recursion can be used to specify processes with infinite behaviour. This is typically achieved by specifying a recursive process of the form $\mathsf{P}(\mathsf{v:V}) = \mathsf{p}$, where P is a process variable, v is a vector of typed variables (where the type is given by V), and p is a process expression that may contain process variables (and in particular variable P). Note that in the next section, we often omit the type V when specifying recursive processes.

Process behaviour can be made to depend on data using the conditional choice operator and a generalised choice operator. The process $b \rightarrow p \diamond q$ denotes a conditional choice between processes p and q: if b holds, it behaves as process p, and otherwise as process q. Process $\sum d{:}D.p(d)$ describes a (possibly infinite) unconditional choice between processes p with different values for variable d.

Example 2. A simple one-place buffer for natural numbers can be represented by a process $\mathsf{Buffer} = \sum m{:}\mathsf{Nat.read}(m) \cdot \mathsf{send}(m) \cdot \mathsf{Buffer}$, where read and send are actions that represent *storing* a value in the buffer and *loading* a buffered value from the buffer. The process below represents the same behaviour:

$$\mathsf{Buffer}(n{:}\mathsf{Nat},b{:}\mathsf{Bool}) = b \rightarrow (\mathsf{send}(n) \cdot \mathsf{Buffer}(b = \mathsf{false}))$$
$$\diamond \; \textstyle\sum m{:}\mathsf{Nat.}\,(\mathsf{read}(m) \cdot \mathsf{Buffer}(n = m, b = \mathsf{true}))$$

In this alternative formalisation of the buffer, variable b is used to keep track of whether the buffer is filled, and, if so, the value currently stored in the buffer is represented by variable n. Note that $\mathsf{Buffer}(b = \mathsf{false})$ is shorthand notation for $\mathsf{Buffer}(n,\mathsf{false})$; *i.e.* in this notation, only updates to parameters are listed.

3.2   A Formal Description of the DEZYNE to mCRL2 Translation

We mainly focus on the transformation of behaviour statements that occur in DEZYNE models to mCRL2; *i.e.* we focus on those statements that correspond to the BehaviourStmt element in the grammar. We omit details about expressions and type declarations, as these map almost one-to-one on mCRL2 types and data structures.

For our transformation, we assume that every statement s in a concrete DEZYNE model has a unique index (*e.g.* a program counter) given by $index(s)$. This index can easily be assigned while parsing the model. Every mCRL2 process equation for a given DEZYNE component (resp. interface specification), generated by our transformation, shares the same list v of typed process parameters. This list contains all variables declared in a DEZYNE component (resp. interface specification). In particular, it includes all global and local variables of the behaviours, all function parameters and local function variables, and a small number of additional variables that are needed as context for the translation. The list of variables v over-approximates the list of variables that may be in scope at any point in the execution of a component (resp. interface specification). The typed list v can also be constructed while parsing the model. We assume that name conflicts have been resolved using appropriate α-renaming.

Our translation of a behaviour statement s is given by $Tr(s, \mathsf{v}, i, j, g)$, where mapping Tr yields a set of mCRL2 process equations, defined by the rules in Table 2 (for basic statements and events), and in Table 3 (for function statements). Here i is always equal to $index(s)$, and j is the index corresponding to the statement that is executed after termination of s, or -1 if there is no such statement; *i.e.* j points to the next continuation. Each statement s with index i has a corresponding process equation $P_i(\mathsf{v})$, where v is the list of typed process parameters. The parameter g determines the current scope in which statement s resides; g can either be the name of a function (in which case s is in the function body of g), or it can have the value $\perp$ (in which case s is not in the scope of any function). The actions inevitable, optional and illegal correspond to the triggers and statement with the same name in DEZYNE. The parameterised actions snd_r and rcv_r are used to send and receive a value t that is set in a reply(t) statement; the snd_r action marks the end of an on e:s_1 statement. The snd_e and rcv_e actions correspond to sending and receiving of events.

In order to bridge the semantic gap between the DEZYNE language and the mCRL2 language, we have added a few statements that are not part of the DEZYNE language. A send_reply statement is inserted at the end of each on e: s_1 statement, to make it explicit that the value that is set using a reply(t) statement inside s_1 is eventually returned. In the DEZYNE language, sending the reply remains implicit. DEZYNE has the requirement that a reply value is set exactly once in an on e: s_1 statement. It is straightforward to extend the translation of Table 2 to check for this by recording the number of executed reply(t) statements in a process parameter. Several other checks, such as *out-of-bounds* checks can be added equally straightforward to our transformation. The choice statement $s_1 \oplus s_2$ and the sequential statement $s_1; s_2$ were introduced to make it explicit that a compound statement that is directly in the scope of an on e:s_1 statement is different from a compound statement inside a behaviour section. The first one acts like a choice between statements, while the latter acts as a sequential composition of statements. Finally the skip statement corresponds to an empty compound statement.

The translation of a behaviour s of a component (resp. an interface specification) is given by $Tr(s, \mathsf{v}_0, i, i, \perp)$, where $i = index(s)$ and v_0 contains the initial values of the global variables of the behaviour, and default values for all other parameters. The continuation variable j is set to i. The effect of this is that the behaviour s will be repeated indefinitely. To reduce the size of the underlying state space, in our implementation of our encoding we reset all non-global variables to their default value at the end of the execution of an on e:s_1 statement.

Example 3. We exemplify the translation on a small part of the DEZYNE model of Fig. 2(left), using fictitious numbers as statement indices. We assume that all events are void events, meaning that these do not return a value.

$$
\begin{aligned}
\mathrm{Controller}_1(\mathsf{s:State}) &= \mathrm{Controller}_2(\mathsf{s}) + \mathrm{Controller}_{12}(\mathsf{s}); \\
\mathrm{Controller}_2(\mathsf{s:State}) &= (\mathsf{s} == \mathsf{Off}) \rightarrow \mathrm{Controller}_3(\mathsf{s}) \diamond \delta; \\
\mathrm{Controller}_3(\mathsf{s:State}) &= \mathrm{Controller}_4(\mathsf{s}) + \mathrm{Controller}_8(\mathsf{s}); \\
\mathrm{Controller}_4(\mathsf{s:State}) &= \mathsf{rcv\_e}(\mathsf{controller.start}) \cdot \mathrm{Controller}_5(\mathsf{s}); \\
\mathrm{Controller}_5(\mathsf{s:State}) &= \mathsf{snd\_e}(\mathsf{actuator.start}) \cdot \mathsf{rcv\_r}(\mathsf{void}) \cdot \mathrm{Controller}_6(\mathsf{s}); \\
\mathrm{Controller}_6(\mathsf{s:State}) &= \mathrm{Controller}_7(\mathsf{s} = \mathsf{Init}); \\
\mathrm{Controller}_7(\mathsf{s:State}) &= \mathsf{snd\_r}(\mathsf{controller.start}, \mathsf{void}) \cdot \mathrm{Controller}_1(\mathsf{s}); \\
\mathrm{Controller}_8(\mathsf{s:State}) &= \mathrm{Controller}_9(\mathsf{s}) + \mathrm{Controller}_{11}(\mathsf{s}); \\
\mathrm{Controller}_9(\mathsf{s:State}) &= \mathsf{rcv\_e}(\mathsf{controller.shutdown}) \cdot \mathrm{Controller}_{10}(s); \\
\mathrm{Controller}_{10}(\mathsf{s:State}) &= \mathsf{Illegal}(); \\
\mathrm{Controller}_{11}(\mathsf{s:State}) &= \mathsf{rcv\_e}(\mathsf{actuator.fail}) \cdot \mathrm{Controller}_{10}(s); \\
\mathrm{Controller}_{12}(\mathsf{s:State}) &= ... \\
& ... \\
\mathrm{Illegal}(\mathsf{s:State}) &= \mathsf{illegal} \cdot \mathsf{Illegal}();
\end{aligned}
$$

Table 2. Mapping Tr, describing the translation of (extended) DEZYNE statements in normal form to mCRL2 processes and process expressions. Note that we used the convention that $i_1 = index(s_1)$ and $i_2 = index(s_2)$, t is a data expression, b is a Boolean expression, e is an event, x is a variable name, T is a type and T_x is the type of x. The process parameter r is an element of v and may contain any value t that is set using a reply(t) statement.

Statement s	Translation $Tr(s, v, i, j, g)$
Basic statements	
skip	$\{P_i(v) = P_j()\}$
$s_1; s_2$	$\{P_i(v) = P_{i_1}()\} \cup Tr(s_1, v, i_1, i_2, g) \cup Tr(s_2, v, i_2, j, g)$
$\{s_1; s_2; \cdots; s_n\}$	$Tr(s_1; (s_2; (\cdots; s_n)), v, i, j, g)$
$s_1 \oplus s_2$	$\{P_i(v) = P_{i_1}() + P_{i_2}()\} \cup Tr(s_1, v, i_1, j, g) \cup Tr(s_2, v, i_2, j, g)$
$\{s_1 \oplus s_2 \oplus \cdots \oplus s_n\}$	$Tr(s_1 \oplus (s_2 \oplus (\cdots; s_n)), v, i, j, g)$
if b then s_1 else s_2	$\{P_i(v) = b \to P_{i_1}() \diamond P_{i_2}()\} \cup Tr(s_1, v, i_1, j, g) \cup Tr(s_2, v, i_2, j, g)$
x = t	$\{P_i(v) = P_j(x = t)\}$
T x = t	$Tr(x = t, v, i, j, g)$
illegal	$\{P_i(v) = \text{Illegal}()\}$ where $\text{Illegal}(v) = \text{illegal} \cdot \text{Illegal}()$
Event related statements	
[b] s_1	$\{P_i(v) = b \to P_{i_1}() \diamond \delta\} \cup Tr(s_1, v, i_1, j, g)$
on e:s_1	$\{P_i(v) = \text{rcv\_e}(e) \cdot P_{i_1}()\} \cup Tr(s_1, v, i_1, j, g)$
reply(t)	$\{P_i(v) = P_j(r = t)\}$
send_reply(e)	$\{P_i(v) = \text{snd\_r}(e, r) \cdot P_j()\}$
x = e	$\{P_i(v) = \text{snd\_e}(e) \cdot \sum x' : T_x.\text{rcv\_r}(e, x') \cdot P_j(x = x')\}$
e	$\begin{cases} \{P_i(v) = \text{snd\_e}(e) \cdot \text{rcv\_r}(\text{void}) \cdot P_j()\} & \text{if e is an 'in' event} \\ & \text{from a required port} \\ \{P_i(v) = \text{snd\_e}(e) \cdot P_j()\} & \text{otherwise} \end{cases}$

Note that the actual typing information for the events would be specified in the interface specifications IController and IActuator, referred to in (but not detailed in) Fig. 2(left). Furthermore, observe that equation Controller$_7$ deals with the send_reply statement which is not part of the DEZYNE language, but which we need to include to signal the end of an on-event statement. □

Formalising the recursive functions of the DEZYNE language proved to be the most involved part of the translation as it required several iterations to find a translation that had a good enough performance for some industrial cases with thousands of deeply nested function calls. One of the complications is that functions can modify the global variables of a behaviour. In our first attempt, we handled these modifications using a separate register process, but it turned out that the additional communication needed for this could cause an unacceptable blow up of the state space for some examples.

Our final solution was to introduce a process parameter c that contains the function call stack, and process parameters rvar$_T$ for each function return type

T that contain function call results. Both c and $rvar_T$ are elements of the list of variables v we maintain in our translation. In each return statement of a function with return type T, the function result is stored in the parameter $rvar_T$. In an assignment statement $x = f(t)$, the function result is retrieved from this parameter $rvar_T$. We ensure that each function body is translated only once. At first sight this may seem problematic, since the translation of a function call depends on the statement where the execution should continue after termination, which is encoded in the parameter j. This problem has been solved by moving the actual mapping of a function call statement with index i to the corresponding continuation j in a separate Return process. The Return process contains a summand $(c \neq [] \wedge head(c) = i) \rightarrow P_j(c = tail(c), x = rvar_T) \diamond \delta$ for each assignment statement $x = f(t)$ with index i. Note that the indices of the function call statements are stored in the function call stack c. In case of a nested function call between mutually dependent tail-recursive functions, it is known that the continuation statement will not change. So in this particular case we do not add the index of the statement to the function call stack c. We determine whether functions are mutually dependent by checking that they are in the same strongly connected component of the function call graph. The restriction to tail-recursive functions ensures that it is not needed to put copies of local function variables on the stack, see e.g. [2]. Details of the formalisation of function call statements can be found in Table 3. For completeness, the translation $Tr(s_f, v, i_f, -1, f)$ of a function body s_f is added to the translation of each function call $f(t)$. In our implementation it is generated only once. Note that the continuation parameter j is set to the undefined value -1, since the actual continuation value of a function call is stored in the Return process.

3.3 Formalising the Execution Model

DEZYNE models that are converted to executable code and subsequently deployed interact with other components following a run-to-completion regime which is guaranteed by the DEZYNE code generation. A faithful analysis of the

Table 3. Mapping Tr, describing the translation of DEZYNE function calls and returns in mCRL2. Note that t is a data expression, s_f is the body of function f, $i_f = index(s_f)$, and d_f is the function parameter of function f. By $c = i \triangleright c$ we denoted that index i is prepended to list c.

Statement s	Translation $Tr(s, v, i, j, g)$
Function call statements	
$f(t)$	$\begin{cases} \{P_i(v) = P_{i_f}(d_f = t)\} & \text{if } f \text{ and } g \text{ are mutually dependent} \\ \{P_i(v) = P_{i_f}(d_f = t, c = i \triangleright c)\} & \text{otherwise} \end{cases}$ $\qquad\qquad\qquad\qquad \cup\ Tr(s_f, v, i_f, -1, f)$
$x = f(t)$	$\{P_i(v) = P_{i_f}(d_f = t, c = i \triangleright c)\} \cup Tr(s_f, v, i_f, -1, f)$
return t	$\{P_i(v) = Return(rvar_T = t)\}$ where T is the return type of f

behaviour of DEZYNE components therefore requires a formalisation of this execution model in mCRL2. This holds particularly true for the compliance test that is conducted, which essentially checks whether the behaviour of a component C, as can be observed from its provided port p, complies with the behaviour that is specified by C's interface specification. Formally, the compliance check decides whether or not the labelled transition system underlying the behaviour of C (when interacting with other components through its required ports r_1 up to r_n, see also Fig. 1) is a correct failures-divergence refinement [6] of the labelled transition system underlying the behaviour of C's interface specification. Relying on an assume-guarantee style of reasoning, the behaviours of the components that C interacts with through ports r_1 up to r_n, are represented by their respective interface specifications (and their underlying labelled transition systems) in all analyses of the behaviour of C in the DEZYNE tool set.

Conceptually, the run-to-completion execution model ensures that component C, when interacting with other components through C's port p and ports r_1 up to r_n, is blocked for unsolicited external stimuli as long as it has not finished dealing with a previous stimulus. External stimuli that come via the required ports are queued in a queue Q. This is not the case for the replies to events submitted to a component via a required port. Unsolicited stimuli arriving at a required port are announced by an optional or inevitable trigger. The execution model furthermore defines the semantic difference between the latter two triggers, by non-deterministically deciding at any point in the execution of C's behaviour that optional triggers become disabled, whereas inevitable triggers cannot be disabled. Such nuances make the effect of the execution model on the interactions between components non-trivial.

Rather than presenting our mCRL2 formalisation of the run-to-completion semantics, we explain its workings using a high-level state diagram of a part of this formalisation, see Fig. 3. The diagram represents how unsolicited stimuli arriving via the provided port are dealt with; the part dealing with unsolicited stimuli arriving via the required port (initiated by an optional or inevitable trigger, which fills buffer Q) is largely the same but lacks, e.g. transitions dealing with sending reply values to the events taken from the queue. The execution model enforces that stimuli at the provided port and optional and inevitable triggers at the required ports are only accepted in state 'Idle' of Fig. 3. In mCRL2, this can be modelled by a blocking synchronisation on actions such as rcv_e, optional and inevitable, using a combination of mCRL2's parallel composition operator ||, its communication and restriction operator and its renaming operator.

The state diagram of Fig. 3 illustrates the flow of events when a stimulus via the provided port arrives. This causes a state change, leading to state 'Processing'. When the component reports that it has finished processing the event (indicated by the snd_r(e,v) action, which sets a value for reply variable r) it moves to state 'Finishing'. Once the component is in state 'Finishing', it will start processing the solicited events that may have arrived in the queue in the meantime. Executing an event e' from the queue (indicated by the rcv_e(e') action)

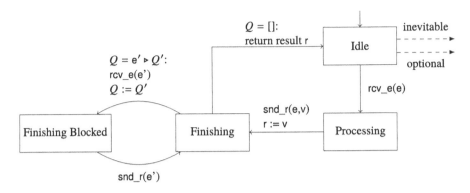

Fig. 3. Schematic overview of the run-to-completion semantics of DEZYNE components.

takes the state diagram to state 'Finished Blocked'; when the component reports it is finished processing this event (indicated by the snd_r(e') action), it returns to state 'Finished'. When the queue is finally empty, the component again returns to the 'Idle' state and returns the value stored in variable r that was determined during the execution of event e. In all non-'Idle' states the component may send out events via its provided port or via its required ports, and, in response to such events, other components may fill the queue with new events; we have omitted these self-loops from the diagram for simplicity.

3.4   Implementing and Validating the Transformation

The model transformation has been implemented using Python. The input of our transformation is a DEZYNE model stored in Scheme format. The Scheme file is parsed into a Python class model of a DEZYNE model, to which our generator is applied. The result is a Python class model of an mCRL2 model. This mCRL2 model is then pretty printed to text format, after which the mCRL2 tools are applied for further analysis.

Our preference for the general purpose programming language Python over a specialised model transformation language such as, *e.g.* QVTo, is motivated by the need to easily make changes to the generator. A scripting language like Python is ideal for that. Since there is a large gap between the DEZYNE language and the process algebra mCRL2, it was clear from the start that the main effort would be to experiment with different ways to do the transformation. The generator and its supporting data structures have been revised many times. What also helped to support making changes is that we made specifications of the translation in an early stage, and kept it in sync with the implementation, ultimately resulting in the specifications of Tables 2 and 3.

Note that the class models of DEZYNE and mCRL2 were stable from the start. The classes were kept very simple, and correspond in a one to one way with UML metamodels of both languages. The mCRL2 classes could even be generated from an input file containing merely 150 lines of text.

We validated the relative correctness of our transformation using a set of test cases provided by Verum, consisting of 168 component models and 224 interface models, including several models taken from industry (see also Sect. 5). For all these cases we were able to establish that the state spaces of the behaviours of the components using our transformation and Verum's transformation were strongly bisimilar. Moreover, using the mCRL2 tool set we could reproduce the outcomes to all checks currently performed by DEZYNE on components, interfaces and their interactions under the run-to-completion semantics on these test cases.

4   Improvements and Enhancements in mCRL2

As the previous section illustrates, from a language point of view, the mCRL2 language is sufficiently expressive for describing the DEZYNE models and its execution semantics. This opens up the possibility to analyse DEZYNE models using the mCRL2 tool set.

The mCRL2 tool set works by parsing, type-checking and subsequently converting an mCRL2 specification to a normal form called a *Linear Process Specification* (LPS). All analyses of the mCRL2 specification are subsequently performed by tools operating on LPSs or its derived artefacts such as state spaces. Analysing the mCRL2 models obtained by translating large DEZYNE models developed in industry led to several feature requests for various tools in mCRL2 but also revealed a few bottlenecks and a thus far undiscovered error in the mCRL2 tool set.

A major enhancement to the mCRL2 tool set concerns the addition of algorithms for deciding several types of refinement relations. This was needed to properly deal with DEZYNE's verification methodology which relies on an assume-guarantee style of reasoning rooted in the notion of *failures-divergence refinement* [6]. While this notion is one of the hallmark features of the FDR tool set (in fact giving it its name), mCRL2 did not support this refinement notion, and it could not be mimicked by any of the many behavioural equivalences that *were* supported by mCRL2. An *anti-chain*-based algorithm, based on [7], for deciding failures-divergence refinement was added to the mCRL2 tool ltscompare.[2] Another enhancement to the tool set concerns the generation of witnesses to divergences—infinite sequences of internal actions—and the generation of counterexamples for failures-divergence refinement and other refinement relations.

The larger DEZYNE models we ran as test cases revealed that mCRL2 was not optimised for dealing with the immense number of recursive process equations obtained from our automated translation. While the complexity of each individual equation was low (some equations just refer to other equations, *e.g.*

---

[2] The option to check for this refinement relation, and other refinement relations such as *trace inclusion, weak trace inclusion, failures, weak failures* and *simulation preorder* is available from mCRL2 revision 13875 and onward. The additions weigh in at approximately 800 lines of code, which include, among others the additional algorithms and test cases for these algorithms.

when translating assignments), the vast number of these equations meant that some basic parts of the algorithms used to convert mCRL2 processes to LPSs needed improvement. Examples include the removal of a linear search through a list of global data variables and the addition of routines to merge similar equations. In particular, *alphabet reduction*, a preprocessing step of linearisation that analyses possible occurrences of multi-actions, has been improved in a number of ways. Due to the occurrence of large blocks of interdependent equations, it turned out to be necessary to cache the alphabet of such equations. Also the sets of possible multi-actions needed to be pruned more aggressively, to deal with their huge sizes. At the same time, an error in the rules underlying the old alphabet reduction algorithm surfaced, which was subsequently fixed.

5   Experiments

In the course of formalising DEZYNE in mCRL2, we have experimented with several different but semantically equivalent (modulo divergence-preserving branching bisimulation) translations. The main criterion, next to correctness, used in our search for a proper formalisation was the scalability of verifying the mCRL2 models resulting from a translation. Typical verifications that are offered by the DEZYNE tool set, and which can be conducted by analysing the appropriate mCRL2 model obtained from translating a DEZYNE model, are absence of deadlock and livelock, out-of-bound checks for variables, invoking events that are marked illegal, and interface compliance of components. As we mentioned before, the latter verification is essentially a check whether the behaviour as can be observed at the provided port of a component is a correct failures-divergence refinement of the behaviour as specified by the interface specification.

While it can be expected that the various ways of formalising a language will have an effect on the size of the underlying labelled transition systems of concrete DEZYNE models, we had initially not expected the effects to be so dramatic. In fact, for small examples, the effects were marginal, but for the models developed in the industry, the effects were surprisingly big. This was particularly true for the compliance checks, which are computationally the most expensive checks carried out by the DEZYNE tool set: the check requires computing a labelled transition system that represents the interaction between a component and the interface specifications for its required ports, given the execution model of Sect. 3.3. To illustrate the differences in scalability for the compliance check, we compare the effect (on time and state space size) of translating functions using a dedicated register process for recording the side effects functions can have on global variables and the translation described in Sect. 3.2, see Table 4.[3] These results clearly indicate that one can easily gain a factor 5 or more for the larger models in terms of speed by choosing an appropriate translation. This also holds for the other types of verification that can be conducted.

---

[3] Unfortunately, we cannot disclose the origin of, nor further details about these industrial models.

Table 4. The effect on the size of the state space and the time to generate the transition system and run the compliance test when translating DEZYNE functions using either a dedicated register process for recording side effects on global variables (translation I) and when translating functions using the rules in Sect. 3.2 (translation II). Time is in seconds; a dash indicates that the computation did not finish within the available time or memory. The models are embedded software control models, developed (and deployed) in industry using Verum's software engineering tool suite. The lines of code for mCRL2 correspond to translation II.

Model	Time (s)		Speedup	# States		Reduction	Lines of code	
	I	II		I	II		DEZYNE	mCRL2
Model 1	155	13	11	715,049	110,773	6	3,133	2,157
Model 2	83	13	6	984,167	43,281	22	2,808	3,616
Model 3	37	10	3	33,488	6,700	4	2,382	2,838
Model 4	27	11	2	822	226	3	2,904	2,482
Model 5	45	11	4	443,379	182,367	2	1,751	2,114
Model 6	135	17	7	1,039,654	323,023	3	4,145	3,114
Model 7	–	18	–	–	74,654	–	4,328	3,161
Model 8	–	21	–	–	101,948	–	4,931	4,434
Model 9	–	35	–	–	215,727	–	5,721	4,645
Model 10	2,069	275	7	36,140,140	10,967,862	3	8,169	8,474

Fig. 4. Visualisations of the state space underlying an interface specification used in 'Model 10'. The symmetry in the two branches at the bottom in the left picture is a telltale sign of symmetry in the behaviour of the interface specification.

It is noteworthy that the verification times we obtain using the mCRL2 model are currently roughly 2–5 times slower than the verification times reported by Verum on the same models. This difference may be due to hardware differences, but we expect that FDR's different state space exploration technique is a main factor, which explores and minimises individual parallel processes before combining these, whereas mCRL2 explores a monolithic model. Indeed, manually mimicking FDR's compositional approach in mCRL2 shows an additional speed-up of a factor 5–10 can be achieved.

Finally, we note that the translation to mCRL2 opens up the possibility to use advanced technology for visually inspecting state spaces and tools to verify more complex properties than the generic ones currently offered by the DEZYNE verification tool set. For instance, for 'Model 10', which models a complex piece of software control in an embedded device of one of Verum's customers, we have verified typical properties relevant in this context such as:

- Invariantly, whenever the system receives an initialisation event, it remains possible to successfully stop production;
- There is an infinite execution in which production is never stopped;
- It is impossible to initialise the system when it is already initialised unless production is stopped.

Such properties are expressed in mCRL2's modal μ-calculus with data, and all three properties listed above are readily verified to hold on 'Model 10'. Moreover, we have verified several liveness properties that are true of the interface specification of 'Model 10' but not of the component itself. Through such properties, the relation between a component and its interface specification can be better understood.

Figure 4 depicts a graphical simulation of a 3D depiction of the state space of one of the interface specifications used in 'Model 10', giving an impression of the type of visualisations that one can use to inspect the state space. Such a visualisation help to, *e.g.* confirm expectations (such as an expected symmetry in the system behaviour).

6   Concluding Remarks

Modelling languages used in the context of model driven engineering have gained traction among industry over the last years. Such languages are predominantly used to generate executable code, but tool sets supporting these languages rarely offer forms of formal verification of the models. The DEZYNE language and associated tool set, developed by Verum, is one of these rare exceptions, with formal verification support offered through a non-documented, proprietary mapping to the FDR tool set [4].

We have described a formalisation of the DEZYNE language in terms of mCRL2 [5], providing a first publicly accessible formal semantics of DEZYNE models and their execution semantics. The formalisation and implementation of the transformation, which was developed in a period of 2 years and took well in excess of 1 man-year of effort, led to improvements and additions in both mCRL2 and the existing DEZYNE to FDR translation, and served as an independent validation of the ideas behind the methodology behind DEZYNE. Moreover, the transformation we developed is a first step to adding more advanced verification and visualisation possibilities to the DEZYNE tool set.

Acknowledgements. Wieger Wesselink and Tim Willemse were funded by the EU-FP7 TTP VICTORIA project (project grant agreement 609491).

References

1. Baeten, J.C.M., Basten, T., Reniers, M.A.: Process Algebra: Equational Theories of Communicating Processes. Cambridge Tracts in Theoretical Computer Science, vol. 50. Cambridge University Press, New York (2010)
2. Clinger, W.D.: Proper tail recursion and space efficiency. In: PLDI, pp. 174–185. ACM (1998)
3. Cranen, S., Groote, J.F., Keiren, J.J.A., Stappers, F.P.M., Vink, E.P., Wesselink, W., Willemse, T.A.C.: An overview of the mCRL2 toolset and its recent advances. In: Piterman, N., Smolka, S.A. (eds.) TACAS 2013. LNCS, vol. 7795, pp. 199–213. Springer, Heidelberg (2013). doi:10.1007/978-3-642-36742-7_15
4. Gibson-Robinson, T., Armstrong, P., Boulgakov, A., Roscoe, A.W.: FDR3: a parallel refinement checker for CSP. Int. J. Softw. Tools Technol. Transf. 18(2), 149–167 (2016)
5. Groote, J.F., Mousavi, M.R.: Modeling and Analysis of Communicating Systems. MIT Press, Cambridge (2014)
6. Roscoe, A.W.: On the expressive power of CSP refinement. Formal Asp. Comput. 17(2), 93–112 (2005)
7. Wang, T., Song, S., Sun, J., Liu, Y., Dong, J.S., Wang, X., Li, S.: More anti-chain based refinement checking. In: Aoki, T., Taguchi, K. (eds.) ICFEM 2012. LNCS, vol. 7635, pp. 364–380. Springer, Heidelberg (2012). doi:10.1007/978-3-642-34281-3_26

Erratum to: Certified Gathering of Oblivious Mobile Robots: Survey of Recent Results and Open Problems

Thibaut Balabonski[6], Pierre Courtieu[1], Lionel Rieg[2],
Sébastien Tixeuil[4,5], and Xavier Urbain[3(✉)]

[1] CÉDRIC, Conservatoire National des Arts et Métiers, Paris, France
[2] Yale University, New Haven, USA
[3] Université de Lyon, Université Claude Bernard Lyon 1,
CNRS, LIRIS UMR 5205, Lyon, France
Xavier.Urbain@liris.cnrs.fr
[4] UPMC Sorbonne Universités, LIP6-CNRS 7606, Paris, France
[5] Institut Universitaire de France, Paris, France
[6] Université Paris-Sud, LRI, CNRS UMR 8623,
Université Paris-Saclay, Paris, France

Erratum to:
Chapter "Certified Gathering of Oblivious Mobile Robots:
Survey of Recent Results and Open Problems" in:
L. Petrucci et al. (Eds.), Critical Systems: Formal Methods
and Automated Verification, LNCS 10471,
https://doi.org/10.1007/978-3-319-67113-0_11

By mistake, the initially published version of chapter 11 omitted the author corrections. This has been updated.

The updated original online version of this chapter can be found at
https://doi.org/10.1007/978-3-319-67113-0_11

Author Index

Printed in the United States
By Bookmasters